THE SURVIVAL OF MAN

THE
SURVIVAL OF MAN

A STUDY IN UNRECOGNISED
HUMAN FACULTY

BY

Sir OLIVER LODGE, F.R.S.

METHUEN & CO.
36 ESSEX STREET W.C.
LONDON

First Published in 1909

DEDICATED TO

THE FOUNDERS OF THE
SOCIETY FOR PSYCHICAL RESEARCH

THE TRUEST AND

MOST PATIENT WORKERS

IN AN UNPOPULAR REGION OF SCIENCE

THAT I HAVE EVER KNOWN

b

" It is mere dogmatism to assert that we do not survive death, and mere prejudice or inertia to assert that it is impossible to discover whether we do or no. We in the West have hardly even begun to inquire into the matter ; and scientific method and critical faculty were never devoted to it, so far as I am aware, previous to the foundation, some quarter of a century ago, of the Society for Psychical Research. . . .

" Alleged facts suggesting *primâ facie* the survival of death . . . are now at last being systematically and deliberately explored by men and women of intelligence and good faith bent on ascertaining the truth. . . .

" I am asking you to take seriously a branch of scientific inquiry which may have results more important than any other that is being pursued in our time."

G. Lowes Dickinson
Ingersoll Lecture on Immortality at Harvard, 1908

And assuredly the religious implications of all these phenomena are worthy of any man's most serious thought. Those who most feel the importance of the ethical superstructure are at the same time most plainly bound to treat the establishment of the facts at the foundation as no mere personal search for a faith, to be dropped when private conviction has been attained, but as a serious, a continuous, public duty. And the more convinced they are that their faith is sound, the more ready should they be to face distrust and aversion,—to lay their account for a long struggle with the *vis inertiæ* of the human spirit.

F. W. H. Myers, *Human Personality*, ii. 225

PREFACE

THE author's conviction of man's survival of bodily death—a conviction based on a large range of natural facts—is well known ; and in this volume some idea can be gained as to the most direct and immediate kind of foundation on which in the future he considers that this belief will in due course be scientifically established.

The author gives an account of many of his investigations into matters connected with psychical research during the last quarter of a century, with an abridgement of contemporary records. His inquiry, following the lines of the Society for Psychical Research, began with experimental telepathy ; but the largest section of the book treats of automatic writing, trance speech, and other instances of temporary lucidity,—for in this department of the subject he considers that the most direct evidence for continued personal existence and posthumous activity will most likely be found.

An account of his experiences in connexion with the controverted and often discredited "physical phenomena" associated with exceptional mental states, and a discussion of the right scientific and philosophic attitude to these puzzling and at first sight incredible facts—which are pressing for inclusion in our scheme of Nature,—are reserved for another volume.

TABLE OF CONTENTS

SECTION I

AIMS AND OBJECTS OF PSYCHICAL RESEARCH

SECTION II

EXPERIMENTAL TELEPATHY OR THOUGHT-TRANSFERENCE

SECTION III

SPONTANEOUS TELEPATHY AND CLAIRVOYANCE

SECTION IV

AUTOMATISM AND LUCIDITY

THE SURVIVAL OF MAN

THE SURVIVAL OF MAN

SECTION I

AIMS AND OBJECTS OF PSYCHICAL RESEARCH

CHAPTER I

THE ORIGIN OF THE SOCIETY FOR PSYCHICAL RESEARCH

PUZZLING and weird occurrences have been vouched for among all nations and in every age. It is possible to relegate a good many asserted occurrences to the domain of superstition, but it is not possible thus to eliminate all. Nor is it likely that in the present stage of natural knowledge we are acquainted with all the workings of the human spirit and have reduced them to such simplicity that everything capable of happening in the mental and psychical region is of a nature readily and familiarly to be understood by all. Yet there are many who seem practically to believe in this improbability; for although they are constrained from time to time to accept novel and surprising discoveries in biology, in chemistry, and in physical science generally, they seem tacitly to assume that these are the only parts of the universe in which fundamental discovery is possible, all the rest being too well known.

I

It is a simple faith, and does credit to the capacity for belief of those who hold it—belief unfounded upon knowledge, and tenable only in the teeth of a great mass of evidence to the contrary.

It is not easy to unsettle minds thus fortified against the intrusion of unwelcome facts ; and their strong faith is probably a salutary safeguard against that unbalanced and comparatively dangerous condition called " open-mindedness," which is ready to learn and investigate anything not manifestly self-contradictory and absurd. Without people of the solid, assured, self-satisfied order, the practical work of the world would not so efficiently be done.

But whatever may be thought of the subject by the majority of people at present, this book is intended to indicate the possibility that discoveries of the very first magnitude can still be made—are indeed in process of being made—by strictly scientific methods, in the region of psychology : discoveries quite comparable in importance with those which have been made during the last century in physics and biology, but discoveries whose opportunities for practical application and usefulness may similarly have to remain for some time in the hands of experts, since perhaps they cannot be miscellaneously absorbed or even apprehended by the multitude without danger.

It has been partly the necessity for caution—the dread of encouraging mere stupid superstition—that has instinctively delayed advance in these branches of inquiry, until the progress of education gave a reasonable chance of a sane and balanced and critical reception by a fairly considerable minority.

But, within the last half century, assertions concerning psychological supernormalities have not only excited general attention, but have rather notably roused the interest of careful and responsible students, both in the domain of science and in that of letters.

Twenty-eight years ago, in fact, a special society with distinguished membership was enrolled in London, with the object of inquiring into the truth of many of these assertions. It was started by a few men of letters and of science who for some years had been acquainted with a number of strange apparent facts— facts so strange and unusual, and yet so widely believed in among a special coterie of ordinarily sane and sensible people, that it seemed to these pioneers highly desirable either to incorporate them properly into the province of ordered knowledge, or else to extrude them definitely as based upon nothing but credulity, imposture, and deceit.

The attempt was to be made in a serious and responsible spirit, a spirit of genuine " scepticism,"—that is to say, of critical examination and inquiry, not of dogmatic denial and assertion. No phenomenon was to be unhesitatingly rejected because at first sight incredible. No phenomenon was to be accepted which could not make its position good by crucial and repeated and convincing tests. Every class of asserted fact was to have the benefit of inquiry, none was to be given the benefit of any doubt. So long as doubt was possible, the phenomenon was to be kept at arm's length : to be criticised as possible, not to be embraced as true.

It is often cursorily imagined that an adequate supply of the critical and cautious spirit necessary in this investigation is a monopoly of professed men of science. It is not so. Trained students of literature—not to mention experts in philosophy — have shown themselves as careful, as exact, as critical, and as cautious, as any professed student of science. They have even displayed an excess of caution. They have acted as a curb and a restraint upon the more technically scientific workers, who—presumably because their constant business is to deal at first hand with new phenomena of one kind or another—have been willing to accept a fresh variety of them upon evidence not *much* stronger than that to which they were already well accustomed. Whereas some of the men and women of letters associated with the society have been invariably extremely cautious, less ready to be led by obtrusive and plausible appearances, more suspicious of possibilities and even impossibilities of fraud, actually more inventive sometimes of other and quasi-normal methods of explaining inexplicable facts. I name no names, but from a student of science this testimony is due : and it is largely to the sceptical and extremely cautious wisdom of some representatives of letters and philosophy, as well as to their energy and enthusiasm for knowledge, that the present moderately respectable position of the subject in the estimation of educated people is due.

The first President was Professor Henry Sidgwick, and in his early Presidential Addresses the following sentences occur :—

It is a scandal that a dispute as to the reality of these phenomena should still be going on, that so many competent witnesses should have declared their belief in them, that so many others should be profoundly interested in having the question determined, and yet that the educated world, as a body, should still be simply in the attitude of incredulity.

Now the primary aim of our Society, the thing which we all unite to promote, whether as believers or non-believers, is to make a sustained and systematic attempt to remove this scandal in one way or another.

If any one asks me what I mean by, or how I define, sufficient scientific proof of thought-reading, clairvoyance, or the phenomena called Spiritualistic, I should ask to be allowed to evade the difficulties of determining in the abstract what constitutes adequate evidence. What I mean by *sufficient evidence* is evidence that will convince the scientific world, and for that we obviously require a good deal more than we have so far obtained. I do not mean that some effect in this direction has not been produced : if that were so we could not hope to do much. I think that something has been done ; that the advocates of obstinate incredulity—I mean the incredulity that waives the whole affair aside as undeserving of any attention from rational beings—feel their case to be not *primâ facie* so strong now as it was.

Thirty years ago it was thought that want of scientific culture was an adequate explanation of the vulgar belief in mesmerism and table-turning. Then, as one man of scientific repute after another came forward with the results of individual investigation, there was a quite ludicrous ingenuity exercised in finding reasons for discrediting his scientific culture. He was said to be an amateur, not a professional ; or a specialist without adequate generality of view and training ; or a mere discoverer not acquainted with the strict methods of experimental research ; or he was not a Fellow of the Royal Society, or if he was it was by an unfortunate accident. We must not expect any decisive effect in the direction at which we primarily aim, on the common sense of mankind, from any single piece of evidence, however complete it has been made. Scientific incredulity has been so long in growing, and has so many and so strong roots, that we shall only kill it, if we are able to kill it at all as regards any of those questions, by burying it alive under a heap of facts. We must keep "pegging away," as Lincoln said ; we must accumulate fact upon fact, and add experiment upon experiment, and, I should say, not wrangle too much with incredulous outsiders about the conclusiveness of any one, but trust to the mass of evidence for conviction. The highest degree of demonstrative force that we can obtain out of any single record of investigation is, of course, limited by the trustworthiness of the investigator. We have done all that we can when the critic has nothing left to allege except that the investigator is in the trick. But when he has nothing else left to allege he will allege that.

We shall, I hope, make a point of bringing no evidence before the public until we have got it to this pitch of cogency.

To many enthusiasts outside and to some of those inside the Society — who, through long acquaintance with the phenomena under investigation, were already thoroughly convinced of their genuine character—this attitude on the part of the founders and leaders of the Society for Psychical Research always seemed wrong-headed, and sometimes proved irritating to an almost unbearable degree. The hostility of the outside world and of orthodox science to the investigation, though at times fierce and scornful, and always weighty and significant, has been comparatively mild— perhaps because fragmentary and intermittent—when compared with the bitter and fairly continuous diatribes which have issued, and still often issue, from the spiritualistic press against the slow and ponderous and repellent attitude of those responsible for the working of the Society.

It has been called a society for the suppression of facts, for the wholesale imputation of imposture, for the discouragement of the sensitive, and for the repudiation of every revelation of the kind which was said to be pressing itself upon humanity from the regions of light and knowledge.

Well, we have had to stand this buffeting, as well as the more ponderous blows inflicted by the other side; and it was hardly necessary to turn the cheek to the smiter, since in an attitude of face-forward progress the buffets were sure to come with fair impartiality; greater frequency on the one side making up for greater strength on the other.

Reply to Religious Critics

There is a persistent class of objector, however, whose attacks are made more in sorrow than in anger, and whose earnest remonstrances are thus sympathetically parried by the founders of the Society :—

One word in reference to another objection, which proceeds from a different quarter. There are not a few religious persons who see no reason to doubt our alleged facts, but who regard any experimental investigation of them as wrong, because they must be the work either of the devil or of familiar spirits, with whom the Bible forbids us to have dealings. . . . What we should urge upon our religious friends is that their scruples have really no place in the present stage of our investigation, when the question before us is whether certain phenomena are to be referred to the agency of Spirits at all, even as a "working hypothesis." . . . Many of us, I think, will be amply content if we can only bring this first stage of our investigation to something like a satisfactory issue; we do not look further ahead; and we will leave it for those who may come after to deal with any moral problems that may possibly arise when this first stage is passed.

There are persons who believe themselves to have certain knowledge on the most important matters on which we are seeking evidence, who do not doubt that they have received communications from an unseen world of spirits, but who think that such communications should be kept as sacred mysteries and not exposed to be scrutinised in the mood of cold curiosity which they conceive to belong to science. Now we do not wish to appear intrusive; at the same time we are anxious not to lose through mere misunderstanding any good opportunities for investigation : and I therefore wish to assure such persons that we do not approach these matters in any light or trivial spirit, but with an ever-present sense of the vast importance of the issues involved, and with every desire to give reverence wherever reverence is found to be due. But we feel bound to begin by taking these experiences, however important and however obscure, as a part of the great aggregate which we call Nature ; and we must ascertain carefully and systematically their import, their laws and causes, before we can rationally take up any definite attitude of mind with regard to them. The unknown or uncommon is not in itself an object of reverence ; there is no sacredness in the mere limitations of our knowledge.

This, then, is what we mean by a scientific spirit ; that we approach the subject without prepossessions, but with a single-minded desire to bring within the realm of orderly and accepted knowledge what now appears as a chaos of individual beliefs.

It is instructive to look back at the original programme issued by the Society, which is now housed at 20 Hanover Square ; and accordingly I make a few quotations from the prelude to its first volume of Proceedings, wherein is contained a statement of its aims and objects :—

PROGRAMME OF THE SOCIETY

From the recorded testimony of many competent witnesses, past and present, including observations recently made by scientific men of eminence in various countries, there appears to be, amidst much illusion and deception, an important body of remarkable phenomena, which are *primâ facie* inexplicable on any generally recognised hypothesis, and which, if incontestably established, would be of the highest possible value.

The task of examining such residual phenomena has often been undertaken by individual effort, but never hitherto by a scientific society organised on a sufficiently broad basis. As a preliminary step towards this end, a Conference, convened by Professor Barrett, was held in London, on January 6th, 1882, and a Society for Psychical Research was projected. The Society was definitely constituted on February 20th, 1882, and its Council, then appointed, sketched out a programme of future work :—

1. An examination of the nature and extent of any influence which may be exerted by one mind upon another, apart from any generally recognised mode of perception.

2. The study of hypnotism, and the forms of so-called mesmeric trance, with its alleged insensibility to pain ; clairvoyance and other allied phenomena.

3. A critical revision of Reichenbach's researches with certain organisations called "sensitive," and an inquiry whether such organisations possess any power of perception beyond a highly exalted sensibility of the recognised sensory organs.

4. A careful investigation of any reports, resting on strong testimony, regarding apparitions at the moment of death, or otherwise, or regard-

ing disturbances in houses reputed to be haunted.

5. An inquiry into the various physical phenomena commonly called Spiritualistic ; with an attempt to discover their causes and general laws.

6. The collection and collation of existing materials bearing on the history of these subjects.

The aim of the Society is to approach these various problems without prejudice or prepossession of any kind, and in the same spirit of exact and unimpassioned inquiry which has enabled Science to solve so many problems, once not less obscure nor less hotly debated. The founders of this Society fully recognise the exceptional difficulties which surround this branch of research ; but they nevertheless hope that by patient and systematic effort some results of permanent value may be attained.

To prevent misconception, it must be expressly stated that Membership of the Society does not imply the acceptance of any particular explanation of the phenomena investigated, nor any belief as to the operation, in the physical world, of forces other than those recognised by Physical Science.

And to this I may add that all seriously interested people are welcome as members, provided they have no selfish or commercial ends to serve by seeking to join. Their interest, and in a minor degree their subscription, tend to promote the object we have in view. Merely superstitious and emotional people would find themselves out of place at our meetings, but otherwise we do not seek to be exclusive. It is a kind of work to which any fair-minded and honest person can, as opportunity offers, contribute his or her share.

CHAPTER II

PRACTICAL WORK OF THE SOCIETY

IN the three earliest years of the present century it fell to my lot to occupy the Presidential Chair of the Society for Psychical Research and to give an Address each year. One of those Addresses—the one for 1903—dealt with the lines of profitable work which seemed at that time to be opening before us ; and, since the general nature of our investigation is there referred to in a preliminary manner, it is useful to reproduce it here as an introduction to the more detailed records which follow.

Our primary aim is to be a Scientific Society, to conduct our researches and to record our results in an accurate and scientific manner, so as to set an example of careful work in regions where it has been the exception rather than the rule, and to be a trustworthy guide to the generation of workers who shall follow.

To be scientific does not mean to be infallible, but it means being clear and honest, and as exact as we know how to be. In difficult investigations pioneers have always made some mistakes, they have no immediate criterion or infallible touchstone to distinguish the more true from the less true, but if they record their results with anxious care and scrupulous honesty and painstaking precision, their mistakes are only less valuable to the next generation than their partially true generalisations; and sometimes it turns out, after a century or so, that mistakes made by early pioneers were no such thorough errors as had been thought, that they had an element of truth in them all the time, as if discoverers were endowed with a kind of prophetic insight whereby they caught a glimpse of theories and truths which it would take several generations of workers to disencumber and bring clearly to light.

Suppose, however, that their errors were real ones, the record of their work is just as important to future navigators as it is to have the rocks and shoals of a channel mapped out and buoyed. It is work which must be done. The great ship passing straight to its destination is enabled to attain this directness and speed by the combined labours of a multitude of workers, some obscure and forgotten, some distinguished and remembered, but few of them able to realise its stately passage. So it is also with every great erection,—much of the work is indirect and hidden;—the Forth Bridge stands upon piers sunk below the water-mark by the painful and long continued labours of Italian workmen in "caissons" full of compressed and heated air.

The study of specifically Natural knowledge was fostered and promoted by the recognition in the reign of Charles II. of a body of enthusiasts who, during the disturbed but hopeful era of the Commonwealth, had met together to discuss problems of scientific interest; and to-day The Royal Society is among the dignified institutions of our land, taking all branches of Natural Philosophy and Natural History—the Physical Sciences and the Biological Sciences—under its wing.

Us it does not recognise; but then neither does it recognise Mental and Moral Philosophy, or Ethics, or

Psychology, or History, or any part of a great region of knowledge which has hitherto been regarded as outside the pale of the Natural Sciences.

It is for us to introduce our subjects within that pale, if it turns out that there they properly belong; and if not, it is for us to do pioneer work and take our place by the side of that group of Societies whose object is the recognition and promotion of work in the mental, the psychological, the philosophical direction, until the day for unification shall arrive.

Half knowledge sees divisions and emphasises barriers, delights in classification into genera and species, affixes labels, and studies things in groups. And all this work is of the utmost practical value and is essentially necessary. That the day will come when barriers shall be broken down, when species shall be found to shade off into one another, when continuity and not classification shall be the dominant feature, may be anticipated by all; but we have no power of hastening the day except by taking our place in the workshop and doing our assigned quota; still less do we gain any advantage by pretending that the day of unification has arrived while as yet its dawn is still in the future.

Popular Mistrust of Science, and its Remedy

Our primary aim is to be a Scientific Society, doing pioneering and foundation work in a new and not yet incorporated plot on which future generations may build, and making as few mistakes as we can reasonably contrive by the exercise of great care. We are not a literary society, though we have had men of letters among our guides and leaders; and we are not a religious society, though some of the members take an interest in our subject because it seems to them to have a bearing on their religious convictions or hopes. I will say a few words on both these points.

First, our relations to literature.

The name of Francis Bacon is a household word in the history of English scientific ideas. I do not mean in the recent, and as it seems to me comic, aspect, that he wrote everything that was written in the Elizabethan era (a matter to which I wish to make no reference one way or the other, for it is completely off my path). But, before that hare was started, his name was weighty and familiar in the history of English scientific ideas; and it is instructive to ask why. Was he a man of Science? No. Did he make discoveries? No. Do scientific men trace back their ancestry to him? No. To Isaac Newton they trace it back, to Gilbert, to Roger Bacon, speaking for those in England; but of Francis Bacon they know next to nothing. Outside England all the world traces its scientific ancestry to Newton, to Descartes, to Galileo, to Kepler; but of Francis Bacon scientific men outside England have scarcely heard, save as a man of letters. Yet the progress of science owes much to him. All unconsciously scientific men owe to him a great debt. Why?

Because he perceived afar off the oncoming of the scientific wave, and because he was able, in language to which men would listen, to herald and welcome its advance.

Scientifically he was an amateur; but he was an enthusiast who, with splendid eloquence, with the fire of genius, and with great forensic skill, was able to impress his generation, and not his own generation alone, with some idea of the dignity and true place of science, and to make it possible for the early pioneers of the Royal Society to pursue their labours unimpeded by persecution, and to gain some sort of recognition even from general and aristocratic Society.

For remember that the term "science" was not always respectable. To early ears it sounded almost as the term witchcraft or magic sounds, it was a thing from which to warn young people ; it led to atheism and to many other abominations. It was an unholy prying into the secrets of Nature which were meant to be hid from our eyes, it was a thing against which the Church resolutely set its face, a thing for which it was ready if need were to torture or to burn those unlucky men of scientific genius who were born before their time. I mean no one Church in particular : I mean the religious world generally. Science was a thing allied to heresy, a thing to hold aloof from, to shudder at, and to attribute to the devil. All which treatment that great and eminent pioneer, Roger Bacon, experienced at the University of Oxford ; because the time was not yet ripe.

How came it that a little later, in the days of the Stuarts, the atmosphere was so different from that prevalent in the days of the Plantagenets ? Doubtless the age of Elizabeth, the patriotism aroused by the Armada and by the great discoveries in geography, had had their vivifying effect ; and the same sort of originality of thought which did not scruple to arraign a king for high treason likewise ventured to set orthodoxy at defiance, and to experiment upon and investigate openly all manner of natural facts. But, in partial contradiction to the expressed opinion of some men of science, I am disposed to agree to a considerable extent with the popular British view that the result was largely due to the influence of the writings of Francis Bacon. He

had accustomed scholars and literary men to the possibilities and prerogatives of scientific inquiry, he had
emphasised the importance and the dignity of experiment, and it is to his writings that the rapid spread of
scientific ideas, discovered as always by a few, became
acceptable to and spread among the many.

Do not let us suppose, however, that the recognition
of science was immediate and universal. Dislike of it,
and mistrust of the consequences of scientific inquiry—
especially in geology and anthropology,—persisted well
into the Victorian era, and is not wholly extinct at the
present day. Quite apart from antipathy to investigation
into affairs of the mind—which is unpopular and mistrusted still, so that good people are still found who will
attribute anything unusual to the devil, and warn young
people from it,—there is some slight trace of lingering
prejudice against the orthodox sciences of Chemistry
and Physics and Biology. They have achieved their
foothold, they are regarded with respect—people do not
disdain to make money by means of them when the
opportunity is forthcoming—but they are not really liked.
They are admitted to certain schools on sufferance, as
an inferior grade of study suited to the backward and
the ignorant; they are not regarded with affection and
enthusiasm as revelations of Divine working to be
reverently studied, nor as subjects in which the youth
of a nation may be wholesomely and solidly trained.

Very well, still more is the time not quite ripe for
our subject; pioneers must expect hard knocks, the
mind of a people can change only slowly. Until the
mind of a people is changed, new truths born before
their time must suffer the fate of other untimely births;
and the prophet who preaches them must expect to be
mistaken for a useless fanatic, of whom every age has

always had too many, and must be content to be literally or metaphorically put to death, as part of the process
of the regeneration of the world.

The dislike and mistrust and disbelief in the validity
or legitimacy of psychical inquiry is familiar : the
dislike of the Natural Sciences is almost defunct. It
survives, undoubtedly—they are not liked, though they
are tolerated—and I am bound to say that part of the
surviving dislike is due not alone to heredity and imbibed
ideas, but to the hasty and intolerant and exuberant
attitude of some men of science, who, knowing themselves to be reformers, feeling that they have a grain
of seed-corn to plant and water, have not always been
content to go about their business in a calm and con-
ciliatory spirit, but have sought to hurry things on by a
rough-shod method of progression, which may indeed
attain its ends, but gives some pain in the process, and
perhaps achieves results less admirable than those which
might have been attained by the exercise of a little
patience, a little more perception of the point of view of
others, a little more imagination, a little more of that
recognition of the insignificance of trifles and of the
transitory character of full-blown fashions which is called
a sense of humour, a little cultivation of the historic
sense.   In a word, a little more general education.

But this is a digression.   I admit the importance
of Francis Bacon in the history of the development of
the national recognition of the natural sciences in
England; and I wish to suggest that in the history
of the psychical sciences we too have had a Bacon,—
and one not long departed from us.   It is possible
that in his two posthumous volumes we have a book
which posterity will regard as a *Novum Organon.*
History does not repeat itself, and I would not draw

2

the parallel too close. It may be that posterity will regard Myers as much more than that,—as a philosophic pioneer who has not only secured recognition for, but has himself formulated some of the philosophic unification of, a mass of obscure and barely recognised human faculty,—thereby throwing a light on the meaning of "personality" which may survive the test of time. It may be so, but that is for no one living to say. Posterity alone, by aid of the experience and further knowledge which time brings, is able to make a judgment of real value on such a topic as that.

Meanwhile it is for us to see that time does bring this greater knowledge and experience. For time *alone* is impotent. Millions of years passed on this planet, during which the amount of knowledge acquired was small or nil. Up to the sixteenth century, even, scientific progress was at the least slow. Recently it has been rapid,—none too rapid, but rapid. The rate of advance depends upon the activities and energies of each generation, and upon the organisation and machinery which it has inherited from its immediate forebears.

The pioneers who created the S.P.R. have left it in trust with us to hand it on to future generations, an efficient and powerful machine for the spread of scientific truth,—an engine for the advancement of science in a direction overgrown with thickets of popular superstition, intermixed with sandy and barren tracts of resolute incredulity. We have to steer our narrow way between the Scylla of stony minds with no opening in our direction, and the Charybdis of easy and omnivorous acceptance of every straw and waif, whether of truth or falsehood, that may course with the currents of popular superstition.

Need for Qualified Investigators

Realising this to be our duty, and perceiving that we have a long period of danger and difficulty before us, it has become evident to persons of clear vision that the Society must be established on a sound and permanent basis, and must endeavour to initiate an attitude of regarding the psychical sciences as affording the same sort of scope to a career, the same sort of opportunities of earning a livelihood, as do the longer recognised sciences,—those which are more specifically denominated "natural," because of the way they fit into our idea of the scheme of nature as by us at present recognised, or at any rate because they deal with facts to which we have gradually grown accustomed.

Any young man who wishes to make money should be warned off the pursuit of pure science at the outset. People who enter the field with that object in view will do neither themselves nor science any good. A certain amount of enthusiasm and pioneering proclivity is essential, but fortunately that has never yet been wanting in our race; witness the hardships willingly entered upon, and the risks run, in Arctic or Antarctic exploration, for nothing more than a living wage. A living wage is however to many a necessity. It has always been recognised that those who labour at the altar should live by the altar; and a minimum of provision for bread and homely needs ought to be at the disposal of a Society like this wherewith to enable a person of ability and enthusiasm to undertake the prosecution of our researches in a definite and continuous and so to speak professional manner. Hitherto we have depended on the spontaneous and somewhat spasmodic work of amateurs, often of wealthy amateurs, before whose minds such questions as salary never even momentarily pass. We shall always have need of services such as theirs. In the more orthodox sciences, in Physics for instance, it has been notorious that throughout last century the best work has often been done by people who—having the means of living otherwise secured to them—were able to devote their time, and often considerable means too, to the prosecution of research. There has been no rule either way. Some of the leaders have been paid a small salary, like Faraday : others have had independent means, like Cavendish and Joule. Always I say we shall depend upon and be grateful for the spontaneous work and help of people of means ; but we must not depend solely upon that, else will young people of genius be diverted by sheer force of circumstance into other channels, and our nascent science will lose the benefit of their powers and continuous work.

We cannot always depend on spontaneous cases alone. They are most important, and are often extremely valuable instances of a spontaneous and purposeful exercise of the faculty we are investigating, and it would be a great mistake to suppose that we have had enough of them. It is essential that we be kept informed of recent well-attested cases, especially of apparitions at or near the time of death ; but we shall not make progress in understanding the laws of the phenomena and disentangling their deeper meaning if we confine ourselves to observation alone. We must experiment, we must endeavour to produce and examine phenomena as it were in a laboratory—such as I have elsewhere foreshadowed (*Journal* S.P.R., vi. 357)—and must submit them to minute investigation.

For instance there is the question of so-called spirit

photography, there are asserted levitations and *apports* and physical movements, none of which have been subjected to adequate scientific examination. Many such cases have been examined and found fraudulent, and there is great difficulty in obtaining the phenomena under prescribed and crucial conditions; but until these things have been submitted to long-continued scientific scrutiny they will make no undisputed impression, they will be either improperly accepted or improperly rejected, and will continue in that nebulous hazy region, the region of popular superstition, from which it is the business of this Society to rescue them; raising them on to the dry land of science, or submerging them as impostures in the waters of oblivion. And I may say parenthetically that we do not care one iota which alternative fate is in store for them: we only want the truth.

Now I know that some few persons are impatient of such an investigation, and decline to see any need for it. They feel that if they have evidence enough to justify their own belief, further inquiry is superfluous. These have not the scientific spirit, they do not understand the meaning of "law." A fact isolated and alone, joined by no link to the general body of knowledge, is almost valueless. If what they believe is really a fact, they may depend upon it that it has its place in the cosmic scheme, a place which can be detected by human intelligence; and its whole bearing and meaning can gradually be made out.

Moreover, their attitude is selfish. Being satisfied themselves, they will help us no more. But real knowledge, like real wealth of any kind, cannot be wrapped up in a napkin; it pines for reproduction, for increase: "how am I straightened till it be accomplished." The missionary spirit, in some form or other, is inseparably associated with all true and worthy knowledge. Think of a man who, having made a discovery in Astronomy,—seen a new planet, or worked out a new law,—should keep it to himself and gloat over it in private. It would be inhuman and detestable miserliness; even in a thing like that, of no manifest importance to mankind. There would be some excuse for a man who lived so much in advance of his time that, like Galileo with his newly invented and applied telescope, he ran a danger of rebuffs and persecution for the publication of discoveries. But even so, it is his business to brave this and tell out what he knows; still more is it his business so to act upon the mind of his generation as to convert it gradually to the truth, and lead his fellows to accept what now they reject.

Those who believe themselves the repositories of any form of divine truth should realise their responsibility. They are bound in honour to take such steps as may wisely cause its perception and recognition by the mass of mankind. They are not bound to harangue the crowd from the nearest platform : that might be the very way to retard progress and throw back the accept-ance of their doctrine. The course to pursue may be much more indirect than that. The way may be hard and long, but to the possessor of worldly means it is far easier than to another. If the proper administration of his means can conduce to the progress of science, and to the acceptance by the mass of mankind of important and vivifying knowledge of which they are now ignorant, then surely the path lies plain.

Argumentum ad Dignitatem

Still however there are persons who urge that a study of occult phenomena is beneath the dignity of science, and that nothing will be gained of any use to mankind by inquisitiveness regarding the unusual and the lawless, or by gravely attending to the freaks of the unconscious or semi-conscious mind.

But—as Myers and Gurney said long ago in *Phantasms of the Living*—it is needful to point out yet once more, how plausible the reasons for discouraging some novel research have often seemed to be, while yet the advance of knowledge has rapidly shown the futility and folly of such discouragement.

It was the Father of Science himself who was the first to circumscribe her activity. Socrates expressly excluded from the range of exact inquiry all such matters as the movements and nature of the sun and moon. He wished—and as he expressed his wish it seemed to have all the cogency of absolute wisdom— that men's minds should be turned to the ethical and political problems which truly concerned them,—not wasted in speculation on things unknowable—things useless even could they be known.

In a kindred spirit, though separated from Socrates by the whole result of that physical science which Socrates had deprecated, we find a great modern systematiser of human thought again endeavouring to direct the scientific impulse towards things serviceable to man ; to divert it from things remote, unknowable, and useless if known. What then, in Comte's view, are in fact the limits of man's actual home and business? the bounds within which he may set himself to learn all he can, assured that all will serve to inform his conscience and guide his life? It is the solar system which has become for the French philosopher what the street and market-place of Athens were for the Greek.

I need not say that Comte's prohibition has been altogether neglected. No frontier of scientific demarcation has been established between Neptune and Sirius, between Uranus and Aldebaran. Our knowledge of the fixed stars increases yearly ; and it would be rash to maintain that human conduct is not already influenced by the conception thus gained of the unity and immensity of the heavens.

The criticisms which have met us, from the side sometimes of scientific, sometimes of religious orthodoxy, have embodied, in modernised phraseology, nearly every well-worn form of timid protest, or obscurantist demurrer, with which the historians of science have been accustomed to give piquancy to their long tale of discovery and achievement.

Sometimes we are told that we are inviting the old theological spirit to encroach once more on the domain of Science ; sometimes that we are endeavouring to lay the impious hands of Science upon the mysteries of Religion. Sometimes we are informed that competent savants have already fully explored the field which we propose for our investigation. Sometimes that no respectable man of science would condescend to meddle with such a reeking mass of fraud and hysteria. Sometimes we are pitied as laborious triflers who prove some infinitely small matter with mighty trouble and pains ; sometimes we are derided as attempting the solution of gigantic problems by slight and superficial means.

Use of Continued Investigation

But the question is reiterated, Why investigate that of which we are sure ? Why conduct experiments in hypnotism or in telepathy ? Why seek to confirm that of which we already have conviction ? Why value well-evidenced narratives of apparitions at times of death or catastrophe, when so many have already been collected in *Phantasms of the Living*, and when careful scrutiny has proved that they cannot be the result of chance coincidence?[1] There is a quite definite answer to this question—an answer at which I have already hinted—which I wish to commend to the consideration of those who feel this difficulty or ask this sort of question.

The business of Science is not belief but investigation. Belief is both the prelude to and the outcome of knowledge. If a fact or a theory has had a *primâ facie* case made out for it, subsequent investigation is necessary to examine and extend it.

Effective knowledge concerning anything can only be the result of long-continued investigation; belief in the possibility of a fact is only the very first step. Until there is some sort of tentative belief in the reasonable possibility of a fact there is no investigation,—the scientific priest and Levite have other business, and pass by on the other side. And small blame to them: they cannot stop to investigate everything that may be lying by the roadside. If they had been sure that it was a fellow creature in legitimate distress they would have acted differently. Belief of a tentative kind will ensure investigation, not by all but by some of the scientific travellers along the road; but investigation is the prelude to action, and action is a long process. Some one must attend to the whole case and see it through. Others, more pressed for time, may find it easier to subscribe their "two pence" to an endowment fund, and so give indirect but valuable assistance.

The object of investigation is the ascertainment of

[1] See the Report of Professor Sidgwick's Committee, *Proceedings* S.P.R., vol. x. p. 394.

law, and to this process there is no end. What, for
instance, is the object of observing and recording
earthquakes, and arranging delicate instruments to
detect the slightest indication of earth tremor? Every
one knows that earthquakes exist, there is no scepticism
to overcome in their case; even people who have
never experienced them are quite ready to believe in
their occurrence. Investigation into earthquakes and
the whole of the motile occurrences in the earth's
crust, is not in the least for the purpose of confirming
faith, but solely for the better understanding of the
conditions and nature of the phenomena; in other
words, for the ascertainment of law.

So it is in every branch of science. At first among
new phenomena careful observation of fact is necessary,
as when Tycho Brahé made measurements of the
motion of the planets and accumulated a store of
careful observations. Then came the era of hypothesis,
and Kepler waded through guess after guess, testing
them pertinaciously to see if any one of them would
fit all the facts: the result of his strenuous life-work
being the three laws which for all time bear his
name. And then came the majestic deductive epoch
of Newton, welding the whole into one comprehensive
system; subsequently to be enriched and extended by
the labours of Lagrange and Laplace; after which the
current of scientific inquiry was diverted for a time
into other less adequately explored channels.

For not at all times is everything equally ripe for
inquiry. There is a phase, or it may be a fashion,
even in Science. I spoke of geographical exploration
as the feature of Elizabeth's time. Astronomical
inquiry succeeded it. Optics and Chemistry were the
dominating sciences of the early part of the nineteenth

century, Heat and Geology of the middle, Electricity and Biology of the later portion. Not yet has our branch of psychology had its phase of popularity ; nor am I anxious that it should be universally fashionable. It is a subject of special interest, and therefore perhaps of special danger. In that respect it is like other studies of the operations of mind, like a scientific enumeration of the phenomena of religion for instance, like the study of anything which in its early stages looks mysterious and incomprehensible. Training and some admixture of other studies are necessary for its healthy investigation. The day will come when the science will put off its foggy aspect, bewildering to the novice, and become easier for the less well-balanced and more ordinarily-equipped explorer. At present it is like a mountain shrouded in mist, whose sides offer but little secure foothold,—where climbing, though possible, is difficult and dangerous.

As a Society we exist to curb venturesome novices, and to support trusted and experienced climbers by roping ourselves together so that we may advance safely and in unison,—guarding ourselves from foolhardy enterprises, but facing such legitimate difficulties as lie in our path, and resolved that, weather and uncontrollable circumstances permitting, our exploration shall continue, and the truth, whatever it may be, be ascertained.

The assuring of ourselves as to facts is one of our duties, and it is better to hesitate too long over a truth than to welcome an error, for a false gleam may lead us far astray unless it is soon detected.

Another of our duties is the making and testing of hypotheses, so as gradually to make a map of the district and be able to explain it to future travellers,

We have to combine the labours of Tycho with those of Kepler, and thus prepare the way for a future Newton ; who has not yet appeared above the psychical horizon.

His advent must depend upon how far we of this and the next few generations are faithful to our trust, how far we work ourselves, and by our pecuniary means enable others to work ; and I call upon those who are simultaneously blessed with this world's goods and likewise inspired with confidence in the truth and value of mental and spiritual knowledge, to bethink themselves whether, either in their lifetime or by their wills, they cannot contribute to the world's progress in a beneficent way, so as to enable humanity to rise to a greater height of aspiration and even of religion ;—as they will if they are enabled to start with a substantial foundation of solid scientific fact on which to erect their edifice of faith.

If it be said that investigation should not be expensive, I would point to what is expended on the investigation of the orthodox sciences. Before Columbus's voyage could be undertaken, the Courts of Europe had to be appealed to for funds. Before astronomical discoveries can be made, large observatories and costly telescopes have to be provided,—and not one only, but many, so that by collaboration of observers in many parts of the world the truth may be ascertained.

Look at the expense of geographical and ethnological exploration to-day. Think of the highly equipped physical laboratories, one of which is maintained at every College or University in the civilised world. And as to chemical laboratories,—remember that every large commercial chemical manufacturing firm in Germany maintains a band of trained and competent chemists, always investigating, in the hope of a new compound or a new process or some little profitable improvement.

Money is not scarce, and if people realised the interest of science to the human race it would be poured out far more lavishly than it is at present. Certain small special sums are now provided for the investigation of disease. The origin of Malaria has been traced, and this disease has some chance of being exterminated, so that the tropical belt of the earth may become open to white habitation. Cancer is being pursued to its lair, without success so far; but funds for researches such as these are bound to be forthcoming. When practical benefits can be definitely foreseen, people feel justified in spending money even on Science; though as a rule that and Education are things on which they are specially economical. Municipal extravagance in any such direction is sternly checked, though in other directions it may be permitted.

And why should not psychical investigation lead to practical results? Are we satisfied with our treatment of criminals? As civilised people are we content to grow a perennial class of habitual criminals, and to keep them in check only by devices appropriate to savages; hunting them, flogging them, locking them up, exterminating them? Any savage race in the history of the world could do as much as that; and if they know no better they are bound to do it for their own protection. Society cannot let its malefactors run wild, any more than it can release its lunatics. Till it understands these things it *must* lock them up, but the sooner it understands them the better; an attempt at comprehension is being made by criminologists in Italy, France,[1]

---

[1] E.g. *Bulletin de l'Institut Général Psychologique*, dirigé par Dr. Pierre Janet, Décembre, 1902 p. 225.

and elsewhere. Force is no remedy : intelligent treatment is. Who can doubt but that a study of obscure mental facts will lead to a theory of the habitual criminal, to the tracing of his malady as surely as malaria has been traced to the mosquito? And once we understand the evil the remedy will follow. Already hypnotic treatment, or treatment by suggestion, occurs to one ; and quite normal measures of moral improvement can also be tried. The fact of imprisonment ought to lend itself to brilliant efforts at reform : such efforts are the only real justification for destruction of liberty. The essence of manhood is to be free—for better for worse, free—and coercion is only justified if it is salutary. It is a great advantage to doctors to have their patients collected compactly in a hospital—and without it medical practice would languish ; it ought to be a similar advantage—a similar opportunity—to have criminals herded together in gaols, and lunatics in asylums. It is unwise and unscientific to leave prisoners merely to the discipline of warders and the preaching of chaplains. That is not the way to attack a disease of the body politic. I have no full-blown treatment to suggest, but I foresee that there will be one in the future. Experiments are already being made in America, in the prisons of Elmira and Concord,—experiments of hope, if not yet of achievemen. Society will not be content always to employ methods of barbarism ; the resources of civilisation are not really exhausted, though for centuries they have appeared to be. The criminal demands careful study on the psychical side, and remedy or palliation will be a direct outcome of one aspect of our researches. The influence of the unconscious or subliminal self, the power of suggestion, the influence of one mind over another, the phenomena of so-called "possession,"—these are not

academic or scientific facts alone: they have a deep
practical bearing, and sooner or later it must be put to
the proof.

Hint to Investigators

To return to the more immediate and special aspect
of our work : one of the things I want to impress upon
all readers, especially upon those who are gifted with a
faculty for receiving impressions which are worth recording, is that too much care cannot be expended in getting
the record exact.   Exact in every particular, especially
as regards the matter of *time*.   In recording a vision or
an audition or some other impression corresponding to
some event elsewhere, there is a dangerous tendency
to try to coax the facts to fit some half-fledged precon-
ceived theory and to make the coincidence in point of
time exact.

Such distortions of truth are misleading and useless.
What we want to know is exactly how the things occurred,
not how the impressionist would have liked them to
occur, or how he thinks they ought to have occurred.
If people attach importance to their own predilections
concerning events in the Universe, they can be set
forth in a footnote for the guidance of any one who
hereafter may think of starting a Universe on his own
account : but such speculations are of no interest to us
who wish to study and understand the Universe as it is.
If the event preceded the impression, by all means let us
know it,—and perhaps some one may be able to detect
a meaning in the time-interval, when a great number
of similar instances are compared, hereafter.   If the
impression preceded the event, by all means let us know
that too, and never let the observation be suppressed
from a ridiculous idea that such anticipation is impossible.

Nor let us exclude well-attested physical phenomena from historical record, on any similar prejudice of impossibility. We want to *learn* what is possible, not to have minds made up beforehand and distort or blink the facts to suit our preconceptions.

If the correspondence in time is exact, then let future students be able to ascertain that also from the record; but the recorder need not make any remark about "allowing for difference of longitude" or anything of that kind, unless indeed he is an astronomer or some one who thoroughly understands all about "time." Arithmetic of that sort can be left to those who subsequently disentangle and criticise the results. The observer may of course indicate his ideas on the subject if he chooses, but his record should be accurate and cold-blooded and precise. Sentences indicating contemporary emotion, in so far as that is part of the facts to be recorded, are entirely in place; but ejaculations of subsequent emotion, speculation as to the cause, or moralisation as to the meaning, are out of place. It may be said that these do no harm, and can easily be ignored by a future student; and that is so in one sense, but their atmosphere is rather apt to spoil the record, to put the recorder into an unscientific frame of mind. And, even when they have biassed him no whit, they suggest to a subsequent reader that they may have biassed him, and so discount unfairly the value of his testimony.

With respect to the important subject of possible prediction, on which our ideas as to the ultimate nature of time will so largely depend, every precaution should be taken to put far from us the temptation or the possibility of improving the original record after the fact to which it refers has occurred, if it ever does occur;

and to remember that though we have done nothing of the sort, and are in all respects honest, and known to be honest and truthful, yet the contrary may be surmised by posterity or by strangers or foreigners who did not know us ; and even our friends may fancy that we did more than we were aware of, in some quite hypothetical access of somnambulic or automatic trance. Automatic writers for instance must be assumed open to this suspicion, unless they take proper precautions and deposit copies of their writings in some inaccessible and responsible custody ; because the essence of their phenomenon is that the hand writes what they themselves are not aware of, and so it is an easy step for captious critics to maintain that it may also have supplemented or amended, in some way of which they were likewise not aware.

The establishment of cases of real prediction, not mere inference, is so vital and crucial a test of something not yet recognised by science that it is worth every effort to make its evidence secure.

Another thing on which I should value experiments is the detection of slight traces of telepathic power in quite normal persons,—in the average man for instance, or, rather more likely perhaps, in the average child. The power of receiving telepathic impressions *may* be a rare faculty existing only in a few individuals, and in them fully developed ; but it is equally possible, and, if one may say so, more likely, that what we see in them is but an intensification of a power which exists in every one as a germ or nucleus. If such should be the fact, it behoves us to know it ; and its recognition would do more to spread a general belief in the fact of telepathy —a belief by no means as yet universally or even widely spread—than almost anything else.

3

One method that has been suggested for detecting faint traces of the power, is to offer to a percipient the choice of one out of two things, and to see whether in multitudes of events the predetermination of a bystander as to which shall be chosen, exerts any influence whatever on the result. Many devices can be made for carrying this out, but experiments of greater interest and novelty will be made if the devices are left to individual ingenuity and experience. Leisure, and patience, and system, and industry, are the requisites : and if I do not myself practise what I preach, in this and other particulars, it is because, whatever I may lack of the others, I am at present conspicuously lacking in the first of these essentials.

BEARING ON ALLIED SUBJECTS

There are many topics on which I might speak : one is the recent advance in our knowlege of the nature of the atom, and the discovery of facts concerning the Ether and Matter which I think must have some bearing,—some to me at present quite unknown bearing,—on the theory of what are called "physical phenomena"; but it is hardly necessary to call the attention of educated persons to the intense interest of this most recent purely scientific subject.

On another topic I might say a few words, viz., on the ambiguity clinging round the phrase "action at a distance," in connection with telepathy. Physicists deny action at a distance, at least most of them do,—I do for one ;—at the same time I admit telepathy. Therefore it is supposed I necessarily assume that telepathy must be conducted by an etherial process analogous to the transmission of waves. That is however a *non-sequitur*.

The phrase "action at a distance" is a technical one. Its denial signifies that no physical force is exerted save through a medium. There must either be a projectile from A to B, or a continuous medium of some kind extending from A to B, if A exerts force upon B, or otherwise influences it by a physical process.

But what about a psychical process? There is no such word in physics; the term is in that connection meaningless. A physicist can make no assertion on it one way or the other. If A mesmerises B, or if A makes an apparition of himself appear to B, or if A conveys a telepathic impression to B; is a medium necessary then? As a physicist I do not know: these are not processes I understand. They may not be physical processes at all.

Take it further :—A thinks of B, or A prays to B, or A worships B.—Is a medium necessary for these things? Absolute ignorance! The question is probably meaningless and absurd. Spiritual and psychical events do not enter into the scheme of Physics; and when a physicist denies "action at a distance" he is speaking of things he is competent to deal with,—of light and sound and electricity and magnetism and cohesion and gravitation,— he is not, or should not be, denying anything psychical or spiritual at all. All the physical things, he asserts, necessitate a medium ; but beyond that he is silent. If telepathy is an etherial process, as soon as it is proved to be an etherial process, it will come into the realm of physics ; till then it stays outside.

There are rash speculators who presume to say that spiritual and psychical and physical are all one. In the higher reaches of Philosophy this may have some meaning—there may be some advantage in thus treating questions of ultimate Ontology,—boundaries and classification must be recognised as human artifices; but for practical purposes distinctions are necessary, and if people unqualified in Metaphysics make these assertions I venture to say that the instinct for simplification has run away with them, that they are trespassing out of bounds and preaching what they do not know, eking out a precarious ignorance with cheap dogmatism.

There is one important topic on which I have not yet spoken,—I mean the bearing of our inquiry on religion. It is a large subject and one too nearly trenching on the region of emotion to be altogether suitable for consideration by a scientific Society. Yet every science has its practical applications,—though they are not part of the science, they are its legitimate outcome,—and the value of the science to humanity must be measured in the last resort by the use which humanity can make of it. To the enthusiast, knowledge for its own sake, without ulterior ends, may be enough,—and if there were none of this spirit in the world we should be poorer than we are;—but for the bulk of mankind this is too high, too arid a creed, and people in general must see just enough practical outcome to have faith that there may be yet more.

That our researches will ultimately have some bearing, some meaning, for the science of theology, I do not doubt. What that bearing may be I can only partly tell. I have indicated in *Man and the Universe*, Chapter II. called " The Reconciliation," part of what I feel on the subject, and I have gone as far in that article as I feel entitled to go. We seek to unravel the nature and hidden powers of man; and a fuller understanding of the attributes of humanity cannot but have some influence on our theory of Divinity itself.

If any scientific Society is worthy of encouragement and support it should surely be this. If there is any object worthy of patient and continued attention, it is surely these great and pressing problems of *whence, what*, and *whither*, that have occupied the attention of Prophet and Philosopher since human history began. The discovery of a new star, of a marking on Mars, of a new element, or of a new extinct animal or plant, is interesting: surely the discovery of a new human faculty is interesting too. Already the discovery of " telepathy " constitutes the first-fruits of this Society's work, and it has laid the way open to the discovery of much more. Our aim is nothing less than the investigation and better comprehension of human faculty, human personality, and human destiny.

SECTION II

EXPERIMENTAL TELEPATHY OR THOUGHT-TRANSFERENCE

CHAPTER III

SOME EARLY EXPERIMENTS IN THOUGHT-TRANSFERENCE

I AM not attempting a history of the subject; and for the observations of Prof. Barrett and others in the experimental transference of ideas or images from one person to another I must refer students to the first volume of the *Proceedings* of the Society, where a number of facsimile reproductions of transferred diagrams and pictures, which are of special interest, will also be found. Prof. Barrett had experimented in conjunction with Mr. William de Morgan so long ago as 1870–73, and he endeavoured to make a communication on the subject to the British Association in 1876, but the subject was unwelcome or the attempt premature, and he naturally encountered rebuff. There was some correspondence on the subject in *Nature* in 1881, and an article in *The Nineteenth Century* for June 1882. All I shall do here is to describe some later observations and experiments of my own.

Suffice it to say that the leading members of the Society for Psychical Research — actuated in the first

instance largely by Prof. Barrett's report—investigated the
matter, and gradually by pertinacious experiment became
convinced of the reality of thought-transference,—taking
due precaution, as their experience enlarged, against the
extraordinary ingenuity and subtle possibility of code
signalling, and discriminating carefully between the
genuine phenomenon and the thought-reading or rather
muscle-reading exhibitions, with actual or partial contact,
which at one time were much in vogue.

Before coming to our conclusion as to Thought-
transference, says Prof. Sidgwick, we considered carefully
the arguments brought forward for regarding cases of
so-called "Thought-reading" as due to involuntary
indications apprehended through the ordinary senses;
and we came to the conclusion that the ordinary experiments, where contact was allowed, could be explained
by the hypothesis of unconscious sensibility to involuntary
muscular pressure. Hence we have always attached
special importance to experiments in which contact was
excluded; with regard to which this particular hypothesis
is clearly out of court.

My own first actual experience of Thought-transference, or experimental Telepathy, was obtained in the
years 1883 and 1884 at Liverpool, when I was invited
by Mr. Malcolm Guthrie of that city to join in an
investigation which he was conducting with the aid of
one or two persons who had turned out to be sensitive,
from among the employées of the large drapery firm of
George Henry Lee & Co.

A large number of these experiments had been
conducted, before I was asked to join, throughout the
Spring and Autumn of 1883, but it is better for me to
adhere strictly to my own experience and to relate only
those experiments over which I had control. Accordingly

I reproduce here a considerable part of my short paper on the subject, originally published in the *Proceedings* of the Society for Psychical Research.

Most of these experiments were confirmations of the kind of thing that had been observed by other experimenters. But one experiment which I tried was definitely novel, and, as it seems to me, important; since it clearly showed that when two agents are acting, each contributes to the effect, and that the result is due, not to one alone, but to both combined. The experiment is thus described by me in the columns of *Nature*, vol. xxx. page 145 :—

An Experiment in Thought-Transference

Those of your readers who are interested in the subject of thought-transference, now being investigated, may be glad to hear of a little experiment which I recently tried here. The series of experiments was originated and carried on in this city by Mr. Malcolm Guthrie, and he has prevailed on me, on Dr. Herdman, and on one or two other more or less scientific witnesses, to be present on several occasions, critically to examine the conditions, and to impose any fresh ones that we thought desirable. I need not enter into particulars, but I will just say that the conditions under which apparent transference of thought occurs from one or more persons, steadfastly thinking, to another in the same room blindfold and wholly disconnected from the others, seem to me absolutely satisfactory, and such as to preclude the possibility of conscious collusion on the one hand or unconscious muscular indication on the other.

One evening last week—after two thinkers, or agents, had been several times successful in instilling the idea of some object or drawing, at which they were looking, into the mind of the blindfold person, or percipient—I brought into the room a double opaque sheet of thick paper with a square drawn on one side and a St. Andrew's cross or X on the other, and silently arranged it between the two agents so that each looked on one side without any notion of what was on the other. The percipient was not informed in any way that a novel modification was being made ; and, as usual, there was no contact of any sort or kind,—a clear space of several feet existing between each of the three people. I thought that by this variation I should decide whether one of the two agents was more active than the other ; or, supposing them about equal, whether two ideas in two separate minds could be fused into one by the percipient.

In a very short time the percipient made the following remarks, every one else being silent : "The thing won't keep still." "I seem to see things moving about." "First I see a thing up there, and then one down there." "I can't see either distinctly." The object was then hidden, and the percipient was told to take off the bandage and to draw the impression in her mind on a sheet of paper. She drew a square, and then said, "There was the other thing as well," and drew a cross inside the square from corner to corner, saying afterwards, "I don't know what made me put it inside."

The experiment is no more conclusive as evidence than fifty others that I have seen at Mr. Guthrie's, but it seems to me somewhat interesting that two minds should produce a disconnected sort of impression on the mind of the percipient, quite different from the single impression which we had usually obtained when two agents were both looking at the same thing. Once, for instance [to take a nearly corresponding case under those conditions], when the object was a rude drawing of the main lines in a Union Jack, the figure was reproduced by the percipient as a whole without misgiving ; except, indeed, that she expressed a doubt as to whether its middle horizontal line were present or not, and ultimately omitted it.

UNIVERSITY COLLEGE, LIVERPOOL,
   5 *June* 1884

It is preferable thus to quote the original record and contemporary mode of publication of an experiment, so as to avoid the risk either of minimising or over-emphasising the cogency of the circumstances. But I wish to say strongly that the experiment was quite satisfactory, and that no reasonable doubt of its validity has been felt by me from that time to this.

REPORT ON THE MAIN SERIES

I now proceed to give my report on the whole series of experiments :—

In reporting on the experiments conducted by me, at the invitation and with the appliances of Mr. Guthrie, I wish to say that I had every opportunity of examining and varying the minute conditions of the phenomena, so as to satisfy myself of their genuine and objective character, in the same way as one is accustomed to satisfy oneself as to the truth and genuineness of any ordinary physical fact. If I had merely witnessed facts as a passive spectator I should not publicly report upon them. So long as one is bound to accept imposed conditions and merely witness what goes on, I have no confidence in my own penetration, and am perfectly sure that a conjurer could impose on me, possibly even to the extent of making me think that he was not imposing on me ; but when one has the control of the circumstances, can change them at will and arrange one's own experiments, one gradually acquires a belief in the phenomena observed quite comparable to that induced by the repetition of ordinary physical experiments.

I have no striking or new phenomenon to report, but only a few more experiments in the simplest and most elementary form of what is called Thought-transference; though certainly what I have to describe falls under the head of "Thought-transference" proper, and is not explicable by the merely mechanical transfer of impressions, which is more properly described as muscle-reading.

In using the term "Thought-transference," I would ask to be understood as doing so for convenience, because the observed facts can conveniently be grouped under such a title; but I would not be understood as implying any theory on the subject. It is a most dangerous thing to attempt to convey a theory by a phrase; and to set forth a theory would require many words. As it is, the phrase describes correctly enough what appears to take place, viz., that one person may, under favourable conditions, receive a faint impression of a thing which is strongly present in the mind, or thought, or sight, or sensorium of another person not in contact, and may be able to describe or draw it, more or less correctly. But how the transfer takes place, or whether there is any transfer at all, or what is the physical reality underlying the terms "mind," "consciousness," "impression," and the like; and whether this thing we call mind is located in the person, or in the space round him, or in both, or neither; whether indeed the term location, as applied to mind, is utter nonsense and simply meaningless,—concerning all these things I obtrude no hypothesis whatsoever. I may, however, be permitted to suggest a rough and crude analogy. That the brain is the organ of consciousness is patent, but that consciousness is located in the brain is what no psychologist ought to assert; for just as the energy of an electric charge, though apparently in the conductor, is not in the conductor, but in the space all round it; so it may be that the sensory consciousness of a person, though apparently located in his brain, may be conceived of as also existing like a faint echo in space, or in other brains, although these are ordinarily too busy and pre-occupied to notice it.

The experiments which I have witnessed proceed in the following way. One person is told to keep in a perfectly passive condition, with a mind as vacant as possible; and to assist this condition the organs of sense are unexcited, the eyes being bandaged and silence maintained. It might be as well to shut out even the ordinary street hum by plugging the ears, but as a matter of fact this was not done.

A person thus kept passive is "the percipient." In the experiments I witnessed the percipient was a girl, one or other of two who had been accidentally found to possess the necessary power. Whether it is a common power or not I do not know. So far as I am aware comparatively few persons have tried. I myself tried, but failed abjectly. It was easy enough to picture things to oneself, but they did not appear to be impressed on me from without, nor did any of them bear the least resemblance to the object in the agent's mind. (For instance, I said a pair of scissors instead of the five of diamonds,—and things like that.) Nevertheless, the person acting as percipient is in a perfectly ordinary condition, and can in no sense be said to be in a hypnotic state, unless this term be extended to include the emptiness of mind produced by blindfolding and silence.

To all appearance a person in a brown study is far more hypnotised than the percipients I saw, who usually unbandaged their own eyes and chatted between successive experiments.

Another person sitting near the percipient, sometimes at first holding her hands but usually and ordinarily without any contact at all but with a distinct intervening distance, was told to think hard of a particular object, either a name, or a scene, or a thing, or of an object or drawing set up in a good light and in a convenient position for staring at. This person is "the agent" and has, on the whole, the hardest time of it. It is a most tiring and tiresome thing to stare at a letter, or a triangle, or a donkey, or a teaspoon, and to think of nothing else for the space of two or three minutes. Whether the term "thinking" can properly be applied to such barbarous concentration of mind as this I am not sure; its difficulty is of the nature of tediousness.

Very frequently more than one agent is employed, and when two or three people are in the room they are all told to think of the object more or less strenuously; the idea being that wandering thoughts in the neighbourhood certainly cannot help, and may possibly hinder, the clear transfer of impression. As regards the question whether when several agents are thinking, only one is doing the work, or whether all really produce some effect, a special experiment has led me to conclude that more than one agent can be active at the same time. We have some right therefore to conclude that several agents are probably more powerful than one, but that a confusedness of impression may sometimes be produced by different agents attending to different parts or aspects of the object.

Most people seem able to act as agents, though some

appear to do better than others. I can hardly say
whether I am much good at it or not. I have not often
tried alone, and in the majority of cases when I have
tried I have failed; on the other hand, I have once or
twice succeeded. We have many times succeeded with
agents quite disconnected from the percipient in ordinary
life, and sometimes complete strangers to them. Mr.
Birchall, the headmaster of the Birkdale Industrial
School, frequently acted; and the house physician at the
Eye and Ear Hospital, Dr. Shears, had a successful
experiment, acting alone, on his first and only visit.
All suspicion of a pre-arranged code is thus rendered
impossible even to outsiders who are unable to witness
the obvious fairness of all the experiments.

The object looked at by the agent is placed usually
on a small black opaque wooden screen between the
percipient and agents, but sometimes it is put on a larger
screen behind the percipient. The objects were kept in
an adjoining room and were selected and brought in
by me, with all due precaution, after the percipient was
blindfolded. I should say, however, that no reliance
was placed on, or care taken in, the bandaging. It was
merely done because the percipient preferred it to merely
shutting the eyes. After remarkable experiments on blindfolding by members of the Society (see *Journal*, S.P.R.,
vol. i. p. 84), I certainly would not rely on any ordinary
bandaging; the opacity of the wooden screen on which
the object was placed was the thing really depended on,
and it was noticed that no mirrors or indistinct reflectors
were present. The only surface at all suspicious was the
polished top of the small table on which the opaque
screen usually stood. But as the screen sloped backwards at a slight angle, it was impossible for the object
on it to be thus mirrored. Moreover, sometimes I

covered the table with paper, and often it was not used at all, but the object was placed on a screen or a settee behind the percipient; and one striking success was obtained with the object placed on a large drawing board, loosely swathed in a black silk college gown, with the percipient immediately behind the said drawing board and almost hidden by it.

As regards collusion and trickery, no one who has witnessed the absolutely genuine and artless manner in which the impressions are described, but has been perfectly convinced of the transparent honesty of purpose of all concerned. This, however, is not evidence to persons who have not been present, and to them I can only say that to the best of my scientific belief no collusion or trickery was possible under the varied circumstances of the experiments.

A very interesting question presents itself as to *what* is really transmitted, whether it is the idea or name of the object or whether it is the visual impression. To examine this I frequently drew things without any name —perfectly irregular drawings. I am bound to say that these irregular and unnameable productions have always been rather difficult, though they have at times been imitated fairly well; but it is not at all strange that a faint impression of an unknown object should be harder to grasp and reproduce than a faint impression of a familiar one, such as a letter, a common name, a teapot, or a pair of scissors. Moreover, in some very interesting cases the idea or name of the object was certainly the thing transferred, and not the visual impression at all; this specially happened with one of the two percipients; and, therefore, probably in every case the fact of the object having a name would assist any faint impression of its appearance which might be received.

As to *aspect*, *i.e.* inversion or perversion,—so far as my experience goes it seems perfectly accidental whether the object will be drawn by the percipient in its actual position or in the inverted or perverted position. This is very curious if true, and would certainly not have been expected by me. Horizontal objects are never described as vertical, nor *vice versâ*; and slanting objects are usually drawn with the right amount of slant.

The two percipients are Miss R. and Miss E. Miss R. is the more prosaic, staid, and self-contained personage, and she it is who gets the best quasi-visual impression, but she is a bad drawer, and does not reproduce it very well. Miss E. is, I should judge, of a more sensitive temperament, seldom being able to preserve a strict silence for instance, and she it is who more frequently jumps to the idea or name of the object without being able so frequently to " see " it.

I was anxious to try both percipients at once, so as to compare their impressions, but I have not met with much success under these conditions, and usually therefore have had to try one at a time—the other being frequently absent or in another room, though also frequently present and acting as part or sole agent.

I once tried a double agent—that is, not two agents thinking of the same thing, but two agents each thinking of a different thing. A mixed and curiously double impression was thus produced and described by the percipient, and both the objects were correctly drawn. This experiment has been separately described, as it is important. See pages 41 and 51.

[*N.B.*—The actual drawings made in all the experiments, failures and successes alike, are preserved intact by Mr. Guthrie.]

Description of some of the Experiments

In order to describe the experiments briefly I will put in parentheses everything said by me or by the agent, and in inverted commas all the remarks of the percipient. The first seven experiments are all that were made on one evening with the particular percipient, and they were rapidly performed.

A.—*Experiments with Miss R. as Percipient*

First Agent, Mr. Birchall, holding hands.   No one else present except myself

Object—a blue square of silk.—(Now, it's going to be a colour; ready.) "Is it green?" (No.) "It's something between green and blue. . . . Peacock." (What shape?) She drew a rhombus.

[*N.B.*—It is not intended to imply that this was a success by any means, and it is to be understood that it was only to make a start on the first experiment that so much help was given as is involved in saying "it's a colour." When they are simply told "it's an object," or, what is much the same, when nothing is said at all, the field for guessing is practically infinite. When no remark at starting is recorded none was made, except such an one as "Now we are ready,"—by myself.]

Next object—a key on a black ground.—(It's an object.) In a few seconds she said, "It's bright. . . . It looks like a key." Told to draw, she drew it just inverted.

Next object—three gold studs in morocco case.—"Is it yellow? . . . Something gold. . . . Something round. . . . A locket or a watch, perhaps." (Do you see more than one round?) "Yes, there seem to be more than one. . . . Are there three rounds? . . . Three rings." (What do they seem to be set in?) "Something bright like beads." [Evidently not understanding or attending to the question.] Told to unblindfold herself and draw, she drew the three rounds in a row quite correctly, and then sketched round them absently the outline of the case; which seemed, therefore, to have been apparent to her though she had not consciously attended to it. It was an interesting and striking experiment.

4

Next object—a pair of scissors standing partly open with their points down.—"Is it a bright object? . . . Something long ways [indicating verticality]. . . . A pair of scissors standing up. . . . A little bit open." Time, about a minute altogether. She then drew her impression, and it was correct in every particular. The object in this experiment was on a settee behind her, but its position had to be pointed out to her when, after the experiment, she wanted to see it.

Next object—a drawing of a right angle triangle on its side.—(It's a drawing.) She drew an isosceles triangle on its side.

Next—a circle with a chord across it.—She drew two detached ovals, one with a cutting line across it.

Next—a drawing of a Union Jack pattern.—As usual in drawing

ORIGINAL   REPRODUCTION

experiments, Miss R. remained silent for perhaps a minute; then she said, "Now I am ready." I hid the object; she took off the hand-kerchief, and proceeded to draw on paper placed ready in front of her. She this time drew all the lines of the figure except the horizontal middle one. She was obviously much tempted to draw this, and, indeed, began it two or three times faintly, but ultimately said, "No, I'm not sure," and stopped.

[END OF SITTING]

Experiments with Miss R.—continued

I will now describe an experiment indicating that one agent may be better than another.

Object—the Three of Hearts.—Miss E. and Mr. Birchall both present as agents, but Mr. Birchall holding percipient's hands at first. "Is it a black cross . . . a white ground with a black cross on it?" Mr. Birchall now let Miss E. hold hands instead of himself, and Miss R. very soon said, "Is it a card?" (Right.) "Are there three spots on it? . . . Don't know what they are. . . . I don't think I can get the colour. . . . They are one above the other, but they seem three round spots. . . . I think they're red, but am not clear."

Next object—a playing card with a blue anchor painted on it slantwise, instead of pips. No contact at all this time, but another lady, Miss R——d, who had entered the room, assisted Mr. B. and Miss E.

as agents. "Is it an anchor? . . . a little on the slant." (Do you see any colour?) "Colour is black . . . It's a nicely drawn anchor." When asked to draw she sketched part of it, but had evidently half forgotten it, and not knowing the use of the cross arm, she could only indicate that there was something more there, but she couldn't remember what. Her drawing had the right slant.

Another object—two pair of coarse lines crossing; drawn in red chalk, and set up at some distance from agents. No contact. "I only see lines crossing." She saw no colour. She afterwards drew them quite correctly, but very small. [It was noticeable that the unusual distance at which the drawing was placed from the agent on this occasion seemed to be interpreted by the percipient as smallness of size.]

Double object.—It was now that I arranged the double object between Miss R——d and Miss E., who happened to be sitting nearly facing one another. [See *Nature*, June 12th, 1884, for the published report of this particular incident which has been reproduced above.] The drawing was a square on one side of the paper, a cross on the other. Miss R——d looked at the side with the square on it. Miss

ORIGINALS   REPRODUCTION

E. looked at the side with the cross. Neither knew what the other was looking at—nor did the percipient know that anything unusual was being tried. Mr. Birchall was silently asked to take off his attention, and he got up and looked out of window before the drawings were brought in, and during the experiment. There was no contact. Very soon Miss R. said, "I see things moving about . . . I seem to see two things . . . I see first one up there and then one down there . . . I don't know which to draw. . . . I can't see either distinctly." (Well anyhow, draw what you have seen.) She took off the bandage and drew first a square, and then said, "Then there was the other thing as well . . . afterwards they seemed to go into one," and she drew a cross inside the square from corner to corner, adding afterwards, "I don't know what made me put it inside."

The next is a case of a perfect stranger acting as agent by himself at the first trial. Dr. Shears, house physician at the Eye and Ear Infirmary, came down to see the phenomena, and Miss R. having arrived before the others, Mr. Guthrie proposed his trying as agent alone. Dr. Shears, therefore, held Miss R.'s hand while I set up in front of him a card: nothing whatever being said as to the nature of the object.

Object—the five of clubs, at first on a white ground. "Is it something bright?" (No answer, but I changed the object to a black ground where it was more conspicuous.) "A lot of black with a white square on it." (Go on.) "Is it a card?" (Yes.) [The affirmative answer did not necessarily signify that it was a playing card; because cards looking like playing cards had been used several times previously, on which objects had been depicted instead of pips.] "Are there five spots on it?" (Yes.) "Black ones." (Right.) "I can't see the suit, but I think it's spades."

Another object at same sitting, but with several agents, no contact, was a drawing of this form—

ORIGINAL   REPRODUCTION

"I can see something, but I am sure I can't draw it. . . . It's something with points all round it. . . . It's a star, . . . or like a triangle within a triangle." Asked to draw it, she expressed reluctance, said it was too difficult, and drew part of a star figure, evidently a crude reproduction of the original, but incomplete. She then began afresh by drawing a triangle, but was unable to proceed.

I then showed her the object for a few seconds. She exclaimed, "Oh yes, that's what I saw. . . . I understand it now." I said, "Well now draw it." She made a more complete attempt, but it was no more really like the original than the first had been. Here it is:

SKETCH MADE AFTER SEEING THE ORIGINAL

Experiments at a Sitting in the room of Dr. Herdman, Professor of Zoology at University College

Object—a drawing of the outline of a flag.—Miss R. as percipient in contact with Miss E. as agent. Very quickly Miss R. said, "It's a little flag," and when asked to draw, she drew it fairly well but "perverted" as depicted in the figure. I showed her the flag (as usual after a success), and then took it away to the drawing place to fetch something else. I made another drawing, but instead of bringing it

ORIGINAL   REPRODUCTION

I brought the flag back again, and set it up in the same place as before, but upside down. There was no contact this time. Miss R——d and Miss E. were acting as agents.

Object—same flag inverted.—After some time, Miss R. said, "No, I can't see anything this time. I still see that flag. . . . The flag keeps bothering me. . . . I shan't do it this time." Presently I said, "Well, draw what you saw anyway." She said, "I only saw the same flag, but perhaps it had a cross on it." So she drew a flag in the same position as before, but added a cross to it. Questioned as to aspect she said, "Yes, it was just the same as before."

Object—an oval gold locket hanging by a bit of string with a little price label attached.—Placed like the former object on a large drawing board, swathed in a college gown. The percipient, Miss R., close behind the said board and almost hidden by it. Agents, Miss R——d and Miss E. sitting in front; no contact; nothing said. "I see something gold, . . . something hanging, . . . like a gold locket." (What shape?) "It's oval," indicating with her fingers correctly. (Very good so far, tell us something more)—[meaning ticket at top]. But no more was said. When shown the object she said, "Oh yes, it was just like that," but she had seen nothing of the little paper ticket.

Next object—a watch and chain pinned up to the board as on a waistcoat.—This experiment was a failure, and is only interesting because the watch-ticking sounded abnormally loud, sufficient to give any amount of hint to a person on the look out for such sense indications. But it is very evident to those witnessing the experiments that the percipient is in a quite different attitude of mind to that of a clever guesser, and ordinary sense indications seem wholly neglected.

I scarcely expected, however, that the watch-ticking could pass unnoticed, though indeed we shuffled our feet to drown it somewhat, but so it was; and all we got was "something bright . . . either steel or silver. . . . Is it anything like a pair of scissors?" (Not a bit.)

I have now done with the selection of experiments in which Miss R. acted as percipient; and I will describe some of those made with Miss E. At the time these seemed perhaps less satisfactory and complete, but there are several points of considerable interest noticeable in connection with them.

B.—EXPERIMENTS WITH MISS E. AS PERCIPIENT

Object—an oblong piece of red (cerise) silk. Agent, Mr. B., in contact.—"Red." (What sort of red?) "A dark red." (What shape?) "One patch." (Well, what shade is it?) "Not a pale red."

Next object—a yellow oblong. Agent as before.—"A dusky gold colour. . . . A square of some yellow shade."

Object—the printed letter r. Told it was a letter; agent as before. —"I can see R." (What sort of R?) "An ordinary capital R."

This illustrates feebly what often, though not always, happens with Miss E.—that the idea of the object is grasped rather than its actual shape.

Another object—a small printed e.—"Is it E?" (Yes.) But, again, she couldn't tell what sort of E it was.

Object—a teapot cut out of silver paper.—Present—Dr. Herdman,

ORIGINAL   REPRODUCTION

Miss R——d, and Miss R., Miss R. holding percipient's hands, but all thinking of the object. Told nothing. She said, "Something light. . . . No colour. . . . Looks like a duck. . . . Like a silver duck. . . . Something oval. . . . Head at one end and tail at the other." [This is not uncommon in ducks.] The object, being rather large, was then moved farther back, so that it might be more easily grasped by the agents as a whole, but percipient persisted that it was like a duck. On being told to unbandage and draw, she drew a rude and "perverted" copy of the teapot, but didn't know what it was unless it was a duck. Dr. Herdman then explained that he had been thinking all the time how like a duck the original teapot was, and, in fact, had been thinking more of ducks than teapots.

Next object—a hand mirror brought in and set up in front of Miss R——d.—No contact at first. Told nothing. She said, "Is it a colour?" (No.) "No, I don't see anything." The glass was then shifted for Miss R. to look at herself in it, holding percipient's hand. "No I don't get this." Gave it up. I then hid the mirror in my coat, and took it out of the room. Dr. Herdman reports that while I was away Miss E. begged to know what the object had been, but the agents refused, saying that I had evidently wished to keep it secret. Half annoyed, Miss E. said, "Oh, well, it doesn't matter. I believe it was a looking-glass."

Next object—a drawing of a right-angled triangle. No contact.— "Is it like that?" drawing a triangle with her finger (no answer). "It's almost like a triangle." She then drew an isosceles triangle.

Next object—a drawing of two parallel but curved lines. No contact.—"I only see two lines," indicating two parallel lines. "Now they seem to close up."

Next object—a tetrahedron outline rudely drawn in projection.—"Is

it another triangle?" (No answer was made, but I silently passed round to the agents a scribbled message, "Think of a pyramid.") Miss E. then said, "I only see a triangle." . . . then hastily, "Pyramids of Egypt. No, I shan't do this." Asked to draw, she only drew a triangle.

Object—a rude outline of a donkey or other quadruped.—Still no contact at first. "Can't get it, I am sure." I then asked the agents to leave the room, and to come in and try one by one. First Miss R——d, without contact, and then with. Next Miss R., in contact, when Miss E. said hopelessly, "An old woman in a poke bonnet." Finally I tried as agent alone, and Miss E. said, "It's like a donkey but I can't see it, nor can I draw it."

General Statements about the Experiments

In addition to the experiments with single percipients, I tried a few with both percipients sitting together— hoping to learn something by comparing their different perceptions of the same object. But unfortunately these experiments were not very successful; sometimes they each appeared to get different aspects or the parts of object, but never very distinct or perfect impressions. The necessity of imposing silence on the percipients, as well as on the agents, was also rather irksome, and renders the results less describable without the actual drawings. I still think that this variation might convey something interesting if pursued under favourable circumstances. Whether greater agent-power is necessary to affect two percipients as strongly as one; or whether the blankness of mind of one percipient re-acts on the other, I cannot say.

With regard to the feelings of the percipients when receiving an impression, they seem to have some sort of consciousness of the action of other minds on them; and once or twice, when not so conscious, have complained that there seemed to be "no power" or anything acting, and that they not only received no impression, but did not feel as if they were going to.

I asked Miss E. what she felt when impressions were coming freely, and she said she felt a sort of influence or thrill. They both say that several images appear to them sometimes, but that one among them persistently recurs, and they have a feeling when they fix upon one that it is the right one.

Sometimes they seem quite certain that they are right. Sometimes they are very uncertain, but still right. Occasionally Miss E. has been pretty confident and yet wrong.

One serious failure rather depresses them, and after a success others often follow. It is because of these rather delicate psychological conditions that one cannot press the variations of an experiment as far as one would do if dealing with inert and more dependable matter. Usually the presence of a stranger spoils the phenomenon, though in some cases a stranger has proved a good agent straight off.

The percipients complain of no fatigue as induced by the experiments, and I have no reason to suppose that any harm is done them. The agent, on the other hand, if very energetic, is liable to contract a headache; and Mr. Guthrie himself, who was a powerful and determined agent for a long time, now feels it wiser to refrain from acting, and conducts the experiments with great moderation.

If experiments are only conducted for an hour or so a week, no harm can, I should judge, result, and it would be very interesting to know what percentage of people have the perceptive faculty well developed.

The experiments are easy to try, but they should be tried soberly and quietly, like any other experiment. A public platform is a most unsuitable place; and nothing tried before a mixed or jovial audience can be of the slightest scientific value. Such demonstrations may be efficient in putting money into the pockets of showmen, or in amusing one's friends; but all real evidence must be obtained in the quiet of the laboratory or the study.

CHAPTER IV

FURTHER EXPERIMENTS IN TELEPATHY

THE next experience of any importance which I had in this kind of experimental telepathy took place during a visit to the Austrian province beyond Tyrol with some English friends during the summer of 1892, and is thus described in the *Proceedings* of the Society for Psychical Research, vol. vii. page 374.

While staying for a fortnight in the house of Herr von Lyro, at Pörtschach am See, Carinthia, I found that his two adult daughters were adepts in the so-called "willing-game," and were accustomed to entertain their friends by the speed and certainty with which they could perform actions decided on by the company; the operator being led either by one or by two others, and preferring to be led by someone to whom she was accustomed. Another lady staying in the house was said to be able to do things equally well, but not without nervous prostration.

On the evening when I witnessed the occurrences nothing done could be regarded as conclusive against muscle-reading, though the speed and accuracy with which the willed action was performed exceeded any muscle-reading that I had previously seen, and left me little doubt but that there was some genuine thought-transference power.

Accordingly I obtained permission to experiment in a more satisfactory manner, and on several occasions tested the power of the two sisters, using one as agent and the other as percipient alternately. Once or twice a stranger was asked to act as agent, but without success.

The operations were conducted in an ordinary simple manner. One of the sisters was placed behind a drawing board, erected by me on a temporary sort of easel, while the other sat in front of the same board ; and the objects or drawings to be guessed were placed on a ledge in front of the board, in full view of the one and completely hidden from the other.

Naturally I attended to the absence of mirrors and all such obvious physical complications. The percipient preferred to be blindfolded, but no precaution was taken with reference to this blindfolding, since we know that it is unsafe to put any trust in bandaging of eyes (*Journal*, i. 84). Agent and percipient were within reach of one another, and usually held each other's hands across a small table. The kind and amount of contact was under control, and was sometimes broken altogether, as is subsequently related.

The ladies were interested in the subject, and were perfectly willing to try any change of conditions that I suggested, and my hope was gradually to secure the phenomenon without contact of any kind, as I had done in the previous case reported ; but unfortunately in the present instance contact seemed essential to the transfer. Very slight contact was sufficient, for instance through the backs of the knuckles ; but directly the hands were separated, even though but a quarter of an inch, the phenomena ceased,—reappearing again directly contact was established. I tried whether I could bridge over the gap effectively with my own, or another lady's hand; but that did not do. I also once tried both sisters blindfolded, and holding each other by one hand, while two other persons completed the chain and tried to act as agents. After a time the sisters were asked to draw, simultaneously and independently, what they had "seen"; but though the two drawings were close imitations of each other, they in this case bore no likeness to the object on which the agents had been gazing. My impression, therefore, is that there is some kind of close sympathetic connection between the sisters, so that an idea may, as it were, reverberate between their minds when their hands touch, but that they are only faintly, if at all, susceptible to the influence of outside persons.

Whether the importance of contact in this case depends upon the fact that it is the condition to which they have always been accustomed, or whether it is a really effective aid, I am not sure.

So far as my own observation went, it was interesting and new to me to see how clearly the effect seemed to depend on contact, and how abruptly it ceased when contact was broken. While guessing through a pack of cards, for instance, rapidly and continuously, I sometimes allowed contact and sometimes stopped it; and the guesses changed, from frequently correct to quite wild, directly the knuckles or finger tips, or any part of the skin of the two hands, ceased to touch. It was almost like breaking an electric circuit. At the same time, partial contact seemed less effective than a thorough hand grasp.

It is perfectly obvious how strongly this dependence

on contact suggests the idea of a code; and I have to admit at once that this flaw prevents this series of observations from having any value as a test case, or as establishing *de novo* the existence of the genuine power. My record only appeals to those who, on other grounds, have accepted the general possibility of thought-trans-ference, and who, therefore, need not feel unduly strained when asked to credit my assertion that unfair practices were extremely unlikely; and that, apart from this moral conviction, there was a sufficient amount of internal evidence derived from the facts themselves to satisfy me that no code was used. The internal evidence of which I am thinking was: (1) the occa-sionally successful reproduction of nameless drawings; (2) the occasional failure to get any clue to an object or drawing with a perfectly simple and easily telegraphed name; (3) the speed with which the guesses were often made.

I wish, however, distinctly to say that none of the evidence which I can offer against a prearranged code is scientifically and impersonally conclusive, nor could it be accepted as of sufficient weight by a sceptic on the whole subject. It is only because, with full opportunity of forming a judgment, and in the light of my former experience, I am myself satisfied that what I observed was an instance of genuine sympathetic or syntonic communication, and because such cases seem at the present time to be rather rare, that I make this brief report on the circumstances.

I detected no well-marked difference between the powers of the two sisters, and it will be understood that one of them was acting as agent and the other as percipient in each case. Sometimes the parents of the girls were present, but often only one or two

friends of my own, who were good enough to invite
the young ladies to their sitting-room for the purpose of experiment; though such experiments are,
when carefully performed, confessedly rather tedious
and dull.

In the early willing-game experiments, such things
were done as taking a particular ring from one person's
hand and putting it on another's; selecting a definite
piece of music from a pile, taking it to the piano, and
beginning to play it. The last item (the beginning to
play) I did not happen to witness, but I was told of it
by several persons as more than could be accounted for
by muscle-reading. A sceptic, however, could of course
object that imperfect bandaging would enable a title to
be read.

One of the things I suggested was aimed at excluding the operation of unconscious muscular guidance as
far as possible, and it consisted in desiring that the lady
while standing in the middle of the room should kick off
her shoes without touching them and begin to sing a
specified song. Success, however, was only partial.
After one or two attempts to wander about the room as
usual, she did shuffle a shoe off, but though she did not
actually touch her feet she stooped so that the held hand
came very near them. She then stood some little time
uncertain what to do next, and at last broke silence by
saying "Shall I sing?"

The first attempt at the more careful experiments
was not at all successful, but novelty of conditions may
fairly be held responsible for that. On the second and
subsequent evenings success was much more frequent:
on the whole, I think, more frequent than failure,—
certainly far beyond chance. I proceed to give a fairly
complete account of the whole series.

The first object was a teapot; but there was no result.

The first drawing was the outline of a box with a flag at one corner; but that produced no impression.

Next, for simplicity, I explained that the object this time was a letter (*Buchstabe*), on which it was correctly guessed E. Another letter, M, was given quite wrong. A childish back-view outline of a cat was given oval like an egg; some other things were unperceived.

On the second evening I began by saying that the object was a colour; on which red was instantly and correctly stated.

A blue object which followed was guessed wrong.

An outline figure of a horse was correctly named. So was the letter B. I then drew a square with a diagonal cross, and a round ring or spot just above the intersection, the whole looking something like the back of an envelope. After a certain interval of silence (perhaps two minutes) the lady said she was ready to draw what she had "seen," and drew the thing almost exactly, except that the spot was put right on the centre of the cross instead of above it, and a superfluous faint vertical stroke was added. Its possible resemblance to an envelope was not detected, nor did the reproduction suggest the idea: it was drawn as, and looked like, a nameless geometrical figure.

The reproductions were nearly always much smaller in size than the originals. The agent did not look on while the reproduction was being made. It is best for no one to look on while the percipient draws, to avoid the possibility of unconscious indications. The original drawings were always made by me, sometimes before, sometimes during, the sitting. These conditions were all satisfactory.

On the third evening I began with a pack of cards, running through them quickly; with 2 reporters, one recording the card held up, the other recording the guess made, without knowing whether it was right or wrong. I held up the cards one after the other and gave no indication whether the guesses were right or wrong. The suit was not attempted, so that the chances of error were, I suppose, 12 to 1.

On comparing the two lists afterwards, out of 16 guesses only 6 were wrong. Full contact was allowed during this series. The lists are reproduced below.

The card guessing is obviously not of the slightest use unless *bona fides* be certain, but, given that, it affords the readiest method of studying the effect of varied conditions, interposed obstacles, and such like. The whole pack was always used and I simply cut it at random and held up the bottom card. About 10 or 12 cards could be got through in a minute.

The following is the list of the first card series. Full contact allowed :—

CARD LOOKED AT				CARD GUESSED
Seven of Spades	.	.	.	Seven
Six of Hearts .	.	.	.	Six
Queen of Spades	.	.	.	King
Nine of Spades	.	.	.	Nine
Three of Spades	.	.	.	Six
Eight of Diamonds	.	.	.	Eight
Ace of Clubs .	.	.	.	Ace
Knave of Diamonds	.	.	.	Queen
Five of Diamonds	.	.	.	Five
Two of Spades .	.	.	.	Ace
Ten of Hearts .	.	.	.	Six
King of Diamonds	.	.	.	King
Ace of Spades .	.	.	.	Ace
Nine of Diamonds	.	.	.	Six
Eight of Hearts	.	.	.	Eight
Four of Spades	.	.	.	Four

Thus, out of the sixteen trials, 10 were correct and 6 were wrong.

Whatever may be the cause of this amount of success, *chance* is entirely out of the question, since the probability of so many successes as ten in sixteen trials, when the individual probability each time is one-thirteenth, is too small to be taken into account.

The theory of such a calculation is given in Todhunter's Algebra, articles 740 and 741 ; but as exactness in such a case is rather tedious and unnecessary, we may over-estimate the total probability by calculating it as follows : $\frac{16!}{10! \, 6!} \left(\frac{1}{13}\right)^{10}$; thus leaving out the factor $\left(\frac{12}{13}\right)^{6}$. This factor would be necessary to give the chance of ten successes *exactly*; but that is needlessly narrow, since there is no particular point in the exact number of 10. The chance of ten *at least* is more like what we have to express.

So an over-estimate of probability is $\frac{8008}{13^{10}}$; that is to say, there is less than one chance in ten million that such a result would occur at perfect random, *i.e.* without any special cause.

Some guesses were made, both with cards and objects, on another evening, without contact, but none were successful. With contact there was success again.

I then went back to simple drawings; with the result that a cross was reproduced as a cross; a figure like 4 petals was reproduced in two ways, one of them being a vague 5-petalled figure.

An object consisting of an ivory pocket measure, standing on end like an inverted V, was drawn fairly well as to general aspect.

A sinuous line was reproduced as a number of sinuous lines. A triangle or wedge, point downward, was reproduced imperfectly.

On other evenings other simple diagrams were tried, such as a face, reproduced as 3 rounds with dots and cross; and a figure like an A with an extra long cross stroke, which could be easily signalled as an A, but which was reproduced correctly as a geometrical diagram with the long stroke prominent.

A circle with 3 radii was reproduced as a circle with roughly inscribed triangle.

The number 3145 was reproduced orally and very quickly as 3146; 715 also quickly as "714, no 715." The written word *hund* was reproduced correctly, but with a capital initial letter.

And being told that they had previously thus reproduced a word in an unknown language (not unknown character), viz., Hungarian, I tried the Greek letters Φαιδω; this, however, was considered too puzzling and was only reproduced as *Uaso*.

A French high-heeled shoe, of crockery, set up as object, was drawn by the percipient very fairly correct, and said to be something like a boot, and a protuberance was tacked on where the heel was.

A white plaster cast of a child's hand, next tried, failed to give any impression. An unlighted candle in candlestick was unsuccessful, and it was objected that there was too much glare of light. Subsequently the percipient said she had seen the general outline of a candlestick but did not think of its being the thing. A teapot and a cup both failed, and two of the drawings did not succeed in stimulating any colourable imitation.

Lastly, another set of card trials were made, with the object of testing the effect of various kinds of contact: a card series being quick and easy to run through.

5

	CARD EXHIBITED TO AGENT	CARD NAMED BY PERCIPIENT
Full contact with both hands . . .	Nine . . .	Nine
	King . . .	King
Contact with tips of fingers only . .	Knave . . .	Two
	Nine . . .	Nine
	Nine . . .	Ten
	Queen . . .	Two
	Eight . . .	Eight
Contact with one finger of one hand .	Five . . .	Six
	Seven . . .	Seven
	Three . . .	Four
	Ten . . .	Six
	Queen . . .	Two
	Ace . . .	Ace
No contact . .	Ace . . .	Four
	Knave . . .	Five
No direct contact, but gap bridged by other person's hand	King . . .	Four
	Four . . .	Eight
	Ten . . .	Seven
Slight contact of knuckles . .	Eight . . .	Six
	Six . . .	Ace
	Two . . .	Two
Full contact again .	Knave . . .	Ace
	Seven . . .	Six
	Three . . .	Three
	Four . . .	Four
	Ace of diamonds .	Ace—red—diamond
	Nine of clubs held sideways	Nine—clubs

The *record* of this series is more complete than that of another varying contact series,—reported below,—but it did not strike me as so instructive at the time; and as it came toward the end of an evening there was probably some fatigue.

The last two entries represent attempts to get the suit as well; but as the particulars are given in stages there is no particular advantage in thus naming a card completely, and it takes a longer time.

On another evening the amount of contact was varied, but I omitted to call out to the reporter the position of the hands with reference to each other.   One hand of each person lay on a table, and I sometimes made them touch, sometimes separated them, all the time going on with the card series.   My impression at the time was (as expressed above) that pronounced failure began directly I broke contact, but that mere knuckle contact was sufficient to permit some amount of success.   [When successes are frequent in the following list, fairly complete contact may be assumed.   At other times I broke and united the two hands as I chose, for my own edification, and was struck with the singular efficiency of contact.]

I can only give the record as it stands.   I believe we began without any contact, but very soon made the hands touch intermittently.

Second Card Series.   Varying amount of contact : sometimes none

CARD SHOWN				CARD GUESSED
2 of Spades	.	.	.	Knave
Ace of Diamonds		.	.	5
Knave of Diamonds		.	.	Knave
10 of Diamonds		.	.	9
6 of Hearts	.	.	.	5
8 of Hearts	.		.	9
9 of Diamonds .		.	.	Ace
King of Diamonds		.	.	King
10 of Hearts	.	.	.	10
9 of Clubs	.	.	.	9
Ace	.	.	.	Ace
Queen	.	.	.	2
Queen	.	.	.	Queen
Knave	.	.	.	Ace
King	.	.	.	King
8	.	.	.	8
8	.	.	.	8
7	.	.	.	8
Ace	.	.	.	Ace
Knave	.	.	.	Knave
7	.	.	.	7
4	.	.	.	4
9	.	.	.	6
Queen	.	.	.	3
King	.	.	.	King

CARD SHOWN					CARD GUESSED
Ace	.	.	.	.	7
Ace	.	.	.	.	5
5	.	.	.	.	10
5	.	.	.	.	4
6	.	.	.	.	7
5	.	.	.	.	3
6	.	.	.	.	6
2	.	.	.	.	3
3	.	.	.	.	6
4	.	.	.	.	4
2	.	.	.	.	8
4	.	.	.	.	5
3	.	.	.	.	4
3	.	.	.	.	Knave

Where lines are drawn it is because I called out some change in the contact; but I made other changes whose occurrence is not recorded.

The only use to be made of the record of this series, therefore, is to treat it as a whole and to observe that out of 39 trials 16 were correct and 23 wrong.

On this occasion there was one reporter who wrote down both what he saw and what he heard; and the operation was so rapid that he had sometimes barely time to do the writing. Towards the end of a series, fatigue on the part of either agent or percipient generally seemed to spoil the conditions.

It is manifest that these experiments should not be conducted too long consecutively, nor repeated without sufficient interval; but if common sense is used there is nothing deleterious in the attempt, and if more persons tried, probably the power would be found more widely distributed than is at present suspected.

I wish to express gratitude to the Fräulein von Lyro and their parents, for the courtesy with which they acquiesced in my request for opportunities of experiment, and for the willingness with which they submitted to dull and irksome conditions, in order to enable me to give as good evidence as possible.

Experiments at a Distance

For more recent experiments, and for experiments conducted over a considerable intervening distance, I must refer to the *Proceedings* of the Society for Psychical Research, vol. xxi., where an account is given of the notable and careful series of observations made by two lady members of the Society, Miss Miles and Miss Ramsden. These ladies, while at their respective homes, or staying in country houses and other places at a distance from each other, endeavoured to transmit an impression of scenes and occupations from one to the other. They kept a careful record both of what they tried to send, and of what was received. And when these records are compared, the correspondence is seen to be beyond and above anything that might be due to chance.

Collusion might rationally be urged as an explanation, by strangers ; but that is not an explanation that can be accepted by those who know all the facts.

When Miss Miles and Miss Ramsden began their experiments in 1905, Miss Miles was living in London, and Miss Ramsden in Buckinghamshire, and the arrangement was that Miss Miles should play the part of agent, Miss Ramsden that of percipient, the times of the experiment being fixed beforehand. Miss Miles noted, at the time of each experiment, in a book kept for the purpose, the idea or image which she wished to convey ; while Miss Ramsden wrote down each day the impressions that had come into her mind, and sent the record to Miss Miles before knowing what she had attempted on her side. Miss Miles then pasted this record into her book opposite her own notes, and in some cases added a further note explanatory of her circumstances at the time; since to these it was found that Miss Ramsden's impressions often corresponded. Whenever it was possible Miss Miles obtained confirmatory evidence from other persons as to the circumstances that had not been noted at the time, and the corroboration of these persons was written in her book. All the original records of these experiments have been submitted to the Editor of the *Proceedings* of the Society for Psychical Research, and have passed that very critical ordeal.

In the second series of experiments, in October and November 1906, Miss Miles, the agent, was staying first near Bristol and afterwards near Malmesbury in Wiltshire; while Miss Ramsden, the percipient, was living all the time near Kingussie, Inverness-shire, and therefore at a distance of about 400 miles from the agent. During the last three days of the experiments, Miss Miles, unknown to Miss Ramsden, was in London.

The general plan of action was that Miss Ramsden should think of Miss Miles regularly at 7 p.m. on every day that an experiment was to be tried, and should write her impressions on a postcard or letter card, which was posted almost always on the next morning to Miss Miles. These postcards or letter cards were kept by Miss Miles and pasted into her notebook, so that the postmarks on them show the time of despatch. And copies of many of these postcards were sent also at the same time to Professor Barrett, who had advised concerning the method of experiment.

Miss Miles on her side had no fixed time for thinking of Miss Ramsden, but thought of her more or less during the whole day, and in the evening noted briefly what ideas had been most prominently before her mind during the day, and which she wished to convey, or thought might have been conveyed, to Miss Ramsden. These notes were made generally on a postcard, which was, as a rule, posted to Miss Ramsden next day. The postcards were afterwards returned to Miss Miles to be placed with her records,—so that here also the postmarks show the date of despatch of the information to Miss Ramsden.

Out of a total of fifteen days' experiments, the idea that Miss Miles was attempting to convey, as recorded on her postcards, appeared on six occasions in a complete or partial form among Miss Ramsden's impressions on the same date. But it also happened that almost every day some of Miss Ramsden's impressions represented, pretty closely, something that Miss Miles had been seeing or talking about on the same day. In other words,—while the agent only succeeded occasionally in transferring the ideas deliberately chosen by her for the purpose, the percipient seemed often to have some sort of supernormal knowledge of her friend's surroundings, irrespective of what that friend had specially wished her to see.

When this happened, Miss Miles at once made careful notes of the event or topic to which Miss Ramsden's statement seemed to refer, and also obtained corroborations from her friends on the spot. Further, when Miss Ramsden gave descriptions of scenes which seemed to Miss Miles like the places where she was staying, she got picture postcards of them, or photographed them, to show how far the descriptions really corresponded.

The actual record is given in the *Proceedings* of the Society for Psychical Research, vol. xxi., together with illustrations, but it must suffice here to quote the critical and judicial opinion of the Editor, which is thus given :—

" After studying all the records, it appears to us that while some of the coincidences of thought between the two experimenters are probably accidental, the total amount of correspondence is more than can be thus accounted for and points distinctly to the action of telepathy between them."

CHAPTER V

SPONTANEOUS CASES OF THOUGHT-TRANSFERENCE

A NEW fact of this sort, if really established, must have innumerable consequences : among other things it may be held to account for a large number of phenomena alleged to occur spontaneously, but never yet received with full credence by scientific authority.

Such cases as those which immediately follow, for instance, we now begin to classify under the head " spontaneous telepathy," and it is natural to endeavour to proceed further in the same direction and use telepathy as a possible clue to many other legendary occurrences also ; as we shall endeavour to show in the next chapter.

Two Cases

As stepping stones from the experimental to the spontaneous cases I quote two from a mass of material at the end of Mr. Myers's first volume, page 674 ; the first concerning a remote connexion of my own.

On the 27th of April, 1889, we were expecting my sister-in-law and her daughter from South America. My wife, being away from home, was unable to meet them at Southampton, so an intimate friend of the family, a Mr. P., offered to do so. It was between Derby and Leicester about 3.30 p.m. My wife was travelling in the train. She closed her eyes to rest, and at the same moment a telegram paper appeared before her with the words, "Come at once, your sister is dangerously ill." During |the afternoon I received a telegram from Mr. P. to my wife, worded exactly the same and sent from Southampton 3.30 p.m. to Bedford. On my wife's arrival home about 9 p.m. I deferred communicating it until she had some refreshment, being very tired. I afterwards made the remark, "I have some news for you," and she answered, "Yes, I thought so, you have received a telegram from Mr. P. !" I said, "How do you know?" She then told me the contents and her strange experiences in the train, and that it impressed her so much that she felt quite anxious all the rest of the journey.

With regard to the above, my wife had no idea of her sister being ill, and was not even at the time thinking about them, but was thinking about her own child she had just left at a boarding school. Also the handwriting my wife saw, she recognised at once to be Mr. P.'s. But then, again, he would have been writing on a white paper form, and the one she saw was the usual brown coloured paper.

Fredk. L. Lodge

In reply to inquiries, Mr. F. Lodge wrote as follows :—

The letter I sent you, with account of vision, I wrote from my wife's dictation. After it occurred in the train she took notice of the hour, and from the time marked on the telegram of its despatch from Southampton, we at once remarked it must have occurred as Mr. P. was filling in a form at Southampton. Mr. P. is now in South America constructing a railway line, and will not return to England for about a year. The occurrence was mentioned to him.

Two years having elapsed, my wife could not say the exact time now, but it was between 3 and 4 p.m., although when it happened, we did notice from the telegram that the time corresponded.

Fredk. L. Lodge

The second case illustrates the communicating of sensations,—a possibility verified in the Liverpool experiments of Mr. Malcolm Guthrie. A pinch or other pain, or a taste caused by some food or chemical, was there often transferred from agent to percipient. Contact was usually found essential for success in these experimental cases ; but, to guard against normal sensation, the agent and percipient were arranged in separate rooms, with a specially contrived and padded small hole in the wall so that they could hold hands through it. Some early experiments of this kind are narrated in the first volume of *Proceedings*, S.P.R., page 275 ; but I myself was present at many others of the same kind.

Here follows an account of the incident which happened to Mr. and Mrs. Arthur Severn ; the narrative having been obtained through the kindness of Mr. Ruskin. Mrs. Severn says :—

BRANTWOOD, CONISTON
October 27th, 1883

I woke up with a start, feeling I had had a hard blow on my mouth, and with a distinct sense that I had been cut, and was bleeding under my upper lip, and seized my pocket-handkerchief, and held it (in a little pushed lump) to the part as I sat up in bed ; and after a few seconds, when I removed it, I was astonished not to see any blood, and only then realised it was impossible anything could have struck me there, as I lay fast asleep in bed, and so I thought it was only a dream !—but I looked at my watch, and saw it was seven, and finding Arthur (my husband) was not in the room, I concluded (rightly) that he must have gone out on the lake for an early sail, as it was so fine.

I then fell asleep. At breakfast (half-past nine), Arthur came in rather late, and I noticed he rather purposely sat farther away from me than usual, and every now and then put his pocket-handkerchief furtively up to his lip, in the very way I had done. I said, 'Arthur, why are you doing that?' and added a little anxiously, 'I know you have hurt yourself! but I'll tell you why afterwards.' He said, 'Well, when I was sailing, a sudden squall came, throwing the tiller suddenly round, and it struck me a bad blow in the mouth, under the upper lip, and it has been bleeding a good deal and won't stop.' I then said, 'Have you any idea what o'clock it was when it happened?' and he answered, 'It must have been about seven.'

I then told what had happened to *me*, much to *his* surprise, and all who were with us at breakfast.

It happened here about three years ago at Brantwood.

JOAN R. SEVERN

The episode is duly authenticated, in accordance with the rule of the S.P.R., by concurrent testimony (*Proc. S.P.R.* vol. ii. p. 128; also *Phantasms*, i. 188.

Another Case

A case of clairvoyance or distant telepathy was told me by my colleague, Professor R. A. S. Redmayne, as having happened in his own experience when he was engaged in prospecting for mines in a remote district of South Africa accompanied only by a working miner from Durham. His account is here abbreviated :—

> So far as they could keep a record of weeks the solitary two used to play at some game on Sundays, instead of working, but on one particular Sunday the workman declined to play, saying he did not feel up to it, as he had just had an intimation of his mother's death,— that she had spoken of him in her last hours saying that she "would never see Albert again."
>
> My informant tried to chaff his assistant out of his melancholy, since it was a physical impossibility that they could receive recent news by any normal means. But he adhered to his conviction, and in accordance with North Country tradition seemed to regard it as natural that he should thus know.
>
> Weeks afterwards complete confirmation came from England, both as to date and circumstance; the words of the dying woman having been similar to those felt at the time by her distant son.

The occurrence made a marked impression on my informant and broke down his scepticism as to the possibility of these strange occurrences.

Fortunately I am able to quote confirmatory evidence of this narrative; for very soon after the verification Professor Redmayne wrote an account of it to his father, and from this gentleman I have received a certified copy of the letter :—

Letter from Professor Redmayne to his Father

Mgagane, nr. Newcastle, Natal,
21st Nov. 1891

I have a curious and startling thing to tell you :—About 6 weeks ago, Tonks said to me one morning, " My mother is dead, Sir. I saw her early this morning lying dead in bed and the relatives standing round the bed ; she said she would never see me again before she died." I laughed at him and ridiculed the matter, and he seemed to forget it, and we thought (no) more of it, but Tonks asked me to note the date which I did not do. Last Wednesday, however, Tonks received a letter from his wife telling him that his mother was dead and had been buried a week, that she died early one Sunday morning about six weeks since and in her sleep ; but before she fell asleep she said she would never see " Albert " again. About a fortnight since I told some people what Tonks had told me, giving it as an instance of the superstitiousness of the Durham pitmen, and they were startled when, the other day, I told them the dream had come true. I will never laugh at anything like this again.

The above is an extract from a letter from my son R. A. S. Redmayne written from Mgagane, Natal, S.A., and dated November 21st [1891].

John M. Redmayne

August 1st, 1902, Harewood, Gateshead

Professor Redmayne has also been good enough to get a certificate from the workman concerned, in the form of a copy of the main portion of the above letter, with the following note appended :—

The above extract correctly relates what occurred to me whilst living in Natal with Mr. Redmayne.

Signed Albert Tonks
Date *August 21st,* 1901

Witness to above Signature N. B. Paddon, Seaton Delaval

Garibaldi's dream of the death of his mother at Nice, when he was in mid-Pacific, is a historical instance of the same kind (G. M. Trevelyan, *Garibaldi and the Thousand,* p. 18).

CHAPTER VI

APPLIED TELEPATHY

An Example of the Influence of Modern Thought on Ancient Superstitions

IT is being made clear, I hope, how the fact of thought-transference—especially of the unconscious or subliminal variety—enables us to admit the possibility of the truth of a large number of occurrences which previously we should have been liable to stigmatise as impossible and absurd. For in truth not only apparitions of the dying and phantasms of the living may tentatively and hypothetically be thus explained, but a number of other phenomena seem likely gradually to fall into their place in an orderly and intelligible Universe when submitted to this rationalising treatment. I do not say that its success is universal. I hold that it may be pressed too far; there are some things which even the greatest extension of it will not explain. Nevertheless when we have a clue we are bound to follow it up to the utmost before abandoning it, and we will therefore enter upon a consideration of as many phenomena as at this stage we can see any chance of beginning rationally to understand. So let us contemplate the subject as reasonably and physically as we can.

By thought-transference I mean a possible communication between mind and mind, by means other than any of the known organs of sense : what I may call a sympathetic connexion between mind and mind ; using the term mind in a vague and popular sense, without strict definition.   And as to the meaning of sympathetic connexion,—let us take some examples :—

A pair of iron levers, one on the ground, the other some hundred yards away on a post, are often seen to be sympathetically connected ;   for when a railway official hauls one of them through a certain angle the distant lever or semaphore-arm revolves through a similar angle.   The disturbance has travelled from one to the other through a very obvious medium of communication—viz., an iron wire or rope.

A reader unacquainted with physics may think " transmission " in this case a misnomer, since he may think the connexion is instantaneous—but it is not. The connexion is due to a pulse which travels at a perfectly definite and measured pace—approximately three miles per second.

The pulling of a knob, followed by the ringing of a bell, is a similar process, and the transmission of the impulse in either of these cases is commonly considered simple and mechanical.   It is not so simple as we think ; for concerning cohesion we are exceedingly ignorant, and why one end of a stick moves when the other end is touched no one at present is able clearly to tell us.

Consider, now, a couple of tuning forks, or precisely similar musical instruments, isolated from each other and from other bodies,—suspended in air, let us say.   Sound one of them and the other responds—i.e. begins to emit the same note.   This is known in acoustics as sympathetic resonance ;   and again a disturbance has travelled through the medium from one to the other. The medium in this case is intangible, but quite familiar, viz., atmospheric air.

Next, suspend a couple of magnets, alike in all respects; pivoted, let us say, on points, at some distance from each other. Touch one of the magnets and set it swinging,—the other begins to swing slightly, too. Once more, a disturbance has travelled from one to the other, but the medium in this case is by no means obvious. It is nothing solid, liquid, or gaseous; that much is certain. Whether it is material or not depends partly on what we mean by "material"—partly requires more knowledge before a satisfactory answer can be given. We do, however, know something of the medium operative in this case, and we call it the Ether—the Ether of Space.

In these cases the intensity of the response varies rapidly with distance, and at a sufficiently great distance the response would be imperceptible.

This may be hastily set down as a natural consequence of a physical medium of communication, and a physical or mechanical disturbance; but it is not quite so.

Consider a couple of telephones connected properly by wires. They are sympathetic, and if one is tapped the other receives a shock. Speaking popularly, whatever is said to one is repeated by the other, and distance is practically unimportant; at any rate, there is no simple law of inverse square, or any such kind of law; there is a definite channel for the disturbance between the two.

The real medium of communication, I may say parenthetically, is still the ether.

Once more, take a mirror, pivoted on an axle, and

capable of slight motion.   At a distance let there be a suitable receiving instrument, say a drum of photographic paper and a lens.   If the sun is shining on the mirror, and everything properly arranged, a line may be drawn by it on the paper miles away, and every tilt given to the mirror shall be reproduced as a kink in the line. And this may go on over great distances; no wire, or anything else commonly called "material" connecting the two stations, nothing but a beam of sunlight, a peculiar state of the ether.

So far we have been dealing with mere physics. Now poach a little on the ground of physiology.   Take two brains, as like as possible, say belonging to two similar animals; place them a certain distance apart, with no known or obvious means of communication, and see if there is any sympathetic link between them. Apply a stimulus to one, and observe whether the other in any way responds?   To make the experiment conveniently, it is best to avail oneself of the entire animal, and not of its brain alone.   It is then easy to stimulate one of the brains through any of the creature's peripheral sense organs, and it may be possible to detect whatever effect is excited in the other brain by some motor impulse, some muscular movement of the corresponding animal.

So far as I know the experiment has hitherto been principally tried on man.   This has certain advantages and certain disadvantages.   The main advantage is that the motor result of intelligent speech is more definite and instructive than mere pawings and gropings or twitchings.   The main disadvantage is that the liability to conscious deception and fraud becomes serious, much more serious than it is with a less cunning animal.

Of course it by no means follows that the experiment

6

will succeed with a lower animal because it succeeds with man; but I am not aware of its having been tried at present except with man.

One mode of trying the experiment would be to pinch or hurt one individual and see if the other can feel any pain. If he does feel anything he will probably twitch and rub, or he may become vocal with displeasure. There are two varieties of the experiment: First, with some manifest link or possible channel, as, for instance, where two individuals hold hands through a stuffed-up hole in a partition-wall; and, second, with no such obvious medium, as when they are at a distance from one another.

Instead of simple pain in any part of the skin, one may stimulate the brain otherwise, by exciting some special sense organ; for instance, those of taste or smell. Apply nauseous or pleasant materials to the palate of one individual and get the receptive person to describe the substance which the other is tasting.

Experiments of this kind are mentioned above, and they have had a fair measure of positive result. But I am not asking for credence concerning specific facts at present. A serious amount of study is necessary before one is in a position to criticise any statement of fact. What I am concerned to show is that such experiments are not, on the face of them, absurd; that they are experiments which ought to be made; and that any result actually obtained, if definite and clear, ought to be gradually and cautiously accepted, whether it be positive or negative.

So far I have supposed the stimulus to be applied to the nerves of touch, or more generally the skin nerves, and to the taste nerves; but we may apply a stimulus equally well to the nerves of hearing, or of

smelling, or of seeing.   An experiment with a sound or
a smell stimulus, however, is manifestly not very crucial
unless the intervening distance between A and B is
excessive; but a sight stimulus can be readily confined
within narrow limits of space.   Thus, a picture can be
held up in front of the eyes of A, and B can be asked
if he sees anything; and if he does, he can be told
either to describe it or to draw it.

If the picture or diagram thus shown to A is one
that has only just been drawn by the responsible experimenter himself; if it is one that has no simple name
that can be signalled; if A is not allowed to touch B,
or to move during the course of the experiment, and
has never seen the picture before; if, by precaution of
screening, rays from the picture can be positively asserted never to have entered the eyes of B; and if,
nevertheless, B describes himself as "seeing" it, however dimly, and is able to draw it, in dead silence on
the part of all concerned; then, I say, the experiment
would be a good one.

But not yet would it be conclusive.   We must consider who A and B are.

If they are a pair of persons who go about together,
and make money out of the exhibition; if they are in
any sense a brace of professionals accustomed to act
together, I deny that anything is solidly proved by such
an experiment; for cunning is by no means an improbable
hypothesis.

Cunning takes such a variety of forms that it is
tedious to discuss them; it is best to eliminate it
altogether.   That can be done by using unassorted
individuals in unaccustomed rooms.   True, the experiment may thus become much more difficult, if not
indeed quite impossible.   Two entirely different tuning

forks will not respond. Two strangers are not usually sympathetic, in the ordinary sense of that word ; perhaps we ought not to expect a response. Nevertheless, the experiment must be made ; and if B is found able to respond, not only to A_1, but also to A_2, A_3, and other complete strangers, under the conditions already briefly mentioned, the experiment may be regarded as satisfactory. I am prepared to assert that such satisfactory experiments have been made.

But the power of response in this way to the uninteresting impression of strangers does not appear to be a common faculty. The number of persons who can act efficiently as B is *apparently* very limited. But I do not make this assertion with any confidence, for so few people have as yet been seriously tried. It is most likely a question of degree. All shades of responsiveness may exist, from nearly o to something considerable.

More experiments are wanted. They are not difficult to try, and sufficient variety may be introduced to prevent the observations from being too deplorably dull. They are, I confess, rather dull.

Before considering them satisfactory or publishing them it would be well to call in the assistance of a trained observer, who may be able to suggest further precautions ; but at first it is probably well to choose fairly easy conditions.

Relations are probably more likely to succeed than are strangers ; persons who feel a sympathy with each other, who are accustomed to imagine they know what the other is thinking of, or to say things simultaneously, and such like vague traditions as are common in most families : such individuals as these would naturally be the most likely ones to begin with, until experiment shows otherwise. The A power seems common

enough ; the B power, so far as I know, is rather rare
—at least to a prominent extent.

It is customary to call A the agent and B the percipient, but there may be some objection to these names.

The name agent suggests activity ; and it is a distinct
question whether any conscious activity is necessary.
Sender and receiver are terms that might be used, but
they labour under similar and perhaps worse objections.
For the present let us simply use the terms A and B,
which involve no hypothesis whatever.

A may be likened to the sending microphone or
transmitter ; B to the receiving telephone.

A to the sounded fork or quivering magnet, B to the
responsive one.

A to the flashing mirror, B to the sensitive sheet.

But observe that in all the cases hitherto mentioned
a third person is mentioned too, the experimenter, C.
A and B are regarded as mere tools, instruments,
apparatus, for C to make his experiments with.

Both are passive till C comes and excites the nerve
of A, either by pinching him, or by putting things in
his mouth, or by showing him diagrams or objects ; and
B is then supposed to respond to A.   It may be objected
that he is really responding to C all the time.   Yes,
indeed, that may sometimes be so, and it is a distinct
possibility to remember.   If something that C is unconsciously looking at is described by B, instead of the
object which is set in front of A, the experiment will
seem a failure.   There are many such possibilities to
bear in mind in so novel a region of research.

But now I want to go on and point out that C is
not essential.   He probably is not an assistance at all,
very likely he is an obstruction, even if he is a serious
and well-intentioned being.   But if D, E, F are present

too as irresponsible spectators, talking or fidgeting, or even sitting still and thinking, the conditions are bad. One can never be sure what F is doing, he may be simply playing the fool. An experiment conducted in front of a large audience is scientifically useless.

Whenever I use the term thought-transference I never mean anything like public performances, whether by genuine persons or impostors. The human race is so constituted that such performances have their value —they incite others to try experiments; but in themselves, and speaking scientifically, public performances are useless, and except when of an exceptionally high order—as they were in the case of the Zancigs—they often tend to obscure a phenomenon by covering it with semi-legitimate contempt.

I fear that some hypnotic exhibitions are worse than useless; in so far as they are conducted, not to advance science, but to exhibit some well known fact again and again, not even to students, but to an idle gaping crowd.

To return, however, to A and B: let us suppose them left alone, not stimulated by any third person; it is quite possible for A to combine the functions of C with his own functions, and to stimulate himself. He may look at a picture or a playing card, or he may taste a substance, or he may, if he can, simply think of a number, or a scene, or an event, and, so to speak, keep it vividly in his mind. It may happen that B will be able to describe the scene of which A is thinking, sometimes almost correctly, sometimes with a large admixture of error, or at least of dimness.

The experiment is virtually the same as those above mentioned, and may be made quite a good one; the only weak part is that, under the circumstances, everything depends on the testimony of A, and A is not always believed.

This is, after all, a disability which he shares with C; and, at any rate, he is able to convince *himself* by such experiments, provided they are successful.

But now go a step further. Let A and B be not thinking of experimenting at all. Let them be at a distance from one another, and going about their ordinary vocations, including somnolence and the other passive as well as active occupations of the twenty-four hours. Let us, however, not suppose them strangers, but relatives or intimate friends. Now let something vividly excite A; let him fall down a cliff, or be run over by a horse, or fall into a river; or let him be taken violently ill, or be subject to some strong emotion; or let him be at the point of death.

Is it not conceivable that if any such sympathetic connexion between individuals as I have been postulating exists,—if a paltry stimulus supplied by a third person is capable in the slightest degree of conveying itself from one individual to another,—is it not conceivable or even probable that a violent stimulus, such as we have supposed A to receive, may be able to induce in B, even though inattentive and otherwise occupied, some dim echo, reverberation, response, and cause him to be more or less aware that A is suffering or perturbed. If B is busy, self-absorbed, actively engaged, he may notice nothing. If he happen to be quiescent, vacant, moody, or half or whole asleep, he may realise and be conscious of something. He may perhaps only feel a vague sense of depression in general; or he may feel the depression and associate it definitely with A; or he may be more distinctly aware of what is happening, and call out that A has had a fall, or an accident, or is being drowned, or is ill; or he may have a specially vivid dream which will trouble him long after he wakes, and may be told to other persons, and written down; or he may think he hears A's voice; or, lastly, he may conjure up an image of A so vividly before his "mind's eye" that he may be able to persuade himself and others that he has seen his apparition:—sometimes a mere purposeless phantom, sometimes in a "setting" of a sort of vision or picture of an event not unlike what is at the time elsewhere really happening.

The Society for Psychical Research have, with splendid perseverance and diligence, undertaken and carried forward the thankless labour of receiving and sifting a great mass of testimony to phenomena such as I have hinted at. They have published some of them in two large volumes, called *Phantasms of the Living*. Fresh evidence comes in every month. The evidence is so cumulative, and some of it is so well established, as to bear down the dead wall of scepticism in all those who have submitted to the drudgery of a study of the material. The evidence induces belief. It is not yet copious enough to lead to a valid induction.

I cannot testify to these facts as I can to the simple experiments where I have acted the part of C. Evidence for spontaneous or involuntary thought-transference must obviously depend on statements received from A and from B, as well as from other persons, some in the neighbourhood of A, others in the neighbourhood of B, together with contemporary newspaper reports, *Times'* obituaries, and other past documents relating to matters of fact, which are available for scrutiny, and may be regarded as trustworthy.

I am prepared, however, to confess that the weight of testimony is sufficient to satisfy my own mind that

such things do undoubtedly occur; that the distance
between England and India is no barrier to the sympathetic communication of intelligence in some way of
which we are at present ignorant; that, just as a
signalling key in London causes a telegraphic instrument to respond instantaneously in Teheran,—which is
an every-day occurrence,—so the danger or death of a
distant child, or brother, or husband, may be signalled,
without wire or telegraph clerk, to the heart of a human
being fitted to be the recipient of such a message.

We call the process telepathy — sympathy at a
distance; we do not understand it. What is the
medium of communication? Is it through the air, like
the tuning forks; or through the ether, like the magnets;
or is it something non-physical, and exclusively psychical?
No one as yet can tell you. We must know far more
about it before we can answer that question,—perhaps
before we can be sure whether the question has a
meaning or not.

Undoubtedly, the scientific attitude, after being
forced to admit the fact, is to assume a physical medium,
and to discover it and its processes if possible. When
the attempt has failed, it will be time enough to enter
upon fresh hypotheses.

Meanwhile, plainly, telepathy strikes us as a spontaneous occurrence of that intercommunication between
mind and mind (or brain and brain), which for want of
a better term we at present style thought-transference.
We may be wrong in thus regarding it, but as scientific
men that is how we are bound to regard it unless forced
by the weight of evidence into some apparently less
tenable position.

The opinion is strengthened by the fact that the
spontaneously occurring impressions can be artificially

and experimentally imitated by conscious attempts to produce them. Individuals are known who can by an effort of will excite the brain of another person at a moderate distance,—say in another part of the same town, or even in some distant place, — so that this second person imagines that he hears a call or sees a face.

These are called experimental apparitions, and appear well established. These experiments also want repeating. They require care, obviously ; but they are very valuable pieces of evidence, and must contribute immensely to experimental psychology.

What now is the meaning of this unexpected sympathetic resonance, this syntonic reverberation between minds ? Is it conceivably the germ of a new sense, as it were,—something which the human race is, in the progress of evolution, destined to receive in fuller measure ? or is it the relic of a faculty possessed by our animal ancestry before speech was ?

I have no wish to intrude speculations upon you, and I cannot answer these questions except in terms of speculation. I wish to assert nothing but what I believe to be solid and verifiable facts.

Let me, however, point out that the intercommunion of minds, the exciting in the brain of B a thought possessed by A, is after all a very ordinary and well known process. We have a quantity of well-arranged mechanism to render it possible. The human race has advanced far beyond the animal in the development of this mechanism ; and civilised man has advanced beyond savages. Conceivably, by thus developing the mechanism, we may have begun to lose the spontaneous and really simpler form of the power ; but the power, with mechanism, conspicuously exists.

I whisper a secret to A, and a short time afterwards I find that B is perfectly aware of it. It sometimes happens so. It has probably happened in what we are accustomed to consider a very commonplace fashion; A has told him. When you come to analyse the process, however, it is not really at all simple. I will not go into tedious details; but when you remember that what conveyed the thought was the impalpable compressions and dilatations of a gas, and that in the process of transmission it existed for a finite space of time in this intermediate and curiously mechanical condition, you may realise something of puzzlement in the process. I am not sure but that we ought to consider some direct sympathy between two minds, without this mechanical process, as really a more simple and direct mode of conveying an idea. However, all dualism is repugnant when pressed far enough, and I do not now wish to insist on any real and essential antithesis between mind and matter, between idea and process. Pass on to another illustration.

Tell a secret to A, in New Zealand, and discover that B, in St. Petersburg, is before long aware of it, neither having travelled. How can that happen? That is not possible to a savage; it would seem to him mysterious. It is mysterious in reality. The idea existed for a time in the form of black scrawls on a bit of paper, which travelled between the two places. A transfer of material occurred, not an aerial vibration; the piece of paper held in front of B's eyes excited in him the idea or knowledge of fact which you had communicated to A.

Not even a material transfer is necessary however; no matter flows along a telegraph wire, and the air is undisturbed by an electric current, but thought-trans-

ference through the etherial medium (with, or indeed
without, the help of a telegraph or telephone wire) is an
accomplished fact, though it would have puzzled our
ancestors of last century.   And yet it is not really new,
it is only the distance and perfection of it that is new.
We all possess an etherial receiving instrument, in our
organ of vision.   The old semaphore system of signalling, as well as the heliograph method, is really a utilisation of the ether for this kind of thought-transference.
Much information, sometimes of momentous character,
may be conveyed by a wink or nod ; or even by a look.
These also are messages sent through the ether.   The
eye is affected by disturbances arriving through the
ether, and by those alone.

Now, then, I say, shut the eyes, stop the ears,
transmit   no   material   substance,   interpose   distance
sufficient to stop all pushing and pulling.   Can thought
or ideas still be transmitted ?   Experiment answers that
they can.   But what the medium is, and how the process
occurs, it remains for further investigation to ascertain.

We reduced our initial three individuals to two ; we
can reduce the two to one.   It is possible for the A and
B functions to be apparently combined in one individual.
Some practice seems necessary for this, and it is a curious
state of things.   It seems assisted by staring at an object
such as a glass globe or crystal—a slight amount of self-
hypnotism probably.   Then you see visions and receive
impressions, or sometimes your hand works unconsciously, as if one part of your brain was signalling to
another part, and your own identity was dormant or
complexed for a time.   But in these cases of so-called
automatic writing, crystal vision, trance-utterance, clairvoyance, and the like, are we quite sure whether it is a
case of A and B at all ; and, if so, whether the subject

before us is really acting as both? I am not sure; I distinctly doubt it in some cases. It is possible that the clairvoyant is responding to some unknown world-mind of which he forms a part: that the real agent is neither himself nor any other living person. This possibility must not be ignored in ordinary cases of apparent thought-transference, too.

Well, now, take a further step. Suppose I discover a piece of paper with scrawls on it. I may guess they are intended for something, but as they are to me illegible hieroglyphics, I carry it to one person after another, and get them to look at it; but it excites in them no response. They perceive little more than a savage would perceive. But not so with all of them. One man to whom I show it has the perceptive faculty, so to speak; he becomes wildly excited; he begins to sing; he rushes for an arrangement of wood and catgut, and fills the air with vibrations. Even the others can now faintly appreciate the meaning. The piece of paper was a lost manuscript of Beethoven!

What sort of thought-transference is that? Where is the A to whom the ideas originally occurred? He has been dead for years; his fossilised thought has lain dormant in matter; but it only wanted a sympathetic and educated mind to perceive it, to revive it, and to make it the property of the world. Idea, do I call it? but it is not only idea: there may be a world of emotion too, thus stored up in matter, ready to be released as by detent. Action of mind on matter, reaction of matter on mind—are these things, after all, commonplaces too?

If so what is not possible?

Here is a room where a tragedy occurred, where the human spirit was strung to intensest anguish. Is there any trace of that agony present still and able to

be appreciated by an attuned or receptive mind? I
assert nothing, except that it is not inconceivable. If
it happen, it may take many forms; vague disquiet,
perhaps, or imaginary sounds or vague visions, or
perhaps a dream or picture of the event as it occurred.
Understand, I do not regard the evidence for these
things as so conclusive as for some of the other
phenomena I have dealt with, but the belief in such
facts may be forced upon us, and you perceive that the
garment of superstition is already dropping from them.
They will take their place, if true, in an orderly universe,
along with other not wholly unallied and already well
known occurrences.

Relics again : is it credible that a relic, a lock of hair,
an old garment, retains any trace of a deceased friend—
represents any portion of his personality? Does not an
old letter? Does not a painting? An "old master" we
call it. Aye, there may be much of the personality of
the old master thus preserved. Is not the emotion felt
on looking at it a kind of thought-transference from the
departed? A painting differs from a piece of music in
that it is constantly incarnate, so to speak. It is there
for all to see, for some to understand. The music requires incarnation, it can be "performed" as we say, and
then it can be appreciated. But in no case without the
attuned and thoughtful mind ; and so these things are,
in a sense, thought-transference, but deferred thought-
transference. They may be likened to telepathy not
only reaching over tracts of space but deferred through
epochs of time.[1]

Think over these great things and be not unduly

---

[1] They are not technical telepathy, as defined, of course, because they
occur through accustomed ways and processes. Technical telepathy is the
attainment of the same result through unaccustomed ways and processes.

sceptical about little things.   An attitude of keen and critical inquiry must continually be maintained, and in that sense any amount of scepticism is not only legitimate but necessary.   The kind of scepticism I deprecate is not that which sternly questions and rigorously probes, it is rather that which confidently asserts and dogmatically denies ; but this kind is not true scepticism, in the proper sense of the word, for it deters inquiry and forbids inspection.   It is too positive concerning the boundaries of knowledge and the line where superstition begins.

Phantasms and dreams and ghosts, crystal-gazing, premonitions, and clairvoyance : the region of superstition?   Yes, hitherto, but possibly also the region of fact. As taxes on credulity they are trifles compared to things with which we are already familiar ; only too familiar, for our familiarity has made us stupidly and inanely inappreciative of them.

The whole of our knowledge and existence is shrouded in mystery : the commonplace is itself full of marvel, and the business of science is to overcome the forces of superstition by enlisting them in the service of genuine knowledge.   And when this is done I do not doubt that some of these forces will be found auxiliary to the sacred cause of religion itself.

SECTION III

SPONTANEOUS TELEPATHY AND CLAIRVOYANCE

CHAPTER VII

APPARITIONS CONSIDERED IN THE LIGHT OF TELEPATHY

THE fact of telepathy having been experimentally established by a large number of experiments conducted by different people, it remains to consider more fully its bearing and significance.

Telepathy means the apparently direct action of one mind on another by means unknown to science. That a thought or image or impression or emotion in the mind of one person can arouse a similar impression in the mind of another person sufficiently sympathetic and sufficiently at leisure to attend and record the impression, is now proved. But the mechanism whereby it is done, or even if there is anything that can be likened to physical mechanism at all, is still unknown. The appearance is as if it were a direct action of mind on mind, or of brain on brain, irrespective of the usual nerves and muscles and organs of sense.

This fact alone—once admitted, after having run the traditional gauntlet of scepticism—serves to explain, at least in a plausible and tentative manner, a number of puzzling phenomena; notably it furnishes a plausible key to the phenomena of apparitions and hallucinations of every kind, whether of sight or of hearing or of touch. It is of especial value in reducing the rudimentary difficulty about the clothes and accessories of so-called "ghosts" to absurdity; since of course a mental impression would represent a person under something like customary, though it may be unexpected, sur-roundings,—just as happens in an ordinary dream.

The word "hallucination" applied to phantasmal appearances in general has been objected to in con-nexion with some of these apparitions; as if it were intended to imply—as it is often mistakenly assumed to imply—that there is no objective reality underlying the apparition whatever. It is, however, fully admitted that some hallucinations may be and indeed are *veridical* (*i.e.* truth-telling); inasmuch as they correspond with some real event, some strong emotion,—due perhaps to an accident or to the illness or decease of the distant and visualised person. They therefore do correspond with some objective reality, just as the image in a looking-glass corresponds with and is veridical evidence of some objective reality; but as to any substantiality about a phantasm—that must be regarded as demanding further investigation. Hypothetically it may differ in different cases; and in no case can it be safe to assume, without special evidence, that it has anything more than a psychological basis.

The question of photography applied to visible phantasms, and to an invisible variety said to be perceived by clairvoyants, is still an open one—at any rate no photographic evidence has yet appeared con-clusive to me. If successful, photography could prove that the impression was not only a mental one, but

7

that the ether of space had been definitely affected in a certain way also, so that the impression had probably become received by the optical apparatus of the eye, and had been transmitted in the usual way to the brain. It would not prove substantiality; since of course it is perfectly easy to photograph the virtual image formed by a looking-glass. Still, genuine photography would indicate a step in advance of telepathy: it would establish one variety of what are called "physical phenomena." There is, in truth, a vast amount of evidence for physical phenomena of this technically supernormal kind; but they have not yet made good their claim to clear and positive acceptance in the way that telepathy has done.

But we are at present not attending to physical phenomena. We need not assume that an apparition has any objective or physical reality. It may be only an impression on the mind of a percipient, analogous to the image or impression caused in one person while another is endeavouring to transfer the image of an object. That which experimentally is found to occur of conscious purpose we think may sometimes occur unconsciously too. We are not sure indeed that the consciousness or will power of the agent has anything to do with it; the transfer is effected we know not how, and it may be wholly an affair of the subconsciousness. If so, a strong emotion even in a distant person may produce an echo or reverberation in the mind of a relative or even a sympathetic stranger, without the agent being in the least conscious of what is happening, and without the percipient in the least understanding the process. He may think that the impression in the mind is real, and may only be undeceived by trying to touch it, or he may perceive that it is no more real than the image in a looking-glass,—or not so real as that,—and yet may feel certain that it corresponds to some sort of psychical reality somewhere.

In that case the impression is called veridical or truth-telling, because it does convey real information, though it does so in a phantasmal or unreal manner. Hallucinations need not necessarily be unreal or phantasmal in every case: that is a matter for further investigation, but it does assuredly clear the ground to treat them as such in the first instance.

PHANTASMS

Examples of apparitions seen by relatives at or very near to the epoch of death are so common that it is hardly worth while to quote any here. The publications of the Society for Psychical Research and the book called *Phantasms of the Living* are full of them; and in most assemblages it will be found that a few of those present are aware of cases of this kind in their own family history.

Part of the scepticism which has surrounded the subject has been undoubtedly due to the difficult notions which are rendered necessary if those apparitions are to be supposed objective realities. Even supposing a human being could thus appear, the apparition of his clothes and simplest accessories must thus become puzzling. Sometimes such figures are seen accompanied by animals, sometimes with their surroundings lightly sketched in as it were,—as for instance part of a ship in the case of a sailor. All these difficulties sink into non-existence directly it is apprehended that the vision is a mental impression produced by a psychical agency, veridical in the sense of corresponding to reality more or less closely, but subjective in the sense of there being no actual bodily presence. This is the kind of rationalising theory on which the Society for Psychical Research started its existence: it must have been the hope of similarly detecting an element of common sense running through a great variety of popular legend that conferred on its pioneers the motive power necessary. Anyhow that was their adopted theory, and accordingly all such apparitions were in the first instance supposed to be due to telepathy from the dying person and were called Phantasms of the Living.

The following is an extract from a Report of one of the Committees:—There is strong testimony that *clairvoyants* have witnessed and described trivial incidents in which they had no special interest, and even scenes in which the actors, though actual persons, were complete strangers to them; and such cases seem properly assimilated to those where they describe mere places and objects, the idea of which can hardly be supposed to be impressed on them by any personality at all. Once more, apparitions at death, though the fact of death sufficiently implies excitement or disturbance in one mind, have often been witnessed, not only by relatives or friends, in a normal state but interested in the event —a case above considered—but by other observers who had no personal interest in the matter.

To secure testimony on these topics we have had to depend on the co-operation of the public, and we have sought far and wide for trustworthy testimony, which we have tested in a stringent manner, never resting satisfied until by inquiry and pertinacious cross-examination, with an examination of contemporary records of various kinds, we have made as sure as is humanly possibly that our witnesses were neither lying nor drawing unduly on their imagination, but that the event happened pretty much as they have narrated or at the time recorded them.

" Phantasms of the Dying " might be a better name for these very numerous cases of apparition or veridical hallucination. Whatever the cause, the fact of their existence has been thoroughly established ; there is a concordance far beyond chance between apparitions which convey the impression of the unexpected death or illness of a distant person, and the actual fact ;—the intelligence being, in this form, impressed on a percipient at a distance, by some apparently unconscious mental activity and by means at present unknown.

Abbreviated Examples

As an instance of a vision with appropriate accessories I might take a case reported more fully in the *Proceedings* of the Society for Psychical Research, vol. iii. page 97—the case of a favourite and devoted Scottish workman who appeared to his employer in what is described as an extraordinarily vivid dream in which the workman appeared with a face of "indescribable bluish pale colour and on his forehead spots like blots of sweat," and earnestly said several times that he had not done the thing which he was accused of doing. When asked what this was, he replied impressively " Ye'll sune ken." Almost immediately afterwards the news of this man's suicide arrived. But the employer felt assured on the strength of his vision that, though dead, the man had not committed suicide ; and said so. Before long it turned out that his assurance was correct, for the workman had drunk from a bottle containing nitric acid by accident. The employer moreover subsequently ascertained that the symptoms exhibited by the phantasmal appearance were such as are appropriate to poisoning by this liquid.

Another case of vision with more detailed accessories is in vol. vii. page 33, communicated by Dr. Hodgson, and may be abbreviated thus :—

Mrs. Paquet on the morning of October 24th, 1889, after her husband had gone to work and the children to school, feeling gloomy, was making some tea for herself, when she saw a vision of her brother,

Edmund Dunn, standing only a few feet away; and her report continues :—

"The apparition stood with back toward me, or rather, partially so, and was in the act of falling forward —away from me—seemingly impelled by two ropes or a loop of rope drawing against his legs. The vision lasted but a moment, disappearing over a low railing or bulwark, but was very distinct. I dropped the tea, clasped my hands to my face, and exclaimed, 'My God ! Ed. is drowned.'

"At about half-past ten a.m. my husband received a telegram from Chicago announcing the drowning of my brother. When he arrived home, he said to me, 'Ed. is sick in hospital at Chicago; I have just received a telegram,' to which I replied 'Ed. is drowned; I saw him go overboard.' I then gave him a minute description of what I had seen. I stated that my brother, as I saw him, was bareheaded, had on a heavy, blue sailor's shirt, no coat, and that he went over the rail or bulwark. I noticed that his pants' legs were rolled up enough to show the white lining inside. I also described the appearance of the boat at the point where my brother went overboard.

"I am not nervous, and neither before nor since have I had any experience in the least degree similar to that above related.

"My brother was not subject to fainting or vertigo.

"AGNES PAQUET"

Mr. Paquet's Statement

"At about 10.30 o'clock a.m., October 24th, 1889, I received a telegram from Chicago, announcing the drowning of my brother-in-law, Edmund Dunn, at 3 o'clock that morning. I went directly home, and wishing to break the force of the sad news I had to convey to my wife, I said to her : 'Ed. is sick in hospital at Chicago; I have just received a telegram.' To which she replied: 'Ed. is drowned; I saw him go overboard.' She then described to me the appearance and dress of her brother as described in her statement, also the appearance of the boat, etc.

"I started at once for Chicago, and when I arrived there I found the appearance of that part of the vessel described by my wife to be exactly as she had described it, though she had never seen the vessel; and the crew verified my wife's description of her brother's dress, etc., except that they thought he had his hat on at the time of the accident. They said that Mr. Dunn had purchased a pair of pants a few days before the accident occurred, and as they were a trifle long, wrinkling at the knees, he had worn them rolled up, showing the white lining as seen by my wife."

STATEMENT OF ACCIDENT

"On October 24th, 1889, Edmund Dunn, brother of Mrs. Agnes Paquet, was serving as fireman on the tug Wolf, a small steamer engaged in towing vessels in Chicago harbour. At about three o'clock a.m., the tug fastened to a vessel, inside the piers, to tow her up the river. While adjusting the tow-line Mr. Dunn fell, or was thrown overboard by the tow-line, and drowned."

In this case, if 3 a.m, signifies Chicago time, the vision must have followed the accident very closely; but it has gradually become clear that some of these cases do not coincide precisely with the epoch of death, but follow it sometimes at so long an interval that another group has to be classified as " Phantasms of the Dead." (See Mrs. Sidgwick's Memoir on the subject in *Proceedings*, vol. iii.)

Again occasionally the hallucinations are collective, so that several people present see the same vision. It is possible to consider these as cases of contagious hallucination : and it is not usually necessary to suppose that the distant person whose image was being seen knew anything about it or was making any conscious effort to communicate.

If indeed he *were* conscious of the attempt, still more if he knew of its success and reception, it would be a feature of greatly added interest ; it would then fall into the class of reciprocal cases—which are rarer.

EXPERIMENTAL APPARITIONS

The fact that such visions can also be produced through the agency of living people—even in health— was proved by the experiments conducted by Mr. S.

H. B., as recorded in *Phantasms of the Living*, vol. i. pp. 104–9, and in *Human Personality*, vol. i. p. 293. This gentleman willed himself or rather his phantom to appear to two ladies, without their knowing of the experiment; and he succeeded in his intention. They both saw him simultaneously, though he did not see them, and his appearance was as of one in evening dress wandering aimlessly about their room, after the traditional manner of " ghosts." This experimental production of a ghost is a particularly instructive case; and many ghostly appearances belong to living people, who are usually unconscious that they are producing any such effect. There appears to be no reason why an apparition should always be of a deceased person. But whether every apparition is of this unsubstantial and purely subjective order, or whether a few proceed to a further degree of reality and belong to what are sometimes spoken of as incipient materialisation, I do not at this stage even discuss. It is sufficient to indicate that a true hypothesis does not close the door to other and more extended ones, if the first is found incompetent to explain all the facts.

For the convenient analogy of conscious and pur- posed Thought-transference must not be pressed too far. Our phenomena break through any attempt to group them under heads of purposely transferred impres- sion; and the words *Telæsthesia* and *Telepathy* were introduced by Mr. Myers to cover all cases of impression received at a distance without the normal operation of the recognised sense organs.

These general terms are found of permanent service; but as regards what is for the present included under them, we must limit and arrange our material rather with an eye to convenience, than with any belief that our classification will ultimately prove a fundamental one.   No true demarcation, in fact, can as yet be made between one class of those experiences and another; we need the record of as many and as diverse phenomena as we can get, if we are to be in a position to deal satisfactorily with any one of them.

The popular term "ghost" may cover a wide range of essentially different phenomena, and the hallucinatory but veridical kind of apparition, which has no close connexion with any particular *place*, is the best established and commonest variety.

Hauntings

The kind of ghost associated with a place—say a room,—and seen by any one who happens to sleep in that room, provided he is fairly wakeful and not too case-hardened against weird influences, constitutes a difficult and at present somewhat unsatisfactory region of inquiry.   The evidence for the existence of this "fixed local" kind of apparition is strong, but hardly conclusive; and this kind is not included among those called "phantasms of the living" nor among hallucinations due to telepathy from the injured or dying.

The Society has not had the opportunity of investigating so-called haunted houses in any considerable number; and many of such cases—even when reported—resolve themselves merely into uncanny noises such as may be accounted for in one of a great many different ways.   I would not be understood as expressing any opinion as to the actual occurrence of this class of phantom—our study of it as yet has been insufficient,—but of the occurrence of visions which coincide fairly in time with some severe shock to the person represented, it is impossible for me to entertain a doubt.

The evidence must certainly depend on human testimony, but immense trouble has been taken to collect such testimony over a wide range of persons, to sift and examine and test it by every means in our power, and then to record it in volumes accessible to the public. Those who have been chiefly occupied for years in this work are able to testify concerning it as follows :—

We have thus accumulated a great body of testimony which it is impossible to overlook or to discard. These facts form a foundation for the beginning of knowledge concerning them.

Our evidence is no shifting shadow, which it may be left to individual taste or temperament to interpret, but more resembles a solid mass seen in twilight which men may indeed avoid stumbling over, but only by resolutely walking away from it. And when the *savant* thus deserts the field, the ordinary man needs to have the nature and true amount of the testimony far more directly brought home to him, than is necessary in realms already mastered by specialists to whose *dicta* he may defer. Failing this direct contact with the facts, the vaguely fascinated regard of the ordinary public is, for all scientific purposes, as futile as the *savant's* determined avoidance. Knowledge can never grow until it is realised that the question " Do you believe in these things?" is puerile unless it has been preceded by the inquiry, " What do you know about them?"

For, in fact, this subject is at present very much in the position which zoology and botany occupied in the time of Aristotle, or nosology in the time of Hippocrates. Aristotle had no zoological gardens or methodical treatises to refer to; he was obliged to go down to the fish-market, to hear whatever the sailors could tell, and look at whatever they could bring him. This spirit of omnivorous inquiry no doubt exposed him to hearing much that was exaggerated or untrue ; but plainly the science of zoology could not have been upbuilt without it.   Diseases afford a still more striking parallel to the phenomena of which we are in quest.   Men of science are wont to make it an objection to this quest that phenomena cannot be reproduced under our own conditions or at our own time.   The looseness of thought here exhibited by men ordinarily clear-headed is surely a striking example of the prepotence of prejudice over education.   Will the objectors assert that all aberrations of function and degenerations of tissue are reproducible by direct experiment?   Can physicians secure a case of cancer or Addison's disease by any previous arrangement of conditions?   Our science is by no means the only one concerned with phenomena which are at present to a large extent irreproducible : all the sciences of life are still within that category, and all sciences whatever were in it once.

CHAPTER VIII

TELEPATHY FROM AN IMMATERIAL REGION

THE phenomenon upon a consideration of which we shall shortly enter is that exhibited in several forms and known under various names, of which the simplest perhaps is *automatic writing*—that is, writing executed independently of the full knowledge and consciousness of the operator—the hand acting in obedience either to some unconscious portion of the operator's mind, or else responding to some other psychical influence more or less distinct from both his normal and his hypernormal personality. Sometimes it takes the form not of writing, but of unconscious speech; and occasionally the person whose hand or voice is being used is himself completely entranced and unconscious for one or two hours together. There is evidently a great deal to be learned about this phenomenon, and many surmises are legitimate respecting it, but it is useless and merely ignorant to deny its occurrence. It is often quite clear that parts of the writings or speech so obtained do not represent the normal knowledge of the automatist; but whence the information is derived is uncertain, and probably in different cases the source is different. The simplest assumption, and one that covers perhaps a majority of the facts, is that the writer's unconscious intelligence or subliminal self—his dream or genius stratum—is at work—that he is in a condition of unconscious and subliminal lucidity, and subject to a sort of hyper-æsthesia.

It has long been known that in order to achieve remarkable results in any department of intellectual activity, the mind must be to some extent unaware of passing occurrences. To be keenly awake and "on the spot" is a highly valued accomplishment, and for the ordinary purposes of mundane affairs is a far more useful state of mind than the rather hazy and absorbed condition which is associated with the quality of mind called genius; but it is not as effective for brilliant achievement.

When a poet or musician or mathematician feels himself inspired, his senses are—at least his common-place and non-relevant attention is — dulled or half asleep; and though probably some part of his brain is in a state of great activity, I am not aware of any experiments directed to test which that part is, nor whether, when in that state, any of the more ordinarily used portions are really dormant or no. It would be interesting, but difficult, to ascertain the precise physio-logical accompaniments of that which on a small scale is called a brown study, and on a larger scale a period of inspiration.

It does not seem unreasonable to suppose that the state is somewhat allied to the initial condition of anæsthesia—the somnambulic condition in which, though the automatic processes of the body go on with greater perfection than usual, the conscious or noticing aspect of the mind is latent, so that the things which influence the person are apparently no longer the ordinary events which affect his peripheral organs, but either something internal or else something not belonging to the ordinarily known physical universe at all.

The mind is always in a receptive state, perhaps, but whereas the business - like wide - awake person receives impressions from every trivial detail of his physical surroundings, the half-asleep person seems to receive impressions from a different stratum altogether ; higher in some instances, lower in some instances, but different always from those received by ordinary men in their every-day state.

In a man of genius the state comes on of itself, and the results are astounding. There are found occasionally feeble persons, usually young, who seek to attain to the appearance of genius by the easy process of assuming or encouraging an attitude of vacancy and uselessness. There may be all grades of result attained while in this state, and the state itself is of less than no value unless it is justified by the results.

By experiment and observation it has now been established that a state not altogether dissimilar to this can be induced by artificial means, *e.g.*, by drugs, by hypnosis, by crystal gazing, by purposed inattention ; and also that a receptive or clairvoyant condition occurs occasionally without provocation, during sleep and during trance. All these states seem to some extent allied, and, as is well known, Mr. Myers has elaborated their relationship in his series of articles on the subliminal consciousness.

Well now, the question arises, What is the source of the intelligence manifested during epochs of clairvoyant lucidity, as sometimes experienced in the hypnotic or the somnambulic state, or during trance, or displayed automatically ?

The most striking cases of which I am now

immediately or mediately cognisant, are the trance
state of Mrs. Piper and the automatism of such writers
as Mrs. Verrall and Mrs. Holland. Without any
apparent lulling of attention at all I am experimentally
assured of the possibility of conveying information
between one mind and another without the aid of
ordinary sense organs; but the cases mentioned are
especially striking, and will serve to narrow the field to
what, after all, may be considered at present the main
points.

Mrs. Piper in the trance state is undoubtedly (I use
the word in the strongest sense; I have absolutely no
more doubt on the subject than I have of my friends'
ordinary knowledge of me and other men),—Mrs.
Piper's trance personality is undoubtedly aware of
much to which she has no kind of ordinarily recognised
clue, and of which in her ordinary state she knows
nothing. But how does she get this knowledge? She
herself when in the trance state asserts that she gets
it by conversing with the deceased friends and relatives
of people present. And that this is a genuine opinion
of hers, *i.e.* that the process feels like that to her
unconscious or subconscious mind—the part of her
which used to call itself Phinuit and now calls itself
" Rector "—I am fully prepared to believe. But that
does not carry us very far towards a knowledge of what
the process actually is.

Conversation implies speaking with the mouth,—and
when receiving or asking information she is momentarily
in a deeper slumber, and not occupied in normal
speech. At times, indeed, slight mutterings of one-
sided questions and replies are heard, or are written,
very like the mutterings of a person in sleep under-
going a vivid dream.

Dream is certainly the ordinary person's nearest approach to the entranced condition; and the fading of recollection as the conscious memory returns is also paralleled by the waking of Mrs. Piper out of the trance. But, instead of a nearly passive dream, it is more nearly allied to the somnambulic state; though the activity, far from being chiefly locomotory, is mainly mental and only partially muscular.

She is in a state of somnambulism in which the mind is more active than the body; and the activity is so different from her ordinary activity, she is so distinctly a different sort of person, that she quite appropriately calls herself by another name.

It is natural to ask, Is she still herself? But it is a question difficult to answer, unless "herself" be defined. It is her mouth that is speaking, or her hand which is writing, and I suppose her brain and nerves are working the muscles; but they are not worked in the customary way, nor does the mind manifested thereby at all resemble her mind. Until, however, the meaning of identity can be accurately specified, I find it difficult to discuss the question whether she or another person is really speaking.

On this point the waking experience of Mrs. Newnham—an automatic writer quoted in *Phantasms of the Living*, vol. i. p. 63—is of assistance. In her case the hand wrote matter not in the writer's mind and which she did not feel that she was writing. Her hand wrote while she was taking the attention of her own conscious mind away from her hand and letting it be guided by her subconscious or by some other mind.

The instructive feature about this case was that the minds apparently influencing the hand were not so much those of dead as of living people. The advantage of this was that they could be catechised afterwards about their share in the transaction ; and it then appeared that they either knew nothing about it or were surprised at it ; for though the communication did correspond to something in their minds, it did not represent anything of which they were consciously thinking, and was only a very approximate rendering of what they might be wishing to convey. They did not seem able to exercise control over the messages, any more than untrained people can control their thoughts in dreams. But we must not jump to the conclusion that this will always be the case ; that the connexion is *never* reciprocally conscious, as when two persons are talking ; but it shows that at any rate it need not be so. Since the living communicant is not aware of what is being dictated, so the dead person need not be consciously operative ; and thus conceivably the hand of the automatist may be influenced by minds other than his own, minds both living and dead (by one apparently as readily as by the other), but not by a conscious portion of the mind of any one ; by the subconscious or dreamy portion, if by any portion at all.

When Phinuit then, or Mrs. Piper in the trance state, reports conversations which she has had with other minds (usually in Phinuit's case with persons deceased), and even when the voice changes and messages come apparently from those very people themselves, it does not follow that they themselves are necessarily aware of the fact, nor need their conscious mind (if they have any) be active in the process.

The signature of an automatist's hand is equivalent to the assertion that Miss X., for instance, is deliberately writing ; Phinuit's statement is equally an assertion that

8

Mr. E. is deliberately speaking; and the one statement may be no more a lie than the other is a forgery, and yet neither need be what is ordinarily called "true."

That this community of mind or possibility of distant interchange or one-sided reception of thoughts exists, is to me perfectly clear and certain. I venture further to say that persons who deny the bare fact, expressed as I here wish to express it without any hypothesis, are simply ignorant. They have not studied the facts of the subject. It may be for lack of opportunity, it may be for lack of inclination; they are by no means bound to investigate it unless they choose; but any dogmatic denials which such persons may now perpetrate will henceforth, or in the very near future, redound to the discredit, not of the phenomena thus ignorantly denied, but of themselves, the over-confident and presumptuous deniers.

We must not too readily assume that the apparent action of one mind on another is really such an action. The impression received *may* come from the ostensible agent, but it *may* come from a third person; or again it *may*, as some think more likely, come from a central mind —some Anima Mundi—to which all ordinary minds are related and by which they are influenced. If it could be shown that the action is a syntonic or sympathetic connexion between a pair of minds, then it might be surmised that the action is a physical one, properly to be expressed as occurring directly between brain and brain, or body and body. On the other hand, the action may conceivably be purely psychological, and the distant brain may be stimulated not by the intervention of anything physical or material but in some more immediate manner,—from its psychological instead of from its physiological side.

The question is quite a definite one if properly expressed: Does the action take place through a physical medium, or does it not?

Guesses at *a priori* likelihood are worthless; if the question is to be answered it must be attacked experimentally.

Now the *ordinary* way in which A communicates with B is through a certain physical mechanism, and the thought of A may be said to exist for a finite time as an etherial or aërial quiver before it reproduces a similar thought in the mind of B. We have got so accustomed to the existence of this intermediate physical process that instead of striking us as roundabout and puzzling it appeals to us as natural and simple; and any more direct action of A on B, without physical mechanism, is scouted as absurd or at least violently improbable. Well, it is merely a question of fact, and perhaps it is within the range of a crucial experiment.

But it may be at once admitted that such an experiment is difficult of execution. If the effect is a physical one it should vary according to some law of distance, or it should depend on the nature of the intervening medium; but, in order to test whether in any given case such variation occurs, it is necessary to have both agent and percipient in an unusually dependable condition, and they should if possible be unaware of the variation which is under test.

This last condition is desirable because of the sensitiveness of the sub-consciousness to suggestion: self-suggestion and other. If the percipient got an idea that distance or interposed screens were detrimental, most likely they would be detrimental; and although a suggestion might be artificially instilled that distance was advantageous, this would hardly leave the test quite fair, for the lessened physical stimulus might perhaps be over-utilised by the more keenly excited organism. Still that is an experiment to be tried among others; and it would be an instructive experience if the agent some day was, say, in India when the percipient thought he was in London, or *vice versâ*.

It is extremely desirable to probe this question of a physical or non-physical mode of communication in cases of telepathy; and if the fact can be established beyond doubt that sympathetic communication occurs between places as distant as India or America and England, or the terrestrial antipodes,—being unfelt between, or in the neighbourhood of the source,—then I should feel that this was so unlike what we are accustomed to in Physics that I should be strongly urged to look to some other and more direct kind of mental relationship as the clue. Some of the recent experiments conducted by Miss Miles and Miss Ramsden (*Proc.*, vol. xxi. pp. 60–93) tend to support such a contention.

This, then, is the first question on which crucial experiments are desirable though difficult.

(1) Is the mechanism of telepathy physical or not?

The second question of which I am thinking is one less easy to state and far less easy (as I think) to resolve. It may be stated thus, in two parts, or as two separate questions :—

(2) Is the power of operating on the minds of terrestrial persons confined to living terrestrial people?

(3) Is the power of operating on or interfering with the rest of the physical universe confined to living material bodies?

I should conjecture that an affirmative answer to Question 1 would render likely an affirmative answer to Questions 2 and 3; but that a negative answer to

Question 1 would leave 2 and 3 entirely open ; because, so far as we at present know, terrestrial people, and people with material bodies, may be the only people who exist.

It is this possibility, or, as many would hold, probability or almost certainty, that renders the strict scientific statement of Questions 2 and 3 so difficult. Yet they are questions which must be faced, and they ought to be susceptible, in time, of receiving definite answers.

That there are living terrestrial people we know ; we also know that there is an immense variety of other terrestrial life ;—though, if we were not so familiar with the fact, the luxuriant prevalence and variety of life would be surprising. The existence of a bat, for instance, or a lobster, would be quite incredible. Whether there is life on other planets we do not know, and whether there is conscious existence between the planets we do not know ; but I see no *a priori* reason for making scientific assertions on the subject one way or the other. It is only at present a matter of probability. Just because we know that the earth is peopled with an immense variety of living beings, I myself should rather expect to find other regions many-peopled, and with a still more extraordinary variety. So also since mental action is conspicuous on the earth I should expect to find it existent elsewhere. If life is necessarily associated with a material carcase, then no doubt the surface of one of the many planetary masses must be the scene of its activity ; but if any kind of mental action is independent of material or physical environment, then it may conceivably be that the psychical population is not limited to the surface of material aggregates or globes of matter, but may luxuriate either in the interstellar spaces or in some undimensional form of existence of which we have no conception.

Were it not for the fact of telepathy the entire question would be an idle one,—a speculation based on nothing and apparently incapable of examination, still less of verification or disproof. But granted the fact of telepathy the question ceases to be an idle one, because it is just possible that these other intelligences, if they in any sense exist, may be able to communicate with us by the same sort of process as that by which we are now learning to be able to communicate with each other. Whether it be true or not, it has been constantly and vehemently asserted as a fact that such communications, mainly from deceased relatives, but often also from strangers, are occasionally received by living persons.

The utterances of Phinuit, the handwriting of Miss A., Mr. Stainton Moses, and others, abound with communications purporting to come from minds not now associated with terrestrial matter.

Very well then ; is a crucial or test experiment possible, to settle whether this claim is well founded or not ?

Mere sentimental messages, conveying personal traits of the deceased, though frequently convincing to surviving friends, cannot be allowed much scientific weight. Something more definite or generally intelligible must be sought.

Of such facts the handwriting of the deceased person, if reproduced accurately by an automatist who has never seen that handwriting, seems an exceptionally good test if it can be obtained. But the negative proof of ignorance on the part of the writer is difficult.

At first sight facts known to the deceased but not known to the automatist, if reported in a correct and detailed manner so as to surpass mere coincidence, would seem a satisfactory test. But here telepathy, which has stood us in good stead so far, begins to operate the other way; for if the facts are known to nobody on earth they cannot perhaps be verified; and if they are known to somebody still alive—however distant he may be—it is necessary to assume it *possible* that they were unconsciously "telepathed" from his mind.

But a certain class of facts may be verified without the assistance or knowledge of any living person,—as when a miser having died with the sole clue to a deposit of "valuables," an automatist's hand, over the miser's signature, subsequently describes the place; or when a sealed document, carefully deposited, is posthumously deciphered. The test in either of these cases is a better one. But still, living telepathy of a deferred kind is not excluded (though to my thinking it is rendered extremely improbable), for, as Mr. Podmore has often urged, the person writing the document or burying the treasure may have been *ipso facto* an unconscious agent on the minds of contemporaries.

Case of Apparently Posthumous Activity

One of the most remarkable instances of this kind, and one which fortunately received the attention of the philosopher Kant, is one in which Swedenborg acted as the Medium, and is thus described by Kant in a letter published as an Appendix to his cautious little book on clairvoyance which has been translated into English under the title, *Dreams of a Spirit Seer.*

Madame Herteville (Marteville), the widow of the Dutch Ambassador in Stockholm, some time after the death of her husband, was called upon by Croon, a goldsmith, to pay for a silver service which her husband had purchased from him. The widow was convinced that her late husband had been much too precise and orderly not to have paid this debt, yet she was unable to find this receipt. In her sorrow, and because the amount was considerable, she requested Mr. Swedenborg to call at her house. After apologising to him for troubling him, she said that if, as all people say, he possessed the extraordinary gift of conversing with the souls of the departed, he would perhaps have the kindness to ask her husband how it was about the silver service. Swedenborg did not at all object to comply with her request. Three days afterward the said lady had company at her house for coffee. Swedenborg called, and in his cool way informed her that he had conversed with her husband. The debt had been paid several months before his decease, and the receipt was in a bureau in the room upstairs. The lady replied that the bureau had been quite cleared out, and that the receipt was not found among all the papers. Swedenborg said that her husband had described to him, how after pulling out the left-hand drawer a board would appear, which required to be drawn out, when a secret compartment would be disclosed, containing his private Dutch correspondence, as well as the receipt. Upon hearing this description the whole company arose and accompanied the lady into the room upstairs. The bureau was opened; they did as they were directed; the compartment was found, of which no one had ever known before; and to the great astonishment of all, the papers were discovered there, in accordance with his description.

It is difficult to attribute this apparently posthumous activity to deferred telepathy from the living burgo-master—*i.e.* deferred from the time when he was engaged in storing the papers—perhaps still more in this case because they were not stored with any view of subsequently disclosing their hiding place. Postponement of the apparently posthumous action for more than a century, so that all contemporaries are necessarily dead, strains this sort of telepathic explanation still more—in fact to breaking point; but such an event is hardly within the reach of purposed experiment. The storage of objects or messages is; and responsible people ought to write and deposit specific documents, for the purpose of posthumously communicating them to some one if they can ; taking all reasonable precautions against fraud and collusion, and also,—which is perhaps a considerable demand,—taking care that they do not forget the contents themselves.

That such forgetfulness is extremely probable has always strongly presented itself to my mind, and has been of force sufficient to prevent my depositing any of these documents with my friends. I am sure that I should forget their contents—forget even that I had written anything—and if reminded should be hopelessly confused as to which sentence I had placed in which envelope.

That the test may fail, owing either to this or to some other reason, is manifested by the following record —which has already been more than sufficiently published and has become well known. As a negative experiment, however, it is my business not to slur it over in any way, so I reproduce the judicial statement in the *Journal* of the Society.

Opening of an Envelope containing a Posthumous Note left by Mr. Myers

On December 13th, 1904, Sir Oliver Lodge invited the Members of the Council and a few other Members of the Society to the Society's Rooms at 20 Hanover Square to witness the opening of a sealed envelope which had been sent to him by Mr. Myers in January 1891 (nearly fourteen years ago), in the hope that after his death its contents might be given by communication through some medium.

It had been decided to open it because various statements made in Mrs. Verrall's automatic script during the last three years had led her to infer that it contained a certain phrase. The apparent references to this posthumous note had begun vaguely, and gradually developed, with some repetition, into what seemed to be a clear and definite statement of what was contained in Sir Oliver Lodge's envelope. The references to the envelope purported to come from Mr. Myers, and were mixed up with writing, some of which appeared to be veridical, relating to other topics, especially with a statement—written before the publication of *Human Personality*—that a certain passage would be found in that book when published. This having been verified, it was hoped that the account given by the script of the contents of the envelope might turn out equally correct.

The meeting was summoned by a circular, of which the annexed is a copy :—

Mariemont, Edgbaston, December 1904

It is probably known to you that some years ago F. W. H. Myers deposited with me an envelope containing some sort of writing or message, to be posthumously deciphered if possible.

It is also known to you that Mrs. Verrall developed the faculty of automatic writing soon after Myers's death. It now appears that she believes herself to have received messages or indications as to the contents of this envelope. This impression of hers may, of course, be mistaken, but the advantage of it is that it is definite, and she is able to put into writing what she thinks the contents of the envelope will be found to be.

That being so, I have taken advice, and find a general consensus of opinion that it is time now to open the envelope and verify or disprove the agreement ; or, if there is partial agreement, to ascertain its amount.

The envelope has been for some time deposited in a bank, but I propose to have it handed back to me some time this week, and to bring it up to London on Tuesday, December 13th, and then, at 4 p.m., in the rooms of the Society for Psychical Research, 20 Hanover Square, after making a statement regarding it and reading Mrs. Verrall's statement of what she believes to be in it, to open it in the presence of a sufficient number of witnesses. I do not propose to do it at a Council meeting, because I think it desirable that one or two outsiders should be present, inasmuch as I wish the event to be known and "counted," whether it turn out successful or the reverse. The only way to avoid chance coincidence is to determine beforehand whether any given event shall "count" or not ; and, subject to anything that may happen between now and then, I propose that this shall count, and that the envelope shall then be opened.

I invite you, therefore, if you think fit, to come to the rooms of the Society on Tuesday, December 13th, at 4 p.m.

It must be understood that the proceedings are confidential, and that the question of subsequent publication must be reserved for the Council or the Society. OLIVER LODGE

Mrs. Verrall first reported to the meeting the conclusions she had been led to form concerning the envelope from her own script, and read the apparently relevant passages. On the envelope being opened, however, it was found that there was no resemblance between its actual contents and what was alleged by the script to be contained in it.

It has, then, to be reported that this one experiment completely failed, and it cannot be denied that the failure is disappointing. But after all, even if this communication of the contents of a sealed envelope had been successfully achieved, the proof to us of mental action on the part of the deceased "agent" would still be incomplete, for it may be that telepathy is not the right kind of explanation of these things at all; it may be that they are done—if ever they are done—by clairvoyance; that the document, though still sealed or enclosed in metal, is read in some unknown or fourth-dimensional manner by the subliminal self.

The existence of such a power as this, however, can be separately tested; because, if straightforward clairvoyance is possible, things unknown to any person living or dead may be read or inspected,—such as a piece of print torn at random out of an unread newspaper and sealed up, or a handful of alphabet letters or figures grasped from a box (p. 221). And in trying this experiment a negative conclusion must not be jumped at too readily. A positive answer might be definite enough; a negative answer can only be a probability. Moreover, it might be unwise to tell an automatist who is endeavouring to decipher the unknown figures that in that collocation they have never been inspected by man,—the knowledge should act as a gratuitously hostile or debilitating suggestion.

But even when such things are read, allowance must be made for some extraordinary possibility of hyperæsthesia—whether it be that of feeling on the part of the person who sealed them up, or of a kind of X-ray vision on the part of the clairvoyant, or some other even more forced hypothesis. Mrs. Sidgwick's paper on the evidence for real clairvoyance is in the *Proceedings*, S.P.R. vol. vii., but I will not quote any of the instances there given. The term clairvoyance ought strictly to be reserved for direct apprehension of hidden things without aid from any human knowledge, but in common practice the term is often applied also to the more numerous cases when some kind of telepathy is possible, provided the circumstances are such as to make a sensitive kind of direct perception not altogether improbable.

If telepathy ever occurs from a supra-mundane and immaterial region, that is to say from a discarnate mind not possessed of a brain, it may be difficult or impossible to distinguish it from clairvoyance. And indeed probably no discrimination would be necessary : that may be what "second-sight" or clairvoyance really is. But from the scientific point of view there is clearly all the difference in the world between recognised telepathy, such as has been proved to occur between one living person and another, and that other more hypothetical kind which has been suspected as occurring between discarnate intelligences, if there are any, and living people. If the process of ordinary experimental telepathy were ever ascertained to be a direct action of brain on brain, then acceptance of the other more hypothetical kind of telepathy would be almost forbidden —at any rate would be rendered extremely difficult. If, however the process of transmission should turn out to be a purely psychical one,—that is a psychological action directly between mind and mind, so that the brains at each end are only the instruments of record and verification,—then the possibility of a transfer of thought between minds unprovided with these appliances—or between one such mind and an embodied mind—is not at all inconceivable. It still has to be established, of course, and the difficulty of proof is still very great; but the effort towards such a proof is a legitimate one. It is that effort which for some years now the Society has been patiently making, and some of the results so far attained will be dealt with in Section IV.

The distinction here drawn, between a comparatively customary, and what may strike us as a more recondite and unexpected, method of communication, may be illustrated by reference to the facts of telegraphy :—

In ordinary telegraphy the message manifestly goes somehow from signalling key to receiving galvanometer; and, if attention is concentrated upon those obvious instruments alone, it might be thought that there was some direct mechanical connexion between them. But the real arrangement is more elaborate than that—a battery or dynamo in the cellar has to be taken into account,—and the actual process of transmission involves some fairly recently discovered properties of the ether of space. The message is conveyed etherially, not by matter at all, it can cross vacuum with perfect ease, though it is sent and received and interpreted by matter. I am speaking of ordinary telegraphy; there is no need to distinguish it from "wireless," in this particular.

I am not denying of course that telegraphic transmission is a physical process. All I imply by the parable is that the first impression of a spectator or critic, that telepathy is a physiological process effected direct between brain and brain, may not be the correct one. For telegraphy had been carried on commercially for years, before it was properly understood; and even now there must remain many things to be discovered about it. So it is hardly likely that in telepathy we have a process which is easily and quickly intelligible; nor is it in the least certain that the mode of transmission can be stated in terms of matter.

Perhaps it cannot be stated even in terms of Ether. The whole idea or imagery of space-relations in respect of mind may be misleading.

CHAPTER IX

EXAMPLES OF APPARENT CLAIRVOYANCE

TO show that some apparent clairvoyance, whether it be due to hyperæsthesia or telepathy or something else, is really possible, I take an instructive little experiment recorded by Mrs. Verrall in *Proceedings*, vol. xi. page 192—which she tried in November 1890 with her daughter, who was then a child aged 7½ years. Other instances will be mentioned later on—see for instance p. 217.

RECOGNITION OF OBJECTS BY TELEPATHY OR HYPERÆSTHESIA PERCIPIENT, H. AGED 7½ YEARS

Mrs. Verrall reports as follows :—

In November, 1890, I tried the following experiment with H. I drew a diagram, which I placed on H.'s forehead, while her eyes were shut, and asked her to describe it. To make the performance more like a game, I went on to ask what colour it was, and what she could see through it. We tried four experiments, three on the afternoon of November 16th, and one at 6.15 on November 30th, with the following results :—

Object drawn.—A triangle.
Result.—H. drew a triangle with her finger in the air. *Right.*
Object drawn.—A triangle with apex cut off.
Result.—H. described and drew an irregular figure, which did not seem to satisfy her, then said it was like an oval dish ⬭. *Wrong.*
Object drawn.—A square.

Result.—H. said : " It's like a window with no cross bars," and drew a four-sided rectangular figure in the air. *Right.*

Object drawn.—A square divided into 4 squares by a vertical and a horizontal line.

Result.—H. said : " It's a diamond." " What else ? " said I, meaning what colour, etc. " It's got a line across it, and another across that. [*Right.*] The colour is pale blue."

When I gave her the diagram, she turned it anglewise and said, " Oh yes, that's right, and the colour was not far wrong." As the diagram was drawn in ink on white paper, I did not understand, and asked what she meant. She said, " Why it's all blue, bluish white inside, and even the ink is blue." The diagram had been dried with blotting paper and was not a very deep black, but I could see nothing blue. Ten minutes afterwards she picked up the paper again and commented on the fact that it was blue, the lines dark bright blue, and the inside pale blue. I burnt the diagram and discontinued the game after observing this persistence of a self-suggested hallucination.

We had previously tried experiments which seemed to show that the child could *feel* the diagram. She could almost always tell whether the right or wrong side of a playing card were placed on her forehead. I was quite unable to distinguish the two sides. I am more inclined to attribute her successes (3 out of 4) to hyperæsthesia than to telepathy.

I will now quote a case which is rather a striking example of the fact that the intelligence operative through unconscious or subliminal processes is superior to that of the normal intelligence of the persons concerned ; so that just as people occasionally seem able to become cognisant of facts or events by means ordinarily closed to them,—a phenomenon which appears akin to the water-dowsing faculty and to the " homing " instincts of animals,—so sometimes they can write poetry or solve problems beyond their normal capacity.

Here for instance is the case of the solution of a mathematical problem by automatic writing—with the pencil not held in the hand, but attached to the heart-shaped piece of board called a " planchette." It is quoted from the record which I communicated at the time to the *Journal* of the Society for Psychical Research, vol. xi.

A Case of Automatic Intelligence

One feature of interest is that both the witnesses are exceptionally competent. The account was written by an old pupil of my own at Bedford College in the seventies—one of the ablest students there,—Miss C. M. Pole, daughter of the late Dr. Pole, F.R.S., the well-known Engineer, Musician, and writer on card-games. Miss Pole is now Mrs. Garrett Smith, living at Magdeburg, and writes as follows :—

In the early part of 1885 I was staying at —— in the house of Mrs. Q., and I and her daughter, Miss Q., B.A. Lond., used to amuse ourselves in writing with a Planchette. We had several Plànchettes (I think four), but we could only get response from one of them, which belonged to Miss Q. In the house with us were some eight or nine others, . . . but for no other pair would the Planchette act. The same one had formerly given good results with Miss Q. and another friend, but I have never written with a Planchette before or since. We got all sorts of nonsense out of it, sometimes long doggerel rhymes with several verses. Sometimes we asked for prophecies, but I do not remember ever getting one which came true, and my impression is that generally when we asked for a prophecy the thing went off in a straight line—running off the table if we did not take our hands off. It often did this, refusing to write at all, and towards the end of my stay there I believe it was always so ; we could get no answer from it. I believe we often asked Planchette who the guiding spirit was ; but I only once remember getting a definite connected answer. Then it wrote that his name was "Jim," and that he had been a Senior Wrangler. After other questions we asked it to write the equation to its own curve [in other words, to express mathematically the outline of the heart-shaped board]. Planchette wrote something like this quite distinctly—

(The curl backwards always denoted that the answer was finished.)

We repeated the question several times, but each time the answer was the same, sometimes more, sometimes less distinct. We interpreted it as $r = \dfrac{a \sin \theta}{\theta}$. . . . I knew just enough to be able to draw the curve represented by the equation. In my first try I made a mistake and believed the curve to be quite a different one, but afterwards I drew [something like] the following [rough sketch]—a double never-ending spiral :

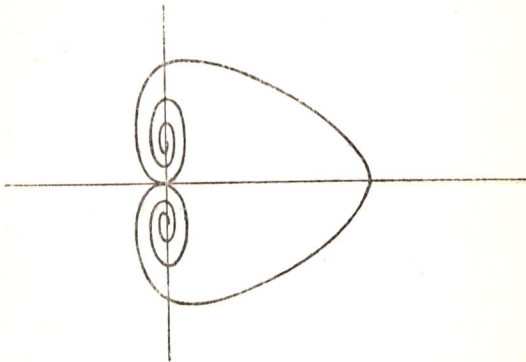

We checked our result by taking the equation to the Mathematical Master at the Boys' College, who drew the same [sort of] curve for us, but we did not tell him where we got the equation from.

I cannot say whether the Planchette we used was really exactly the shape of the outside curve; I should rather fancy that with the heart shape the resemblance ended. I am *quite sure* that I had never seen the curve before, and therefore the production of the equation could not have been an act of unconscious memory on my part. Also I most certainly did not know enough mathematics to know how to form an equation which would represent such a curve, or to know even of what type the equation must be. But I had come across such equations and drawn the curves represented by them ;—for instance, afterwards I found in my notebook the spiral $r\theta = \tfrac{1}{2}\pi a$, and the cardioid $r = a\,(1 + \cos\theta)$. We had used no text-book, and in the full notes of the lectures I had attended, these were the two curves I found most similar to Planchette's. If my brain produced the equation written by Planchette, it must have been that I unconsciously formed an equation like some I had seen before, which by a curious coincidence chanced to represent a heart-shaped curve.

I know that we were both quite unconscious of any influence we may have exercised on the Planchette.   Cecilia Garrett Smith

Magdeburg, *November* 1903

I (O. L.) made inquiries about Miss Q., and found that she was well known to friends of mine, and was a serious and responsible and trustworthy person, so I wrote some further questions to her, and received the following reply :—

March 23rd, 1904

. . . As far as Miss Pole and I were concerned, it was quite bonâ-fidê, and was not open to any suspicion of practical joking or setting traps for each other. It is true that when we wrote planchette, it was never with any serious motive, such as with the object of testing the unconscious mind, or for any scientific purpose, but merely for the fun of the thing. We used to ask it to prophesy future events, and to make up poetry, and all purely for amusement, after the manner of schoolgirls. Nevertheless, all that was written was quite in good faith.

The equation written did not come within the mathematical knowledge I then possessed, which was limited to the mathematics necessary for the London B.A. Pass Degree. I knew of course that every curve could be represented by an equation, and I was familiar with polar co-ordinates in which the equation was written. But the only equations I could then identify were those of the conic sections. Miss Pole had read some elementary Differential, and knew more than I did, but my impression is that her knowledge was not sufficient to enable her to trace curves.

Certainly neither of us perceived from the appearance of the equation that the reply was the correct one, but that I think would have been too much to expect, even if our knowledge had been much higher than it was.

I did not know sufficient at that time to attempt to plot the curve. I believe Miss Pole did attempt it, but if so, her attempts were un-successful. We were not satisfied that the equation did represent a curve like the outline of the planchette till we had asked our mathe-matical master to trace it for us. (This was done without telling him any of the facts of the case.)

I do not remember that we ever closely compared the curve he drew in tracing the equation with the actual planchette in question. We did not take the matter very seriously, and were quite content when we saw that the solution was at all events approximately true.

On *now* tracing the curve represented by the equation, I am inclined to think that it very closely resembles the shape of the actual planchette used, from my memory of it. (The planchette is no longer in existence.) . . .

To this I (O. L.) add that the equation which would naturally occur to any one is the cardioid $r = a\,(1 + \cos\theta)$; but it is quite likely, as Mrs. Garrett Smith says, that although as a student she was undoubtedly aware of this curve, she might not, some years afterward, be able to reproduce it on demand.

The equation written by Planchette is not a familiar one and certainly would not be likely to occur to her, nor would it have occurred to me; but the sketch given does not profess to be an exact representation of the curve corresponding to the equation written by the planchette, but only represents her recollection of its general character.

Mr. J. W. Sharpe, of Bournemouth, has been good enough to draw out an accurate graph of the curve, and here is his drawing on a reduced scale.

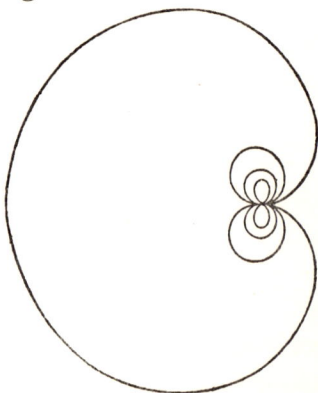

It is to be remembered that the equation $r = a\,\dfrac{\sin\theta}{\theta}$ was given by planchette, as representing mathematically the shape of its own outline or boundary; the intelligence controlling its movements being represented as that of a Cambridge Wrangler.

With regard to his drawing Mr. Sharpe observes that the curve does not consist of two sets of spirals, as at first depicted roughly, but of two sets of loops, all passing through the cusp and touching one another there, and all contained within the outer heart-shaped boundary. The loops meet only at the cusp, and there is an infinite number of them. They decrease in area without limit, ultimately sinking into the point of the cusp.

The equation very well represents the ordinary form of a planchette. But if it had accidentally been reversed into $r = a \dfrac{\theta}{\sin \theta}$, the curve would have been entirely different and entirely unlike any planchette outline.

Mr. Sharpe thinks it very unlikely that either of the automatists had ever seen an accurate graph of the equation given in their writing. It is of course much more difficult to invent an equation to fit a given curve (which was the feat performed by the writing in this case) than, when the equation is given, to draw the curve represented by it.

Power of Unseen Reading

In illustration of supernormal power of a still more excessive kind I quote from the automatic writings of Mr. Stainton Moses—well known as a master for many years in University College School, London—who for a great part of this period used to write automatically in the early morning in solitude. A great number of these writings have been published and are well known to all students of the subject; but the following incident is of a surprising character and is an example, though an exceptionally strong one, of the power of reading letters, etc., possessed in some degree by one or two of the "controls" of Mrs. Piper and of many another medium in history.

The following script was obtained by Mr. Stainton Moses while he was sitting in Dr. Speer's library and discoursing with various supposed communicators through his writing hand :—

See *Proceedings*, *S.P.R.*, vol. xi. p. 106.

S. M. Can you read?

"No, friend, I cannot, but Zachary Gray can, and Rector. I am not able to materialise myself, or to command the elements."

S. M. Are either of those spirits here?

"I will bring one by and by. I will send . . . Rector is here."

S. M. I am told you can read. Is that so? Can you read a book?

(Handwriting changed.) "Yes, friend, with difficulty."

S. M. Will you write for me the last line of the first book of the Æneid?

"Wait——*Omnibus errantem terris et fluctibus æstas.*" [This was right.]

S. M. Quite so. But I might have known it. Can you go to the book-case, take the last book but one on the second shelf, and read me the last paragraph of the ninety-fourth page? I have not seen it, and do not even know its name.

[With a little delay the following writing came.]

"I will curtly prove by a short historical narrative, that Popery is a novelty, and has gradually arisen or grown up since the primitive and pure time of Christianity, not only since the apostolic age, but even since the lamentable union of kirk and state by Constantine."

(The book on examination proved to be a queer one called "*Roger's Antipopopriestian*, an attempt to liberate and purify Christianity from Popery, Politikirkality, and Priestrule." The extract given above was accurate, but the word "narrative" substituted for "account.")

S. M. How came I to pitch upon so appropriate a sentence?

"I know not, my friend. It was done by coincidence. The word was changed in error. I knew it when it was done, but would not change."

S. M. How do you read? You wrote more slowly, and by fits and starts.

"I wrote what I remembered and then went for more. It is a special effort to read, and useful only as a test. Your friend was right last night; we can read, but only when conditions are very good. We will read once again, and write, and then impress you of the book :—'Pope is the last great writer of that school of poetry, the poetry of the intellect, or of the intellect mingled with the fancy.' That is truly written. Go

and take the eleventh book on the same shelf. [I took a book called *Poetry, Romance, and Rhetoric.*] It will open at the page for you. Take it and read, and recognise our power, and the permission which the great and good God gives us, to show you of our power over matter. To Him be glory. Amen."
(The book opened at page 145, and there was the quotation perfectly true. I had not seen the book before : certainly had no idea of its contents. S. M.) [These books were in Dr. Speer's library :—F. W. H. M.]

To this Mr. Myers pertinently appends the note :—

It is plain that a power such as this, of acquiring and reproducing fresh knowledge, interposes much difficulty in the way of identifying any alleged spirit by means of his knowledge of the facts of his earth life.

Dream Lucidity

To illustrate the fact that extra or supernormal lucidity is possible in dreams, a multitude of instances might be quoted from the publications of the Society for Psychical Research. Almost at random I quote two,—the first a short one of which the contemporary record is reported on by a critical and sceptical member of the Society, Mr. Thos. Barkworth, in the *Journal* of the Society for Dec. 1895.

G. 249. Dream.

The following is a case which was noted at the time, before it was known to be veridical.

It was received by Mr. Barkworth, who writes concerning it :—

"West Hatch, Chigwell, Essex, *August 24th,* [1895]

" It has been often made a subject of reproach by persons who distrust the S.P.R. that the evidence we obtain is seldom, if ever, supported by written records demonstrably made before the dream or the hallucination had been verified by subsequently ascertained facts. Indeed, a Mr. Taylor Innes, writing in the *Nineteenth Century* some years ago, went so far, if I remember rightly, as to assert that no such case could be produced up to the time he wrote. It must certainly be admitted that in provokingly numerous instances it is found that the alleged letter or diary has been destroyed.

"The following experience of the Rev. E. K. Elliott, Rector of Worthing, who was formerly in the navy, and who made the entry in his diary as quoted when he was cruising in the Atlantic out of reach of post or telegraph, will therefore be found of interest. The diary is still in his possession.

T. B.

Extract from diary written out in Atlantic, January 14th, 1847

" Dreamt last night I received a letter from my uncle, H. E., dated January 3rd, in which news of my dear brother's death was given. It greatly struck me.

" My brother had been ill in Switzerland, but the last news I received on leaving England was that he was better.

"The 'January 3rd' was very black, as if intended to catch my eye.

"On my return to England I found, as I quite expected, a letter awaiting me saying my brother had died on the above date.

" E. K. ELLIOTT "

Worthing

The second case I quote is a much longer and more elaborate one, and we owe its receipt to Dr. Hodgson while in America.

There are many partially similar records of people becoming aware of an accident in which some near relative was injured or killed : and it is noteworthy that the emotion caused by injury seems as likely to convey such an impression as anything pertaining to death itself ; but the point of the following narrative is that a complete stranger became impressed with facts which were happening at a distance, without the slightest personal interest in any one concerned—so that it seems to make in favour of a general clairvoyant faculty rather than for any spiritistic explanation. The prefix P. 224 is merely a classificatory reference number.

P. 224. Dream.

The following case has some resemblance to Mrs. Storie's experience, of which an account was published in *Phantasms of the Living*, vol. i. p. 370, except that the person whose fate was represented in the dream was in the case here printed entirely unknown to the dreamer. The account is written by Mr. H. W. Wack, Attorney, and comes to us through the American Branch of the Society.

"Court House, St. Paul, Minn., *February 10th*, 1892

"I believe I have had a remarkable experience. About midnight on the 29th day of December, headsore and fatigued, I left my study where I had been poring over uninspiring law text, and, climbing to my chamber door, fell into bed for the night.

"Nothing unusual had transpired in my affairs that day, and yet, when I gave myself to rest, my brain buzzed on with a myriad fancies. I lay an hour, awake, and blinking like an over-fed owl. The weird intonation of an old kitchen clock fell upon my ears but faintly, as it donged the hour of two. The sound of the clock chime had hardly died when I became conscious [of] my position in a passenger coach on the St. Paul, Minneapolis and Omaha railroad. I was journeying to Duluth, Minnesota, from St. Paul, in which latter place I had gone to sleep. I was aware that I had been on the train about four hours and that I was somewhere near the town of Shell Lake, Wis., distant from St. Paul about eighty miles. I had often been over the road, and as I peered through the coach window, I recognised, in the moonlit scene, features of country and habitation I had seen before. We were plunging on, almost heedlessly as it seemed, when I fancied I heard and was startled from my reverie by a piercing shriek, which was protracted into a piteous moaning and gasping, as if some human creature were suffering some hideous torture.

"Then I felt the train grind heavily to an awkward stop. There was a sudden commotion fore and aft. Train men with lanterns hurried through my car and joined employés near the engine. I could see the lights flash here and there, beside and beneath the cars ; brake-men moved along the wheels in groups, the pipe voice of the con-ductor and the awe-stricken cry of the black porter infused a livening sense to a scene which I did not readily understand. Instinctively I concluded that an accident had happened, or perhaps that a break to the train had occasioned this sudden uprising of train men. A minute later I was out upon the road bed. The brusque and busy search and the disturbed manner of the attendants did not propitiate elaborate inquiry from a curious passenger, so I was appeased to be told, in very ugly snappish English, that if I had eyes I might see for myself that 'some one got killed, I reckon.' Everybody moved and acted in a spirit of stealth, and each, it appeared, expected a horrible 'find.'

The trucks were being examined from the rear of the train forward. Blood splotches were discovered on nearly all the bearings under the entire train. When the gang reached one of the forward cars, all lights were cast upon a truck which was literally scrambled with what appeared to be brains—human brains, evidently, for among the clots were small tufts of human hair. This truck, particularly, must have ground over the bulk of a human body. Every fixture between the wheels was smeared with the crimson ooze of some crushed victim. But where was the body, or at least its members? The trucks were covered only with a pulp of mangled remnants. The search for what appeared of the killed was extended 500 yards back of the train and all about the right-of-way with no more satisfactory result than to occasionally find a blood-stained tie.

"All hands boarded the train; many declaring that it was an unusual mishap on a railroad which left such uncertain trace of its victim. Again I felt the train thundering on through the burnt pine wastes of northern Minnesota. As I reclined there in my berth, I reflected upon the experience of the night, and often befuddled my sleepy head in an effort to understand how a train, pushing along at the rate of thirty miles an hour, could so grind and triturate a vital bulk, staining only trucks behind the engine, unless the killed at the fatal time were upon the truck or huddled closely by it. I concluded, therefore, that the being destroyed under the train had been concealed near the bespattered fixtures of the car. I had read of death to tramps stealing rides by hiding themselves under or between cars, and finally I dismissed meditation—assured that another unfortunate itinerant had been crushed out of existence. Horrible! I shuddered and awoke—relieved to comprehend it all a *dream*.

"Now the fact that the foregoing is an accurate statement of a dream experienced by me is not a matter for marvel. Taken alone, there is nothing remarkable in the time at which this vision blackened my sleep. The spell was upon me between two and three o'clock in the morning—of that I am certain. I am positive of the time, because, when I awoke, I heard the clock distinctly, as it struck three.

"On the morrow, I,—who usually forget an ordinary dream long before breakfast—recounted to the family the details of the night's distraction. From my hearers there followed only the ordinary comments of how ghastly and how shocking the story was as told and how strange the nature of the accident—*that no parts of the body had been found*. The latter circumstance was, to me also, quite an unusual feature of railroad casualty.

"The evening following the night of the dream (December 30th), at 5 o'clock, I returned to my home, stepped into my study, and, as I am in the habit of doing, I glanced at a page of the *St. Paul Dispatch*, a daily evening newspaper. It had been casually folded by a previous reader, so that in picking it up flatly, the article which first fixed my attention read:

"'Fate of a tramp. Horrible death experienced by an unknown man on the Omaha Road. His remains scattered for miles along the track by the merciless wheels.

"'Duluth, December 30.—Every truck on the incoming Omaha train from St. Paul this morning was splashed with blood. Train men did not know there had been an accident till they arrived here, but think some unfortunate man must have been stealing a ride between St. Paul and this city. Train men on a later train state that a man's leg was found by them at Spooner, and that for two miles this side the tracks were scattered with pieces of flesh and bone. There is no possible means of identification.'

"Here was an evident verification of all that transpired in my mind between two and three o'clock on the previous night. I reflected, and the more I pondered the faster I became convinced that I had been in some mysterious form, spirit or element, witness of the tragedy reported in the columns of the press—that my vision was perfect as to general details, and the impression complete and exact to time, place, and circumstance. The next morning I scanned the pages of the *Pioneer Press* of December 31st, and read the following paragraph:—

"'Unknown man killed, Shell Lake, Wis. Special telegram, December 30th.—Fragments of the body of an unknown man were picked up on the railroad track to-day. Portions of the same body were also found on over 100 miles of the railroad. He is supposed to have been killed by the night train, but just where is not known.'

"With this came the conviction to me that, living and asleep, 100 miles from the place of the killing, I had been subjected to the phantom-sight of an actual occurrence on the Omaha railroad, as vivid and in truth as I have stated it above.

"I have not written this account because Mark Twain and other authors have published in current magazines their experiences in what is termed Mental Telepathy or Mental Telegraphy. On the contrary, having read a number of those articles, I have hesitated to utter, as authentic, what I now believe to be a material and striking evidence of the extent, the caprice, and the possibilities of this occult phenomenon.

"HARRY W. WACK"

In reply to Dr. Hodgson's inquiries, Mr. Wack wrote :—

"St. Paul, *February 20th*, 1892

"My Dear Sir,—Replying to your valued favour of the 15th inst., I will say that you *are right* in understanding that my account of the dream submitted to your Society is a true narrative.

"I reaffirm every word of it, and give you my solemn assurance that, as I have stated, I informed the family and friends of the dream and its details, before I had the first suspicion that the public press ever had contained or ever would contain a report of such an actual occurrence.

"If desirable I will make affidavit as to the truth of the substance of the narrative in your hands.

"I enclose a few corroborative letters, the signatures to which I procured yesterday, February 19th. If these serve you, well and good.

"Harry W. Wack"

The following were the corroborative letters enclosed :—

(1)   "St. Paul, *February 20th*, 1892

"Gentlemen,—Referring to an account of a dream submitted to you by Mr. Harry Wack of this city which I have read, I beg leave to add the following facts corroborative of the narrative.

"After careful consideration of the article, I find that the story of the dream on December 29th–30th is in substance identical with that which was related by Mr. Wack at breakfast on the morning of December 30th, 1891. On that occasion Mr. Wack stated that he had been agitated the previous night by a dream of unusual features, and then, at the request of those present, he recited what now appears in his article, which I have just perused for the first time. On the evening of December 30th, 1891, when Mr. Wack discovered the newspaper item, he again mentioned the dream and called my attention to the newspaper item, and several of the family discussed the matter. On the morning of December 31st, another newspaper clipping bearing on the same matter was debated by the family.

"Aside from the unusual features and hideousness of the dream, there was nothing to startle us, until the newspaper accounts developed the affair in a mysterious sense. The first version of the dream was given in the morning of December 30th. The first newspaper dispatch appeared and was discovered in the evening of the same day. This I know of my own knowledge, being present on each occasion.

"Mrs. Margaret B. Macdonald"

(2)   "St. Paul, Minn., *February 20th*, 1892

"Gentlemen,—I have read the letter of Mrs. Macdonald, with whom I visited on December 29th, 30th, 31st, and days following, and with your permission I will say that I also was present at breakfast when Mr. Wack mentioned the dream, and at dinner (6 p.m.) when Mr. Wack called our attention to the newspaper item, which he then declared was a positive verification of the dream he experienced the night before. I have read the account of the dream, and I believe it to be precisely as I understood it from Mr. Wack's account given on the morning of December 30th, 1891.

"Rose B. Hamilton"

(3)   "St. Paul, *February 20th*, 1892

"Gentlemen,—Having read the foregoing letters of Mrs. Macdonald and Miss Rose B. Hamilton, and being familiar with the facts and incidents therein set forth, I would add my endorsement to them as being in strict accord with the truth.

"Mr. Wack stated his dream as he has written of it in the article which I understand he has submitted to you, on the morning of December 30th, 1891. He came upon and drew our attention to the newspaper articles in the evening of December 30th, and on the morning of December 31st, 1891. It was these newspaper dispatches which made the dream interesting, and thereafter it was freely discussed.

"C. E. McDonald"

Mr. H. W. Smith, an Associate Member of the American Branch, writes to Dr. Hodgson in connection with the case:—

"Office of Smith & Austrian, Commission Merchants,
"290, E., 6th Street, Produce Exchange,
"St. Paul, Minn., *April 14th*, 1892

"My Dear Sir,—It has been impossible for me to accept Mr. Wack's invitation to meet at his house the witnesses he cited in his communication to you. I have already written you of my preliminary interview with Mr. Wack, and it confirms in my own mind the high opinion which I previously held of him through our acquaintanceship, extending over a series of years. There is no reasonable doubt in my mind that the statement he makes is substantially correct, at least as respects any and all allegations of fact. Of course the application of these facts to an unknown force is a matter upon which I cannot speak.

"Herbert W. Smith"

Instances like this are by no means solitary, and whatever view we take of them we have to include them in the roll of facts demanding explanation—an explanation which may not be readily forthcoming. It may be presumed that as far as they go they make against the spiritistic hypothesis in any simple or direct form ; and that is why in a book like this it is necessary to emphasise them.

Meanwhile all we are sure of is that information is obtained by some mediums which is entirely beyond their conscious knowledge, and occasionally beyond the conscious knowledge of everyone present. But as to how this lucidity is attained we are as yet in the dark ; though we must ultimately proceed to consider the possibility that it is by some sort of actual communication from other intelligences, akin to the conveyance of information in the accustomed and ordinary human way, by rumour, by conversation, and by the press.

Incidents that seem to point to some form of supernormal communication are exemplified in the experiments of Dr. van Eeden of Bussum, in Holland, with Mrs. Thompson at Hampstead,—a lady who is referred to more particularly in Section IV. of this book. (See his paper on sittings with Mrs. Thompson in *Proceedings*, S.P.R., vol. xvii., especially pp. 86–7 and 112–115). Dr. van Eeden, having cultivated the power of controlling his own dreams, so as to be able to dream of performing actions which he had planned while awake, arranged with Mrs. Thompson that he would occasionally call "Nelly" (her "control") in his dreams after returning to Holland, and that if she heard him calling she should tell Mr. Piddington, who was in charge of the sittings, at his next sitting. On three occasions, in January and February 1900, some success was obtained in these experiments ; that is, "Nelly" stated that she had heard Dr. van Eeden calling, and had "been to see him"; the dates she gave were approximately, though not exactly, the same as those recorded in his diary of dreams; but on each occasion she gave details, which were afterwards verified, as to his circumstances at the time. On a fourth occasion (April 19th, 1900), when "Nelly" stated that she had been to see Dr. van Eeden, he had no dream of her at the time, but she gave a description of his condition which corresponded with what it had been during the early part of the same month.

A case of a somewhat similar kind is the one recorded in Dr. Hodgson's report on Mrs. Piper (*Proceedings*, vol. viii. p. 120), where Mr. M. N. in America relates that Mrs. Piper's control, "Dr. Phinuit," had said that he would visit Mr. N.'s dying father in England about certain matters connected with his will, and where later on it was reported by those attending the dying father that he had complained of the presence of an obtrusive old man. (This case is quoted below, see page 146.)

CLAIRVOYANCE OF THE DYING

The extra lucidity of the dying is a thing so often asserted that it has become almost a commonplace, and sometimes, as in the case of children, it would seem to eclipse mere imagination—as for instance when a dying child welcomes, and appears to be welcomed by, its deceased mother. But these visions and auditions, which are unmistakably common, are usually of things beyond our ordinary cognisance, so that for the most part they have to be relegated to the category of the unverifiable. Occasionally, however, we have records of a kind of clairvoyant faculty whereby terrestrial occurrences also are perceived by persons who in health had no such power; and these are worthy of attention,—

especially those which are reciprocal, producing an impression at both ends of a terrestrial line, as if the telepathic and less material mode of communication had in their case already begun.

The extant descriptions of dying utterances are very much like the utterances in the waking stages of Mrs. Piper's trance, to be subsequently mentioned—and these do not appear to be random or meaningless sayings, but do really correspond to some kind of reality, since in them the appearance of strangers is frequently described correctly and messages are transmitted which have a definite meaning. Moreover, the look of ecstasy on Mrs. Piper's face at a certain stage of the waking process is manifestly similar to that seen on the faces of some dying people; and both describe the subjective vision as of something more beautiful and attractive than those of earth.

Whether the dying really have greater telepathic power as agents, which is what is assumed in the ordinary telepathic explanation of Phantasms of the Living, is doubtful, but that they sometimes have greater sensibility as percipients seems likely; and sometimes the event which they are describing is likewise apprehended by another person at a distance,—thus appearing to demonstrate reciprocal telepathic influence. There is a small group of cases illustrative of the reciprocal clairvoyance of the dying,—I can only quote an illustrative case or two from the few which are well evidenced : *i.e.* which come up to the standard of the Society for Psychical Research in this matter — but I omit the authentication in quoting them, and I also abbreviate, as I only here wish to indicate the kind of thing.

The writer of the following account is Colonel B., a well-known Irish gentleman. He explains that his wife engaged to sing with her daughters a Miss X., who was training as a public singer but who ultimately did not come out in that capacity, having married a Mr. Z.

Six or seven years afterwards Mrs. B., who was dying, in the presence of her husband spoke of voices she heard singing, saying that she had heard them several times that day, and that there was one voice among them which she knew, but could not remember whose voice it was.

"Suddenly she stopped and said, pointing over my head," says Colonel B., "'Why, there she is in the corner of the room; it is Julia X.; she is coming on; she is leaning over you; she has her hands up; she is praying; do look; she is going.' I turned but could see nothing. Mrs. B. then said, 'She is gone.' All these things [the hearing of singing and the vision of the singer] I imagined to be the phantasies of a dying person.

"Two days afterwards, taking up the *Times* newspaper, I saw recorded the death of Julia Z., wife of Mr. Z. I was so astounded that in a day or so after the funeral I went up to —— and asked Mr. X. if Mrs. Z., his daughter, was dead. He said, 'Yes, poor thing, she died of puerperal fever. On the day she died she began singing in the morning, and sang and sang until she died.'"

The case next quoted is a curious incident connected with a deceased child, obtained in one of the bereaved mother's sittings with Mrs. Piper in America, at a time when Phinuit was in control.

It is the concluding portion of a long and striking series of communications, extremely characteristic of identity, which are quoted both in *Human Personality*, vol. ii. 245–7, and in *Proc.* S.P.R., vol. xiii. pp. 386–9. The mother's testimony is thus reported :—

The remarks made at her second sitting suggest that "the little book" in the child's mind was not this one. " Kakie wants the little bit of a book mamma read by her bedside, with the pretty bright things hanging from it—mamma put it in her hands—the last thing she remembers." Mrs. Sutton states that this was a little prayer book with a cross and other symbols in silver attached to ribbons for marking the places, and that it was sent to her by a friend after Kakie had ceased to know any one except perhaps for a passing moment. Mrs. Sutton read it when Kakie seemed unconscious, and *after Kakie's death* placed it in her hands to prevent the blood settling in the nails. She adds later that Mrs. Piper's hands, when the book was asked for at the sitting, were put into the same position as Kakie's.

There is also evidence of reciprocity of an unusual kind in connection with the Piper case ; for " Phinuit " has been described as perceived by a dying person at a distance, in correspondence with the assertion of Phinuit that he would go and talk to this same person about unfair clauses in his will.

The account of this curious episode is from an American gentleman who had had a good deal of experience in Piper sittings, and who does not want his name disclosed. Of three examples of what he calls pre-dictions, thus obtained, I select this one, as it illustrates the kind of reciprocal experience of which I am now speaking. The account is corroborated by Mrs. " M.N."

April 5th, 1889

. . . About the end of March of last year I made [Mrs. Piper] a visit (having been in the habit of doing so, since early in February, about once a fortnight). [As Phinuit] told me that the death of a near relative of mine would occur in about six weeks, from which I should realise some pecuniary advantages, I naturally thought of my father, who was advanced in years, and whose description Mrs. Piper had given me very accurately some week or two previously. She had not spoken of him as my father, but merely as a person nearly connected with me. I asked her at that sitting whether this person was the one who would die, but she declined to state anything more clearly to me. My wife, to whom I was then engaged, went to see Mrs. Piper a few days afterwards, and she told her (my wife) that my father would die in a few weeks.

About the middle of May my father died very suddenly in London from heart failure, when he was recovering from a very slight attack of bronchitis, and the very day that his doctor had pronounced him out of danger. Previous to this Mrs. Piper (as Dr. Phinuit) had told me that she would endeavour to influence my father about certain matters connected with his will before he died. Two days after I received the cable announcing his death, my wife and I went to see Mrs. Piper, and she [Phinuit] spoke of his presence, and his sudden arrival in the spirit-world, and said that he (Dr. Phinuit) had endeavoured to persuade him in those matters while my father was sick. Dr. Phinuit told me the state of the will, and described the principal executor, and said that he (the executor) would make a certain disposition in my favour, subject to the consent of the two other executors, when I got to London, England. Three weeks afterwards I arrived in London; found the principal executor to be the man Phinuit had described. The will went materially as he had stated. The disposition was made in my favour, and my sister, who was chiefly at my father's bedside the last three days of his life, told me that he had repeatedly complained of the presence of an old man at the foot of his bed, who annoyed him by discussing his private affairs. . . .

(" M.N.")

A similar illustration of reciprocity occurred in the case of the lady called " Elisa Mannors," whose near relatives and friends concerned in the communications were known also to Mr. Myers.

On the morning after the death of her uncle, called F. in the report, she described an incident in connection with the appearance of herself to her uncle on his death-bed. Dr. Hodgson's account of this is in *Proceedings*, S.P.R., vol. xiii. p. 378, as follows :—

The notice of his [F.'s] death was in a Boston morning paper, and I happened to see it on my way to the sitting. The first writing of the sitting came from Madame Elisa, without my expecting it. She wrote clearly and strongly, explaining that F. was there with her, but unable to speak directly, and that she wished to give an account of how she had helped F. to reach her. She said that she had been present at his death-bed, and had spoken to him, and she repeated what she had said, an unusual form of expression, and indicated that he had heard and recognised her. This was confirmed in detail in the only way possible at the time, by a very intimate friend of Madame Elisa and myself, and also of the nearest surviving relative of F. I showed my friend the account of the sitting; and to this friend, a day or two later, the relative, who was present at the death-bed, stated spontaneously that F. when dying saw Madame Elisa who was speaking to him, and he repeated what she was saying. The expression so repeated, which the relative quoted to my friend, was that which I had received from Madame Elisa through Mrs. Piper's trance, when the death-bed incident was, of course, entirely unknown to me.

WRITING OF FOREIGN LANGUAGES

Instances in which foreign languages unknown to the medium are written or spoken are comparatively rare.

At a sitting in 1892, when Madame Elisa Mannors was "communicating," some Italian was written by request, the lady being as familiar with Italian as with English, but only two or three common words were decipherable. The first names of sitter and communicator were given, and the last name was both written and afterwards given by G.P. to Phinuit. Some of the writing was of a personal character, and some about the watch [concerning which inquiry had been made]; and G.P. stated correctly, *inter alia*, that the sitter's mother was present (in "spirit") with the communicator, and that he himself did not know her. The real names are very uncommon. The Italian for "It is well, Patience," was whispered at the end of the sitting as though by direct control of the voice by Madame Elisa.

Further attempts were made to speak and write Italian, but not much was said, and the writing was not very legible. Concerning this Dr. Hodgson remarks :—

As I have mentioned elsewhere (Report, pp. 293, 332), the intelligence communicating by writing is not conscious of the act of writing. The chief difficulty apparently in getting another language written by the hand is that strange words tend to be written phonetically unless they are thought out slowly letter by letter. The writing is usually much more legible now than it was during the period of the records from which I am quoting, when there was frequently much difficulty in deciphering even the simplest English words. It was therefore not surprising that so little of the Italian written by Madame Elisa was decipherable.

This does not appear to be a strong case, but the next one seems to me better :

Dr. Hodgson reports the following case in a sitting which a Mr. Vernon Briggs had with Mrs. Piper in October 1893 (*Proc.* S.P.R. xiii. 337 ; or *Hum. Pers.* ii. 244).

The communication purported to come from a Honolulu boy named Kalua, who became much attached to Mr. Briggs, during a six months' stay of Mr. Briggs in Honolulu in 1881, and who followed Mr. Briggs back to Boston under somewhat romantic circumstances in 1883. He was soon sent back to his native island, but again returned to Boston, where he was shot in 1886, in a sailor's Bethel, whether intentionally or not was unknown. There was some suspicion against a Swede who was imprisoned, but there was no evidence against him, and he was finally discharged. The Swede said that Kalua had accidentally shot himself with a revolver, and eventually confessed that after the accident he had himself hidden the revolver behind a flue, where, after taking part of the chimney down, it was found. Mr. Briggs had taken a handkerchief belonging to Kalua with him to the sitting. Kalua had been shot through the heart, and there was some confusion apparently about the locality of the suffering, "stomach" and "side" being mentioned, under what appeared to be the direct control of the voice by "Kalua," and Mr. Briggs asked if it was Kalua. Phinuit then spoke for "Kalua," who said that he did not kill himself, that he had been gambling with the other man who disputed with him and shot him, but did not mean to, and who threw the revolver "into the hot box where the pepples are" (meaning the "furnace" and the "coals"), and hid his purse under the steps where he was killed. "Kalua" also said there was shrubbery near it. The cellar of the house was examined, but no purse was found, and there was no shrubbery in the cellar. "Kalua" tried to write Hawaiian, but the only "ordinary" words deciphered were "lei" (meaning *wreaths*, which he made daily for Mr. Briggs) which was written clearly and frequently, and an attempt at "aloha"-greeting. Phinuit tried to get the answer to the question where Kalua's father was, but could only succeed in getting "Hiram." But the writing gave the answer "Hawaiian Islands." In reply to the question which one, the answer in writing was Kawai, but Phinuit said Tawai. The word is spelt Kawai, but is pronounced Tawai by the natives of the island itself and in the island where Kalua was born. The natives of the other islands call it Kawai.

Cases in which the lucidity or clairvoyant faculty is not limited to the present, but apparently anticipates the future, are sufficiently important to deserve a separate chapter.

It is extremely difficult to contemplate such a faculty. Hitherto we have dealt only with knowledge of the present and the past.

CHAPTER X

PREVISION

BUT assertions are made that there is a kind of lucidity occasionally attainable by healthy people which is beyond the powers of *any* ordinary intelligence, even aided by telepathy; inasmuch as knowledge is sometimes exhibited not only of occurrences at a distance but also of events which have not yet happened, and which could not by any process of reasoning be inferred.

Is it possible to become aware of events before they have occurred, by means other than ordinary scientific prediction?

The anticipation of future events is a power not at all necessarily to be expected on a Spiritistic or any other hypothesis; it is a separate question, and will have important bearings of its own. An answer to this question in the affirmative may vitally affect our metaphysical notions of "Time," but will not of necessity have an immediate bearing on the existence in the universe of intelligences other than our own. A cosmic picture gallery (as Mr. Myers calls it), or photographic or phonographic record of all that has occurred or will occur in the universe, may conceivably—or perhaps not conceivably—in some sense exist, and may be partly open and dimly decipherable to the lucid part of the automatist's or entranced person's mind.

But the question for us now is whether we can obtain clear and unmistakable proof of the existence of this foreseeing power in any form. It is not an easy thing to establish beyond any kind of doubt. Casual and irresponsible critics have said that documentary evidence, such as a postmark on a letter which detailed an event either not yet happened or certainly not known by ordinary methods at the date of the postmark (like a recent shipwreck in mid-ocean for instance), would be proof positive to them of something occult. A writer in *The Nineteenth Century* goes so far as to say that a document thus officially verified by a Post Office clerk would be worth thousands of pounds to the British Museum. If so it would be singularly easy to get rich. I believe that a postmark on an envelope would satisfy some of these critics, but a postmark on the document itself would be entirely convincing.

I wonder some enterprising forger has not endeavoured to gull a leading journal by an elaborate account, say, of the *Victoria* disaster, or the Santander explosion, or the Messina earthquake, written on foolscap paper transmitted blank through the post, at small cost, in preparation for any such striking event; or perhaps on paper subsequently covered with previous postmarks by a genial Post Office friend, and decorated with red tape by a live Government clerk!

The feeling that everything done by a Post Office official is conclusive, is of the same order as the opinion that barristers or criminal judges or medical practitioners are the only people fit to investigate unusual mental phenomena, because their practice makes them familiar with the warpings of the human mind.

But to consider the case of a medical practitioner; as I understand a doctor's business, it is to cure an abnormality if he can, not to prolong and investigate it. True, a doctor may be a scientific man in addition, but *qua* physician he is out of his element as a general investigator, and as a leading practitioner he has very little spare time. Were it not so, the record against the profession—the attitude the main body of doctors has taken or used to take to everything new—would be not only pitiful, as it is, but essentially disgraceful. To this day I expect that in some countries there are promising subjects, some for investigation and some for psychical cure, lost both to science and to themselves within the walls of asylums.

But about this question of postmarks. Let it not be thought that I claim that their evidence is worthless. As evidence subsidiary to testimony they may be very valuable, and every effort should be made to get them; my contention only is that they do not dispense with testimony.

This I hold is the function of all circumstantial evidence, or of any automatic record; it lessens the chance of self-delusion or over-exuberant imagination, it can never be held to guard against fraud. If a couple of friends by interchanging letters, with their dates verified in some cold blooded official manner, are able to establish foreknowledge of events such as could hardly be guessed or inferred, then their testimony is strengthened by the date-marks to this extent :—Either the things happened as they say, or they are in some sort of collusion to bear false witness and deceive. One could only grant them the loophole of self-deception on the alternative of something very like insanity.

That is how these automatic records, photographs and the like, may be so valuable—as supplementary to human testimony—never as substitutes for it.

ANTICIPATION OF EVENTS

Have we any trustworthy evidence at all as to the power of foreseeing unpredictable events? Strange to say, we have, but it is not yet sufficient in volume to justify any generalisation: it is only enough to cause us to keep an open mind, even in this direction, and be ready critically to scrutinise future evidence as it arrives. Mrs. Sidgwick's paper on the evidence for Premonitions is in vol. v. of *Proceedings* S.P.R.

I attach no high importance to predictions of illness and death: they may represent an unusual power of diagnosis, but need not represent anything more. Besides, a great number of these predictions fail; so much so that a prediction of this kind now hardly perturbs an experienced person who receives it.

And even the successful prevision of an accident must be attributed as a rule to accidental concordance unless it is accompanied by an exceptional amount of detail.

The following case is contained in Mrs. Sidgwick's paper, *Proceedings*, vol. v. p. 333. It is from an engine-driver who was interviewed afterwards by an agent of the S.P.R. in America.

[In 1853] I was firing a locomotive, a fine new passenger engine, built for speed, and just from the shop. I thought myself lucky to be on such a fine engine, and was proud of my position. One night, May 29th, 1853, I dreamed that the train ran through a shallow cut, and came out on a high stone bridge, over which the train passed, and then the engine turned over down the bank some 70 feet, into the river. I mentioned my dream the next morning to the family

with whom I was living. The lady [now dead] told me I was going
to be killed, but I told her that in my dream I had assurance that I
should not be hurt. On the second morning after my dream, we
were sent over a part of the road with which I was not familiar, and
presently came to a shallow cut, and I saw a number of men ahead
on the track. The engineer was near-sighted and did not see them.
I called to him to stop the engine; he tried to do so, but the track
was wet, and seeing that part of the track ahead had been taken up,
he jumped from the engine. I remained on it and tried to stop it.
Before this could be done, we were on a stone bridge, and I could
not get off. The engine left the track, and at the other end of the
bridge turned over twice before it reached the bottom, and I with it,
receiving but a small scratch *how* I do not know. I climbed the bank,
and looking back, saw just what I had seen in my dream. The bridge
was 200 feet long, with five stone arches, 54 feet high, and the bank
down which the engine rolled 70 feet.

THE MARMONTEL CASE

The perception of incidents at a distance is common
enough, but the perception of incidents in the future is
rare. The following selection from experiences of this
kind received by Mrs. Verrall must serve as an example
of the few trustworthy cases I know of (*Proc.* S.P.R.,
vol. xx. p. 331).

On December 11th, 1901—*i.e.* towards the end of the
first year in which Mrs. Verrall had developed the power
of automatic writing—her hand wrote as follows :—

Nothing too mean, the trivial helps, gives confidence. Hence this.
Frost and a candle in the dim light. Marmontel, he was reading on a
sofa or in bed—there was only a candle's light. She will surely remember this. The book was lent, not his own—he talked about it.

Then there appeared a fanciful but unmistakable
attempt at the name Sidgwick.

No meaning was conveyed by the above, but the
concluding effort naturally suggested that Mrs. Sidgwick
should be applied to. This was done; and her reply,

received on December 17th, said that she could make nothing of it but would report if the name Marmontel turned up.

Mrs. Verrall was now away from home and had decided to abandon writing till her return.   But all the 17th she was so disturbed by a desire to write that she made time, and that evening obtained the following :—

I wanted to write.   Marmontel is right.   It was a French book, a Memoir I think.   Passy may help, Souvenirs de Passy, or Fleury. Marmontel was not on the cover—the book was bound and was lent— two volumes in old-fashioned binding and print.   It is not in any papers —it is an attempt to make some one remember—an incident.

Soon after my return to Cambridge—Mrs. Verrall reports—about December 25th, 1901, I was looking through a list of books—which I had glanced at before December 11th — and found an advertisement of " Marmontel, *Moral Tales*, selected and translated by G. Saintsbury."   This, strange though such an admission may seem, was, as far as I could remember, my first conscious knowledge of Marmontel as a French writer.

So ends the record of the obtaining of the script. The sentence in the first portion " She will surely remember this" is a characteristic *sotto voce* remark which is not infrequent in these scripts,—having the same sort of signification as the terminal sentence of the second portion.   It means that Mrs. Verrall herself will surely remember having obtained the writing, when at some future time the incident described is referred to.

Now begins the verification by quite unexpected means.

In January 1902 Mrs. Verrall happened to write to a friend of hers named Mr. Marsh, asking him to come for a week-end visit ; and he replied fixing March 1st.   She had had no recent communication with him since June

1901. On February 23rd she sent him a post card to remind him of his visit, and he replied with a letter on February 24th.

Mrs. Verrall then reports as follows :—

On March 1st Mr. Marsh arrived, and that evening at dinner he mentioned that he had been reading Marmontel.   I asked if he had read the *Moral Tales*, and he replied that it was the *Memoirs*.   I was interested in this reference to Marmontel, and asked Mr. Marsh for particulars about his reading, at the same time explaining the reasons for my curiosity.   He then told me that he got the book from the London Library, and took the first volume only to Paris with him, where he read it on the evening of February 20th, and again on February 21st.   On each occasion he read by the light of a candle ; on the 20th he was in bed, on the 21st lying on two chairs.   He talked about the book to the friends with whom he was staying in Paris.   The weather was cold, but there was, he said, no frost.   The London Library copy is bound, as most of their books are, not in modern binding, but the name " Marmontel " is on the back of the volume.   The edition has three volumes ; in Paris Mr. Marsh had only one volume, but at the time of his visit to us he had read the second also.

I asked him whether " Passy " or " Fleury " would " help," and he replied that Fleury's name certainly occurred in the book, in a note ; he was not sure about Passy, but undertook to look it up on his return to town, and to ascertain, as he could by reference to the book, what part of the first volume he had been reading in Paris.   He is in the habit of reading in bed, but has electric light in his bedroom at home, so that he had not read " in bed or on a sofa by candlelight " for months, until he read Marmontel in Paris.

On his return to town Mr. Marsh wrote to me (March 4, 1902), that on February 21st while lying on two chairs he read a chapter in the first volume of Marmontel's Memoirs describing the finding at Passy of a panel, etc., connected with a story in which Fleury plays an important part.

It will thus be noted that the script in December, 1901, describes (as [presumably] past) an incident which actually occurred two and a half months later, in February, 1902,—an incident which at the time of writing was not likely to have been foreseen by any one. I ascertained from Mr. Marsh that the idea of reading Marmontel occurred to him not long before his visit to Paris. It is probable that had he not seen me almost immediately upon his return, when his mind was full of the book, I should never have heard of his reading it, and therefore not have discovered the application of the scripts of December 11th and 17th.

The description is definite, and in the main accurate. There are, however, errors :—Though the weather was cold, it does not seem to have been actually freezing on either of the two nights in question ; the book was not in two volumes only, as seems implied, though only two volumes had been read when the incident was related to me ; the name Marmontel was on the back of the book, though not on the face of the cover ; the binding, though not modern, can hardly be described as old fashioned. But the reference to Passy and Fleury— names which, so far as I can discover are not together in any passage of Marmontel's Memoirs except that read by Mr. Marsh on February 21st—is a precise and, I think, remarkable coincidence.

Two other points may be noted :—

(1) That the script on December 17th did not accept the suggestion that the name Marmontel had anything to do with Mrs. Sidgwick ;

(2) The omission to give any name to the reader of Marmontel.

This latter kind of reticence is characteristic of the script ; and, although it may be superficially regarded from a sarcastic point of view, it is really essential to the verification of the prevision, because if Mr. Marsh's name had been given, Mrs. Verrall would naturally have written to him a premature inquiry, which would have spoilt the whole thing.

But inasmuch as she had no inkling of Mr. Marsh in connexion with it, that gentleman was left unconsciously to carry out the anticipation, entirely ignorant of it and uninfluenced by it.

The anticipation received in December was fulfilled in February and was reported on in March.

The fact that the anticipation was received in December is proved by the preservation of Mrs. Sidgwick's letter of December 17th saying that she could make nothing of it, but that if the name turned up in some manuscripts she was then reading she would let Mrs. Verrall know.

Discussion of Possibility

In his book Mr. Myers contemplated the occurrence of prevision, and dealt with it in many an eloquent passage. The following is too eloquent for the incident just quoted, but it serves to illustrate his view of the possibility of such things :—

Few men have pondered long on these problems of Past and Future without wondering whether Past and Future be in very truth more than a name—whether we may not be apprehending as a stream of sequence that which is an ocean of co-existence, and slicing our subjective years and centuries from timeless and absolute things. The precognitions dealt with here, indeed, hardly overpass the life of the individual percipient. Let us keep to that small span, and let us imagine that a whole earth-life is in reality an absolutely instantaneous

although an infinitely complex phenomenon. Let us
suppose that my transcendental self discerns with equal
directness and immediacy every element of this phenomenon; but that my empirical self receives each
element mediately, and through media involving different
rates of retardation; just as I receive the lightning more
quickly than the thunder. May not then seventy years
intervene between my perceptions of birth and death
as easily as seven seconds between my perceptions of
the flash and the peal? And may not some intercommunication of consciousness enable the wider self
to call to the narrower, the more central to the more
external, "At such an hour this shock will reach you!
Listen for the nearing roar!"

But let us consider whether there is any way of
regarding the fulfilment of a meaningless anticipation
—such as this of the Marmontel case, just quoted—
without trenching on so difficult a question as the
reality of time?

I can only suggest something of the nature of
hypnotic suggestion, automatically effected. An outside
or, let us say, a subliminal intelligence gets the record
made by Mrs. Verrall that an unspecified man will
read Marmontel on a frosty night lying on a sofa by
candle light, etc., and then sets to work to try and
secure that within the next two or three months some
man shall do it—some one who is sufficiently a friend of
Mrs. Verrall to make it reasonably likely that in subsequent conversation she may sooner or later hear of the
circumstance.

I make the suggestion for what it is worth, as the
only way that occurs to me of avoiding still more
difficult notions;—provided of course we do not dismiss
the whole thing as invention—which is preposterous,—
or as chance, which in my judgment is put out of court

by the amount of detail, and by other incidents of the same *general* nature as this one which have also occurred in Mrs. Verrall's script.

It may be asked what possible object there can be in thus predicting a perfectly unimportant and common-place incident.

The object, to those associated with the work of the Society for Psychical Research, is manifest enough.

During the lifetime of Professor Sidgwick and Mr. Myers we often discussed what sort of evidence could be regarded as conclusive as to the existence of super-normal, even if not posthumous, intelligence. And it was agreed that prediction of future events of an insignificant kind, such as could not be inferred or deduced by however wide a knowledge of con-temporary events,—incidents which were outside the range of any amount of historical or mathematical or political skill,—would be conclusive, if obtained in quantity sufficient to eliminate chance. It did not at all follow that such anticipations were *possible*,—so far as we could tell they might be beyond not only normal but supernormal powers,—but if possible it was realised that they would be singularly satisfactory.

Accordingly it is eminently characteristic of an intelligence purporting to be associated in any way with the late Professor Sidgwick or the late Mr. Myers that attempts of that kind should be made. Several attempts have now been made with more or less success, and I have selected one of them. Others will be found in Mrs. Verrall's paper (*Proceedings*, vol. xx.) in the chapter called "Future Events."

SECTION IV

AUTOMATISM AND LUCIDITY

CHAPTER XI

AUTOMATIC WRITING AND TRANCE SPEECH

WE now enter upon the more detailed consideration of a group of facts, in which of late years
the Society has been remarkably prolific—and
the general truth of which is accepted without hesitation
by all the prominent members; who, though they differ
in their interpretation, yet receive the evidence with
practical unanimity as to its interest and importance—
receive it, that is to say, with all the unanimity that we
desire or expect.

At the end of last chapter we were discussing the
possibility of the rather vague and ill-defined hypothesis
that vistas of unlimited information lie open to people
in a clairvoyant state, as if during unconsciousness a
psychical region were entered wherein the ordinary
barriers between soul and soul, or mind and mind, are
broken down. Even this surmise must not be rejected
without examination, if we are driven to it, but it is not
a known *vera causa*. A hypothesis of this kind is
referred to at the end of Chapter VIII.

Naturally it is only when all normal means of
obtaining information have been scrupulously avoided
that any problem arises; and the first hypothesis that

must be made, whenever normal explanations thoroughly break down, is that telepathy of some kind is occurring from some living person and is influencing the sensitive mind or brain of the unconscious or partially unconscious operator, after the fashion of an objectified and sympathetic dream.

This hypothesis is extremely elastic, and can be stretched to cover an immense area; indeed, to get beyond it, and definitely find a region which it will not cover, is exceedingly difficult. For twenty years at least members of the society have been intimately acquainted with excellent and astonishing examples of trance speaking and automatic writing, and yet they have hesitated to make full use of all this material, and have refrained from proceeding in the direction towards which it undoubtedly points, so long as there was a chance—even a remote chance—that an established variety of telepathy or some extension of it might constitute a sufficient explanation. Some of us hold that telepathy from living people is still sufficient—or at least as sufficient as it has ever been—and that no further step beyond it need be taken. Others are beginning to be impressed with the idea—not without qualms and surviving hesitation—that the time has come, or is coming, when it may be legitimate and necessary to take a further step, and to admit, at any rate as a tentative hypothesis, the view which undoubtedly the phenomena themselves suggest — the view they have all the time been, as it were, forcing upon us. This is the hypothesis of actual telepathic or telergic influence from some outside intelligence— the surviving intelligence, apparently, of some of those who have recently lived on this planet, and who are now represented as occasionally, under great difficulties and discouragements, endeavouring to make known the fact that they can communicate with us, by aid of such intervening mechanism as is placed at their disposal— namely, the brain nerve and muscle of an automatist or medium. The assertion made is that, during the temporary suspension of the normal control, discarnate intelligences can with difficulty make use of these organs for the purpose of translating their own thought into mechanical movement, and so pro- ducing some kind of speech or writing in the physical world. Such utilisation of physiological apparatus, by an intelligence to which it does not normally belong, is what is called *motor automatism*, or "telergy," or popularly — when of an extreme kind — "possession."

It does not by any means follow that the agent or intelligence, active in this unusual experience, is necessarily that of a departed person, but that is undoubtedly the form which the phenomenon often takes; so if we resign ourselves to be guided by it at all, we may as well try how far the claim openly and persistently made will carry us, before definitely discarding it. And if we are going to try it at all, I urge that we had better try it frankly and thoroughly : it had better be accepted provisionally as a working hypothesis and pressed as far as it will go. That is the way to test any provisional hypothesis. Hesitate as long as you like before giving a theory even provisional and tentative acceptance ; but, once having determined on testing a key or theoretical solution, then utilise it to the utmost. Try it in all the locks ; and if it continually fails to open them, reject it ; but do not hesitate each time over the insertion of the key. Hesitate before accepting a working hypothesis, not after. If false, its

falseness will become apparent by its failure and inability to fit the facts.

Mr. Myers himself pointed out in *Human Personality*,
vol. i. p. 250, that if we allow ourselves to contemplate such a hypothesis it will at least fit in with
many other facts; the innovation that we are called
upon to make is to suppose that segments of the personality can operate in apparent separation from the
organism. "Such a supposition, of course, could not
have been started without proof of telepathy, and could
with difficulty be sustained without proof of survival
of death. But, given telepathy, we have *some* psychical
agency, connected with man, operating apart from his
organism. Given survival, we have an element of his
personality—to say the least of it—operating when
his organism is destroyed. There is therefore no very
great additional burden in supposing that an element
of his personality may operate apart from his organism,
while that organism still exists.

"*Ce n'est que le premier pas qui coûte.* If we have
once got a man's *thought* operating apart from his body
—if my fixation of attention on the two of diamonds
does somehow so modify another man's brain a few
yards off that he seems to see the two of diamonds
floating before him—there is no obvious halting place
on *his* side till we come to "possession" by a departed
spirit, and there is no obvious halting place on *my* side
till we come to "travelling clairvoyance," with a
corresponding visibility of my own phantasm to other
persons in the scenes which I spiritually visit."

MIND AND BODY

So let us consider in the first place what occurs
during the ordinary process of speaking or writing—
speaking or writing of the most normal or commonplace
kind. An idea is conceived in the mind, but in order

to achieve some effect in the material world it must move matter. The movement or rearrangement of matter is all that we ourselves are able to accomplish in the physical universe : the whole of our direct terrestrial activities resolve themselves into this, the production of changes of motion.

But a thought belongs to a different order of existence,—whatever it is, it is not material ; it is neither matter nor force ; it has no direct power over matter ; directly and unaided it can move nothing. How then can it get itself translated in terms of motion ? How can it, from the psychical category, produce a physical effect ?

Physiology informs us, not indeed of the whole manner of the achievement, but of part at least of the method.

The thing that can move matter is called muscle. In muscle is located the necessary energy, which only requires to be stimulated into activity in order to be transformed into visible motion and transferred in any required direction.

In a living body means are provided for stimulating its muscles, in the shape of an intricate arrangement of nerve fibres, which, when themselves excited in one of many ways, can cause the muscle to contract. This part of the process is not indeed fully understood, but it is familiarly known. The excitation of the nerves *may* be a mere random tweaking, or irritation, by a mechanical or electric goad ; but in a living organism it can also be produced in a more meaningful and economical fashion, by the discharge of energy from a central cell, such as exists in the cortex or grey matter of the brain. This process may also be considered as comparatively though not completely understood : the central ganglion is clearly the direct means of getting the nerve excited, the muscle contracted, and the direct motion produced. But what is it that stimulates the brain? What is it that desires the particular motion and liberates energy from the appropriate brain cell? In some cases it is mere reflex action: it is some stimulus which has arrived from the peripheral nerve-endings, so as to evoke response in a central ganglion— say, in the spine or the cerebellum; whence the stimulus has proceeded to a neighbouring cell and so to the efferent nerve fibres. In that case no consciousness is involved; the psychical element is absent; there is no intelligence or will in the process, nor any necessary sensation. The wriggling of a worm, and many contortions of the lower animals, may be—shall we say may be hoped to be?—of this order.

But I am not taking the case of reflex and unconscious action; I am definitely postulating a thought or idea conceived in the mind—operating, so to speak, on the will—and determining that there shall be a response in the material world. By what means the stimulus gets out of the psychical region into the physical, and liberates energy from the brain centre, I have not the remotest idea; nor, I venture to say, has any one.

The operation is at present mysterious. But conspicuously it occurs; it is evidently a rational and I should say an ultimately intelligible process,—a process, that is to say, on which discovery is possible, though at present there has been no discovery concerning it. Somehow or other the connexion is established; and by long habit it seems to be established in normal cases without difficulty—nay, rather with singular ease, as when a pianist executes in miraculous fashion a complicated sonata.

Things may go wrong, energy may be liberated in the wrong direction, the wrong muscles may be stimulated, so that stammering and contortions result. Or the mental connexion may be in a state of suspense, the mind may be unable to get at the right centre, so to speak, and may refrain from acting on any for a time; in which case we have hesitation, aphasia, feebleness of many kinds, up to paralysis. Or these effects may be due to faults and dislocation in the physiological mechanism,—faults which can perhaps be discovered and set right. If the brain centres are fatigued, also, the response is weak and uncertain. But when everything physiological is in good health, and when the conscious self is in good condition, with a definite thought that it wants to convey, then it appears to be able to play upon the brain, as a musician plays upon a keyboard, and to get its psychical content translated into terms of mechanical motion; so that other intelligences, sufficiently sympathetic and suitably provided with receptive mechanism, can be made more or less aware of the idea intended to be conveyed. Which means that, by aid of their nerve fibres and brain centres, mechanical movements can be translated back into thought once more.

That is the usual process, from mind to mind through physiological apparatus and physical mechanism. The physical mechanism is a neutral intermediary of non-living matter, belonging to nobody; or rather belonging equally to everybody. We can all throw the air into vibration; and at some public meetings everybody does so, at one and the same time, with some resulting confusion. We can all write with ink; and if need be we can dip our pens into our neighbour's inkstand and use his desk, though with some loss of convenience ;—we find it difficult to lay our hands upon his notepaper, and it is not efficacious if, on finding his cheque-book, we proceed to fill up and sign his cheques. The *identity* of the scribe then becomes an important consideration. Pretended identity in such cases may perturb the social conscience, and be stigmatised not merely as unrecognised and wrongful possession, but as fraud.

Thus of all existing forms of matter there are certainly some which can be used intelligently though temporarily by people to whom they do not belong. But whatever may be the undiscriminating communism of the main part of the physical universe, the physiological part is undoubtedly appropriated by individuals ; body No. 1 belongs definitely to operator No. 1, and body No. 2 to operator No. 2. And the common idea —I might say the common-sense idea—is that operator No. 1 is entirely limited to control over his own physiological apparatus, and has no means of getting at the apparatus of another person, in any direct manner, or otherwise than through neutral physical means. That is the natural *prima facie* notion, based upon ordinary experience ; but it need not be exactly true or complete,—facts may turn up which suggest something different or supplementary.

As a matter of fact, telepathy has suggested—without any necessary reference to the physiological part of the business—that mind can act directly on mind, and can thereby indirectly operate on the physical world through the organism of another person. But cases also occur where the *mind* of the second person appears to be left out of the process altogether ; he may be thinking his own thoughts or doing nothing particular,—in a state of unconsciousness perhaps, or at any rate of inattention,—and yet his physiological mechanism may be set in action, and his physical neighbourhood affected in such a way as to suggest a stimulus proceeding not from himself at all, but from the mind of another person ; who in this case must be conceived as operating not upon the second mind, but directly upon its brain. Or if not upon the brain, then perhaps upon some other portion of the nervous system,—say, upon spinal or other ganglia not essentially or necessarily associated with consciousness, and not arousing any consciousness, but stimulating the parts usually controlled by the sub-consciousness,—the parts which regulate the beating of the heart, the respiration of the lungs, the digestion or secretions of the body.

Assuming that such a thing is possible, assuming that a mind can operate, not only as usual on its own body, not only telepathically as supposed on another mind, but directly and telergically upon another body, then that is exactly what is meant by a case of incipient or partial possession.

So far, it may be said, we have no *a priori* reason to doubt its occurrence, and no *a priori* reason to expect it. We know nothing about the connexion between mind and body, except that the brain is the specially appropriate organ or instrument for the purpose ; and accordingly we are not entitled to any *a priori* views. We know that each organism is usually appropriated by, and belongs to, the special psychical character or unit which commonly employs it ; just as a violin belongs to a special operator, who might resent any other person, especially a novice, attempting to play upon it. The desk of an author is his private property, from which a certain class of literature usually emanates ; and he might not like to see it used for works of fiction, or scandalous gossip, or the advocacy of vaccination, or vegetarianism, or Christian Science, or tariff reform. But that proves nothing as to the impossibility of so utilising it. The power may exist, but may be in abeyance, or be recognised as inappropriate and inconvenient, or even as dangerous and illegal.

But if the power exist, it is a fact worth knowing. If it is possible for the normal operator to go out for a walk and leave his writing mechanism open to the casual tramp or the enterprising visitor, it is a definite fact that we may as well know.

Now as to the power of dislocation or suspension of the usual connexion between mind and body, it is supposed more or less to occur during sleep; it is certainly supposed to occur during trance; and, in case of what is called travelling clairvoyance, it would appear to be in some sort a demonstrable fact.

Anyhow, it is orthodox—not scientifically orthodox, but religiously orthodox—to maintain that the connexion between ourselves and our organism is only temporary, and that at what we call "death" we shall give up this material mode of manifestation for ever: so that the body resolves itself into its original elements. And it is usually supposed that, after having lost control of our appropriate and normally possessed bodily organs, even though we still persist as psychical entities, we have in our new state no means of operating upon the physical world. No more can we move pieces of matter; no more can we stimulate ideas in the minds of our friends when we are "dead." No, not unless one of three things happens.

First, the telepathic power may continue; and we may operate directly on their conscious or unconscious minds, in such a way as to cause *them* to produce some physical effect or record, by normal means, through their own accustomed mechanism.

Second, a materialising power may continue, analogous to that which enabled us, when here on the planet, to assimilate all sorts of material, to digest it and arrange it into the organism that served us as a body. It is extraordinarily difficult to conceive of such a power, and impossible to suppose that it can be a direct power of a psychical agency unaided by the re-productive activity of any other unit already incarnate; because such a power would imply a control of mind over matter which by hypothesis we conceive does not in fact exist, save through the mechanism of a brain. Such action we might well consider to be miracle.

Still something of the kind has been asserted to occur; though always, I believe, in the presence of some peculiarly disposed organism or medium.

Thirdly, a telergic power, analogous to that which we have already supposed occasionally active, may exist; enabling the psychical unit to detect and make use of some fully developed physiological mechanism, not belonging to it—a fully developed brain, shall we say, with nerves and muscles complete;—so that, during temporary vacation by the usual possessor, these may be utilised for a time, and may achieve, in an unpractised and more or less blundering fashion, some desired influence upon the physical world. In such a case the operator may be understood as contriving to utter in speech or writing something like the message which he intends to convey to his otherwise occupied and in-accessible but still beloved friends.

Affection need not be the only motive, however, which causes a given operator to take all the trouble, and go through the process of using other people's writing materials,—at the risk of rousing superstition and fright or being ejected by medical treatment. Occasionally it may be a scientific interest surviving from the time in this life when he was a keen and active member of the S.P.R. ; so that he desires above all things to convey to his friends, engaged on the same quest, some assurance, not only of his continued individual existence,—in which, on religious grounds, they may imagine that they already believe,—but of his retention of a power to communicate indirectly and occasionally with them, and to produce movements even in the material world,—by kind permission of an organism, or part of an organism, the temporary use or possession of which has been allowed him for that purpose.

Identity

The question of identity is of course a fundamental one. The control must prove his identity mainly by reproducing facts which belong to *his* memory and not to that of the automatist. And notice that proof of identity will usually depend on the memory of trifles. The objection, frequently raised, that communications too often relate to trivial subjects, shows a lack of intelligence, or at least of due thought, on the part of the critic. The object is to get, not something dignified, but something evidential : and what evidence of persistent memory can be better than the recollection of trifling incidents which for some personal reason happen to have made a permanent impression ? Do we not ourselves remember domestic trifles more vividly than things which to the outside world seem important ? Wars and coronations are affairs read of in newspapers — they are usually far too public to be of use as evidence of persistent identity; but a broken toy, or a family joke, or a schoolboy adventure, has a more personal flavour, and is of a kind more likely to be remembered in old age, or after a rending shock.

In fiction this is illustrated continually. Take the case of identification of the dumb and broken savage, apparently an Afghan prowler, in *The Man Who Was.* What was it that opened the eyes of the regiment, to which he had crawled back from Siberia, to the fact that twenty years ago he was one of themselves? Knowledge of a trick-catch in a regimental flower-vase, the former position of a trophy on the wall, and the smashing of a wineglass after a loyal toast. That is true to life: it is probably true to death also.

That is the kind of evidence which we ought to expect, and that is the kind of evidence which not infrequently we get. We have not been able to hold it sufficient, however. The regiment in Kipling's tale never thought of unconscious telepathy from themselves, as spoiling the testimony to be drawn from the uncouth savage's apparent reminiscence: such an explanation would have been rightly felt to have been too forced and improbable, and exaggeratedly sceptical. But when it comes to proof of surviving existence and of memory beyond the tomb, we are bound to proceed even to this length, and to discount the witness of anything that is in our own minds; or, as some think, in the mind of any living person.

Thus is the difficulty of incontrovertible proof of identity enormously increased. Even when the evidence enables a hidden thing to be discovered of which no one living possessed the secret—as in Swedenborg's discovery of the dead burgomaster's private papers above quoted, p. 119—deferred telepathy is sometimes adduced as preferable to what must then seem to most, as it did to Swedenborg, if not to Kant, the only rational explanation.

CHAPTER XII

PERSONAL IDENTITY

IN illustration of the remarks made at end of last chapter, the following is a favourable instance of the mode in which evidence is given to prove identity in cases of automatic writing : it was described by Mr. Stainton Moses to Edmund Gurney and F. W. H. Myers, while it was still fresh, on his first meeting with them, May 9th, 1874. It is to be understood that he was an automatic writer, and one of those who could, as it were, "converse" with the script as it emanated from his own unconscious hand. He was accustomed alternately to write a conscious question and then to receive an unconscious or subliminal answer—his hand being apparently guided by an intelligence not his own. The record runs thus :—

On the evening of April 8th, 1874, while at Bedford with his father and mother, Mr. Stainton Moses, who had been receiving messages about ancient religions during the day, began to ask a question, " I should like——," when a meaningless drawing was made in place of intended words.

Q. What is all that ? And why was I stopped ?

A. " A spirit wished to communicate, and we are commanded to permit her. She is not able to write with ease, but will communicate through us. Her name is Fanny Westoby. Do you know the name ? "

Q. I do not remember.

A. "Your mother knows her well. She is a cousin of hers. She passed from your earth May 15th last."

Q. Was she married.

A. "Yes, her maiden name was Kirkham."

Q. Fanny Kirkham. Yes, I have a dim remembrance. She used to live at Markby.

A. "She says that she was born in Alford, in the house now occupied by Sam Stevenson. She then lived at Markby, and, having married, at Belchford. She passed away at Horncastle, at 63 years of age. You do not remember her, when, in the year 1845, you went to see her at Markby. Her mother, Elizabeth Kirkham, was then just released from a lingering illness, and your mother had gone to condole with her cousin. You were taken round the farm, and rode on a goat (she is anxious on this point), and she threw you in sport into a heap of wheat which was being threshed. The result was that you were severely bitten by the harvest bug. She is very anxious that you should recall this to your mother."

Q. I will, but is it wise?

A. "You will not be able to induce her to search into this matter, but you may satisfy yourself that what is said is true."

Q. Has she any message?

A. "She says, 'I lost much of my opportunity for progress through the gratification of bodily appetite, which cast me back. My course of progress is yet to come. I find my present life not very different from yours. I am nearly the same. I wish I could influence Mary, but I can't get near her."

Q. Can she assure me that she is F. W.?

A. "She can give you no further evidence. Stay, ask your father about Donnington and the trap-door."

Q. I have not the least idea what she means. All the better. I will ask. Any more? Is she happy?

A. "She is as happy as may be in her present state."

Q. How did she find me out?

A. "She came by chance, hovering near her friend [*i.e.* Mrs. Moses], and discovered that she could communicate. She will return now."

Q. Can I help her?

12

A. " Yes, pray.   She and all of us are helped when you devote your
     talents willingly to aid us."

Q. What do you mean?

A. " In advocating and advancing our mission with care and judg-
     ment.   Then we are permeated with joy.   May the Supreme
     bless you.   + Rector "

On this Mr. Stainton Moses comments thus :—I
have inquired of my mother and find the particulars
given are exactly true.   She wonders how I remember
things that occurred when I was only 5 years old!   I
have not ventured to say how I got the information,
believing that it would be unwise and useless.   My
father I can get nothing out of about the trap-door.   He
either does not remember, or will not say.

April 9th, 1874.   My father has remembered this
incident.   A trap-door led on to the roof in the house he
occupied at Donnington.   The house was double roofed,
and a good view could be had from it.   F. K. on a visit
wanted to go there, and got fixed halfway, amid great
laughter.

[We have verified Mrs. Westoby's death in the
Register of Deaths.—F. W. H. M.]

It is indeed seldom that particulars of date, place,
and circumstance are given so glibly and fully as this.
Communicators themselves usually appear confused about
these more precise details ; but an ostensible reporter,
having obtained the information from them at leisure,
can sometimes quote it through an automatist with fair
accuracy, as in the case above.

————————

Another striking case is that of the lady known here
as " Blanche Abercromby " ; though in this case the con-
cealment of real name removes some of the interest that
would otherwise be felt in it.   When the communication
arrived through Mr. Stainton Moses's hand he was not
aware of her death—nor did he know her at all well ; in

fact he had only met her and her husband once at some
séance, and had been annoyed at the strongly expressed
disbelief of her husband in the possibility of such things.

The communicating purports to be a hasty *amende*,
at the earliest, posthumous, opportunity. Mr. Myers
examined this case carefully, being much interested in
some features of it. The pages of the notebook in
which the writing occurred had been gummed down and
marked " private," nor had they apparently been mentioned to any one at the time. But years later, after the
death of Mr. Stainton Moses, this and other books came
into Mr. Myers's hands, and with the consent of the
executors he opened this portion.

He was surprised to find a written communication
entirely characteristic of a lady known to him, here
called Blanche Abercromby, who had died on a Sunday
afternoon about twenty-five years ago at a country
house about two hundred miles from London. He
found that it was on the very same evening near midnight that the supernormal intimation of the death had
reached Mr. Stainton Moses at his secluded lodgings
in the north of London : and that afterwards the lady
had ostensibly written a few lines herself. The evidence
of the handwriting, which was in one point peculiar, is
specifically testified to, not only by Mr. Myers, but by
a member of the family, and by an expert (see *Human
Personality*, vol. ii. p. 231, or *Proc.* S.P.R. xi. 96 *et seq.*).
It is unlikely that Mr. Moses had ever seen her writing.

The chances necessary to secure a verification of
this case were more complex that can here be fully
explained. This lady, who was quite alien to these
researches, had been dead about twenty years when
her posthumous letter was discovered in Mr. Moses's
private notebook by one of the very few surviving

persons who had both known her well enough to recognise the characteristic quality of the message, and were
also sufficiently interested in spirit identity to get the
handwritings compared and the case recorded.

The entries in the MS. book will now be quoted.
The communications began with some obscure drawings,
apparently representing the flight of a bird; then in
answer to a question as to the meaning it went on :—

A. "It is a spirit who has but just quitted the body. Blanche Abercromby in the flesh. I have brought her. No more. M."

Q. Do you mean ——?
   No reply. [Sunday night about midnight. The information is
   unknown to me.]
   (On Monday morning the script continues):—

Q. I wish for information about last night. Is that true? Was it
   Mentor?

A. "Yes, good friend, it was Mentor, who took pity on a spirit that
   was desirous to reverse former errors. She desires us to say
   so. She was ever an inquiring spirit, and was called suddenly
   from your earth. She will rest anon. One more proof has
   been now given of continuity of existence. Be thankful and
   meditate with prayer. Seek not more now, but cease. We do
   not wish you to ask any questions now.
                                     † I : S : D. × RECTOR "

A week later some matter of what must be called
non-evidential quality appears; but in this instance I
propose to quote it because this is an important case.

Q. Can you write for me now?

A. "Yes, the chief is here."

Q. How was it that spirit [Blanche Abercromby's] came to me?

A. "The mind was directed to the subject, and being active, it projected itself to you. Moreover, we were glad to be able to
   afford you another proof of our desire to do what is in our
   power to bring home to you evidence of the truth of what we
   say."

Q. Is it correct to say that the direction of thought causes the spirit
   to be present?

A. "In some cases it is so. Great activity of spirit, coupled with anxiety to discover truth and to seek into the hidden causes of things, continue to make it possible for a spirit to manifest. Moreover, direction of thought gives what you would call direction or locality to the thought. By that we mean that the instinctive tendency of the desire or thought causes a possibility of objective manifestation. Then by the help of those who, like ourselves, are skilled in managing the elements, manifestation becomes possible. This would not have been possible in this case, only that we took advantage of what would have passed unnoticed in order to work out another proof of the reality of our mission. It is necessary that there should be a combination of circumstances before such a manifestation can be possible. And that combination is rare. Hence the infrequency of such events, and the difficulty we have in arranging them : especially when anxiety enters into the matter, as in the case of a friend whose presence is earnestly desired. It might well be that so ready a proof as this might not occur again."

Q. Then a combination of favourable circumstances aided you. Will the spirit rest, or does it not require it?

A. "We do not know the destiny of that spirit. It will pass out of our control. Circumstances enabled us to use its presence : but that presence will not be maintained."

Q. If direction of thought causes motion, I should have thought it would be so with our friends and that they would therefore be more likely to come.

A. "It is not that alone. Nor is it so with all. All cannot come to earth. And not in all cases does volition or thought cause union of souls. Many other adjuncts are necessary before such can be. Material obstacles may prevent, and the guardians may oppose. We are not able to pursue the subject now, seeing that we write with difficulty. At another time we may resume. Cease for the present and do not seek further.

† I : S : D. Rector "

A few days later, Mr. Moses wrote :—

Q. The spirit B. A. began by drawing. Was it herself?

A. "With assistance. She could not write. One day if she is able to return again, she will be more able to express her thoughts. . . ."

(A few days later.)

A. A spirit who has before communicated will write for you herself. She will then leave you, having given the evidence that is required.

"I should much like to speak more with you, but it is not permitted. You have sacred truth. I know but little yet. I have much, much to learn.—Blanche Abercromby.

"It is like my writing as evidence to you."

The statement that the writing of this particular message is like that of the lady's, was long afterwards verified with some care and trouble by Mr. Myers, and is correct. The *amende*, and the sentence "I have much, much to learn," are characteristic.

Attempts have been made, and are still made from time to time, to explain all this sort of thing—some of it by the recrudescence of lapsed memory, some of it by telepathy, and some of it by clairvoyance. If such attempts are regarded as successful how can it be possible, by any means, to get over the difficulty and to establish the identity of any communicator? I reply

(*a*) by gradually accumulated internal evidence, based on pertinacious and careful record;

(*b*) by cross correspondences, or the reception of unintelligible parts of one consistent and coherent message, through different mediums;

(*c*) by information or criteria specially characteristic of the supposed communicating intelligence; and, if possible, in some sense new to the world.

Cross-correspondence—that is, the reception of part of a message through one medium and part through another—is good evidence of one intelligence dominating both automatists; especially if the parts separately are unintelligible, so that they cannot be rationally signalled either by normal or supernormal means. And if the message is characteristic of some one particular deceased person, and is received through people to whom he was not intimately known, then it is fair proof of the continued intellectual activity of that personality. If further we get from him a piece of literary criticism which is eminently in his vein and has not occurred to ordinary people—not to either of the mediums, and not even to the literary world, but which on consideration is appreciated as sound as well as characteristic criticism, showing a familiar and wide knowledge of the poetry of many ages, and unifying apparently disconnected passages in some definite way,—then I say the proof, already striking, would tend to become crucial.

These, then, are the kinds of proof at which the Society is aiming. These are the kinds of proof which are in process of being attained.

CHAPTER XIII

BEGINNING OF THE CASE OF MRS. PIPER

THE most famous of recent thorough automatists, or trance speaking and trance writing mediums, is undoubtedly Mrs. Piper of Boston, U.S.A. With her an enormous amount of work has been done ; and the *Proceedings* of the Society, both in the past and in future years, will bear witness to the richness and fertility of this case, as well as to the industry with which it has been pursued and its various stages studied. To give anything like a full account of even my own work in this direction—the merest fraction of the whole —would need much more space than it would be wise to expend on it in this book, so I shall select only such small portions as will give some idea of what happens, and refer students who wish to pursue the matter further to the *Proceedings* of the Society for Psychical Research.

As a prelude to the Report on the 1890 English series of sittings, which were the first that the Society published, Mr. Myers at that time wrote an Introduction from which I will make a few extracts, because they illustrate the kind of view which that experienced investigator at that time took of these in some respects novel phenomena.

Mr. F. W. H. Myers's Early Testimony

On certain external or preliminary points, all who have had adequate opportunity of judgment, are decisively agreed ; but on the more delicate and interesting question as to the origin of the trance-utterances we cannot unite in any absolute view. We agree only in maintaining that the utterances show that knowledge has been acquired by some intelligence in some supernormal fashion ;—and in urging on experimental psychologists the duty of watching for similar cases, and of analysing the results in some such way as we have endeavoured to do.

The study of trance-utterances, indeed, is at first sight distasteful ; since real and pretended trance-utterances have notoriously been the vehicle of much conscious and unconscious fraud. But we urge that, just as the physical and psychical phenomena of hysteria —long neglected as a mere jungle of trickeries—are now analysed with adequate security against deception, and with most fruitful results, so also these utterances are now capable of being rationally studied,—thanks to the advance in the comprehension of automatic phenomena which French and English effort during the last few years has achieved.

These utterances, although they often occur in hysterical subjects, seem to have no necessary connection with hysteria. Nor again have we any real ground for calling them morbid *per se*, although their excessive repetition may lead to morbid states. All that we can safely say is that they are a form of automatism ; that they constitute one of many classes of phenomena which occur in sane subjects without entering the normal waking consciousness or forming part of the habitual chain of memory.

In previous discussions automatism has been divided into active and passive types ; active automatism consisting of such phenomena as automatic writing and trance-utterance—passive, of hallucinations of sight, hearing, etc. "The automatism may be called *active* if it finds a motor channel, *passive* if it finds a sensory channel, but the impulse whence it originates may be much the same in the one case as in the other."

The unsubstantial character of trance-utterances in general is fully admitted. "Trance-addresses are eminently barren of fact; they generally show little more than a mere power of improvisation, which may either be fraudulently practised, or may be a characteristic faculty of the unconscious self."

When, therefore, we were informed by trusted witnesses,—by Professor William James, who is a physician as well as a psychologist, and by Mr. Hodgson, whose acumen in the detection of imposture has been proved in more fields than one,—that the utterances of Mrs. Piper's trance did in their view unquestionably contain facts of which Mrs. Piper in her waking state was wholly ignorant, some inquiry into the character of this trance seemed to fall in the direct line of our work.

However the specific trance-utterances may be interpreted, the case as a whole is a rare and remarkable one. It is an instance of automatism of that extreme kind where the upheaval of sub-conscious strata is not merely *local*, but affects, so to say, the whole psychical area;—where a secondary consciousness not only crops up here and there through the primary, but for a time displaces it;—where, in short, the whole personality appears to suffer intermittent change.

These trances cannot always be induced at pleasure. A state of quiet expectancy or "self-suggestion" will usually bring one on; but sometimes the attempt altogether fails. We never attempted to induce the trance by hypnotism. We understand, indeed, that Mrs. Piper has never been deeply hypnotised, although Professor Richet tried on her some experiments of suggestion in the waking state, and found her somewhat "suggestible." On the other hand, the trance has occasionally appeared when it was not desired.   The first time that it occurred (as Mrs. Piper informs us) it came as an unwelcome surprise.   An instance of this kind occurred at Cambridge.   Before going to bed she had, at my request, says Mr. Myers, and for the first time in her life, been looking into a crystal, with the desire to see therein some hallucinatory figure which might throw light on the nature of the mysterious secondary personality. She saw nothing; but next morning she looked exhausted, and said that she thought that she had been entranced during the night.   The next time that she went into a trance Phinuit [which is the name she used to be known by when in the trance] said he had come and called, and no one had answered him.   It appeared as though the concentration of thought upon the crystal had acted as a kind of self-suggestion, and had induced the secondary state, when not desired.

The trance when induced generally lasted about an hour.   On one occasion in my house, and I believe once at least in America, it only lasted for about a minute. Phinuit only had time to say that he could not remain, and then the habitual moaning began, and Mrs. Piper came to herself.

There was often a marked difference between the first few minutes of a trance and the remaining time. On such occasions almost all that was of value would be told in the first few minutes; and the remaining talk would consist of vague generalities or mere repetitions of what had already been given.   Phinuit, as will be seen, always professed himself to be a spirit communicating with spirits; and he used to say that he remembered their messages for a few minutes after "entering into the medium," and then became confused. He was not, however, apparently able to depart when his budget of facts was empty.   There seemed to be some irresponsible letting-off of energy which must continue until the original impulse was lost in incoherence.

Mrs. Piper's case has been more or less continuously observed by Professor James and others almost from the date of the first sudden inception of the trance, some twenty-five years ago. Dr. Hodgson was in the habit of bringing acquaintances of his own to Mrs. Piper, without giving their names ; and many of these have heard from the trance-utterance facts about their dead relations, etc., which they feel sure that Mrs. Piper could not have known. Dr. Hodgson also had Mr. and Mrs. Piper watched or "shadowed" by private detectives for some weeks, with the view of discovering whether Mr. Piper (at that time alive and employed in a large store in Boston, U.S.A.) went about inquiring into the affairs of possible "sitters," or whether Mrs. Piper received letters from friends or agents conveying information. This inquiry was pushed pretty closely, but absolutely nothing was discovered which could throw suspicion on Mrs. Piper,—who is now aware of the procedure, but has the good sense to recognise the legitimacy—I may say the scientific necessity—of this kind of probation.

It was thus shown that Mrs. Piper made no discoverable attempt to acquire knowledge even about persons whose coming she had reason to expect. Still less could she have been aware of the private concerns of persons brought anonymously to her house at Dr. Hodgson's choice.

We took great pains, continues Mr. Myers, to avoid giving information in talk ; and a more complete security is to be found in the fact that we were ourselves ignorant of many of the facts given as to our friends' relations, etc. In the case of Mrs. Verrall, for instance, no one in Cambridge except Mrs. Verrall herself could have supplied the bulk of the information given ; and some of the facts given Mrs. Verrall herself did not know. As regards my own affairs, says Mr. Myers, I have not thought it worth while to cite *in extenso* such statements as might possibly have been got up beforehand; since Mrs. Piper of course knew that I should be one of her sitters. Such facts as that I once had an aunt, "Cordelia Marshall, more commonly called Corrie," might have been learnt,—though I do not think that they were learnt,—from printed or other sources. But I do not think that any larger proportion of such accessible facts was given to me than to an average sitter, previously unknown; nor were there any of those subtler points which could so easily have been made by dint of scrutiny of my books or papers. On the other hand, in my case, as in the case of several other sitters, there were messages purporting to come from a friend who has been dead many years, and mentioning circumstances which I believe that it would have been quite impossible for Mrs. Piper to have discovered.

I am also acquainted with some of the facts given to other sitters, and suppressed as too intimate, or as involving secrets not the property of the sitter alone. I may say that so far as my own personal conviction goes, the utterance of one or two of these facts is even more conclusive of supernormal knowledge than the correct statement of dozens of names of relations, etc., which the sitter had no personal motive for concealing.

On the whole, I believe that all observers, both in America and in England, who have seen enough of Mrs. Piper in both states to be able to form a judgment, will agree in affirming (1) that many of the facts given could not have been learnt even by a skilled detective; (2) that to learn others of them, although possible, would have needed an expenditure of money as well as of time which it seems impossible to suppose that Mrs. Piper could have met; and (3) that her conduct has never given any ground whatever for supposing her capable of fraud or trickery. Few persons have been so long and so carefully observed; and she has left on all observers the impression of thorough uprightness, candour, and honesty.

Mrs. Piper and the Press

It may be within the knowledge of some readers that in the year 1901 absurdly misleading articles appeared in the *American Press*, and were copied in some of the English papers, to the effect that Mrs. Piper had "confessed" and exploded her whole fabric.

The articles belong to the discreditable side of transatlantic newspaper enterprise, and it is discouraging that they should not have been more readily assessed at their true worth. I find that the misconception thus started is occasionally still found surviving, so I quote the critical and judicial utterance of the Editor of the *Journal* of the Society for Psychical Research on the subject, which set the matter completely at rest so far as all members of the Society were concerned.

Since issuing the November *Journal*, a copy of the article on Mrs. Piper published in the *New York Herald* of October 20th [1901] has reached us. The first part of this is signed by Mrs. Piper herself, the second part consisting of comments and opinions on her case. The article begins by saying that Mrs. Piper intends to give up the work she has been doing for the S.P.R., in order to devote herself to other and more congenial pursuits; and it goes on to say that it was on account of her own desire to understand the phenomena that she first allowed her trances to be investigated and placed herself in the hands of scientific men with the understanding that she should submit to any tests they chose to apply; also that now, after fourteen years' work, the subject not being yet cleared up, she feels disinclined for further investigation. As to her own view of the phenomena, she says : — "The theory of telepathy strongly appeals to me as the most plausible and genuinely scientific solution of the problem. . . . I do not believe that spirits of the dead have spoken through me when I have been in the trance state. . . . It may be that they have, but I do not affirm it."

The Editor of *Light* states in his issue of November 30th, 1901, that he has received a letter from Mrs. Piper in which she "explains that, having heard that the *New York Herald* people had, in a preliminary announcement, advertised her name with the word 'Confession' above it, she at once forbade the publication of the article altogether. The result was that she received a telegram from the *Herald* counselling her to 'sleep calm!' and assuring her that the word 'Confession' had only been used in the way of 'advertising smartness' and would not appear in the *Herald* article. This telegram Mrs. Piper has sent for our inspection, and we have it still."

Dr. Hodgson has sent us cuttings from two Boston papers bearing on this report. The *Boston Advertiser* of October 25th, 1901, says that Mrs. Piper dictated the following statement to a representative of theirs :—

"I did not make any such statement as that published in the *New York Herald* to the effect that spirits of the departed do not control me. . . . My opinion is to-day as it was eighteen years ago. Spirits of the departed may have controlled me and they may not. I confess that I do not know. I have not changed. . . . I make no change in my relations."

Now, comparing all these statements together, it will be seen that, neither in the original report in the *Herald* nor anywhere else has any revelation been made which could in any way affect the evidential value of Mrs. Piper's trance phenomena. Her honesty is not in question, and the *Herald* speaks of her throughout in highly laudatory terms. It represents her as holding a certain view of the phenomena—a view which is really incompatible with the supposition that they are fraudulent.   Mrs. Piper's later utterances show that, although the *Herald's* report was garbled and post-dated, she still expresses a preference for the telepathic over the spiritistic hypothesis.   It is well known to all members of the S.P.R., and it is hardly necessary for us to repeat, that these two hypotheses have always been kept before the minds of those investigators who have sat with her ; and since little value would be attached to her opinion in favour of the spiritistic hypothesis, it cannot fairly be urged that her opinion on the other side should weigh with us.   Mrs. Piper, in fact, as we have already said, is not in a more favourable, but even in a less favourable, position for forming an opinion than those who sit with her, since she does not afterwards remember what passes while she is in trance.

On the other hand, the allegation of the *Herald* that Mrs. Piper had determined finally to discontinue her sittings is shown to be unfounded.   The sittings had been suspended for some months owing to her health ; but one was held, as Dr. Hodgson informs us, on October 21st (the day after the article in the *Herald* appeared), and it was then arranged to resume them after an interval of three months.

To sum up, it is clear that Mrs. Piper has neither said nor done anything to diminish the value of evidence obtained through her, that the report in the *New York Herald* was misleading, and that her relations with the Society and Dr. Hodgson continued on the same footing as before.

CHAPTER XIV

PROFESSOR WILLIAM JAMES'S EARLY TESTI-
MONY TO MRS. PIPER

ALTHOUGH Mrs. Piper was brought by the Society to England in the autumn of 1889, she was of course known to members of the Society in America before then, and, so far as we were concerned, may be said to have been " discovered" by Professor William James in 1885. His early experience of her sittings, and his testimony as to the way in which his initial scepticism was broken down, are very interesting; and I shall here make a few quotations from a short paper of his which was included in the *Proceedings* of the Society along with my first Report of the Piper Case.

Professor William James's Statement

" I made Mrs. Piper's acquaintance in the autumn of 1885. My wife's mother, Mrs. Gibbens, had been told of her by a friend, during the previous summer, and, never having seen a medium before, had paid her a visit out of curiosity. She returned with the statement that Mrs. P. had given her a long string of names of members of the family, mostly Christian names, together with facts about the persons mentioned and their

13

relations to each other, the knowledge of which on her part was incomprehensible without supernormal powers. My sister-in-law went the next day, with still better results, as she related them. Amongst other things, the medium had accurately described the circumstances of the writer of a letter which she held against her forehead, after Miss G. had given it to her. The letter was in Italian, and its writer was known to but two persons in this country.

"I may add that on a later occasion my wife and I took another letter from this same person to Mrs. P., who went on to speak of him in a way which identified him unmistakably again. On a third occasion, two years later, my sister-in-law and I being again with Mrs. P., she reverted in her trance to these letters, and then gave us the writer's name, which she said she had not been able to get on the former occasion.

"But to revert to the beginning. I remember playing the *esprit fort* on that occasion before my feminine relatives, and seeking to explain by simple considerations the marvellous character of the facts which they brought back. This did not, however, prevent me from going myself a few days later, in company with my wife, to get a direct personal impression. The names of none of us up to this meeting had been announced to Mrs. P.; and Mrs. J. and I were, of course, careful to make no reference to our relatives who had preceded. The medium, however, when entranced, repeated most of the names of 'spirits' whom she had announced on the two former occasions, and added others. The names came with difficulty, and were only gradually made perfect. My wife's father's name of Gibbens was announced first as Niblin, then as Giblin. A child Herman (whom we had lost the previous year) had his name spelt out as Herrin. I think that in no case were both Christian and surnames given on this visit. But the *facts predicated* of the persons named made it in many instances impossible not to recognise the particular individuals who were talked about. We took particular pains on this occasion to give the Phinuit control no help over his difficulties and to ask no leading questions. In the light of subsequent experience I believe this not to be the best policy. For it often happens, if you give this trance-personage a name or some small fact for the lack of which he is brought to a standstill, that he will then start off with a copious flow of additional talk, containing in itself an abundance of 'tests.'

"My impression after this first visit was, that Mrs. P. was either possessed of supernormal powers, or knew the members of my wife's family by sight and had by some lucky coincidence become acquainted with such a multitude of their domestic circumstances as to produce the startling impression which she did. My later knowledge of her sittings and personal acquaintance with her has led me absolutely to reject the latter explanation, and to believe that she has supernormal powers.

"I also made during this winter an attempt to see whether Mrs. Piper's medium-trance had any community of nature with ordinary hypnotic trance.

"My first two attempts to hypnotise her were unsuccessful. Between the second time and the third, I suggested to her 'control' in the medium-trance that he should make her a mesmeric subject for me. He agreed. (A suggestion of this sort made by the operator in one *hypnotic* trance would probably have some effect on the next.) She became partially hypnotised on the third trial; but the effect was so slight that I ascribe it rather to the effect of repetition than to the suggestion made. By the fifth trial she had become a pretty good hypnotic subject, as far as muscular phenomena and automatic imitations of speech and gesture go ; but I could not affect her consciousness, or otherwise get her beyond this point. Her condition in this semi-hypnosis is very different from her medium-trance. The latter is characterised by great muscular unrest, even her ears moving vigorously in a way impossible to her in her waking state. But in hypnosis her muscular relaxation and weakness are extreme. She often makes several efforts to speak ere her voice becomes audible ; and to get a strong contraction of the hand, for example, express manipulation and suggestion must be practised. The automatic imitations I spoke of are in the first instance very weak, and only become strong after repetition. Her pupils contract in the medium-trance. Suggestions to the 'control' that he should make her recollect after the medium-trance what she had been saying were accepted, but had no result. In the hypnotic-trance such a suggestion will often make the patient remember all that has happened.

" No sign of thought-transference—as tested by card and diagram guessing—has been found in her, either in the hypnotic condition just described, or immediately after it ; although her 'control' in the medium-trance has said that he would bring them about. So far as tried (only twice), no right guessing of cards in the medium-trance. No clear signs of thought-transference, as tested by the naming of cards, during the waking state. Trials of the 'willing game,' and attempts at automatic writing, gave similarly negative results. So far as the evidence goes, then, her medium-trance seems an isolated feature in her psychology. This would of itself be an important result if it could be established and generalised, but the record is obviously too imperfect for confident conclusions to be drawn from it in any direction.

" Here I dropped my inquiries into Mrs. Piper's mediumship for a period of about two years, having satisfied myself that there was a genuine mystery there, but being over-freighted with time-consuming duties, and feeling that any adequate circumnavigation of the phenomena would be too protracted a task for me to aspire just then to undertake. I saw her once, half-accidentally, however, during that interval, and in the spring of 1889 saw her four times again. In the fall of 1889 she paid us a visit of a week at our country house in New Hampshire, and I then learned to know her personally better than ever before, and had confirmed in me the belief that she is an absolutely simple and genuine person. No one, when challenged, can give ' evidence ' to others for such beliefs as this. Yet we all live by them from day to day, and practically I should be willing now to stake as much money on Mrs. Piper's honesty as on that of anyone I know, and am quite satisfied to leave my reputation for wisdom or folly, so far as human nature is concerned, to stand or fall by this declaration.

" And I repeat again what I said before, that, taking everything that I know of Mrs. P. into account, the result is to make me feel as absolutely certain as I am of any personal fact in the world that she knows things in her trances which she cannot possibly have heard in her waking state, and that the definitive philosophy of her trances is yet to be found. The limitations of her trance-information, its discontinuity and fitfulness, and its apparent inability to develop beyond a certain point, although they end by rousing one's moral and human impatience with the phenomenon, yet are, from a scientific point of view, amongst its most interesting peculiarities, since where there are limits there are conditions, and the discovery of these is always the beginning of explanation."

The most recent utterance of Professor William James on the subject is published in the *Proceedings* of the S.P.R. for June 1909 (Part LVIII.), and it contains an account of conversations carried on through Mrs. Piper since Dr. Hodgson's death with what purported to be Dr. Hodgson's surviving personality—together with Professor James's critical comments thereupon. I do not quote, since the publication can easily be obtained.

CHAPTER XV

THE AUTHOR'S FIRST REPORT ON MRS. PIPER

M^Y own first Report on this case appeared in 1890, soon after the close of Mrs. Piper's first visit to England, and it ran as follows :—

ACCOUNT OF SITTINGS WITH MRS. PIPER

Formal Report

At the request of Mr. Myers I undertook a share in the investigation of a case of apparent clairvoyance.

It is the case of a lady who appears to go off into a trance when she pleases to will it under favourable surroundings, and in that trance to talk volubly, with a manner and voice quite different from her ordinary manner and voice, on details concerning which she has had no information given her.

In this abnormal state her speech has reference mainly to people's relatives and friends, living or deceased, about whom she is able to hold a conversation, and with whom she appears more or less familiar.

By introducing anonymous strangers, and by catechising her myself in various ways, I have satisfied myself that much of the information she possesses in the trance state is not acquired by ordinary commonplace methods, but that she has some unusual means of acquiring information. The facts on which she discourses are usually within the knowledge of some person present, though they are often entirely out of his conscious thought at the time. Occasionally facts have been narrated which have only been verified afterwards, and which are in good faith asserted never to have been known ; meaning thereby that they have left no trace on the conscious memory of any person present or in the neighbourhood, and that it is highly improbable that they were ever known to such persons.

She is also in the trance state able to diagnose diseases, and to specify the owners or late owners of portable property, under circumstances which preclude the application of ordinary methods.

In the midst of this lucidity a number of mistaken and confused statements are frequently made, having little or no apparent meaning or application.

Concerning the particular means by which she acquires the different kinds of information, there is no sufficient evidence to make it safe to draw any conclusion. I can only say with certainty that it is by none of the ordinary methods known to Physical Science.

OLIVER J. LODGE

May, 1890

In order to gain experience, my wife had invited Mrs. Piper to our house in Liverpool between the dates December 18th and December 27th, 1889 ; and again between the dates January 30th and February 5th, 1890, when she sailed for New York.

During these days we had twenty-two sittings, and I devoted my whole time to the business, being desirous of making the investigation as complete and satisfactory as possible while the opportunity lasted.

Mrs. Piper pretends to no knowledge as to her own powers, and I believe her assertion that she is absolutely ignorant of what she has said in the trance state. She appears to be anxious to get the phenomenon elucidated, and hopes by sitting to scientific investigators to have light thrown on her abnormal condition, about which she expresses herself as not quite comfortable.   She perfectly appreciates the reasonableness of withholding information ; assents with a smile to a sudden stop in the middle of a sentence, and in general is quite uninquisitive.   All this innocency may, of course, be taken as perfection of acting, but it deprives her of the great advantage (assuming fraudulent intention for the moment) of controlling the circumstances after the manner of a conjurer ; and prevents her from being the master of her own time and movements.   The control of the experiments was thus entirely in my own hands, and this is an essential ingredient for satisfactory testimony.

The initial question to be satisfactorily answered, before anything can be held worth either investigating or recording, concerns the honesty of Mrs Piper herself.

That there is more than can be explained by any amount of either conscious or unconscious fraud—that the phenomenon is a genuine one, however it is to be explained—I now regard as absolutely certain ; and I make the following two statements with the utmost confidence :—

(i.) Mrs. Piper's attitude is not one of deception.

(ii.) No conceivable deception on the part of Mrs. Piper can explain the facts.

[I went on to enumerate eight possibilities of imposture against which we were on our guard: but matters have advanced far beyond that now, and it is useless to dwell upon this discarded part of the subject.]

Cheating being eliminated, and something which may briefly be described as a duplex or trance personality being conceded, the next hypothesis is that her trance personality makes use of information acquired by her

in her waking state, and retails what it finds in
her sub-consciousness without any ordinary effort of
memory.

It is an interesting question whether any facts
instilled into the waking Mrs. Piper can be recognised
in the subsequent trance speech.   My impression
at one time was that the trance information is
practically independent of what specific facts Mrs.
Piper may happen to know.   The evidence now
seems to me about evenly balanced on either side.
Whether the trance speech could give, say, scientific
facts, or a foreign language, or anything in its nature
entirely beyond her ken, I am unable to say.   [Further
information on these points is now accessible, but not
anything finally conclusive.   It appears that unknown
details and incidents can certainly be obtained, but
hardly information on some alien and recondite subject,—at least without great difficulty.]   So far as
my present experience has gone, I do not feel
sure how far Mrs. Piper's knowledge or ignorance of
specific facts has an appreciable influence on the communications of her trance personality.   But certainly the
great mass of facts retailed by this personality are wholly
outside of Mrs. Piper's knowledge ; in detail, though not
in kind.

The personality active and speaking in the trance is
apparently so distinct from the personality of Mrs. Piper
that it is permissible and convenient to call it by another
name.   It does not differ from her as Hyde did from
Jekyll, by being a personification of the vicious portion
of the same individual.   There is no special contrast,
any more than there is any special similarity.   It strikes
one as a different personality altogether ; and the name
by which it introduces itself when asked, viz., " Dr.

Phinuit," is as convenient as any other, and can be used wholly irrespective of hypothesis.

I would not, in using this name, be understood as thereby committing myself to any hypothesis regarding the nature of this apparently distinct and individual mind. At the same time the name is useful as expressing compactly what is naturally prominent to the feeling of any sitter, that he is not talking to Mrs. Piper at all. The manner, mode of thought, tone, trains of idea, are all different. You are speaking no longer to a lady, but to a man, an old man, a medical man. All this cannot but be vividly felt even by one who considered the impersonation a consummate piece of acting.

Whether such a man as Dr. Phinuit ever existed I do not know, nor from the evidential point of view do I greatly care. It will be interesting to have the fact ascertained if possible; but I cannot see that it will much affect the question of genuineness. For that he did not ever exist is a thing practically impossible to prove. While, if he did exist, it can be easily supposed that Mrs. Piper took care enough that her impersonation should have so much rational basis.

Proceeding now on the assumption that I may speak henceforth of Dr. Phinuit as of a genuine individual intelligence, whether it be a usually latent portion of Mrs. Piper's intelligence, or whether it be something distinct from her mind and the education to which it has been subjected, I go on to consider the hypotheses which still remain unexamined.

And first we have the hypothesis of fishery on the part of Dr. Phinuit, as distinguished from trickery on the part of Mrs. Piper. I mean a system of ingenious fishing: the utilisation of trivial indications, of every intimation—audible, tactile, muscular—and of little shades of manner too indefinable to name ; all these, excited in the sitter by skilful guesses and well-directed shots, and their nutriment extracted with superhuman cunning.

Now this hypothesis is not one to be lightly regarded, or ever wholly set aside. I regard it as, to a certain extent, a *vera causa*. At times Dr. Phinuit does fish ; occasionally he guesses ; and sometimes he ekes out the scantiness of his information from the resources of a lively imagination.

Whenever his supply of information is abundant there is no sign of the fishing process.

At other times it is as if he were in a difficult position,—only able to gain information from very indistinct or inaudible sources, and yet wishful to convey as much information as possible. The attitude is then as of one straining after every clue, and making use of the slightest indication, whether received in normal or abnormal ways : not indeed obviously distinguishing between information received from the sitter and information received from other sources.

I am familiar with muscle-reading and other simulated " thought-transference " methods, and prefer to avoid contact whenever it is possible to get rid of it without too much fuss. Although Mrs. Piper always held somebody's hand while preparing to go into the trance, she did not always continue to hold it when speaking as Phinuit. She did usually hold the hand of the person she was speaking to, but was often satisfied for a time with some other person's, sometimes talking right across a room to and about a stranger, but preferring them to come near. On several occasions she let go of everybody, for half-hours together, especially when fluent and kept well supplied with " relics."

I have now to assert with entire confidence that,

pressing the ingenious-guessing and unconscious-indication hypothesis to its utmost limit, it can only be held to account for a very few of Dr. Phinuit's statements.

It cannot in all cases be held to account for medical diagnosis, afterwards confirmed by the regular practitioner. It cannot account for minute and full details of names, circumstances, and events, given to a cautious and almost silent sitter, sometimes without contact. And, to take the strongest case at once, it cannot account for the narration of facts outside the conscious knowledge of the sitter or of any person present.

Rejecting the fishery hypothesis, then, as insufficient to account for many of the facts, we are driven to the only remaining *known* cause in order to account for them :—viz., thought-transference, or the action of mind on mind independently of the ordinary channels of communication.

I regard the fact of genuine "thought-transference" between persons in immediate proximity (not necessarily in contact) as having been established by direct and simple experiment ; and, except by reason of paucity of instance, I consider it as firmly grounded as any of the less familiar facts of nature such as one deals with in a laboratory. I speak of it therefore as a known cause, *i.e.* one to which there need be no hesitation in appealing in order to explain facts which without it would be inexplicable.

The Phinuit facts are most of them of this nature, and I do not hesitate to assert confidently that *thought-transference is the most commonplace explanation to which it is possible to appeal.*

I regard it as having been rigorously proved before, and as therefore requiring no fresh bolstering up ; but to the many who have not made experiments on the subject, and are therefore naturally sceptical concerning even thought-transference, the record of the Phinuit sittings will afford, I think, a secure basis for faith in this immaterial mode of communication,—this apparently direct action of mind on mind.

But, whereas the kind of thought-transference which had been to my own knowledge experimentally proved was a hazy and difficult recognition by one person of objects kept as vividly as possible in the consciousness of another person, the kind of thought-transference necessary to explain these sittings is of an altogether freer and higher order,—a kind which has not yet been experimentally proved at all. Facts are related which are not in the least present to the consciousnes of the sitter, and they are often detailed glibly and vividly without delay ; in very different style from the tedious and hesitating dimness of the percipients in the old thought-transference experiments.

But that is natural enough, when we consider that the percipient in those experiments had to preserve a mind as vacant as possible. For no process of inducing mental vacancy can be so perfect as that of going into a trance, whether hypnotic or other. Moreover, although it was considered desirable to maintain the object contemplated in the consciousness of the agent, a shrewd suspicion was even then entertained that the sub-conscious part of the agent's mind might be perhaps equally effective.

Hence one is at liberty to apply to these Phinuit records the hypothesis of thought-transference in its most developed state : vacuity on the part of the percipient, sub-conscious activity on the part of the sitter.

In this form one feels that much can be explained. If Dr. Phinuit tells a stranger how many children, or brothers, or sisters he has, and their names; the names of father and mother and grandmother, of cousins and of aunts; if he brings appropriate and characteristic messages from well-known relatives deceased; all this is explicable on the hypothesis of free and easy thought-transference from the sub-consciousness of the sitter to the sensitive medium of the trance personality.[1]

So strongly was I impressed with this view that after some half-dozen sittings I ceased to feel much interest in being told things, however minute, obscure, and inaccessible they might be, so long as they were, or had been, within the knowledge either of myself or of the sitter for the time being.

At the same time it ought to be constantly borne in mind that this kind of thought-transference, without consciously active agency, has never been experimentally proved. Certain facts not otherwise apparently explicable, such as those chronicled in *Phantasms of the Living*, have suggested it, but it is really only a possible hypothesis to which appeal has been made whenever any other explanation seems out of the question. But until it is actually established by experiment, in the same way that conscious mind action has been established, it cannot be regarded as either safe or satisfactory; and in pursuing it we may be turning our backs on some truer but as yet perhaps unsuggested clue. I feel as if this caution were necessary for myself as well as for other investigators.

[1] For instance, in the course of my interviews, all my six brothers (adult and scattered) and one sister living were correctly named (two with some help), and the existence of the one deceased was mentioned. My father and his father were likewise named, with several uncles and aunts. My wife's father and stepfather, both deceased, were named in full, both Christian and surname, with full identifying detail. I only quote these as examples; it is quite unnecessary as well as unwise to attach any evidential weight to statements of this sort made during a sojourn in one's house.

On reading the record it will be apparent that while
"Phinuit" frequently speaks in his own person, relating
things which he himself discovers by what I suppose we
must call ostensible clairvoyance, sometimes he represents
himself as in communication—not always quite easy and
distinct communication, especially at first, but in communication—with one's relatives and friends who have
departed this life.

The messages and communications from these persons
are usually given through Phinuit as a reporter. And
he reports sometimes in the third person, sometimes in
the first. Occasionally, but very seldom, Phinuit seems
to give up his place altogether to the other personality,
friend or relative, who then communicates with something of his old manner and individuality; becoming
often impressive and realistic.

This last I say is rare, but with one or two personages
it occurs, subject to reservations to be mentioned directly;
and when it does, Phinuit does not appear to know what
has been said. It is quite as if he in his turn evacuated the
body, just as Mrs. Piper had done, while a third personality
utilises it for a time. The voice and mode of address are
once more changed, and more or less recall the voice
and manner of the person represented as communicating.

The communications thus obtained, though they
show traces of the individuality of the person represented
as speaking, are frequently vulgarised; and the speeches
are more commonplace, and so to say "cheaper," than
what one would suppose likely from the person himself.
It can, of course, be suggested that the necessity of
working through the brain of a person not exceptionally
educated may easily be supposed capable of dulling the
edge of refinement, and of rendering messages on abstruse
subjects impossible.

CHAPTER XVI

EXTRACTS FROM PIPER SITTINGS

AND now might follow a detailed report of the sittings which at that date (1889–1890) I held with Mrs. Piper in my house at Liverpool, all of which were taken down very fully; some of them verbatim by a stenographer introduced on those occasions. For in those days communication was conducted entirely by the voice; writing being quite exceptional and limited to a few words occasionally. Whereas in more recent years communication is for the most part conducted by writing only, and the need for stenography has practically ceased.

My detailed report appears in the *Proceedings* of the Society, vol. vi., but it occupies a great deal of space, and would be merely tiresome if reproduced in any quantity. Accordingly I propose to make only a few extracts, quoting those incidents which demonstrate one or other of the following powers; or which illustrate by way of example the general character of the sittings at that time,—regarded rather from the dramatic than from the evidential point of view.

The powers just referred to are the following :—

(1) The perception of trivial events simultaneously occurring at a distance.

14

(2) The reading of letters by other than normal means.

(3) The recognition of objects and assignment of them to their respective owners.

(4) Perception of small and intimate family details in the case of complete strangers.

(5) The statement of facts unknown at the time to any person present ;

(6) With perhaps a supplement illustrating apparent ignorance of some facts within Mrs. Piper's normal knowledge, and likewise — what are frequent—instances of erroneous statement concerning facts which are well-known to, and in the mind of, the sitter.

Among sitters, I may mention Dr. Gerald Rendall, late of Trinity College, Cambridge, then Principal of University College, Liverpool. He was introduced as Mr. Roberts, and a sitting was immediately commenced. The names of his brothers were all given correctly at this or at the evening sitting of the same day, with many specific details which were correct.

He brought with him a locket, and received communications and reminiscences purporting to come from the deceased friend whom it commemorated, some of them at present incompletely verified by reason of absence of persons in America, some of them apparently incorrect, but those facts which he knew correctly stated in such a way as to satisfy him that chance guessing and all other commonplace surmises were absurdly out of the question.

Another sitter was Prof. E. C. K. Gonner, then Lecturer on Economics at University College, Liverpool, introduced as Mr. McCunn, another colleague with whom therefore he might on a fraudulent hypothesis be confused. He brought a book belonging to his mother, still living in London, and had many correct details concerning her family and surroundings related to him.

Many of his own family were also mentioned; but, whether because of the book or otherwise, his mother's influence seemed more powerful than his own; and, several times, relatives, though otherwise spoken of correctly, were mentioned in terms of their relationship to the elder generation. Phinuit, however, seemed conscious of these mistakes and several times corrected himself; as for instance: "Your brother William—no, I mean your uncle, her brother."

This Uncle William was a good instance. He had died before Prof. Gonner was born, but he had been his mother's eldest brother, and his sudden death had been a great shock to her—one in fact from which she was a long time recovering. Phinuit described him as having been killed with a hole in his head, like a shot hole, and yet not a shot, more like a blow :—the fact being that he met his death in a Yorkshire election riot, a stone striking him on the head.

Speaking of deaths, I may also mention the case of my wife's father, who died when she was a fortnight old in a dramatic and pathetic fashion. Phinuit described the circumstances of his death rather vividly. The cause of death of her stepfather also, which was perfectly definite, was also precisely grasped. The fall of her own father down the hold of his ship and his consequent leg-pain were clearly stated. My wife was present on these occasions, and of course had been told of all these family incidents, and remembered them.

As an illustration of the facility with which in those days Dr. Phinuit arrived at the relatives and their peculiarities of a complete stranger, I take the case of two sittings on the same day at which a medical man practising in Liverpool was introduced without notice by the false name of Dr. Jones. During the sitting the name, tastes, and defect of one little deaf and dumb daughter, "Daisy," of whom he was very fond, were vividly stated. My children are not acquainted with his.

I may say that Dr. C. was almost entirely silent. Occasionally he assented with a grunt, but I found afterwards that he was assenting to wrong quite as much as to right statements. I hardly ever knew what was right and what wrong as I took the notes. He was thus an excellent though trying sitter. Phinuit was in one of his most loquacious moods, or he would not have progressed so well. Towards the end one could see he began to get tired of his own monologue. The following is a very abbreviated record :—

Sitting No. 42. *Monday morning, December 23rd*

Present: Dr. C. (introduced as Dr. Jones) and O. J. L.

[The following is an abstract of the correct, or subsequently corrected or otherwise noteworthy, statements. The false ones are similarly collected and appear later, page 215.]

"You have a little lame girl, lame in the thigh, aged 13; either second or third. She's a little daisy. I do like her. Dark eyes, the gentlest of the lot; good deal of talent for music. She will be a brilliant woman; don't forget it. She has more sympathy, more mind, more—quite a little daisy. She's got a mark, a curious little mark, when you look closely, over eye, a scar through forehead over left eye. The boy's erratic; a little thing, but a little devil. Pretty good when you know him. He'll make an architect likely. Let him go to school. His mother's too nervous. It will do him good. [This was a subject in dispute.] You have a boy and two girls and a baby; four in the body. It's the little lame one I care for. There are two mothers connected with you, one named Mary. Your aunt passed out with cancer. You have indigestion, and take hot water for it. You have had a bad experience. You nearly slipped out once on the water. [Dangerous yacht accident last summer. Above statements are correct except the lameness. See next sitting.]

He came again the same evening and brought his wife. This time, unfortunately, they were admitted by a servant, who announced their names. Phinuit did not mention it, however. The full account of these sittings is long, and would require a great deal of annotation to make the details clear. For the sake of brevity, I propose merely to abstract them. There are a number of erroneous statements, some of them to be partially accounted for by the fact that Dr. and Mrs. C. are cousins (a fact which I did not know, and which Phinuit did not ascertain); so he mixed their relatives at the second sitting. The family seems to be a very large one. I quote later the misstatements, but first I pick out the correct ones or those which require comment.

Sitting No. 43. Monday evening, December 23rd

Present: Dr. and Mrs. C. and O. J. L. [Statement correct when not otherwise noted.]

"How's little Daisy? She will get over her cold. But there's something the matter with her head. There's somebody round you lame and somebody hard of hearing. That little girl has got music in her. This lady is fidgety. There are four of you, four going to stop with you, one gone out of the body. One got irons on his foot. Mrs. Allen, in her surroundings is the one with iron on leg. [Allen was maiden name of mother of lame one.] There's about 400 of your family. There's Kate; you call her Kitty. She's the one that's kind of a crank. Trustworthy, but cranky. She will fly off and get married, she will. Thinks she knows everything, she does. [This is the nurse-girl, Kitty, about whom they seem to have a joke that she is a walking compendium of information.] (An envelope with letters written inside, N—H—P—O—Q, was here handed in, and Phinuit wrote down B—J—R—O—I—S, not in the best of tempers.) A second cousin of your mother's drinks. The little dark-eyed one is Daisy. I like her. She can't hear very well. The lame one is a sister's child. [A cousin's child, the one *née* Allen, really.] The one that's deaf in her head is the one that's got the music in her. That's Daisy, and she's going to have the paints I told you of. [Fond of painting.] She's growing up to be a beautiful woman. She ought to have a paper ear. [An artificial drum had been contemplated.] You have an Aunt Eliza. There are three Maries, Mary the mother, Mary the mother, Mary the mother. [Grandmother, aunt, and granddaughter.] Three brothers and two sisters your lady has. Three in the body. There were eleven in your family, two passed out small. [Only know of nine.] Fred is going to pass out suddenly. He married a cousin. He writes. He has shining things. *Lorgnettes.* He is away. He's got a catchy trouble with heart and kidneys, and will pass out suddenly." [Not the least likely. I have inquired and find that the "Fred" supposed to be intended is still alive in 1909. O. J. L.]

NOTE.—The most striking part of this sitting is the prominence given to Dr. C.'s favourite little daughter, Daisy, a child very intelligent and of a very sweet disposition, but quite deaf; although her training enables her to go to school and receive ordinary lessons with other children. At the first sitting she is supposed erroneously to be lame, but at the second sitting this is corrected and explained, and all said about her is practically correct, including the cold she then had. Mrs. Piper had had no opportunity whatever of knowing or hearing of the C. children by ordinary social means. We barely know them ourselves. Phinuit grasped the child's name gradually, using it at first as a mere description. I did not know it myself. Dr. Phinuit is lavish with predictions, such as the one at the end, which frequently, I think usually, fail. I deeply regret to say that his predictions regarding Daisy are likewise false, for she caught the influenza, and the announcement of her death is in to-day's paper.—*June,* 1890.

A list of particulars like this makes very dull reading, but evidentially it is as good as can be. No possible normal means can be suggested by which these things were obtained, nor was there any fishing or guidance by the sitter.

The only normal explanation is that they were hit upon by chance, but that is perfectly absurd, as any one will realise who will go through these incidents and try to apply them to himself or to any friend known to him. As a matter of fact they do not apply, and cannot apply

in their entirety, to anybody but the person for whom
they were intended.

Of course this is by no means a solitary instance of
the detection of appropriate family details, and perhaps
it is not so striking as some others, but it is a sound
instance that came directly within my own observation.

The doctor himself was characteristically sceptical
about the whole thing, but permits me to append the
following note of his on the case, written some time
later :—

"The trance state seemed natural; but had more
voluntary movement than I had ever seen in an epileptic
attack. The entire change in Mrs. Piper's manner and
behaviour is unlike an intentional effort, and it is possible
she herself believes that the conditions mean something
outside of herself. With regard to the result, the misses
seem to balance the hits, and the 'reading' is not so
impressive as the 'sitting.' After reading over your
notes I think they consist of a certain amount of thought-
reading and a large amount of skilful guessing."

I find myself unable to agree with the hasty statement that "the misses balance the hits," since even
numerically they are distinctly fewer; and if the result
were due to chance they ought to be out of all comparison fewer.

The following is a summary of the *false* assertions
made during the two sittings :—

At first sitting :—

"Your lady's Fanny; well, there is a Fanny. [No.] Fred has
light hair, brownish moustache, prominent nose. [No.] Your thesis
was some special thing. I should say about lungs." [No.]

At second sitting :—

"Your mother's name was Elizabeth. [No.] Her father's lame.
[No.] Of your children there's Eddie and Willie and Fannie or Annie

and a sister that faints, and Willie and Katie (no, Katie don't count) [being the nurse], and Harry and the little dark-eyed one, Daisy. [All wrong except Daisy.] One passed out with sore throat. [No.] The boy looks about eight. [No, four.] Your wife's father had something wrong with leg; one named William. [No.] Your grandmother had a sister who married a Howe—Henry Howe. [Unknown.] There's a Thomson connected with you [no], and if you look you will find a Howe too. Your brother the captain [correct], with a lovely wife, who has brown hair [correct], has had trouble in head [no], and has two girls and a boy." [No, three girls.]

As another instance of the disentangling of the relatives of a stranger, I take the case of a shorthand clerk whom I had borrowed once or twice from the College Registrar to take down what was said *verbatim*. He sat at a distance taking notes, but Phinuit presently began to refer to him, told him that his brother had had a tooth out (which was true) and told him to inquire about a George Edward H. who had hurt his hand at a party, but who has not been recognised. Then he said—

"There seems to be some of that fellow's friends about here whom I can't avoid. There's a lot, and I can't get things straight. You will have to let me talk to him and get all his influence, and then I will talk to the rest of you. I can't help it. Get out. You don't mind me, do you?"

[Exeunt O. J. L., A. L., and M. L.]

(Clerk now came and took one hand, taking brief notes with the other.)

"Your relations make me get mixed; they confuse me when I'm talking to the Captain, so if I mention anyone belonging to you you must tell me, that we may keep things straight. There's an old lady in the spirit talking to me, and her influence disturbs me. [Grandmother died a few years ago.] Ask your brother if he don't know those people at party, and that fellow who hurt his hand, George Edward H., and he's got a brother Fred. You have a cousin Charley [true] that stops in your home [no, his brother used to], and a cousin named Harry. [True.] There are six in your family, four boys and two girls. [Correct.]

The sister is Minnie. [Correct.] She is cranky, stupid sometimes [true], but she will grow out of that. Your mother has a pain in her head sometimes. [No.] Minnie is musical. [Not particularly.] One brother writes a great deal. [I do myself.] Your name is Ed. [Correct.] Your grandmother keeps calling Ed. You ask about those people I told you of, and you will find it's true. [Have made diligent inquiries ineffectually.] I want the Captain. See you, Captain, that fellow's straight. Now, then, Alfred and Marie. Got straightened out a little bit? That's all right. Here, Alfred, I've got to talk to you. All the rest skip." ["Captain" was the nickname by which Phinuit usually addressed O. J. L.]

As an instance of reading a letter, which had indeed passed through my mind in the way recorded, but which was not read in any normal manner by the medium, I take the following case.

(A chain was handed to Phinuit by O. J. L., the package having been delivered by hand to O. J. L. late the previous evening. He had just opened the package, glanced at the contents, and hastily read a letter inside, then wrapped all up again and stored them. The chain had been sent by Mrs. John Watson from Sefton Drive; it had belonged to Dr. Watson's father.)

"This belongs to an old gentleman that passed out of the body— a nice old man. I see something funny here, something the matter with heart, paralytic something. Give me the wrappers, all of them." [*i.e.*, The paper it came in; a letter among them. Medium held them to top of her head, gradually flicking away the blank ones. She did not inspect them. She was all the while holding with her other hand another stranger, a Mr. Lund, who knew nothing whatever about the letter or the chain.]

"Who's dear Lodge? Who's Poole, Toodle, Poodle? Whatever does that mean?"

O. J. L.: "I haven't the least idea."

"Is there J. N. W. here? Poole. Then there's Sefton. S-e-f-t-o-n. Pool, hair. Yours truly, J. N. W. That's it; I send hair. Poole. J. N. W. Do you understand that?"

O. J. L.: "No, only partially."

"Who's Mildred, Milly? something connected with it, and Alice; and with him, too, I get Fanny. There's his son's influence on it."

[Note by O. J. L.—I found afterwards that the letter began "Dear Dr. Lodge," contained the words "Sefton Drive," and "Cook" so written as to look like Poole. It also said "I send you some hair," and finished "yours sincerely J. B. W."; the "B" being not unlike an "N." The name of the sender was not mentioned in the letter, but at a subsequent sitting it was correctly stated by Phinuit in connexion with the chain.]

This reading of letters in an abnormal way is very curious, and is a very old type of phenomenon. Kant and Hegel were both familiar with it : only it was then called "reading with the pit of the stomach." Now it seems usually done with the top of the head.

I had a few other cases—less distinct than the above —and I again refer here to the little experiment made by Mrs. Verrall as reported on page 127, as well as to page 133.

———————

One of the best sitters was a friend who for several years was my next-door neighbour at Liverpool, Isaac C. Thompson, F.L.S., to whose name indeed, before he had been in any way introduced, Phinuit sent a message purporting to come from his father. Three generations of his and of his wife's family, living and dead (small and compact Quaker families), were, in the course of two or three sittings, conspicuously mentioned, with identifying detail ; the main informant representing himself as his deceased brother, a young Edinburgh doctor, whose loss had been mourned some twenty years ago. The familiarity and touchingness of the messages communicated in this particular instance were very remarkable, and can by no means be reproduced in any printed report of the sitting. Their case is one in which very few mistakes were made, the details standing out vividly correct, so that in fact they found it impossible not to believe that their relatives were actually speaking to them. This may sound absurd, but it correctly represents the impression produced by a favourable series of sittings, and it is for that reason I mention it now. Simple events occurring elsewhere during the sitting were also detected by Dr. Phinuit in their case, better than in any other I know of. A full report of this rather excellent case has had to be omitted for lack of space.

There was a remarkable little incident towards the end of my series of sittings, when this friend of mine was present. A message interpolated itself to a gentleman living in Liverpool, known, but not at all intimately known, to both of us, and certainly outside of our thoughts—the head of the Liverpool Post-office, Mr. Rich. The message purported to be from a son of his who had died suddenly a few months ago, and whom I had never seen; though Isaac Thompson had, it seems, once or twice spoken to him.

This son addressed I. C. T. by name, and besought him to convey a message to his father, who, he said, was much stricken by the blow, and who was suffering from a recent occasional dizziness in his head, so that he felt afraid he should have to retire from business. Other little things were mentioned of an identifying character; and the message was, a few days later, duly conveyed. The facts stated were admitted to be accurate; and the father, though naturally inclined to be sceptical, confessed that he had indeed been more than ordinarily troubled at the sudden death of his eldest son, because of a recent unfortunate estrangement between them which would otherwise have been only temporary.

The only thought-transference explanation I can reasonably offer him is that it was the distant activity of his own mind, operating on the sensitive brain of the medium, of whose existence he knew absolutely nothing, and contriving to send a delusive message to itself!

One thing about which the son seemed anxious was a certain black case which he asked us to speak to his father about, and to say he did not want lost. The father did not know what case was meant: but I have heard since, indirectly, that on his death-bed the son was calling out about a black case, though I cannot learn that the particular case has been securely identified.

Contemplating these and such-like communications, I could not help feeling that if it be really a case of thought-transference at all, it is thought-transference of a surprisingly vivid kind, the proof of which would be very valuable, supposing it were the correct explanation of the phenomenon.

But I felt doubtful if it were the correct explanation. One must not shut one's eyes to the *possibility* that in pursuing a favourite hypothesis one may after all be on the wrong tack altogether.

Every known agency must be worked to the utmost before one is willing to admit an unknown one: and indeed to abandon this last known link of causation as inadequate to sustain the growing weight of facts was an operation not to be lightly undertaken. And yet I felt grave doubts whether it would really suffice to explain the facts; whether indeed it went any distance toward their explanation.

Things were sometimes told to me and to others so entirely foreign to our conscious thought that at first they were not recognised as true or intelligible, and only gradually or by subsequent explanation was the meaning clearly perceived. But something of the same experience is gone through in dreams; one sometimes feels surprised at the turn a dream conversation is taking,

and has the feeling also occasionally of learning something new.   Hence this argument is not of much strength
taken alone.

Another argument bases itself on the mistakes which
Dr. Phinuit sometimes unaccountably made.   One noteworthy instance is called attention to by one of my
sitters, whose father, in the midst of much that was
correct and striking, was reported as saying that his
name was John.   Now his son, the sitter, was vividly
conscious that his deceased father's name was not John,
but was Peter.   No knowledge of this, however, was
shown by Phinuit; though, by subsequently several
times quoting the name as Thomas, he seemed to show
consciousness that there had been an error somewhere.

The only explanation of this that I can suggest,
beyond mere bungle and error, is that *I* was in the room
also taking notes, and though I of course knew the
surname, I was quite ignorant of the Christian name.

Undoubtedly, therefore, the hypothesis of thought-
transference has to be wriggled and stretched a little;
though we may be willing to stretch it to any required
length, so long as it does not actually snap.   But feeling
that it did not really commend itself, I endeavoured
to apply some crucial tests.

And the first was a few children's alphabet letters,
pinched up at random, put in a pill box without looking, and sealed by me in the presence of Prof. Carey
Foster a month or so previously.   This box I now
handed to "Phinuit" and asked him what was inside
it, telling him at the same time that no one knew, and
requesting him to do his best.

He immediately asked for a pencil, and holding the
box to Mrs. Piper's forehead, shaking it a little at intervals, as if to disentangle the contents and bring them

more clearly before him, wrote down some letters on a bit of cardboard held for him.

I thanked him, and next morning for better security, asked him to try again. He did, and wrote down just the same letters, even to the extent of saying which way they happened to face in the box.

I wrote two accounts of the contents of the box, one to Mr. Myers and one to Prof. Carey Foster, under seal, telegraphing to him to know if he were at home and ready to receive the box, assure himself that it had not been tampered with (though indeed it had not been out of my possession all the time), and then to open it and write out the letters and their aspects, in full detail, before opening my sealed account. He replied, "Yes," and I sent him the box registered and insured.

All the letters were wrong but two : though as it happens the *number* of letters was nearly correct.

According to chance, if they had been pinched from a single alphabet, two should have been guessed right. The box from which they had been pinched contained many alphabets, but practically the conclusion of the experiment was utterly negative. The letters had not been read (*Proc*. S.P.R. vi. 494).

This experiment inclined me strongly to *some* thought-transference explanation, as distinct from what seemed to me the more unknown and vague region of clairvoyance.

If the letters themselves could be really directly perceived, the fact that they existed in nobody's mind could not matter. But if *minds* only could be read, then it was essential that someone somewhere should be cognisant of the letters. I do not mean that it would do to base so clear a conclusion on the result of one negative experiment. It is an experiment which I want to repeat,—though Phinuit doesn't much care for this kind of thing and says it strains him,—but it seemed to me to strengthen the hypothesis of thought-transference from some mind or other. So I set to work to try and obtain, by the regular process of communication which suits this particular medium, facts which were not only out of my knowledge but which never could have been in it.

In giving an account of these experiments, fully reported at the time though now some twenty years old, I must enter on a few trivial details concerning my own relations. The occasion is the excuse.

It happened that an uncle of mine in London, then quite an old man, the eldest of a surviving three out of a very large family, of which my own father was one of the youngest, had a twin brother who died some twenty or more years ago. I interested him generally in the subject, and wrote to ask if he would lend me some relic of this brother. By morning post on a certain day I received a curious old gold watch, which the deceased brother had worn and been fond of; and that same morning—no one in the house having seen it or knowing anything about it—I handed it to Mrs. Piper when in a state of trance.

I was told almost immediately that it had belonged to one of my uncles—one that had been mentioned before as having died from the effects of a fall—one that had been very fond of Uncle Robert, the name of the survivor—that the watch was now in possession of this same Uncle Robert, with whom its late owner was anxious to communicate. After some difficulty and many wrong attempts Dr. Phinuit caught the name, Jerry, short for Jeremiah, and said emphatically, as if impersonating him, "This is my watch, and Robert is my brother, and I am here. Uncle Jerry, my watch." All this at the first sitting on the very morning the watch had arrived by post, no one but myself and a shorthand clerk who happened to have been introduced for the first time at this sitting by me, and whose antecedents are well known to me, being present.

Having thus ostensibly got into communication through some means or other with what purported to be Uncle Jerry, whom I had indeed known slightly in his later years of blindness, but of whose early life I knew nothing, I pointed out to him that to make Uncle Robert aware of his presence it would be well to recall trivial details of their boyhood, all of which I would faithfully report.

He quite caught the idea, and proceeded during several successive sittings ostensibly to instruct Dr. Phinuit to mention a number of little things such as would enable his brother to recognise him.

References to his blindness, illness, and main facts of his life were comparatively useless from my point of view ; but these details of boyhood, two-thirds of a century ago, were utterly and entirely out of my ken. My father himself had only known these brothers as men.

"Uncle Jerry" recalled episodes such as swimming the creek when they were boys together, and running some risk of getting drowned ; killing a cat in Smith's field ; the possession of a small rifle, and of a long peculiar skin, like a snake-skin, which he thought was now in the possession of Uncle Robert.

All these facts have been more or less completely verified. But the interesting thing is that his twin brother, from whom I got the watch, and with whom I was thus in correspondence, could not remember them all. He recollected something about swimming the creek, though he himself had merely looked on. He had a distinct recollection of having had the snake-skin, and of the box in which it was kept, though he did not know where it was then. But he altogether denied killing the cat, and could not recall Smith's field.

His memory, however, was decidedly failing him, and

he was good enough to write to another brother, Frank, living in Cornwall, an old sea captain, and ask if he had any better remembrance of certain facts—of course not giving any inexplicable reasons for asking. The result of this inquiry was triumphantly to vindicate the existence of Smith's field as a place near their home, where they used to play, in Barking, Essex; and the killing of a cat by another brother was also recollected; while of the swimming of the creek, near a mill-race, full details were given, Frank and Jerry being the heroes of that foolhardy episode.

I may say here that Dr. Phinuit has a keen "scent" —shall I call it?—for trinkets or personal valuables of all kinds. He recognised a ring which my wife wears as having been given "to me for her" by a specified aunt just before her death; of which he at another time indicated the cause fairly well. He called for a locket which my wife sometimes wears, but had not then on, which had belonged to her father 40 years ago. He recognised my father's watch, asked for the chain belonging to it, and was still unsatisfied for want of some appendage which I could not think of at the time, but which my wife later on reminded me of, and Phinuit at another sitting seized,—a seal which had been usually worn with it, and which had belonged to my grandfather.

He pulled my sister's watch out of her pocket and said it had been her mother's, but disconnected the chain and said that didn't belong, which quite right. Even little pocket things, such as fruit-knives and corkscrews, he also assigned to their late owners; and once he quite unexpectedly gripped the arm of the chair Mrs. Piper was sitting in, which had never been mentioned to him in any way, and said that

15

it had belonged to my Aunt Anne.   It was quite
true : it was an old-fashioned ordinary type of arm-
chair which she valued and had had re-upholstered
for us as a wedding present 12 years ago.   Phinuit, by
the way, did not seem to realise that it was a chair :
he asked what it was, and said he took it for part
of an organ.

But perhaps the best instance of a recognised object
was one entrusted to me by the Rev. John Watson, at
that time quite a recent friend of mine, with whom I had
been staying recently in Italy,—a chain which had
belonged to his father.   It is the chain referred to in
connexion with the episode of reading a letter related on
page 217 above.

The package was delivered by hand one evening at
my house, and, by good luck, I happened to meet the
messenger and receive it direct.   Next morning I
handed it to Dr. Phinuit, saying only, in response to
his feeling some difficulty about it, that it did not belong
to a relative.   He said it belonged to an old man and had
his son's influence on it.   He also partially read a letter
accompanying it—as described at page 217.   Next sitting
I tried the chain again, and he very soon reported the
late owner as present, and recognising the chain but not
recognising me.   I explained that his son had entrusted
me with it ; on which Phinuit said the chain belonged
now to John Watson, away for health, a preacher, and
a lot of other details all known to me, and all correct.
The old gentleman was then represented as willing to
write his name.   A name was written in the backward
manner Phinuit sometimes affects.   It was legible afterwards in a mirror as James Watson.   Now, the name
of his father I was completely ignorant of.

I explained to the communicator that his son desired
to hear from him, and asked him to be good enough to
prove his identity.

Whereupon, at intervals, a number of specific though trivial facts were mentioned. They were frequently admitted to be trivial in an apologetic way, but nevertheless would serve as good evidence; better than more conspicuous ones indeed. I took them down as well as I could, knowing absolutely nothing of the correctness or incorrectness of most of them. Such facts as I did know were nearly all correct. Hence I had good hopes of another crucial test here.

If what I knew was stated correctly, while all those things which I did not know should turn out inaccurate or false, I should be forcibly impelled towards a direct thought-transference explanation for this entire set. But, on the other hand, if these things of which I had absolutely never heard or dreamt should turn out true, then some further step must be taken.

Unfortunately the result is not so simple and crucial as I had expected it to be. A stranger always encounters some difficulty in getting at facts. The father's name turned out to be not James but John—the same as that of the son: and although the facts stated concerning the son, my friend, were practically all correct, I learned three weeks later, when I got a reply from Egypt where he was travelling, that the statements about the father were all wrong. Thus then they become valueless, except as strengthening the evidence for thought-transference from myself; for it was the facts of which I was ignorant that were wrong. But Dr. Watson told me later that James was the name of his *grandfather*, and that the statements would have a truer ring if they had purported to come from the grandfather instead of from the father. And I understood that the chain—which was the ostensible link of connexion—had belonged to both.

PERCEPTION OF EVENTS AT A DISTANCE

As an instance of the perception of things happening at a distance, I take the case of what may be called "Charley and the bird." This insignificant episode was in nobody's mind or knowledge in this country. It had happened in Canada during the time that Mrs. Piper was in England, and its occurrence was only ascertained by subsequent special inquiry.

The message purported to come from my deceased Aunt Anne, of whom this "Charley," living in Canada, was the adopted son.

She said that she was very sorry that Charley ate the bird—the chicken—and made himself sick. He has had a trouble with his stomach. Her Charley. And he has been troubled for some little time. The bird made him sick. Some kind of bird. Quite sick. It troubled him a good deal. You write and ask him. But it is so. You will find it was. He will tell you. [This message was received on 26 Dec. 1889.]

Sequel added September, 1890.—Concerning the episode recorded above : I wrote to a cousin who had emigrated last October to join her brother (the "Charley" referred to) in Manitoba, asking her if he had eaten any particular bird about Christmas time which had disagreed with him. Only recently have I got full information on the subject, the unsportsmanlike character of the act possibly, but more likely the difficulty of realising any sense in the inquiry, being responsible for some of the delay. The evidence now obtained is as follows :—

"The boys shot a prairie hen as they were coming home one night, near the beginning of December, out of season, when there was a fine for killing these birds. So we had to hide it. It was hung for about a fortnight, and a few days before Christmas we ate it, Charley eating most. The bird didn't make him ill, but he was ill at the time, having the grippe. He went to town either that night or next day, and was certainly worse when he returned."

Another instance of perception of an event happening at a distance occurred as the result of an experiment which my friend Mr. Gonner had arranged at an early sitting.   He had combined with his sister in London to coax their mother into doing something unusual at a certain hour on a certain day, for reasons to be afterwards explained.   We found afterwards that the selection of an unusual proceeding consisted in driving round Regent's Park in a hansom cab in the wet.   And this is what she was doing during the time her son was sitting at Liverpool, while the medium held a little book of hers.   He had carefully not arranged or suggested anything as a suitable proceeding, but he had a presentiment that some not very striking occurrence would probably be deemed sufficient.   It is impossible to say that the idea of a possible outdoor excursion may not have been latent in his mind.

We were completely ignorant of what was going on in London, but Dr. Phinuit described the surroundings of this lady and a younger lady who was with her— described her as being over-persuaded to go out, though she didn't want to, and as going clearly through the operation of outdoor dressing : several minute actions, such as opening a box, taking up a photograph from dressing-table to look at, and so on, being mentioned correctly.   But there it stopped.   We did not get to Regent's Park and the cab, though that was the stage reached while he was speaking, but Phinuit stopped short at the stage reached just about when the sitting began ; though he spoke as if he was describing the present moment.   More experiments of this nature are wanted, and very likely have been made by others.   I do not pretend that this experiment by itself is conclusive, but it is useful as far as it goes.

It was a carefully arranged experiment, planned by Mr. Gonner and myself in Liverpool, and carried out in a satisfactory manner through the kind aid of his relations in London.   The problem was to remove thought-transference to as many orders of remoteness as possible. He therefore wrote to his sister, Miss Gonner, giving her full particulars of what was wanted. Their mother was to be requested to decide on and do something uncommon at a specified hour without letting Miss Gonner know what it was; neither was she to have any inkling whatever as to a reason for the request, nor to know that it was connected with her son. I find that all this was scrupulously done. With the aid of Miss Ledlie (the lady correctly described and named as "Annie" by Phinuit), who likewise knew nothing whatever as to reasons, the mother was prevailed upon to accede to the request; and she accordingly decided to go out under perfectly unlikely circumstances, accompanied by Miss Ledlie, both ladies being very much puzzled to account for the singular and vague request on the part of Miss Gonner. The latter lady, who was the only one of the trio who had any idea of the reason, purposely absented herself from the house before any decision was made as to what should be done. The driving round the park on a wet Saturday morning, though sufficiently incongruous to astonish even the cabman, was an unfortunately passive kind of performance to select; but considering the absence of every kind of information or clue to the reason for doing anything, the wonder is that anything whatever was done. Miss Ledlie reports that after Miss Gonner had left the house she and Mrs. Gonner decided what to do, and a vehicle was sent for. Just about 11 she ran upstairs to see if Mrs. Gonner was ready, and saw her come out of her room to a landing cupboard, take a box out of it, put it on a ledge, open it and take out a muff, very much as described by Phinuit half an hour later. She had her cloak and things on then, and the cloak is troublesome to hook, so that there would be a good deal of apparently fixing things round the neck. The taking up and looking at the photograph would almost certainly be done before going out, though it was not actually seen. The "taking up a pencil to write," and the "brushing something," if by "something" is meant a garment, are unlikely actions. Although the success was far from complete, Phinuit distinctly left us in Liverpool with the impression that "going out" was the thing selected to be done.

The following is the record of this part of the sitting at Liverpool.

Present—O. J. L. as recorder and Prof. Gonner as sitter.

O. J. L. "Tell him about his mother and what she's doing now. It's very important."

Ha, ha! I'll tell you why it's important, because he don't know it himself. I read your thoughts then. I can't generally.

Your mother is just this minute fixing her hair, putting a thing through her hair (indicating) in a room with a cot in it, up high. Did you know she had some trouble with her head?

Sitter. " No."

Long distance between you and your mother, separation between you. She's in another place. [Yes, in London.] . . . She's fixing something to her throat and putting on a wrap here, round here, and now she has lifted up the lid of a box on a stand. (11.30) . . .

There's been some news, some correspondence reached the large building where your mother is. She has had a cold. A young lady is with her, and I should think it's her daughter; a very nice girl. She draws somewhat, and needlework and reads a great deal, a pretty girl with light hair and bluish eyes. She's speaking to your mother at this minute. [This is all practically correct, except the relationship.]

Sitter. " Is her hair long or short? "

How do you mean? It's fuzzy light hair. She's a little pale, sort of smiling; nice teeth. Your mother is going out. Your mother had trouble in leg, kind of rheumatic. There's a young lady, not Annie, with light hair, light complexion, good influence. [This is the daughter.]

Thus Phinuit described all three ladies—all in fact who were directly or indirectly concerned in the episode —and described them correctly. Whatever this power is due to, it is certainly beyond chance.

The following are part of Professor Gonner's Notes :—

Notes by the Sitter.—In preparation for the interview I had written and asked my sister to persuade my mother to do something that was unusual for her between the hours of eleven and twelve Saturday morning; and to observe what she did. My mother was not to know, and did not know, that she was doing this at my request. Saturday morning, at a few minutes before eleven, she prepared herself for going out to take a drive in a hansom cab, this striking her as an unusual procedure, as it was raining. Such preparation involved touching the head in the putting on of her bonnet, of her neck and shoulders when she put on her cloak. Then she was specially observed to take her muff-box from her wardrobe, to place it on a table, lift the lid, and take her muff out. On her dressing-table there stands a small photograph of my father, which she very frequently takes up and looks at intently. Whether she did this on the occasion in question cannot be ascertained, as it is one of those ordinary actions the performance of which makes no impression. She cannot, however, be said to have been suffering from her head. There is a wooden half-tester in her room, which might conceivably be called a "cot."

There is here a general correspondence between her actions at three or four minutes to eleven, and those attributed to her by the medium at 11.25–11.30. But the séance was beginning at eleven, and the medium began at once with my mother. It is then an interesting matter to examine whether she was trying to discover what my mother was engaged upon at the moment or to recall her actions as she last perceived them.

The episode of Miss Ledlie's hair not having been cut short, when Mr. Gonner, having been told in fun that it had, felt dissatisfied with Phinuit's reply implying that there was nothing special to say about its length— dissatisfaction which he expressed to me,—is likewise good as against ordinary thought-transference.

Comment

If experiments like this can be got to succeed definitely, we seem driven to suppose that actions can be detected, or the mind of a neutral unconscious person read, at any distance,—connexion being established by some link, such as a book, a bit of jewellery, an old letter, or a lock of hair, and sometimes no connexion being established at all.

So even if the hypothesis of disembodied telepathic activity could be intelligently granted I do not see that it would explain all the facts. Not, for instance, Phinuit's skill in recognising diseases, reading letters, and describing contemporary events. Ordinary thought-transference does better for some of these; but it does not serve for all.

If we reject every kind of telepathic explanation, it seems as if we should be driven to postulate direct clairvoyance; to suppose that in a trance a person is able to enter a region where miscellaneous information of all kinds is readily available; where, for instance, time and space are not; so that everything that has happened, whether at a distance or close at hand, whether long ago or recently, can be seen or heard and described. Unknown letters in a box, for instance (which, though not read in my case, p. 221, are said to be sometimes read, cf. p. 133), might be read on this hypothesis by harking back to the time before they were put in; or, if we assume it possible to see the future also, by looking forward to the time when they were taken out. A fourth dimension of space is known to get over difficulties like this, and an omnipresent time is very like a fourth dimension.

I see no way of evading such an elastic hypothesis as this! It could explain anything and everything; but is it not rather like postulating omniscience, and considering that an explanation? It is all very well to call a thing clairvoyance, but the thing so called stands just as much in need of explanation as before.

Undoubtedly Mrs. Piper in the trance state has access to some abnormal sources of information, and is for the time cognisant of facts which happened long ago or at a distance; but the question is how she becomes cognisant of them. Is it by going up the stream of time and witnessing those actions as they occurred; or is it through information received from the still existent actors, themselves dimly remembering and relating them; or, again, is it through the influence of contemporary and otherwise occupied minds holding stores of forgotten information in their brains and offering them unconsciously to the perception of the entranced person ; or, lastly, is it by falling back for the time into a one Universal Mind of which all ordinary consciousnesses, past and present, are but portions ? Opinions may differ as to which is the least extravagant supposition.

Possibly some hypothesis more simple than any of these may be invented, but at present I feel as if it were unlikely that any one explanation will fit all the facts. It rather feels as if we were at the beginning of what is practically a fresh branch of science ; and that to pretend to frame explanations, except in the most tentative and elastic fashion for the purpose of threading the facts together and suggesting fresh fields for experiment, is as premature as it would have been for Galvani to have expounded the nature of Electricity, or Copernicus the laws of Comets and Meteors.

CHAPTER XVII

DISCUSSION OF PIPER SITTINGS

UNLESS the evidence, of which the merest sample has now been given, be held to constitute a sufficiently strong proof that the performances of this particular " medium " are neither lucky shots nor explicable by cunning and imposture, it is premature to examine further into their significance. But as soon as these preliminary suppositions can be unreservedly dismissed, the best plan is to dismiss them thoroughly and waste no more time over them.

From this point of view the next hypothesis is that the information is derived from the sitter's mind in some way or other : *e.g.* (*a*) by question and answer ; (*b*) by muscular and other semi-occult and unconscious signalling ; (*c*) by direct mind-reading, or influence of the sitter's thought, conscious or otherwise, acting on the entranced person as percipient. I do not propose critically to distinguish between these three methods, although the first is very ancient, the second only recently recognised in its full development and power, while the third is only in process of being accepted by scientific men.

A large number of instances can be easily found which are not explicable by either (*a*) or (*b*), and to all those who have hitherto spent any labour over the records it has become clear that either (*c*) or some even less admissible hypothesis is necessary to explain a large portion of the results.

Let it be clearly understood that the first question is whether any reading of the mind *of the sitter* can be considered sufficiently efficacious. That *some* mind is read I should think most probable; the question is not between mind-reading and something quite distinct; it is between reading the mind of the sitter and reading the mind of some one else.

There are three methods of reading the mind of the sitter, labelled above (*a*), (*b*), and (*c*). Methods of extracting information from *distant* persons are fewer. Correspondence is one; telepathy may, I suppose, be assumed to be another. The only method known to science of extracting information from *deceased* persons is the discovery of documents.

Now, in respect of correspondence and documents it is comparatively easy to be assured as to the use or non-use of these methods in any particular case. Eliminating them, if anything is obtained inexplicable by the agency of the sitter, it is to telepathy that we must look for a possible explanation. Telepathy from distant persons if that is in any way feasible, telepathy from deceased persons only as a last resort, but telepathy of some kind, as distinct from any conceivable method of extracting information from persons present : that seems to be the alternative hypothesis, to an examination of which we find ourselves forced by an attentive study of the records.

The question therefore largely turns upon proof of identity : proof of the genuineness of the identity claimed by the communicator. Now if you met a stranger in a railway-carriage who professed to have

returned from the Colonies where he had met your
friends or relations, of whom he showed knowledge
in some decided ways, it would not at first occur
to you to doubt his veracity, even though he was a
little hazy about the names of relatives, and occasionally mixed things up; nor would you stigmatise him
as a deceiver if he occasionally made use of information
supplied by yourself in course of conversation. But
directly it was suggested that he might be a thought-
reader, detailing to you the unconscious contents of
your own mind, it would not be easy rigorously
to disprove the suggestion, especially if subsequent
access to the friends chiefly mentioned were denied
you. This is, however, very nearly, the problem
before us.

Only occasionally does the question forcibly arise;
most facts asserted are, of course, within the knowledge
of the sitter, and none of those are of any use for the
purpose of discrimination; but every now and then
facts, often very trivial but not within the knowledge of
the sitter, have been asserted, and have been more or
less clearly verified afterwards; and in order to assist a
special study of these data, with the view of examining
how far they are really valuable, I made an index to
them, which I published in the *Proceedings*, vol. vi.
p. 647, as an Appendix to the Report of the early Piper
sittings. To that index a student may refer.

EPISODES NORMALLY SELECTED FOR IDENTIFICATION

Concerning the means of identification naturally
adopted by living people who are communicating with
each other at a distance by telephone, under conditions
in which they are debarred from communicating their

names, or, what is the same thing, under conditions in which their names might be understood as being falsely given, Professor Hyslop made some interesting experiments which are thus reported in the *Journal* of the Society for Psychical Research (vol. ix.) :—

In an introduction he explains the object and the method of these experiments, about which there was nothing supernormal at all. A telegraph line was arranged between two buildings of the Columbia University, and a couple of friends or acquaintances were taken independently to each end of the line, only one of them knowing who was at the other end ; and this one (the communicator) was to send messages, at first vague but increasing in definiteness, while the other person was to guess until he could guess correctly and assuredly who it was that was at the other end of the line. The replies and guesses were likewise telegraphed by an assistant stationed with the receiver, for the guidance of the sender. Professor Hyslop's objects in carrying out an extensive series of this kind of experiment are thus stated by himself :—

" I may now summarise the several objects of the whole series of experiments. The first of these objects was not intimated to any one. I was extremely careful not to breathe it to any one, not even to my assistants, so that the results might be entirely spontaneous and without the influence of suggestion from me.

" I. To test the extent to which intelligent persons would spontaneously select trivial and unimportant incidents for the purpose of identification—that is, incidents that were not connected, or not necessarily connected, with the main habits of their lives.

" II. To test the accuracy of the identification in connection with both individual and collective incidents, and especially to test how slight or how definite the incident had to be in order to suggest rightly the person it was intended to represent.

"III. To test the success and personal assurance of the receiver of the messages in guessing who is the true sender, in spite of some messages that are misleading or even false, but the bulk of which involves sufficient cumulative facts to overcome the natural scepticism and confusion caused by incoherences and contradictions.

"IV. To study the sources of misunderstanding that might arise under such circumstances when one party was ignorant of the intentions of the other, and the causes of illusion in identification which we can determine in my experiments, and which are likely to occur in the Piper case."

And he proceeds :—

"In regard to the first of these objects, it is very interesting to observe the uniformity with which perfectly intelligent persons spontaneously chose what would generally be considered trivial incidents in order to identify themselves. This seemed naturally to recommend itself to them, perhaps for the reason that trivial circumstances represent far more isolation than any chosen from the main trend of life, though I noticed no consciousness of this fact in any one. It was simply the instinctive method which every one tended to adopt. The records show very distinctly that, if left to themselves, men will naturally select unimportant incidents for proof of their identity, and it is one of the most interesting features of this choice that the individual relied wholly upon the laws of association to recall what was wanted, after deciding on the nature of the incidents to be chosen. Very often there were interesting illustrations of those capricious revivals in memory of remote incidents which not only resemble so much the incidents in the Piper sittings in triviality, but also represent the caprices and incoherences of associative recall, intelligible to the subject on reflection, but hardly so to the outside observer. At any rate, the results in this regard completely remove all objections to the Piper phenomena from the standpoint of the triviality of the incidents chosen for identification ; and that is an accomplishment of some worth."

I may further add that though the incidents serving for identification sounded vague to bystanders or readers of the record, yet when they were explained from the point of view of both sender and receiver they were perceived to be distinct enough, and to justify the leap of identification taken upon them.   And this fact is of interest in connection with the Piper record, where it has been often felt by readers or note-takers that sitters identify their relatives too easily and fancifully ; for in Professor Hyslop's experiments the identification is often performed on still slighter grounds—often on what would superficially appear no legitimate ground at all— and yet it turns out, when both ends of the line are catechised (as they can *not* be catechised in the real Piper case), that these incidents are perceived to be of force adequate to support the conclusion based upon them.   I have been constantly struck, while taking notes for a stranger at a Piper sitting, with the apparently meaningless incidents which were being referred to ; and yet afterwards, when I saw the annotations, I realised their meaning and appropriateness.

Further, in answer to Professor Sidgwick's tentative objection that the sitters in the Hyslop experiments were only *playing* at identification, and therefore were naturally in a more or less frivolous mood, whereas on a spiritistic hypothesis the Piper communicators would be serious and emotional and not so likely to refer to trivial incidents : we may imagine the case of a wanderer not able to return to his home, but able to communicate with it for a few minutes by telephone.

In however strenuous and earnest a spirit he might be,
—indeed, both ends of the line might be,—yet when
asked to prove his identity and overcome the dread of
illusion and personation, he would instinctively try to
think of some trifling and absurd private incident ; and
this might very likely be accepted as sufficient, and
might serve as a prelude to closer and more affectionate
messages, which, previous to identification, would be out
of place.   And I feel bound to say that my own experience of the Piper sittings leads me to assert that this
kind of genuinely dignified and serious and appropriate
message does ultimately in many cases come,—but not
until the preliminary stages (stages beyond which some
sitters seem unable to get) are fairly passed.

16

CHAPTER XVIII

SUMMARY OF DR. HODGSON'S VIEWS

OF all men at that time living, undoubtedly Dr. Hodgson had more experience of Mrs. Piper's phenomena than any other — for he devoted years of his life to the subject and made it practically his sole occupation. He did this because, after preliminary study, he recognised its great importance. He was by no means a credulous man—in fact he was distinctly sceptical, and many have been the spurious phenomena which he detected and exposed. In some respects he went, in my judgment, too far in his destructive career—he disbelieved in Mrs. Thompson, for instance, and he practically for the time annihilated Eusapia Palladino, the famous "physical" medium— but hyper-scepticism is far more useful to the development of the subject than hyper-credulity, and when such a man is, after adequate study, decidedly and finally convinced, his opinions deserve, and from those who knew him received, serious attention.

Not that we must be coerced into acceptance, any more than into rejection, of facts, by any critical judgment passed upon them by others; but undoubtedly his views are entitled to great weight. Accordingly I extract some of them from a paper which he published in the *Proceedings*, vol. xiii., in the year 1898; and I begin with his summary of the kind of statements made by the ostensible communicators as to the way the phenomenon appeared to them—on their side—statements which I judge were partially accepted by him as true. (But see p. 263.)

The statements of the "communicators" as to what occurs on the physical side may be put in brief general terms as follows. We all have bodies composed of "luminiferous ether" enclosed in our flesh and blood bodies. The relation of Mrs. Piper's etherial body to the etherial world, in which the "communicators" claim to dwell, is such that a special store of peculiar energy is accumulated in connection with her organism, and this appears to them as "a light." Mrs. Piper's etherial body is removed by them, and her ordinary body appears as a shell filled with this "light." Several "communicators" may be in contact with this light at the same time. There are two chief "masses" of it in her case, one in connection with the head, the other in connection with the right arm and hand. Latterly, that in connection with the hand has been "brighter" than that in connection with the head. If the "communicator" gets into contact with the "light" and thinks his thoughts, they tend to be reproduced by movements in Mrs Piper's organism. Very few can produce vocal effects, even when in contact with the "light" of the head, but practically all can produce writing movements when in contact with the "light" of the hand. Upon the amount and brightness of this "light," *cæteris paribus*, the communications depend. When Mrs. Piper is in ill-health the "light" is feebler, and the communications tend to be less coherent. It also gets used up during a sitting, and when it gets dim there is a tendency to incoherence even in otherwise clear communicators. In all cases, coming into contact with this "light" tends to produce bewilderment, and if the contact is continued too long, or the "light" becomes very dim, the consciousness of the communicator tends to lapse completely.

Then floods of excited emotion at the presence of incarnate friends, dominant ideas that disturbed him when he was incarnate himself, the desire to render advice and assistance to other living friends and relatives, etc., all crowd upon his mind; the sitter begins to ask questions about matters having no relation to what he is thinking about, he gets more and more bewildered, more and more *comatose*, loses his "grasp" of the "light," and drifts away, perhaps to return several times and go through a similar experience (pp. 400–1).

For the several years during which the personality calling itself Phinuit continued to control the voice in the trance, after the development of the "automatic writing," the personalities controlling respectively the *hand* and the *voice* showed apparently a complete independence.

The sense of hearing for the "hand" consciousness *appears* to be in the hand, and the sitter must talk to the hand to be understood. I do not profess (says Dr. Hodgson) to be able to give any satisfactory explanation of some of the processes which I am describing.

The thoughts that pass through the consciousness controlling the hand tend to be *written*, and one of the difficulties apparently is to prevent the writing out of thoughts which are not intended for the sitter. Other "indirect communicators" frequently purport to be present, and the "consciousness of the hand" listens to them with the hand as though they were close by, as it listens to the sitters, presenting the palm of the hand, held in slightly different positions for the purpose by different "direct communicators," so as to bring usually the region of the junction between the little finger and the palm towards the mouth of the sitter. The writing at its best is liable to include occasionally remarks not intended to be written, words apparently addressed by an "indirect communicator" to the consciousness of the hand, or by the consciousness of the hand to an "indirect communicator," or by "indirect communicators" to one another; or, in worse cases, where the power of inhibition seems to have been almost entirely wanting, the wandering thoughts of the "direct communicator" are apparently reproduced in incoherent fragments, mixed up with his attempts at replies to questions of the sitter, and bits of conversation, as it were, between him and other "indirect communicators."

Phinuit, for example, claims to have done much work, while the hand has been used for writing, in keeping back, so to speak, various other would-be communicators. Interruptions, nevertheless, were frequent enough until the advent of the group connected with "W. Stainton Moses," and the establishment of their supervision. Whatever else has been done, it seems to me that one result of this change has been to make the way clearer, and freer from interruptions and from the admixture of apparently foreign elements that prevailed so largely in earlier sittings. The new "controls" claim to have both the desire and the power to exclude "inferior" intelligences, whom they speak of as "earth-bound spirits," from the use of the "light," and, as a matter of fact, the perturbations referred to have practically disappeared.

That the exclusion of influences that are continually changing—and that may be otherwise not conducive to the clearest results—is a desirable thing, is also perhaps indicated by the methods which we have found most successful in forms of ordinary telepathic experiment. We there take into consideration the attitude of mind of agent and percipient; we give the percipient a chance to receive impressions of one object before we hurry him along to another; we have regard to what may be the extremely sensitive state of his "telepathic faculty," whatever that may be, and whether it resides in his subliminal consciousness or not.

Similarly, if we find a particularly good agent and a particularly good percipient, we should think it wise to give them the best opportunity possible, in long series of experiments, to get better results, and, by varying the conditions, to ascertain if possible what are the limits of, and what the causes most conducive to, clear telepathic communication.

And so I think (says Dr. Hodgson) that in Mrs. Piper's and similar cases, the introduction of persons more or less indiscriminately may not be a condition for general success, but a condition for perpetual blundering. We can all use telephones *now*; but when Reis and Bell and Blake and others were making experiments on lines that eventually led to satisfactory instruments, they would hardly have thought it worth while to let the general public spend their time in listening to more or less inarticulate noises through their incipient receiving apparatus.

Sometimes, shortly before the hand starts writing, Phinuit gives notice that some one is "going to talk with you himself." Sometimes the hand is "seized," and passes through its convulsive vagaries while Phinuit gives no sign, but talks on with the sitter continuously, even after the writing has started. To give an extreme instance of this, at a sitting where a lady was engaged in a profoundly personal conversation with Phinuit concerning her relations, and where I [H.] was present to assist—knowing the lady and her family very intimately,—the hand was seized very quietly and, as it were, surreptitiously, and wrote a very personal communication to myself, purporting to come from a deceased friend of mine, and having no relation whatsoever to the sitter ; precisely as if a caller should enter a room where two strangers to him were conversing, but a friend of his also present, and whisper a special message into the ear of the friend without disturbing the conversation.

In the case of a new communicator, however, Phinuit frequently requests the sitter to "talk to *him*," *i.e.*, to the hand-writer [who is not Phinuit but "G. P." or "Rector" or some one else], though Phinuit is not averse from keeping up the oral conversation as well, if this is desired. Indeed he seems to prefer this, and when the sitter turns to pay attention to the hand, Phinuit frequently makes some such enigmatical remark as "I'll help him," or "I'll help to hold him up." At other times Phinuit will request that an article should be given to himself, so that he might have something to engage his attention, and I have known him to blurt out something about the article in the middle of the sitting, while the writing is still going on. At any time, apparently, under these circumstances, Phinuit can be evoked from his silence by talking into the ear, and will at once resume the communication while the writing continues without a break.

It occurred to me (continues Dr. Hodgson) that possibly the left hand might also write, and that it might be possible to get both hands writing and Phinuit speaking, all at the same time on different subjects with different persons; and I remarked to Phinuit that I hoped some day to get a separate "control" of each finger and toe of the medium's body, while he could manage the voice. On February 24th, 1894, the "Edmund Gurney" control wrote in the course of some remarks about certain "mediums": "In these cases there is no reason why various spiritual minds cannot express their thoughts at the same time through the same organism." I then referred to my proposed experiment with the two hands, and said that I would arrange to try it some time, with "Gurney" using one hand and "George Pelham" the other, but that I was not prepared to make the experiment at that time. At my next sitting, February 26th, 1894, when I was unprepared and was alone, an attempt, only very partially successful, was made to write independently with both hands at the very beginning of the sitting. On March 18th, 1895, another attempt, much more successful, was made, when I was accompanied for the purpose by Miss Edmunds. Her "deceased sister" wrote with one hand, and G. P. with the other, while Phinuit was talking,—all simultaneously on different subjects. Very little, however, was written with the left hand. The difficulty appeared to lie chiefly in the deficiencies of the left hand as a writing-machine.

After having endeavoured as best I could to follow the writing of thousands of pages with scores of different writers, after having put many inquiries to the communicators themselves, and after having analysed numerous spontaneously occurring incidents of all kinds, I have no sort of doubt whatever but that the consciousness producing the writing,—whatever that consciousness be, whether Mrs. Piper's secondary personality or the real communicator as alleged,—is *not conscious of writing*, and that the thoughts that pass through "his" mind tend to be reproduced in writing by some part of the writing mechanism of Mrs. Piper's organism. This writing mechanism is far from perfect, and it frequently produces words that cannot be read. This entails a repetition of the word and checks the thought of the communicator, already reduced to the necessity of thinking his words at the slow rate of writing, and of excluding other thoughts that he does not wish written, in a state when he has already been steeped into a state of partial sleep by coming into relation with an organism not his own, for the purpose of manifesting in my physical world.

Regarding these phenomena, then, as supernormal, I may first emphasise the fact that it is much more difficult now to suppose that the supernormal knowledge exhibited has its source in the minds of living persons, than it was in the earlier years of Mrs. Piper's trances, when practically the only intermediary was the Phinuit personality.

With the advent of the G. P. intelligence, the development of the automatic writing, and the use of the hand by scores of other alleged communicators, the problem has assumed a very different aspect. The dramatic form has become an integral part of the phenomenon. With the hand writing and the voice speaking at the same time on different subjects and with different persons, with the hand writing on behalf of different communicators at the same sitting, with different successive communicators using the hand at the same sitting, as well as at different sittings, it is difficult to resist the impression that there are here actually concerned various different and distinct and individually coherent streams of consciousness. To the person unfamiliar with a series of these later sittings, it may seem a plausible hypothesis that perhaps one secondary personality might do the whole work, might use the voice and write contemporaneously with the hand, and pretend in turn to be the friends of the various sitters; might in short be a finished actor with telepathic powers, producing the impression not only that he is the character he plays, but that others are with him also, though invisible, playing their respective parts. I do not, however, think it at all likely that he would continue to think it plausible after witnessing and studying the numerous coherent groups of memories connected with different persons, the characteristic emotional tendencies distinguishing such different persons, the excessive complication of the acting required, and the absence of any apparent bond of union for the associated thoughts and feelings indicative of each individuality, save some persistent basis of that individuality itself.

But here objectors arise.

"Why," they will say, "if discarnate persons are really communicating, do they not give us much more evidence? We ourselves, if put in the witness-box here and cross-examined, could do vastly better even than G. P., and why have so few others been able to show even an approximation to such clearness as he exhibited? Why all the incoherence and confusion and irrelevancy?"

In all cases I should expect at first a confusion in understanding *me*, as well as a confusion in manifesting *to me*. If the cessation from manifestation has been very complete and has lasted a very long time, I should expect a greater bewilderment, for a short time at least, when it began again to manifest. These deficiencies and bewilderments I should expect to be much more marked if such a consciousness, instead of trying to manifest itself once more through its own organism with which it had practised for years, were restricted for its manifestations to *another* organism. In such an event I should expect the manifestations to partake in the first instance of the same lack of inhibitory control, the same inability to appreciate my injunctions and questions, the same dreamy irrelevancy that characterises all the manifestations, in my physical world, of a consciousness that has temporarily ceased to manifest therein and begins once more to reveal itself in what I call the waking state,—varying in individual cases as I find they do in ordinary life,—whether it be after ordinary sleep, or prolonged coma, or anæsthetisation, etc.—but with a tendency for the incoherency of the manifestations to be much more pronounced, inasmuch as the consciousness is trying to regain its wakefulness towards me by an unwonted way. Whether such a consciousness could ever regain its complete former fulness in my world through another organism seems highly improbable. What I should expect to find is that through another organism it could *only partially wake*. Hence I must suppose that even the best of direct "communicators" through Mrs. Piper's trance is *partly asleep*. This is the first point, says Dr. Hodgson, which I wish to emphasise.

Again, that persons just "deceased" should be extremely confused and unable to communicate directly, or even at all, seems perfectly natural after the shock and wrench of death. Thus in the case of my friend Hart, he was unable to write the second day after death. In another case a friend of mine, whom I may call D., wrote, with what appeared to be much difficulty, his name and the words, "I am all right now. Adieu," within two or three days of his death. In another case, F., a near relative of Madame Elisa, was unable to write on the morning after his death. On the second day after, when a stranger was present with me for a sitting, he wrote two or three sentences, saying, "I am too weak to articulate clearly;" and not many days later he wrote fairly well and clearly, and dictated also to Madame Elisa, as amanuensis, an account of his feelings at finding himself in his new surroundings. Both D. and F. became very clear in a short time. D. communicated later on, frequently, both by writing and speech, chiefly the latter, and showed always an impressively marked and characteristic personality. Hart, on the other hand, did not become so clear till many months later. I learned long afterwards that his illness had been much longer and more fundamental than I had supposed. The continued confusion in his case seemed explicable if taken in relation with the circumstances of his prolonged illness, including fever, but there was no assignable relation between his confusion and the state of my own mind.

Returning to the actual circumstances, I say that *if* the "spirits" of our "deceased" friends do communicate as alleged through the organisms of still incarnate persons, we are *not* justified in expecting them to manifest themselves with the same fulness of clear consciousness that they exhibited during life. We should on the contrary expect even the best communicators to fall short of this for the two main reasons : (1) loss of familiarity with the conditions of using a gross material organism at all—we should expect them to be like fishes out of water or birds immersed in it ; (2) inability to govern precisely and completely the particular gross material organism which they are compelled to use. They learned when living to play on one very complicated speaking and writing machine, and suddenly find themselves set down to play on another of a different make.

There are, indeed, three kinds of confusion that need to be distinguished by the investigator : (1) the confusion in the "spirit," whether he is communicating or not, due primarily to his mental and bodily conditions when living ; (2) the confusion in the "spirit" produced by the conditions into which he comes when in the act of communicating; (3) the confusion in the result due to the failure of complete control over the writing (or other) mechanism of the medium. (2) and (3) are increased very much by the failures of sitters to understand the process. Thus when a "Mrs. Mitchell" control was requested to repeat words which we had difficulty in deciphering, she wrote :—

No, I can't, it is too much work and too weakening, and I cannot repeat—you must help me and I will prove myself to you. I cannot collect my thoughts to repeat sentences to you. My darling husband, I am not away from you, but right by your side. Welcome me as you would if I were with you in the flesh and blood body. [Sitter asks for test.] * * * I cannot tell myself just how you hear me, and it bothers me a little . . . how do you hear me speak, dear, when we speak by thought only? Your thoughts do not reach me at all when I am speaking to you, but I hear a strange sound and have to half guess. . . .

Of such confusions as I have indicated above I cannot find any satisfactory explanation in "telepathy from the living" (continues Dr. Hodgson), but they fall into a rational order when related to the personalities of the "dead." (Cf. also pp. 305, 309, 314.)

The persistent failures of many communicators under varying conditions ; the first failures of other communicators who soon develop into clearness in communicating, and whose first attempts apparently can be made much clearer by the assistance of persons professing to be experienced communicators ; the special bewilderment, soon to disappear, of communicators shortly after death and apparently in consequence of it ; the character of the specific mental automatisms manifest in the communications ; the clearness of remembrance in little children recently deceased as contrasted with the forgetfulness of childish things shown by communicators who died when children many years before,—all present a definite relation to the personalities alleged to be communicating, and are exactly what we should expect if they are actually communicating under the conditions of Mrs. Piper's trance manifestations. The results fit the claim.

On the other hand these are not the results which we should expect on the hypothesis of telepathy from the living. If the hypothesis of telepathy from the living is acted upon in anything like the ordinary experimental way, the supernormal results will be lessened. If the investigator persistently refuses to regard the communications as coming from the sources claimed, he will not get the best results. If, on the other hand, he acts on the hypothesis that the communicators are "spirits" acting under adverse conditions, and if he treats them as he would a living person in a similar state, he will find an improvement in the communications.

And having tried the hypothesis of telepathy from the living for several years, and the "spirit" hypothesis also for several years,—says Dr. Hodgson,—I have no hesitation in affirming with the most absolute assurance that the "spirit" hypothesis is justified by its fruits, and the other hypothesis is not.

Note added October 1909

A book has just been sent me from America, published by Sherman French & Co., under the title *Both Sides of the Veil*, which contains a supplementary account of Mrs. Piper and her phenomena from the pen of Miss Robbins,—a lady who has had considerable experience of sittings, being very sympathetic to the controls, and who often acted as confidential stenographer for Dr. Hodgson as well as for some important Civic Officials in Boston. Sometimes she was allowed to sit alone with Mrs. Piper, especially for voice sittings, taking her own notes. It is a selection from these records of her own that she has now printed, prefacing it with an Introduction and Description written in an earnest and believing spirit. Her point of view and mental attitude are somewhat different from ours, and hence her record is usefully supplementary, since she sets forth the obvious appearance of the phenomenon in a consecutive and readable manner.

Without endorsing her estimate of value throughout, I can heartily commend the book to the attention of those who, without being too critical, feel an interest in the manner and the substance of communications thus received, and who would like to hear more of them.

CHAPTER XIX

RECENT PIPER SITTINGS. GENERAL INFORMATION

THE preceding account of my own sittings dates from 1889–90. I saw Mrs. Piper again on 9 Nov. 1906 at Liverpool, where she had just arrived from America, and was staying in the house of Mrs. Isaac Thompson of Liverpool, whose acquaintance she had made on her previous visit to this country. Another series of sittings then began, but at a rate of only two or three per week instead of two a day, and of the general character of these I now propose to give an account.

Since our first English experience with Mrs. Piper a great mass of material had been accumulated in America, under the management of Dr. Hodgson, and the manner of the sittings had somewhat changed. In the old days communication had always been made with the voice, and any writing done was only brief and occasional. Communications are now almost entirely in writing, and only under exceptional circumstances is the voice employed.

The manner of preparation was as follows. A quiet room was selected in which interruption need not be feared; a fire was provided for warmth, and the windows were open for ventilation. A comfortable chair was placed near a table, on which was a pile of from four to six cushions or pillows, on which the medium sitting in the chair and leaning forward could securely rest the side of her head when sleep came on, —not burying her face in the cushions, but turning it to the left side so as to be able to breathe during the trance.   If it ever happened that the pillows incommoded the breathing, they had to be adjusted and pressed down by the experimenter in charge, so that air obtained free access to the mouth and nose.   On the right hand side of the pillows, either on the same or on a small sub-sidiary table, the writing materials were arranged, namely a large pad or block-book ($10'' \times 8''$) of 100 blank sheets all numbered in order, and four or five pencils of soft lead, 2 B or 3 B, properly cut and ready.

It was the duty of the experimenter in charge to record all that the sitter said.   This could generally be done sideways on the same sheet without interfering with the medium's hand.   He also had to arrange the pad so that the hand could conveniently write upon it; and to tear off the sheets as they were done with.   No attempt was made to economise paper; the automatic writing was large and scrawling, and did not often begin at the top of the page.   Sometimes a good deal of writing was obtained on a single page, sometimes only a few lines, and occasionally only a few words.   The tearing off of the old sheet was quickly done; and the hand waited the moment necessary; though sometimes, when in the midst of an energetic message, it indicated momentary impatience at the interruption.

Mrs. Piper and her daughters often had breakfast with the family, though occasionally she breakfasted in her room.   On ordinary days she went shopping or sight-seeing, or was otherwise ordinarily occupied; but on sitting days she went back after breakfast to her own room to be quiet.   At the time fixed for the sitting, say 10 or 10.30 a.m., Mrs. Piper came into the arranged room and seated herself in the chair in front of the pillows; then the experimenter in charge sat down on a chair near the table, leaving a vacant chair between him and the medium, for the sitter; who at my sittings was sometimes present from the first, but at those held in London was introduced only after the trance had come on.   Mrs. Piper sat with her hands on the pillows in front of her; about five minutes of desultory conversation followed, then heavy breathing began, and the head of the medium presently dropped on to her hands on the pillows and turned itself with its face to the left.

Then almost at once the right hand disengaged itself and fell on the table near the writing materials.   After about 30 seconds of complete quiescence, this hand alone "woke up" as it were; it slowly rose, made the sign of the cross in the air, and indicated that it was ready to write.

The experimenter then gave the hand a pencil, placing it between fore and middle fingers; it was at once grasped, and writing began.   First a cross was drawn, and then the word "Hail" was written, followed usually by "We return to earth this day with joy and peace"; or "We greet you friend of earth once again, we bring peace and love"; or some such semi-religious phrase, signed "R," which stands for "Rector," the ostensible amanuensis.

In the old days the control had styled itself "Phinuit"; now Phinuit never appears, and the control calls itself Rector.

In the old days the tone was not so dignified and serious as it is now: it could in fact then be described as rather humorous and slangy; but there was a serious

17

under-current constantly present even then; the welcomes and farewells were quaint and kindly—even affectionate at times—and nothing was ever said of a character that could give offence. I judge that stupid familiarity or frivolity on the part of a sitter—for which, however, there was no excuse—would have been at once rebuked and checked.

In the old days the going into trance seemed rather a painful process, or at least a process involving muscular effort; there was some amount of contortion of the face, and sometimes a slight tearing of the hair; and the same actions accompanied the return of consciousness. Now the trance seems nothing more than an exceptionally heavy sleep, entered into without effort—a sleep with the superficial appearance of that induced by chloroform; and the return to consciousness, though slow and for a time accompanied by confusion, is easy and natural.

A sitting used to last only about an hour; and on the rare occasions when there is a voice sitting now, an hour is the limit; but a writing sitting seems less of a strain, and was often allowed to last as much as two hours, though not more.

In the old days, when sittings were more frequent, there were degrees of intensity about them. Occasionally, though rarely, trance declined to come on at all; and sometimes, even when it did, the loss of consciousness seemed less than complete. Under present conditions the trance is undoubtedly profound, and the suspension of normal consciousness unmistakably complete. Once, but only once in my recent experience, the trance refused to come on, and the attempt at a sitting had to be abandoned till next day.

Usually after purposely placing herself under the familiar conditions to which she is accustomed, Mrs.

Piper is able to let herself go off without trouble or delay.

Great care was taken of the body of the medium, both now and previously, by the operating intelligence. She was spoken of usually as "the light," sometimes as "the machine," though the word "machine" commonly signified only the pencil.

If anything went wrong with the breathing, or if there was insufficient air in the room, or if the cushions slipped so as to make the attitude uncomfortable, the hand wrote "something wrong with the machine," or "attend to the light," or something of that sort; and the experimenter amended the arrangements before the writing went on. The whole thing was as sensible and easy as possible, as soon as the circumstances and conditions were understood. Each experimenter, of course, handed down all the information and Hodgsonian tradition of this kind to the next, so that all the conditions to which Mrs. Piper was accustomed could be supplied beforehand, and so that no injury would happen to her bodily health.

The following illustrates the care taken of the physical conditions and the way they are spoken of. It is an extract from a sitting held by Mr. Dorr at Boston in 1906.

(Rector interrupting a "Hodgson" communication.) Friend, you will have to change the conditions a moment.
[At the beginning of the sitting only one of the two windows in the room was open a very little way. A few moments previous to this time H. J. Jr. noticing that the room was a little close had opened the other window, and G. B. D. had nearly closed it again.]
G. B. D. What is wrong with the conditions? Do you want more air or less?
Well, there will have to be a change in the surroundings, there

will have to be more strength, what is it, air, yes, air. And a good deal more just now. Hodgson takes a good deal of strength when he comes, but he is all right, he understands the methods of operation very well. (The window was now opened wide). That is better. Now the light begins to get clear. All right, friend.

As the time drew near to the two-hour limit, which has been set as a period beyond which it is undesirable to persist, and sometimes at the end of about an hour and a half, or an hour and three quarters, from the commencement, the experimenter in charge gave a hint that the sitting must terminate soon; or else the controls indicate the same thing, and they then begin to clear up and take farewell. A sitting usually concludes as it began, with the writing of a serious sentence invoking the blessing of the Most High upon the sitter and the group.

The coming out of the trance was gradual, and semi-consciousness lasted for several minutes, during which muttered sentences were uttered, and the eyes, if open at all, only glared in sleep-walking fashion; until almost suddenly they took on a natural appearance, and Mrs. Piper became herself. Even then, however, for half an hour or so after the trance had disappeared, the medium continued slightly dazed and only partly herself. During this time her eldest daughter usually took charge of her. But the trance itself was so familiar to them all that the daughters were not the least anxious, and in another room went on with their letters or needlework unconcerned. After a sitting, one of them was usually called and took her mother for a stroll in the garden. Then everybody had lunch together and talked of ordinary topics, nothing being said about the sitting, and no ill result of any kind being experienced. It seemed a normal function in her case. The experimenter meanwhile had collected the papers and arranged them in order, and had removed the pencils and other appliances. Subsequently it was his business to write out legibly all the material accumulated during the two hours of sitting, to annotate it sufficiently, and send it to a typewriter.

The actual record is of course preserved for exact reference whenever necessary. A record was also made of the remarks of Mrs. Piper during the period of awaking from trance. These were more or less mumbled and difficult to hear, but they were often a continuation of what had been obtained during trance, and generally contained useful passages ; though part of them nearly always consisted of expressions of admiration for the state or experience she was leaving, and of repulsion—almost disgust—at the commonplace terrestrial surroundings in which she found herself. Even a bright day was described as dingy or dark, and the sitter was stared at in an unrecognising way, and described as a dull and ugly person, or sometimes as a negro. Presently, however, the eyes became intelligent, and she recognised some one—usually Lady Lodge first—and then with a smile welcomed her by name, and speedily came to.

Coming to ordinary social details : it is not an impertinence, but is justified by the special circumstances of the case, to state that the family is an admirable one, and that we regard them as genuine friends.

At the time of Mrs. Piper's first visit her daughters were children. Now they are grown up, and are very useful to their mother. Nothing in any way abnormal or unusual is to be noticed about them, and their mother expresses it as her sincerest wish that they will not develop her power. For though she must realise the value of her services to science, she cannot but feel that it to some extent isolates her and marks her out as peculiar among her neighbours in New England, and that the time spent in the trance state must have made a distinct inroad on her available lifetime. This however is to some extent the case with any occupation, and it is as the duty specially allotted to her that she has learnt to regard her long service, now extending over a quarter of a century.

In speaking of messages received from a certain "control," it is not to be understood in general that that control is actually manipulating the organism; it may be always, and certainly is in general, merely dictating through an amanuensis as it were,—the actual writer or speaker being either "Rector" or "Phinuit," who again may or may not be a phase of Mrs. Piper's personality.

In the old days, undoubtedly, the appearance was sometimes as if the actual control was changed—after the fashion of a multiple personality; whereas now I think it is nearly always Rector that writes, recording the messages given to him as nearly as he can, and usually reporting in the first person, as Phinuit often did. I do not attempt to discriminate between what is given in this way and what is given directly, because it is practically impossible to do so with any certainty; since what appears to be direct control is liable to shade off into obvious reporting. That is to say, if a special agency gets control and writes for a few minutes, it does not seem able to sustain the position long, but soon abandons it to the more accomplished and experienced personality, Rector. In the recent series there appeared very little evidence of direct control other than Rector.

We shall speak however of the "Gurney control," the "Hodgson control," etc., without implying that these agents—even assuming their existence and activity—are ever really in physical possession of the organism ; and, even when they are controlling as directly as possible, they may perhaps always be operating telepathically on it rather than telergically— operating, that is to say, through some stratum of the mind, rather than directly on any part of the physical organism. It is rather soon as yet to make definite assertions regarding the actual method of control,—there are too many unknown quantities about the whole phenomenon,—at the same time Dr. Hodgson has thought it worth while to report the general aspect of the phenomenon as it is said to appear to the *Communicators* themselves ; he does this on page 400 of *Proc.* xiii. (A portion is quoted above on page 243). And in the next few pages he goes on to indicate his own independent view of what is occurring,—giving a detailed description which my own smaller experience, as far as it goes, tends in a general way to confirm. Readers interested in these particulars may here conveniently refer to further remarks on the subject in Chapter XI.

Further Details

In the old days Mrs. Piper sat upright in her chair, with head somewhat bowed and eyes closed, and with both hands available for holding objects or a hand of the sitter. Now her head reclines throughout on a cushion, with her face turned away. The right hand alone is active, being engaged nearly all the time in writing, with intervals of what looks like listening. The dramatic activity of the hand is very remarkable : it is full of intelligence, and can be described as more like an intelligent person than a hand (cf. pp. 272 and 313). It turns itself to the sitter when it wants to be spoken to by him ; but for the most part, when not writing, it turns itself away from the sitter, as if receiving communications from outside, which it then proceeds to write down ; going back to space—*i.e.* directing itself to a part of the room where nobody is—for further information and supplementary intelligence, as necessity arises (cf. p. 134).

When Mrs. Piper in trance wrote a name in the old days—as Phinuit did sometimes—the writing was usually mirror-writing ; but sometimes she wrote a name on paper held to her forehead, so that the pencil was turned towards her face : in that case the writing was ordinary. If this should happen to have been so consistently, it is curious. But now that Rector writes, voluminously, the mirror-writing only crops up occasionally ; and usually the only reversal consists in giving the letters of a name in inverted order, *e.g.* *Knarf* instead of *Frank*.

One other point deserves to be here mentioned :—

In the days of Phinuit considerable facility was shown in dealing with strangers. Persons introduced anonymously had their relations enumerated, and their family affairs referred to, in a remarkably quick and clever way : so much so that they sometimes thought that their special case must have been " got up " beforehand. The facility for dealing with strangers in this way is now much less marked. The introduction of a stranger now makes things slow and laborious, and is on the whole discouraged; for although the old characteristics continue to some extent, the tests now given are mainly of a different kind. The early procedure was useful at the beginning, and it continued useful for a good many years till a case for investigation was firmly established; but it must have seemed tedious to prolong that method further, so the group of controls associated with Rector assured Dr. Hodgson that they would take the trance in hand and develop it on better and higher lines.

As to how far the change is an improvement, there have been at times some differences of opinion; but in view of the remarkable tests recently given under what, though of several years' standing, may be called the new régime,—tests which have been and are being dissected out by Mr. Piddington,—there can be but little doubt about the reality of the improvement now.

CHAPTER XX

THE ISAAC THOMPSON CONTROL

I SHALL first take as an example of the present style of communication a continuation of the case of the Isaac Thompson family, which is referred to on pp. 218 and 225.

Members of this family had made the acquaintance of Mrs. Piper, as there stated, during her stay with us in Liverpool in 1890. In the interim, in 1903, Isaac Thompson had died, and they were anxious to get into communication with him if possible.

The first attempt at reaching this control through Mrs. Piper occurred during a business visit of the son, Edwin Thompson, to America in 1906; when Dr. Hodgson introduced him as a stranger—not by name— to Mrs. Piper in trance at her house near Boston.

The effort was, I consider, not really successful; partly in all probability owing to the inexperience of the sitter. The position is a very difficult one. He had had no previous experience of the sittings; because in 1889, when Mrs. Piper was in Liverpool, he was only eight years old. Besides, the character of the sittings had changed, and the writing of Rector is not at all easy for a novice to read.

Suffice it therefore to say that Edwin Thompson was introduced anonymously by Dr. Hodgson after the trance had begun on Monday, 11th December 1905, at Boston. Messages purported to come from his father, who seemed to wonder how his son had "managed to find him." It was however a poor sitting, and evidentially is best treated as nearly blank.

Undoubtedly there ought to have been another sitting without delay, to clear up this unsatisfactory interview, which clearly established nothing whatever; though I believe that Mr. E. Thompson is on the whole more satisfied with it than these remarks of mine would suggest; but unfortunately he had to return to England immediately, and at the next sitting he was not present. From some points of view—however unfortunate it undoubtedly was—this absence of any connecting link at ensuing sittings held by Dr. Hodgson or others in America may be held to strengthen the evidence, provided anything further was obtained—as it was; since now the facts could hardly be supposed to be obtained from the sitter; American strangers naturally knowing nothing about the family, and Dr. Hodgson being a complete stranger to them all, except E. T., whose slight acquaintance he had only just made.

The sitter on 12th December 1905 was a Miss M., who the same evening sent a special delivery letter to Dr. Hodgson conveying a message entrusted to her by the control George Pelham. She wrote :—

> "'There was a message for you,' George saith. 'Tell Hodgson
> that name the gentleman in the spirit tried to get was Agnes.'
> They said you would know, and it was the day before."

This evidently refers to a name "Anna" attempted near the end of the omitted sitting. The name Agnes is quite appropriate—being the name of a daughter—and would have been jumped at by Edwin Thompson if it had occurred while he was present as sitter. It is noteworthy that "Agnes" was a name that Phinuit in the old days had always boggled over, pretending he could not pronounce it ; his best attempt being something like Annese or Anyese, see vol. vi., p. 478 ; but when taken unawares he could pronounce it well enough, though he quickly changed it to Adnes before repeating it. (See p. 509, vol. vi. *Proc.* S.P.R.)

On the next day, 13th December 1905, Dr. Hodgson had a sitting ; when Rector, after script relating to other matters had been obtained, wrote as reported below :—

Sitting with Mrs. Piper in America, 13*th December* 1905. *Present—Dr. R. Hodgson alone.*

Didst thou receive the message from George?

R. H. Yes, last night, thank you.

Have you the influences of the young man's father?

R. H. No.

It seems almost an injustice to us not to have met him once more, as it would be a great help to the communicator himself and all on our side.

R. H. I have explained all to him, and he will send me some articles of his father after he returns to England. He had no more time here, and is already on his way back. He had no opportunity, before leaving home, to know what he ought to do.

We understand, and since the spirit is now waiting with our good and faithful co-worker George [Pelham] we shall after preliminary matters are cleared up listen to what he hath to say.

R. H. I shall be glad.

That young man hath some significant light himself.

(Scrawls were now made, ending "help me.")

R. H. Kindly tell me anything you wish.

I hold this bottle in my hand for identification. . . . Bottle . . in my hand.

R. H. Yes?

I had much to do with them when in your world.

R. H. Who are you?

I used to be address [sic] Dr.   I got.

[He had medical ambitions, and was partner in Thompson &
Capper.   O. J. L.]

(G. P. communicating.)   He is trying very hard.   let him dream
it out H and he will be all right.

If he says anything clearly, congratulate him help him by words
of encouragement only, remember he has nothing or no
one except yourself to attract him here.

R. H. Yes.   Is he the young man's father?

he is surely.   Agnes is his daughter.

R. H. Yes?

So he tells me.

R. H. Shall I talk to him?

Just encourage him a little by telling him who you are etc.
what your object is etc.   It will help him greatly.

R. H. I will explain in answer to your inquiry who I am,—that I am
an old friend of Professor Lodge.

L o d g e.

R. H. Yes.

What my old neighbour in Liv. .

(Excitement in hand which cramps and twists about.)

calm friend   (Between sp.)

Li . .

(Excitement stops the writing again.)

D r u g s . .

Do not go.   Wait for me.

L i v e r s t o o l.

R. H. *Liverpool*, you mean.

I say so.

I say say   I say so   I say so   I say so [sic.] . .

R. H. Yes I understand.

I say so.

Liverstool [Livestool?]

R. H. Liver-pool.

P o o l.   R [R = Rector.]

I live   I live   I had three daughters one son [true]
(scrawls over sheet) . .

I want to help them all all all.   God help me to help them to
understand that I am alive.

R. H. Yes?

I am confused [confussed]   No doubt but I will be better soon

it is so hard to understand.   You look so heavy, a black
cloud comes over you and I can scarcely see you.   Do you
know me?

R. H.   I do not know you personally, but I now know your son who
came with me.   Did you not see the lady in England with
Professor Lodge through whom you are now communicating?   I mean the light?

Oh I cannot tell you yet, wait until I find my way about.

R. H.   Don't . .

Tell me all about yourself first, I want to get acquainted with
you.

R. H.   Yes I will.   Kindly listen.

I'll do my best. because I want to reach my family.   very very
much.

R. H.   I am interested in psychical work and sent Mrs. Piper many
years ago to England,—don't you remember seeing Mrs.
Piper?

Piper?

R. H.   Yes, and the . .

(Perturbation in hand)

Oh yes I remember Piper.   Was Mrs. Piper a Medium, an
American lady?

R. H.   Yes.

Oh yes   Oh yes I do   I do, but I'll find her out and come to
you if it is a possible thing.   What is your name?

R. H.   My name is Hodgson, Richard Hodgson.

Can't you spell it for me?

R. H.   H o d g s o n.

Oh he is telling me   thank you greatly.

Let me think.

I am so anxious to understand all about this then I can talk
with you.

R. H.   Well, now, Mr . .

Where are we?   I left my body some time ago.   Where are
you?

R. H.   This is America where I am now.

America?

R. H.   Yes.

Well well that is very interesting to me.

You are in the body?

R. H.   Yes I am.

Well? happy?

R. H. Yes, both, thank you.

Splendid   I begin to understand.

R. H. Well now I will tell you more about myself and Lodge.

My wife is better thank you   I am watching over them.   but my business will be better in time.   I am trying to take care of it for the children.

R. H. Yes.   Mr . . did you [say] that there were three daughters and one son in the body?

Yes . .

My wife wore *glasses* . . spectacles we called them I think.

R. H. You mentioned her eye trouble.

Oh may be so, it was on my mind.

Who is the lady with my boy?

R. H. I don't know anything about her.

No . .

Well I understand.   I had a business called . .

sounds like D R U G S.

I am helping all I can [this was evidently Rector]

(Hand to Sp. 1.)

he must rest + . . [this is the signature of Imperator]

R. H. I shall be so pleased for you to come again and send any messages you wish to your family.

he will return in a moment friend but I command him to go for a moment.   + R.

(Thump of hand.)

Mrs. . kindly

Your friend George is the very best helper we have.

R. H. I am very grateful to him.

Did his spirit seem any clearer? R.

R. H. Yes I should judge that he will probably be a very clear communicator shortly.

talk with him in general when he comes whether he gives you a chance or not. . . chance or not . . he is very earnest but he does not understand yet our methods.

R. H. No.

I say I shall return and help you.

was very very glad I came.

R. H. Thank you very much.

I could not understand while you were here but I could see him after you left.   T——

R. H.   I understand.

Waking Stage

(During the waking stage Mrs. Piper said)

. . Thompson [sic.] . . with you all.
[This was the first time the name had been mentioned.]
Before I let you go . . you must take this over to Mr. Hodgson.
Tell him . .

R. H.   "Tell him"?

Tell Mrs. Thompson I'm very glad to be here.   It is better so.
I am grateful for all God has done to help me.
. . the truth will find its way.
Farewell.   fare thee well . . peace . . .

(Pause.)

There were two gentlemen resembling each other.   One was
George, the other was another man looked something like
him.

This is an improvement on what had been obtained
at the sitting before, and indicates considerable anxiety
on the part of the Isaac Thompson control to manifest
himself, since this time he had to overcome the difficulty
of talking to a complete stranger; and save for the
mention of my name as a common friend of Hodgson
and himself, it is doubtful if anything could have been
got.   The excitement which the hand displays, as here
at the mention of Lodge and Liverpool, is characteristic.
On such occasions it twists and squirms about and
frequently breaks the point of the pencil by pressure
against the paper.   It is as if the nerves conveyed too
strong a stimulus to the muscles, so that until the excitement abates no writing can go on (cf. also pp. 313
and 314).

The bottles and drugs mentioned are symbolic of his
profession.   (See p. 525, *Proc.* vol. vi., and cf. a similar
case near foot of page 554, vol. vi.)   The things said
are all true and appropriate.

One of the most curious episodes is the way in which

Mrs. Piper's name is introduced.   R. Hodgson says, in order to introduce himself,

R. H. I am interested in psychical work and sent Mrs. Piper many
      years ago to England,—don't you remember seeing Mrs.
      Piper?

      Piper?

R. H. Yes, and the . .

                (Perturbation in hand.)

      Oh yes I remember Piper.   Was Mrs. Piper a Medium an
      American lady?

R. H. Yes.

      Oh yes   oh yes I do   I do, but I'll find her and come to you if
      it is a possible thing.   What is your name?

R. H. My name is Hodgson, Richard Hodgson.

      Can't you spell it for me?

R. H. H o d g s o n.

      Oh he is telling me   thank you greatly."

The perturbation in hand thus begins again when the name Piper is remembered, and then the Thompson control speaks of her as a medium he had known, and says he will try to find her now in order to communicate.

When it is remembered that the whole thing is being obtained through Mrs. Piper's body, the curiosity of the position is obvious.

The sentence "oh he is telling me, thank you greatly" signifies that whereas the Thompson control had been trying to understand with difficulty what Dr. Hodgson was saying, he was now being told on his own side by G. P. or Rector, whom he thanks;—all this by-play being, now as often, automatically recorded by the writing hand.

The way in which he receives the information that Hodgson is in America,—where in 1884 Isaac Thompson had been with me alone for nine weeks,—is also very natural; and his inquiry as to whether Hodgson is a living person or not is curious.

18

It is quite true that Mrs. Thompson wore spectacles, though of course this was within Mrs. Piper's own knowledge.   In the previous set (p. 524, vol. vi.) a sister of Mr. Thompson's was represented as unfamiliar with them and wanting them taken off.   This also was a correct apprehension of fact at the date referred to.

"The lady with my boy" may well refer to his son's engagement : though that was not in Mrs. Piper's normal knowledge, and presumably not in Dr. Hodgson's either.   But of course this sort of thing can be guessed ; and E. T. in his own sitting had clearly hinted it.

In fact although there is nothing very much obtained, and little that can be called really evidential, because of Mrs. Piper's previous normal knowledge,—provided any clue to the particular family had been conveyed during Edwin Thompson's sitting, in the course of which, though he had certainly not given his name, I observe that he had mentioned the name "Theodora" and also spoken of "the business,"—there is nothing that is inapplicable or foreign to the person represented, or in the least untrue, as soon as communication really began ; and there is much in the dramatic details that I find distinctly interesting.

Waking Stage

While coming out of trance Mrs. Piper usually speaks, or rather mutters, at intervals ; and her words are taken down, or such of them as can be heard.   It is worth while to quote one record of these ejaculations—which sometimes convey interesting residual information,—and I select the following as a fairly typical case of an unimportant and unevidential but characteristic coming to.

Notes intruded in square brackets are added merely

in order to place the reader in the same sort of position as regards understanding the significance of these subconscious utterances as a recorder finds himself in after an experience of many sittings.

I am aware that such explanations may irritate a certain group of people who have been all their lives familiar with trance speeches of one kind or another; but in the first place I must beg them to observe that when I explain things I am not assuming ignorance on the part of specialists. It would be impossible to write in an explanatory fashion on any branch of even the most orthodox science if thereby one ran the risk of offending specialists. In ordinary subjects it is safe silently to assume that experienced people will understand that their knowledge is taken for granted. Besides, trances are by no means identical : each has distinctive features. Mrs. Piper's trance has itself undergone modification in the course of the nineteen years since I first knew her ; and it may be useful to quote the kind of phrases employed by her during recovery—if only as a psychological study. They are seldom identical, but they have a strong family likeness. Here then they are, on an occasion after one of the sittings with the Isaac Thompson family :—

> "I saw you before. It is fearful. [This means that she dislikes changing from her trance state and coming back to ordinary surroundings.]
>
> They are going away. It's awful. Too bad. Snap. [This refers to a sensation which she calls a snap in the head, which nearly always precedes a return to consciousness. Sometimes it heralds almost a sudden return ; and she is always more conscious after a snap than she was before ; but often it takes two snaps to bring her completely to. What the snap is I do not know, but I expect it is something physiological. It is not audible to others, though Mrs. Piper half seems to expect it to be so.]

What are all the people doing?

[Probably some of the sitters were moving about and leaving the room, under the mistaken impression that the snap meant that interest was over.]

I saw a man in the light, which looked like Mr. Thompson. Kept waving his hand. The man with the cross was helping him out.

["The man with the cross" is intended to signify Imperator.]

The moon was shining [or it may have been the 'sun.' It only signifies that her recent surroundings have been bright and luminous.]

Has an old lady with him. She is helping him read something. I could see his face perfectly.

Noise. [probably something going on outside.] They were talking to me. I came in on a cord, a silver cord. They were trying to tell me something about the children in the body. Lovely place.

Buzzing in my head. Another snap.

Miss Thompson. I thought you were small. Looking through opera glasses at wrong end. You grew larger. Did you hear my head snap? It breaks.

I forgot where we were sitting.

Why Mrs. Thompson, I didn't know you were there. My cold."

[Mrs. Piper was troubled with a cold at this time. Her intelligence was now normal.]

In further illustration of the waking stage, showing how similar it was in 1906 to what it is now, and as a further description of the curious "snap" sensation, I subjoin an extract from the termination of a sitting with Henry James, Junior, and Mr. Dorr in America in 1906.

I thought you were a stranger.
Well, did you hear my head snap?

H. J. Jr.   No.

Didn't hear it? It is a funny sound. Don't you hear it at all? Sounds like wheels clicking together and then snaps. There it is again.

G. B. D.   Now you are really back.

CHAPTER XXI

GENERAL REMARKS ON THE PIPER SITTINGS

FOR a further account of these sittings my paper in vol. xxiii. of the *Proceedings* of the Society for Psychical Research must be referred to. It would take too much space to quote further here. I must be satisfied with a few comments.

It is noteworthy how natural it is for a sitter to ignore all the normal knowledge which Mrs. Piper must undoubtedly possess, and to treat her as a separate individual when in the trance state. Her controls exhibit the same tendency ; and, while of course nothing evidential can be made to depend upon the supposition, it does appear to be really true that that knowledge has little or no influence on the knowledge shown by the controls.

I surmised this at an earlier stage—as recorded on page 202—and subsequent experience has only confirmed the impression.

As a minor instance of this fact may be mentioned the surprise and eagerness shown by the Isaac Thompson control when after some delay he was told that Mrs. Isaac Thompson was present at the first sitting subsequently held in her house in Liverpool. For of course Mrs. Piper had known perfectly well the people likely to be present at the sitting, and had seen them assemble ;

it was no news to her.   But indeed everything tends to
show that during thorough trance the normal consciousness is in abeyance.   And, although it is true that we
cannot claim anything as evidential when it comes out
in the trance if it had ever been known to Mrs. Piper, I
myself am unable to trace much, if any, connexion
between the trance knowledge and her normal knowledge.   For instance, a sitter introduced by name is no
more likely to have his name mentioned during a sitting
than one who is introduced as an anonymous stranger.
I make a general statement of this kind believing that
careful analysis will bear it out, and as a challenge to
any one who will bestow time and labour upon the work
of analysing the records from this point of view.   It
seems to me a desirable piece of work for someone to
undertake.

Of course a sceptic may say that this kind of *kenosis*
is due to mere cunning; but the time for suspicion of
that kind is over with most of us investigators.   It is
a genuine piece of psychological information that we
now desire, not anything analogous to detective work.
Detective work is necessary in its proper time and place,
but there are cases which have run that gauntlet, and
require more advanced treatment.   The Piper case is
one of them.

When I speak of "Mrs. Piper's normal knowledge,"
I mean of course knowledge acquired in her ordinary
state.   Knowledge acquired while in the trance state is
certainly reproducible when in that state, but it appears
not to be accessible in her ordinary state; and *vice versa*.
I do not call that "normal knowledge."

The controls themselves feel that they have no
direct access to the normal Mrs. Piper; so, if they want
to communicate with her, they must utilise some other

agency,—for instance, they send messages through her own daughter, with whom they occasionally communicate during trance.   To illustrate this, I extract a small fragment from a quantity of serious conversation which took place between them and Dr. Hodgson's executors soon after his death.   Mr. Dorr was conducting the sitting and speaking the remarks labelled G.B.D.

G. B. D. We are anxious that the light in the future should not go
adrift and astray, and anxious that past relations should not
be wholly interrupted by any change of environment or other.
     Well, no one could be more anxious about these
things or more concerned than we ourselves are,
and it hath disturbed us not a little to see the conditions
on the earthly side.   We are not quite pleased with them,
because the light cannot know itself, it cannot understand
itself.   It is shut off from communication with us on our
side and it must remain in ignorance of the methods which
we pursue in our endeavours to reach the mortals on the
earthly side.
G. B. D. But through the daughter, Alta, I have felt that you might in
a sense reach her.
     Yes, that is the only way.

I do not adduce this as evidence, but as illustrative of how the phenomenon represents itself; for when it does so consistently it is reasonable to suppose that something true is indicated.

It will be observed in many of the records how natural it is for a sitter, or for the experimenter in charge, to challenge a "control" to furnish some evidence of his identity, or to demand from him a sudden answer to a specific question.

It is quite natural, and I suppose inevitable: but that it also is to some extent unreasonable, must be admitted. Trivial domestic incidents are not constantly in one's thoughts, and only when in a reminiscent and holiday mood, or under the stimulus of friendly chat, does any vivid recollection of such incidents normally occur.

It is a common experience that characteristic touches, specific phrases and sparkling sayings, are most likely to come out in the give and take of lively conversation. Silent and solitary brooding, though it may generate valuable and even brilliant ideas in a few cases, does not as a rule lead to anything specially personal, or identifying; rather the contrary,—such ideas seem to spring up impersonally, or to be supplied from outside, so to speak.

It is proverbially difficult to control thoughts to order, and a communicator suddenly asked to remember an identifying circumstance, or to send an appropriate message, may feel rather as a person feels when set in front of a phonograph and told to "say something brilliant for posterity." Under these conditions any one with the gift might compose some half-doggerel verse perhaps, or might remember some poetry more or less accurately,—and indeed that is what it appears the controls sometimes actually do—but usually there would be hesitation, requests for delay, and fishing for suggestions,—something like what we find in the records. The controls unfortunately cannot be assisted by the give and take of friendly and stimulating conversation; for, under the conditions of a sitting, the intercourse on our side is nearly all "take" and very little "give." It is admittedly dangerous for a sitter to talk freely, because the conditions then become "loose," and more may be inadvertently given away than was intended, so that thereafter nothing obtained, however otherwise good, can be considered evidential. But then—it must also be admitted—no conversation can be in the full sense stimulating or satisfactory if its animation is hampered by a constant desire to withhold information, lurking in the background.

In order to be human a conversation should be whole-hearted and free from *arrières pensées* on both sides : but under evidential conditions that seems quite impossible. It is one of the many disadvantages under which the investigation of the subject inevitably labours.

Trivial Recollections, and Relics

It will by some people—who might otherwise be in favour of some form of spiritistic hypothesis—be thought absurd that reference should be made under such circum-stances to trifles like ordered but undelivered pictures, and to trivialities like the possession of a handkerchief or other relic. The usual excuse is that these things are mentioned for purposes of identification ; but though there may be some truth in that view, there is in my judgment more reason than that for such incidents ; and they are not contradictory of the notion of survival. The fate of objects once regarded with affection, or even interest, and possessing any kind of personal association, does not seem to have suddenly become a matter of indifference. Scattered through all the sittings are innumerable instances of this sort of curious memory of and interest in trifles ; so that it would be merely tedious to refer to pages where they occur. Every experienced sitter knows that such references are the commonest of all. What is the explanation? I am not prepared with a full explanation ; but, granted the most completely spiritistic hypothesis, it would appear that the state after death is not a sudden plunge into a stately, dignified, and specially religious atmosphere. The environment, like the character, appears to be much more like what it is here than some folk imagine. This may be due to the effort and process incidental to the condition of semi-return, under which alone communication is possible : it appears to involve something less than full consciousness. But it goes rather further than this, since a few of the controls when recently deceased (a pious old lady in particular is in my mind) have said that the surroundings were more "secular" than they expected ; they have indeed expressed themselves as if a little disappointed, though they nearly always say that the surroundings are better than they are here. Anyhow, there appears to be no violent or sudden change of nature ; and so any one who has cared for trinkets may perhaps after a fashion care for them still.

But there must be more than that even. Objects *appear* to serve as attractive influences, or nuclei, from which information may be clairvoyantly gained. It appears as if we left traces of ourselves, not only on our bodies, but on many other things with which we have been subordinately associated, and that these traces can thereafter be detected by a sufficiently sensitive person. This opens a large subject which I have touched upon once or twice already in other papers—never with any feeling of certainty or security—and which requires careful handling lest its misunderstanding pave the way for mere superstition.

But to return to common sense, and without assuming anything of this kind, even hypothetically, how do we know that we are right in speaking of some things as trifles and other things as important ? What is our scale or standard of value ?

No one expects people to be wholly indifferent as to the posthumous disposal of their property, provided it amounts to several thousand pounds. They make careful wills, and would, if they knew, be perhaps displeased if the provisions were not adhered to, or if their final will was lost.

Very well, on what scale shall we estimate property, and how shall we measure its value?

It is conceivable that, seen from another side, little personal relics may awaken memories more poignant than those associated with barely recollected stocks and shares.

That at any rate is the kind of idea which naturally suggests itself in connexion with the subject. Our terrestrial estimate of the comparative importance of things is not likely to be cosmically sufficient or perennially true.

However that may be, it is clear that the various Piper controls do not estimate the importance of property by any standard dependent on pounds sterling. As a variant on old letters, old lockets, and other rubbish, in which Phinuit seemed to take some interest, I once gave him a five-pound note. It was amusing to see how at first he tried to read it—in his usual way by applying it to the top of the medium's head ;—and then on realising the sort of thing it was, how he crumpled it up and flung it into a corner with a grunt, holding out his hand for something of interest. Needless to say, I did not share in this estimate of value, and, after the sitting, was careful to rescue the despised piece of paper from its perilous position.

CHAPTER XXII

THE MYERS CONTROL

NOW let us enter upon the episodes where F. W. H. Myers was supposed to be controlling, or at least communicating, while I was present. I shall begin, however, with communications received not through Mrs. Piper, but through other mediums. Most of the Piper-Myers messages were obtained, and must be dealt with, by Mr. Piddington ; because they often involve cross-correspondences, which belong to his department of the work. Moreover, in the recent series of sittings I had but few conversations with the Myers control as modified or represented by Mrs. Piper—what we call the "Piper-Myers" or Myers$_P$. I fear I did not give him many chances, and one day was rather rebuked by Rector for not affording the Myers$_P$ control more opportunity for utterance. This was because I usually had something else ready that I wanted to try. So neither from Myers$_P$ nor from Hodgson$_P$ did I get very much in these recent sittings.

And of course in the old days, 1889–90, both had been in full vigour of life.

But it so happens that long before Mrs. Piper arrived, and very soon after Mr. Myers's death, I had had a couple of unexpected and exceptional sittings with the well-known Mrs. Thompson, at that time still living at Hampstead. (It is hardly necessary to say that she has no connexion with the Mrs. Isaac Thompson referred to as a sitter with Mrs. Piper in previous chapters.) She had suspended sitting altogether ; but she kindly allowed myself and my wife to sit twice with her,—she said she felt impelled to do so,—on two occasions when she happened to be visiting friends in or near Birmingham.

Mrs. Thompson was so well acquainted with Mr. Myers and his family that no evidential importance can be attached to remarks and messages concerning that family, obtained through her mediumship, however natural they may be. These are therefore all omitted. Reference to trivial facts and domestic affairs are good as evidence only in the case of unknown strangers : in other cases they are only of use as contributing to the dramatic character and personal expression of the whole. From this point of view I regret some omissions, which nevertheless have been considered necessary.

Mrs. Thompson's trance is an easy trance, not so complete or striking as Mrs. Piper's, but it is a state of suspension, or partial suspension, of ordinary consciousness, and is accompanied by a change of voice and manner.

In the sitting which follows, " Myers " was represented as controlling and speaking for part of the time, but the sittings began with the " Nelly " control, and when the Myers control is not manifestly intended to be speaking, the words may be taken as emanating either from Nelly or from one or other of Mrs. Thompson's ordinary controls —it does not matter which, since I am not studying Mrs. Thompson's phenomena, but am giving what appear to be messages from or about Myers, who died on 17 January 1901.

FIRST THOMPSON SITTING AT EDGBASTON

The first appearance of a Myers control in my experience was on Thursday, 19 February 1901, that is to say just about a month after F. W. H. Myers's decease. Present, only myself and wife with Mrs. Thompson. At 6 o'clock the control "Nelly" began. She had been incredulous about his death, and indeed had declared that she could not find him anywhere and did not believe that he had come over. See J. G. P.'s paper, *Proceedings*, vol. xviii. p. 240, also 238. But now she was just beginning to admit the fact :—

Tuesday, 19th February 1901. *Sitting with Mrs. Thompson at* 225 *Hagley Road, Birmingham. Notes by O. J. L. and M. L.*

6.0 *p.m.* (*"Nelly" control speaking.*)

> I was allowed to go on his birthday to see him. He will have plenty of work to do, for he has promised to send messages to 74 people.
>
> All the people said he was dead, but I did not believe it; and though I saw him, I thought he only came over for his birthday like in a vision. But I see him now. It *is* the truth, it *is* the truth (excitedly). Let us see if he can talk sense. He was talking on the platform with you. It was at a station by a racecourse. [I had met him at Liverpool; seen him off from the landing stage to America. But this is unimportant.] He will come when he is more wakened up — before 9 o'clock. You be ready at 25 minutes to 9. He will be awake by then. He would rather think and realise for a little space by himself. He is sensible, for a spirit.
>
> Before you came, mother was praying. She said "Come and tell the truth for truth's sake."
>
> (At 6.30 Mrs. Thompson came to.)

Then we had dinner, and at 8.30 the Control "Nelly" appeared again, saying

What is the matter with the little girl's throat? her ear seems to have made her throat ache. One of yours—a twinkle one.

[This is of course a mere friendly interlude. One of my twin daughters was often troubled with ear-ache about this time.]

(Here there was an incipient attempt at a Myers control, and an incident at a Club was referred to. Then another control said)

Do you know he feels like the note-taker, not like the spirit that has to speak. I think he will speak presently.

(A short interval of apparent discomfort, and then "Myers" purported to communicate)

Lodge, it is not as easy as I thought in my impatience. Gurney says I am getting on first rate. But I am short of breath.

Oh, Lodge, it is like looking at a misty picture. I can distinctly feel I ought to be taking a note of it. I do not feel as if I were speaking, but it is best to record it all.

Tell them I am more stupid than some of those I had to deal with. Oh, Lodge, what is it when I see you? Was it the Albemarle Club we went to when I talked about —— oh, it leaves off.

Sidgwick knows I am with him. He said that he saw me in the morning of —— Oh dear, it always leaves off in the interesting places.

I can hear myself using Rosa Thompson's voice.

I want to convince Sidgwick. He says "Myers, now we are together, you convince me that I am sending my messages, and that she is not getting them from us some way." He still wants me to show him. He says he saw me in the morning of the day he went to Trevelyan. He met Trevelyan, and he saw me first. I am trying to show him the way. It is funny to feel myself talking when it is not myself talking. It is not my whole self talking. When I am awake I know where I am. Do you remember the day I was with you here? When I went home that day I was ill. I had such a bad night. It is in my diary. It was in May, I think. I was very ill. [This about Trevelyan seems to refer to an incident dealt with by Mr. Piddington. See *Proc.* vol. xviii. pp. 239, 241.]

[The description of the feeling of the control while engaged in communication agrees closely with that of Dr. Hodgson based upon his experience of Mrs. Piper. See for instance vol. xiii. pp. 366, 380, 404, 405. And the forgetfulness immediately following may be compared with statements in Chap. XVIII. above, especially p. 252.]

O. J. L. Do you want to say anything about the Society?

What Society?

O. J. L. You remember the S.P.R.

Do not think that I have forgotten. But I have. I have forgotten just now. Let me think. You know, Lodge, when you have wanted a thing thirty or forty years, and at last got it, you do not think of much else beside. Let me think, and bit by bit give it you. I used to get better evidence when I let them say what they wanted to say.

They tell me it was my best love that Society. They will help me.

What did Battersea say about it?

O. J. L. I do not know.

I am going to talk to you clearly and very distinctly in April. I do not know my Mother's name now. . . .

What James gave me to make me sleep did not do me any good.

There is plenty of good matter in those papers that I left . . . if it is gone through. You remember the discussion there was over Hyslop's paper and its length? If it is put in too much detail, there is too much of it; and yet if you put it fully it is there for those who want it full; and you can pick out the points too. . . .

I was confused when I came here. I groped my way as if through passages, before I knew I was dead. I thought I had lost my way in a strange town, and I groped my way along the passage. And even when I saw people that I knew were dead, I thought they were only visions.

I have not seen Tennyson yet by the way. [Cf. p. 295.]

I am going to be bold and prophesy already. I am going to see you in April. I am going to know who I am by then.

O. J. L. And will you then read what you wrote in the envelope?

What envelope?—I shall be told.

Ernest does not mind now. What do they mix me up with him for? (Jocularly.) Do they think I want to shine in his glory?

[This was evidently a reference to the *Times* obituary notice, which I had written, but to which some one in the *Times* office appended a supplementary statement that F. W. H. M. had been a joint translator of Homer together with Walter Leaf and Andrew Lang; whereas it is public and general knowledge that this was only true of his brother Ernest.] (Cf. incident on p. 146.)

I wanted you to do for me what I did for Sidgwick. [*i.e.* write a notice in the Society's *Proceedings*; see p. 342 below.]

O. J. L. I am going to; and so are Richet and James.

Ah, Richet: Yes, Richet knows me; and James will do it well.

I never finished those letters I was writing—letters to be published.

[Probably meaning the book *Human Personality*.]

[Then the control seemed to change, and it went on]:—

He says he must stay and try and help. He says, Bless him when he has so much to do. He says " Brothers I have none excepting Lodge." He wants Lodge to be President if he dare spare the work; but he says " Do not rope yourself, but keep the group, keep the group together. It will soon take care of itself."

O. J. L. We are trying to get Rayleigh.

That would be splendid, but that is too good to hope for. I think it will be you. (Cf. p. 341.) Thank you for being helpful to him. You have helped him. Man's sympathy is more helpful than anything else, and with sympathy everything slips into place. Among the things which are not evidential you get things which are. They must take it all. Those that seek only the evidential things will not get them.

There are so many he would like to help. He promised, and he will have to.

When he comes in April he will remember a great deal more. He will remember what he wrote for you in the envelope.

(Trance ends about 10.30 p.m.)

19

The impersonation at this sitting was really a remarkably vivid and lifelike one. It occurred only a month after the death of F. W. H. Myers, and the state of confusion in which the Myers control found itself seemed very natural. Indeed it would be difficult for me to invent an experience or a communication more reasonable, under the supposed circumstances, or more what we might suppose to be "natural," than what we actually got. The necessity for still "convincing Sidgwick" struck us as amusingly characteristic; so did several other little traits, such as that Myers "felt as if he ought to be taking notes"—a point on which F. W. H. M. was always specially insistent. And as to his temporary forgetfulness of the existence of the S.P.R., though it will probably be pounced upon as an absurdity by scoffers, and though it was of course quite unexpected, yet even that struck us at the time as humanly natural and interesting. And indeed so it does now. (Compare Hodgson's statement on p. 252.) With the portions omitted, and everything taken into account, this sitting seems to me about the best of the Myers sittings in which I have been immediately concerned. Without being strictly evidential, it was in fact as convincing as anything that could be imagined of that kind.

This was in February 1901. A further communication was promised for April, but no opportunity for another sitting came until May 8th, and then it came quite unexpectedly and without being arranged for. In fact at that time it was unlikely that any sitting would occur, since we had all been definitely told that Mrs. Thompson's sittings were suspended,—or rather that they were intended henceforth to cease.

Second Thompson Sitting at Edgbaston

On May 8th, 1901, Mrs. Thompson happened to come to Birmingham again, to see her connexions there; and she incidentally visited us at our temporary home in the Hagley Road.

I made the following contemporary notes, and it seems to me worth while to reproduce them as a representation of the circumstances of the case at this time.

From O. J. L.'s Note-book, 9 May, 1901

After dinner Mrs. Thompson spontaneously asked Mrs. Lodge to take her up into my study, saying as she went upstairs that she felt only half conscious, and as if she were going off.

Upstairs we three alone sat and talked for some time.

At last "Nelly" appeared and notes began: Mrs. Lodge taking them as well as myself. Mrs. Lodge spoke no word during the trance from first to last.

The sitting was dim and unsatisfactory, and in most respects apparently at the time a failure. It lasted about an hour and a half, one continuous trance, and at the end Mrs. Thompson was much agitated; not exhausted, but weepy; saying how much she disliked the idea of coming back to consciousness and leaving the conditions in which she had just been. She said she had no recollection of what had been said; and this appeared to be the case. She also told me, before the sitting began, that of late she had been quite unconscious of any communications, that is to say, she could not remember their contents, but that she was under the impression that during the last month or so she had had three or four trances when no one was there, at different times, and that once she found herself waking on the floor with a feeling of great satisfaction and contentment.

She further said that the sudden cutting off of all attempts at communication had been a great blow to her, and seemed to upset her physically to some extent. Also that she had been promised something for her birthday, April 22nd,—evidently connecting it with me. "Nelly" had indeed promised me a sitting in April [as recorded in last sitting], though not for any particular date. But it seems she had expected it on the 22nd. However I had no sitting in April—nothing till this May 8th.

The difficulties of clear utterance at times rendered it necessary for me to help the ideas out, or anticipate them as far as I could. My notes aim at recording the sense of what was intended, and can only be of interest to those who understand.

Additional Note written on 11 May, 1901

The above was dictated before copying the notes, and gives my contemporary impression of the sitting; but on reading over the notes I find them better than I expected; and now think that though at the time it seemed a bad sitting to everybody concerned, it is not really bad; though the utterances were so feeble and confused that to a novice it would have been nearly all gibberish. A little gibberish remains undeciphered in places; but is recorded in case any meaning can be attached to it. I do not think it is gibberish really,— only as heard and taken down. It probably had sense if it could have been heard and understood, though most likely not at all important sense.

Second Sitting with Mrs. Thompson at 225 *Hagley Road,*
Birmingham, 8 *May,* 1901, *from* 9.0 *till* 10.30 *p.m.*
Present—O. J. L. and M. L., both taking notes.

(Nelly speaking.)

> P'fessor Lodge, what is that umbrella they have put up and
> made it all dark ? I wish they would take it away.
> (Further indications followed that she had tried to communi-
> cate but found it dark.)
> [This evidently refers to the suspension of sittings ; Mrs.
> Thompson, for some private reason, had declined to
> sit for the last few months, and only did it now as
> a special favour, and because she felt internally urged
> to do so.]
> I have not seen Mr. Myers, not once ; I have not seen him since
> they put that umbrella up.

Nelly then appealed to me to try and believe her and receive her
statements sympathetically and not with an undercurrent of suspicion,
explaining that such undercurrent befogged her, and that she could
give me better things if I was sympathetic. I asked her not to regard
me as in any way hostile, and she said " No, I don't feel like that to
any of the Marshall family." This remark was not amplified, nor did
it seem understood by Nelly herself.

It is perhaps worth noting incidentally that my grandmother and
my wife's father were both Marshalls, though no relation whatever to
each other, nor to Frederic Myers's relations of that name.

Nelly then sent a few messages to Mr. Piddington, and incidentally
remarked that she felt as if in a pound in the middle of a field, and
as if she could not see clearly the people on the other side of the en-
closure, and that communication was very difficult and not clear to-day.

Then followed some convulsive movements and a sort of internal
colloquy of which only fragments were audible. They appeared
however to indicate a confused conversation between Nelly and Mr.
Myers, Nelly asking him to " come in," and Mr. Myers saying that
he had been told not,—that he had understood the communications
were suspended for a time.

But this was only an impression gathered from the confused
mutterings. A further impression was that Mr. Myers mistrusted the

presence of a third person, and was being reassured by Nelly that it
was only Mrs. Lodge :—

> It's only Mrs. Lodge whom you love.
> No I don't love her.
> It's only Lodge's wife, who will help.
> More than I anticipated much more.

With other barely intelligible fragments of internal colloquy.

Ultimately the conversation with me began again, but in a very
halting and indistinct fashion—no marked personality at all—somewhat
as if Nelly were half giving messages and half personating Mr. Myers,
and doing both badly and with difficulty.

The following however are my notes of what was said :—

> Mr. Myers is worrying about something connected with Mr.
>   Sidgwick, something that was not understood or that was
>   not put down.   He [H. S.] had some Jews in College and
>   he could not do it on a Saturday.
> Tell Fielding that he is doing something that is waste of
>   time.   *The Times* said something about it and said it was
>   valuable.
> [But I understood the communicator to mean that it was
>   not.   I do not know what work is being referred to.]
> The first shock to my dearest hopes.
> So stupid not to tell them what I wished.
> The time was gradually passing.
> You know Sidgwick and I had many disappointments like this
>   [when communications would not come clear?]
> I thought I should do better, but I cannot.
> We had many, a year, a hundred, at Newcastle.   Bitter
>   disappointments.
> But when I can give pound　　[muddle]
> Given a grain and found as much as would have been, for
>   Sidgwick, in that hundred.
> Mrs. Sidgwick was cold on a brick floor.
> A hundred results nil.
> It is true Lodge it is true.
> I tried on the Sunday with—
> I saw the receptacle, but not this one.   It was Hodgson and
>   Smith and I.   We were all in my room together, and I
>   told him.
> I told him I would find no difficulty, if he were in difficulty, in
>   putting things straight ;

But it is.

[Meaning that it was much harder than he thought.]

I thought I knew better than be such a miserable failure. I
thought I would come and read it.

[Apparently or *possibly* meaning the sealed letter.]

I had gone away. I thought I was not to communciate now.
It is not the time now.

I wished you would all write to me. I was so far away. I
pined to hear from you all.

My philosophy did not help me much.

I feel just as lonely. Lodge, it is just as they say, you grope
in fog and darkness.

I do not know, when I come to talk to you, about the other
side.

But I must do as I promised.

I feel I am selfish still.

I wanted it for my own satisfaction.

Further indications that the conditions under which he was were
not altogether to his liking, not at least when trying to communicate;
and also further statements that he could not very clearly realise the
conditions on that side when he was trying to communicate, and that
now he was wishful to pass on and up and not stay to redeem his
promises.

Is the typhoid better?

What are you doing in this place?

[Apparently meaning strange and unfamiliar surroundings,
the temporary house in Birmingham which I had taken,
and which he had never seen.]

I had plenty of this kind of unsatisfactory experience [meaning
bad sittings.]

James went with me.

I seemed to be taken from all my pain and suffering into
light.

I hardly like to tell you what I wanted to do, it seems so
selfish now, but I wanted to go and talk to Tennyson,
whom I idolised. (Cf. p. 288.) But I was told that I must
suffer for my promises, and then I could have what I
wanted.

I wish I had not been taken so far; it makes it difficult to
communicate.

Then—referring as I thought at the time, to Mrs. Thompson's unexpected and undesired trance which she had told me of, when she woke up and found herself on the floor, but perhaps more probably referring to one of the incidents mentioned by Mr. Piddington in *Proc.*, vol. xviii. pp. 147, 148—the control went on,

> I did not throw her on the floor.
>
> It was Talbot—Talbot Forbes.
>
> It was not I. I wanted her to know I was there, but Talbot only wanted her to tell his Mother.
>
> Why does she [meaning apparently the Medium] pray to me and beg me to come, when she knows I want to be cleansed from earth first? I do not want her to fetch me back at all times.
>
> They keep on calling me. I am wanted everywhere. I hear them calling, and I cannot tell who it is at first.
>
> They tell me I am wanted. But I want to concentrate in a few places, or in one place, and not to be split up.
>
> Do appeal to them not to break me up so, and leave me not clear in one spot.
>
> I am only one now, and the noise of you all calling makes me feel I cannot. Someone is calling me now.
>
> What did Miss Edmunds want with me? On Friday she called.
>
> [A letter from America referring to this, May 3rd, arrived later.]
>
> Tell Richet I shall meet him in Rome. I shall speak to him in Rome on the third day of the Congress.
>
> I heard them describing how I died, and I could not stop them.
>
> [Referring apparently to some unpublished Piper sittings in America.]
>
> I could not say it, but they were translating like a schoolboy does his first lines of Virgil—so terribly confused and inaccurate. But somehow I could not help it. It was not me communicating, yet I saw it going on. They had something from me on the 15th.
>
> I tried to communicate on *a* 15th.
>
> [These things are referred to in Mrs. Verrall's report. *Proc.*, vol. xx. pp. 207–9. See also notes below.]
>
> I tried by writing.
>
> Moses—Stainton Moses.

They mixed the deaths up—his death and my death.   It applies to him and not to me.

[Apparently referring to some unpublished and to me unknown account of the death-bed.]

How easy to promise and how difficult to fulfil.

Make one appeal to them to let me be at rest for two or three weeks after they get the note.   After Hodgson hears that I have tried, however badly, ask him not to call me, and tell him that if he does, they will not let me hear him.   I have gone back from where I was that night.   I could hear what she (the Medium) was saying, and keep a check on it, but now I cannot hear what is being said : I can only think the things, and false things may creep in without my knowing it.

Have you ten days work in a week ?   I cannot protect you from the calls upon you as they may protect me.

Do you not think, Mrs. Lodge, he has ten days work a week ?

(Then the Nelly Control reappears.)

P'fessor Lodge, do you know I have seen such a funny thing.   I have seen Mr. Myers talking as if to a stick right through Mother's body ; and while he was talking to it some one came up and touched it, and it all got confused, and he could not think why it went funny.

He seems to have to talk through this stick, and yet it keeps on being interfered with by other people.

I wish Mother was not so wicked ; because when Mr. Myers wants to go to sleep and be quiet, Mother will not let him.   She will call him.   You must tell her not to.   Tell her it is wicked to call him.   When he wants to go to sleep and be quiet she keeps him back.   She must not do it.

[I promised to give her the message ; which I did after the trance, and she then admitted that she thought of him frequently and urgently, but that she would try to refrain.]

(Nelly went on,)

Do you know last Monday when I went to Dr. Van Eeden's house ; he called for me and we went.   Mr. Myers came and told me he was calling. We both went, yes, on Monday. He has got an impression that Mr. Myers helped him to call me. Mr. Myers said "Let us go and see 'old Whiskers' in his little bed and laugh at him." He is much more lively when he is talking to me, and much more wakened up than when he is talking down that stick. [Cf. *Proc.* S.P.R., vol. xviii. p. 201. See also chapter IX. above.]

But he does seem worried, he gets no rest. Some one has called him in a glass bottle—yes, a crystal.

Oh yes, and he said it was not he that wrote when Miss Rawson wrote and said he told her. But it was not he that was writing. You know when ; Miss Rawson wrote two very full sheets in the middle of a Gurney letter. He said it was not he, but neither was it fraud. He does not want you to stop the phenomenon. He wants to study it. You are not to say that it was wrong and get it stopped. He likes to watch the somnambulistic thing at work. It is not he that is doing it, and yet he is looking on.

He does not see how it is worked, but he finds this more interesting than the genuine communications.

He did not rattle the curtains either. Eva—now do not think I am talking about Mrs. Myers, but Mrs. Eva ; they had a shaking of the curtain, and thought it was he. It was not he, but it was not cheating, and he does not want you to make them think that they are cheats. He does not know how it is worked, but he is studying, and he thinks it will help a great deal if he can understand how the cheating things that are not cheats are done. It is not cheating, and yet it is not him doing it. . . . There was no stick that went through any one's body there.

He says that others tell him it was just the same with them.

Sometimes when he thought they were communicating they were not, and yet they knew about it.

He says he is finding out how honest non-phenomena are to be accounted for.

Apparently dishonest phenomena are phenomena of extreme [interest ?] apart from the spirit which purports to be communicating.

[This last part was slowly recited by Nelly, like a lesson not understood by her.]

I can't help what he says.

I must go now.

(End of sitting, 10.30 p.m.)

Notes on this Sitting

Some of the remarks reported above seem to indicate a connexion with statements made in Mrs. Verrall's automatic writing of the same period, about which Mrs. Thompson knew nothing. Thus there appears a certain similarity between the remark " Mr. Myers is worrying about something connected with Mrs. S." and the attempts—misunderstood at the time—in Mrs. Verrall's script between April 19 and May 8, as related in *Proceedings*, vol. xx. pp. 195–198, to describe where Mrs. Sidgwick was to look for something of the nature of a book. Again " I tried on the Sunday with—I saw the receptacle but not this one " may perhaps be connected with the sudden impulse on Sunday, March 17th (*Proceedings*, vol. xx. p. 221), which induced Mrs. Verrall to write automatically and which produced the first reference to Mrs. Forbes in what eventually became a long series of cross-correspondences between those two automatists.

Finally, there seems a close correspondence between the above remarks as to difficulties produced by simultaneous efforts at communication and similar observations in Mrs. Verrall's script of the same day and approximately the same hour (*Proceedings*, vol. xx. pp. 207–209). Thus in Mrs. Thompson's sitting the Myers control speaks of " the noise of you all calling makes me feel I cannot. Someone is calling me now "; he also says " false things may creep in "; and the Nelly control describes how, just before, "someone came up and touched" the stick through which communication was being made, "and it all got confused." While Mrs. Verrall's automatic script of Monday, May 8th, 10–10.30 p.m., concludes as from the Myers control with the words : "falsehood is never far away. What do you want with me. I cannot . . . No power, doing something else to-night. Note hour." The initial "H" with which the message is there reported as signed was a substitution for the real initial, because that purported to represent F.W.H.M. ; and in those early days of Mrs. Verrall's writing it was thought safer, and at any rate less sensational, to treat this as mere impersonation.

The correspondence can be shown by a statement in parallel columns, as follows (see also p. 306) :—

May 8, 1901

Mrs. Thompson Birmingham 9–10.30 p.m.	Mrs. Verrall Cambridge 10–10.30 p.m.
1. "I cannot."	1. "Non possum (I cannot)." "No power."
2. "Some one is calling me now."	2. "Doing something else to-night."
3. "Let me be at rest."	3. "Desine (leave off)."
4. "False things may creep in."	4. "Falsehood is never far away."

The utterances of Mrs. Thompson were not known to Mrs. Verrall when she wrote the script reported in her paper, *Proc.*, vol. xx. ; but the correspondence is mentioned in her paper on pages 207 *et seq.*

Further Notes on the Thompson Myers Sittings

The rather strikingly worded complaints and requests recorded above (p. 296 and 297), as received through Mrs. Thompson—

> "They keep on calling me. I am wanted everywhere. . . . Do appeal to them not to break me up so. . . .
> How easy to promise and how difficult to fulfil. Make one appeal to them to let me be at rest for two or three weeks."

also correspond with something to the same effect independently received through another lady, called Miss Rawson, three months earlier ; and constitute what may be fairly considered a very simple kind of cross-correspondence. This message, received on Feb. 7th, 1901, purported to come from Edmund Gurney, who was represented as speaking through Miss Rawson as follows :—

> "I have come to warn you for my friend to implore you not to let them call him. He gets no rest day or night. At every sitting 'Call Myers! Bring Myers'; there's not a place in England where they don't ask for him ; it disturbs him, it takes away his rest. For God's sake don't call him. It is all right for him to come of his own accord. . . . What we want for him now is to rise, and to forget the earthly things. He can't help any more. His life was given to it, and that must be the help. He was allowed just to say that he continued. That was his great desire, but it will help nobody that he should be called back, and made to hover near the earth. In fact it will only make him earthbound.

I am tempted to quote here, from page 213 of *Proc.*, vol. xxi., a different though not altogether dissimilar extract from the script of Mrs. Holland in India which was written on January 5th and 6th, 1904, by the Myers$_H$ control :—

"Oh if I could only get to them—could only leave you the
proof positive that I remember—recall—know—continue. . . .
I have thought of a simile which may help you to realise the
'bound to earth condition' which persists with me.   It is a
matter very largely of voluntary choice—I am, as it were,
actuated by the missionary spirit; and the great longing to
speak to the souls in prison—still in the prison of the flesh—
leads me to 'absent me from felicity awhile.'"

This clearly expresses the idea of "service" which I
wish to emphasise, and it is a reverberation and later
expansion of the thought in the extracts already quoted,
which had not been published and were not known to
Mrs. Holland.   But the long post-dating of this last
communication destroys any claim to consideration as a
cross-correspondence.   Besides it was only an explanation of why the messages still willingly continued;
whereas the other two—so soon after the death—are
full of earnestness and anxiety.

General Remarks, Addressed to Religious Objectors

Good and earnest though moderately intelligent
religious people sometimes seek to pour scorn upon the
reality of any of these apparent communications—not
for any scientific reason, but for reasons born of
prejudice.   They think that it is not a worthy occupation
for "just men made perfect" "who have entered into
felicity" to be remembering trivial and minute details,
under circumstances of exceptional difficulty, for the
purpose of proving to those left behind the fact of
survival and the continuance of personal identity.   It
is taken for granted that saints ought to be otherwise
occupied in their new and lofty and favoured conditions.
What may or may not be possible to saints, it is

hardly for me or other gropers among mere terrestrial facts to surmise : nor am I anxious to imagine that all our communicators belong to the category of "perfected and glorified saints,"—it seems to me, I confess, singularly unlikely ; nor is it necessary to suppose that such exercises as we report—even if they are fully and entirely what they pretend to be—constitute any large proportion of the activity of the people who are professedly concerned in their production—people who are confessedly far from perfection and who have still much to learn.   And as regard dignity and appropriateness,— does it not sometimes happen that an Archbishop or a Savant is found willing to play a frivolous childish game, and otherwise to disport himself, in spite of his being on the brink of eternity, in a world of sorrow and sin ?

But seriously, is it not legitimate to ask these good people whether, if an opportunity of service to brethren arises, an effort to seize it may not be made even by a saint ?   Whether this notion of perennial service is not in accordance with their own doctrines and beliefs ? and whether they are not impressed by that clause in the creed of most Christians which roundly asserts that their Master descended into Hades ? for purposes which in another place are suggested.   Whereby they may learn that, even after such a Life and Death as that, Felicity was not entered into save after an era of further personal service of an efficient kind.   Those who interpret the parables in such a way as to imagine that dignified idleness is the occupation of eternity— that there will be nothing to do hereafter but idly to enjoy the beatific contemplation and other rewards appropriate to a well-spent life or to well-held creeds,— free from remorse of every kind, and without any call for future work and self-sacrifice,—such people will probably some day find themselves mistaken, and will realise that as yet they have formed a very inadequate conception of what is meant by that pregnant phrase "the Joy of the Lord."

Further Comments

Those who think that there is anything sensational or specially emotional in these communications are mistaken. The conversation is conducted on the same lines as a telephonic conversation: it is liable to the same sort of annoying interruptions, and likewise to the same occasional surprising gleams of vividness,—a happy turn of phrase, for instance, a tone of the voice, and other unmistakable and unexpected revelations of identity—forged or real—such as may be conveyed by an appropriate nickname or by some trivial reminiscence. When this happens, and when relatives are present, their emotions are certainly perturbed.

These remarks are general, and are applicable to this whole group reported on by me : they are not limited in their application to any one particular series.

I have not the slightest interest in attempting to coerce belief of any kind. The facts will make different kinds of appeal to different people, and to some they will not appeal at all. These will regard the whole business with contempt and pity. They are within their rights in doing so if they have conscientiously read this and the other records. As a rule however that is where they are apt to fail ; and when a person's knowledge of a subject is small, we may be pardoned for holding his opinion concerning it in light esteem.

Among the messages the most interesting to me are

the concluding observations, part of which were carefully and laboriously reported by the " Nelly " control,—the words (repeated below) sounding odd in a childish voice.

(*Myers*) " I could not say it, but they were translating like a schoolboy does his first lines of Virgil—so terribly confused and inaccurate. But somehow I could not help it. It was not me communicating, yet I saw it going on. . . . I can only think the things, and false things may creep in without my knowing it."

(*Nelly*) " He said it was not he, but neither was it fraud. He does not want you to stop the phenomenon, he wants to study it. You are not to say it was wrong and get it stopped. He likes to watch the somnambulistic thing at work. It is not he that is doing it, and yet he is looking on. He does not see how it is worked, but he finds this more interesting than the genuine communications. He did not rattle the curtains either . . . but it was not cheating, and he does not want you to make them think that they are cheats. He does not know how it is worked, but he is studying and he thinks it will help a great deal if he can understand how the cheating things that are not cheats are done. . . .

[And then came the laborious sentence]

" He says he is finding out how honest non-phenomena are to be accounted for. Apparently dishonest phenomena are phenomena of extreme [interest] apart from the spirit which purports to be communicating."

Whatever their origin, these words do, in my judgment, represent the truth about a good many of these phenomena—that is to say, that they are not precisely what their surface-aspect implies, yet neither are they fraud. They are attempts at doing something rather beyond the power of the operators,—who arrive approximately at their aim without achieving what they want exactly. They are trying to get something definite through, let us say, and something like it comes. Occasionally they hardly know how it comes, it is a puzzle to them as to us, and often they don't know what

20

it is that we have got; but sometimes they too seem to be spectators, aware of the result, and to be worried by the misconception and misunderstanding which they see will arise, but which they are powerless to prevent,—except, as here, by trying to instruct us and awaken our intelligences into a condition in which we too can understand and grapple with the unavoidable difficulties of the situation.

"I can only think the things": seems to me likely to be an accurate description of the method. It is a telepathic method, and the reproduction by voice or pen is a supplementary and only barely controllable process (cf. also pp. 252 and 308).

It was characteristic also of Myers to feel as if he were the note-taker, not the communicator, and that he ought to be putting it all down (p. 287). Another amusing episode was the persistence of Prof. Sidgwick's incredulity (p. 287), so that he was represented as asking to be convinced that he was himself communicating, and that the medium was not "getting it out of him somehow."

The coincidence in time between the termination of this sitting at Birmingham and some writing obtained by Mrs. Verrall at Cambridge, as exhibited in the analytical statement above, on p. 300, is very remarkable and worth careful notice—especially when the unexpected character of the Thompson sitting is taken into account. It really makes an effective cross-correspondence.

These observations terminate this account of communications received through the mediumship of Mrs. Thompson. An immense mass has been obtained through her in the past (see Reports in vols. xvii. and

xviii. of *Proceedings*, S.P.R.), but so far as I know these
two sittings are among the last which she has given.
We owe her thanks for the time and opportunity which
she has freely accorded to members of the Society for
scientific purposes.

In concluding this chapter, which I regard as an
important one, I claim that these utterances represent a
genuine psychological phenomenon, and are therefore of
interest to students of psychical matters, from any point
of view.   It is just possible that a hostile critic may here
find part of the pabulum necessary for making every
effort at studying matters of the kind appear ridiculous.
Whether this portion, or the subsequent commonplace
dialogue carried on through Mrs. Piper, or such few of the
"unverifiable" communications as have been reported
in our *Proceedings* (such, for instance, as that on 181
above) will appear the more humorous when regarded
from the scoffer's point of view, I am unable to judge.
Nor need the question deeply concern us.

CHAPTER XXIII

THE MYERS AND HODGSON CONTROLS IN RECENT PIPER SITTINGS

AS to Myers and Hodgson controls through Mrs. Piper—like the Gurney control in the old days —I do not propose to report the communications I received. They were not so good as some of those received by others, partly because I did not give these controls much chance. Indeed "Rector" complains of this as follows :—

> Myers has had very little opportunity or encouragement to prove his identity.

O. J. L. Yes, that is fairly true so far.

> And now if the opportunity can be given him, no one on our side is more desirous of proving his identity than Myers. Understand?

O. J. L. Yes, I quite understand.

> He understands, and wishes very much to communicate with a few of his real friends. R. It should be given him in any case, as he is intelligent, clear, and understands the necessity of so doing.

In Mrs. Holland's script of 16th April 1907 a description is given by the Myers$_H$ control of one of the difficulties of communication.

> "I want you to understand me but I have so few chances to speak—it's like waiting to take a ticket and I am always pushed away from the pigeon-hole before I can influence *her* mind—No the scribe's——"

Only one of the English sittings in 1907 was conducted on similar lines to those in the old days,—that is to say, as a voice sitting,—a talking, not a writing, sitting : and it was less unlike those of the old Phinuit days than I had expected.

In fact there was distinct recurrence of what in the old days used to be called "fishing," when Phinuit was groping in tentative fashion for a name and hoping for help from the sitter.

But in truth I have long wanted to exonerate Phinuit from most of the blame in this matter. The "fishing" procedure had to be admitted, and indeed emphasised, like all other weak spots; and Phinuit had not been trained to eschew normal help and to take precautions against it, as Mrs. Thompson's "Nelly" had been trained; but I always felt that his haziness and tentative approach to things probably represented a genuine difficulty, and was part of the phenomenon which needed study; so I am interested in reading in Dr. Hodgson's Report, p. 382, vol. xiii., the following judicial pronouncement :—

"It was out of the automatic dreameries of persons in some such conditions as those which I have illustrated above, that Phinuit in my present view so often had to fish his facts; and I think that assent to correct statements, and other clues from the sitters—besides helping the 'communicator'—were probably of great service to Phinuit, enabling him to 'cast his line' for those mental automatisms that specially concerned the sitter.

"Much light seems to me to have been thrown upon Phinuit's mistakes and obscurities and general method of trying to get at facts, in what were on the whole bad sittings, by comparison of the results obtained from the various communicators writing directly or using G.P. as amanuensis ; and I feel pretty sure that much of Phinuit's 'fishing' was due to the confusions of the more or less comatose communicators, whose minds had let loose, so to speak, a crowd of earthly memories."

MANNER OF THE STAINTON MOSES GROUP

It will be of interest to those familiar with the script of Stainton Moses to see the names of his old controls cropping up. Not only Imperator and Rector, but "Prudens" also, who appears to act as an accomplished messenger. I conjecture, however, that whatever relationship may exist between these personages and the corresponding ones of Stainton Moses, there is little or no identity. For instance, a "Doctor" is represented as communicating or controlling, but he appears neither to have, nor to claim, any connexion with the non-medical "Doctor" of Stainton Moses ; sometimes at any rate this Piper one is called "Dr. Oliver," and is probably intended to represent a deceased medical man of Boston. It is rather a puzzle to me why Mrs. Piper's personalities should have assumed the same set of names. In general characters they are similar ; but I see no very close resemblance in detail. And hitherto the Piper "Imperator" has not given to us the same old earth-name as did the original "Imperator" to Stainton Moses. So that it would appear as if they did not very seriously pretend to be identical.

It is seldom nowadays that there is any marked change of control, such as occurred with Phinuit sometimes. The utterances appear to consist of first-person-reporting on the part of Rector, who speaks or writes after the fashion of a dignified and gentle old man.

It may be noted that in America, with the advent

of the Stainton Moses controls, the atmosphere of a
sitting sometimes became rather markedly "religious."
This can be illustrated by the following close of an
American Voice-Sitting in 1906, reported to me by Mr.
Dorr :—

> (" Hodgson " terminating his communication)
> Well, I will be off.   Good-bye for the present.
> (Rector resumes.)   All right.   That is first-rate.   Took him a
>   long time to turn round and get out.   He dislikes to go
>   more than anybody I ever saw.   The last moment he kept
>   talking to me and talking to me.   He could not give it up.

> PRAYER
>
> Father, in Thy kindness guide Thy children of earth, bestow
>   Thy blessings on them, teach them with Thy presence and
>   Thy power to receive suffering, pain, illness and sorrow,
>   teach them to know that Thy presence is always with them.
>   May Thy grace and everlasting love be and abide with them
>   now and evermore.
> Farewell.   We depart, friends, and may the blessings of God
>   be bestowed on you.   Farewell.

MANNER OF THE HODGSON CONTROL

The atmosphere of a sitting is always serious, but
only occasionally solemn ; usually it is of an even tenor,
and sometimes it is hearty and jovial.   The following
is a characteristic Hodgson greeting extracted from a
sitting with Mr. Dorr and Henry James, Jr., at Boston
in 1906 :—

> Ha !   Well, I did not expect to see you so soon.
> Good morning, Harry !
> I am delighted to see you.
> H. J. Jr.   Is that you, Mr. Hodgson ?
> Yes, it is a great delight to me to see your face once more.
>   How is everything with you, first rate ?

H. J. Jr. Very well.
> Why, I feel as though I was one among you. Hello, George !

G. B. D. Hello !
> You people don't appreciate my spirit of fun ! But I am Hodgson, and I shall be Hodgson to the end of all eternity, and you cannot change me no matter what you do.

H. J. Jr. I think we appreciate it, Mr. Hodgson.
> Well, I hope you do—if you don't, you have lost something, because I am what I am, and I shall never be anything else, and of all the joyous moments of my whole existence, the most joyful is when I meet you all.

This sort of thing is of course not in the least evidential, and yet if I were asked to invent some scheme of salutation more natural and characteristic of Hodgson's personality I should not be able to improve upon it.

To illustrate the manner of the Hodgson control in my own experience the following brief extract must serve :—

At the Eighth Sitting on 23 Nov. 1906 (present : O. J. L. alone), " Isaac Thompson " wrote a good deal, but the following came from Hodgson$_P$ *:—*

> I am Hodgson, but I cannot take Rector's place to-day. However I will make a poor attempt to speak through him.

O. J. L. Very glad to see you.
> Here's ditto. Do I understand that Mrs. Piper is in England ?

O. J. L. Yes, she is, and is staying in my house.
> Capital. If I were in the body it would not be so.
> However I am glad it is so.

O. J. L. She is here, well and happy, with Alta and Minerva.
> Good, first rate. I am glad.
> Will you take a message to Billie Newbold for me, safe ?

O. J. L. Yes, I will send it through William James.

. . . .

> Do you wish me to take a message for you ?
> Ask slowly ; remember we cannot hear as well as you can.

I am so glad to be on this side.

O. J. L. Well, Hodgson, I do want to ask you something. You know when I am talking to you I am talking to the hand; but I want to know whether it is through the hand you hear. Suppose I stopped up your medium's ears with cotton wool, would it make any difference? Would the message still come?

I think it would, try it.

O. J. L. Very well, I will another time.

First rate, I permit it; first rate.

But after all I did not try the experiment ; for it is exceedingly difficult to secure complete deafness by plugging the ears—even with putty. Moreover the necessary manipulation of the medium's head during trance seemed rather repellent. It is an experiment worth trying, however, if we could be sure of a clear result. If I could have been sure of a crucial test I would have had it done ; but hyperæsthesia would have to be allowed for in the positive direction—possibly also inhibitory suggestion in the negative,—and on the whole I felt that no definite deduction could be made, whatever the result. Nevertheless the experiment ought to be made by some competent person.

Manner of the Impersonation Generally

As illustrating the dramatic activity of the hand in an extreme case—though it is always very marked, for the hand is full of "personality" (p. 264)—I quote the following contemporaneous note made by Mrs. Sidgwick during a sitting in which the Myers$_P$ control, at length after much effort, had just succeeded in giving *Abt Vogler* as the name of a poem he was referring to.

"The hand is tremendously pleased and excited and thumps and gesticulates. The impression given is like

that of a person dancing round the room in delight at
having accomplished something."

But indeed the writing which immediately followed
this success is worth quoting.   The record runs thus :—

> "(Rector communicating)
> He pronounced it for me again and again just as you did,
>   and he said Rector get her to pronounce it for you and
>   you will understand, he whispered it in my ear.
>
> E. M. S. Just as you were coming out?
> Just as I left the light.
> Voglor, yes.
>
> E. M. S. Good.
>   (Myers communicating)
> Now dear Mrs. Sidgwick in future have no doubt or fear of
>   so-called death as there is none as there is certainly
>   intelligent life beyond it."

With regard to the misspelling which occurs here
and elsewhere, the difficulty is readily imaginable, but it
is thus expressed by Rector, later, when he is repeating
the name of a poem.   The record runs thus :—

> "Abt ABT. Volg.
> (Hand expresses dissatisfaction with this.)
> Vogler.
>   (Rector communicating)
> You see I do not always catch the letters as he repeats them.
>   R.
>
> E. M. S. No, I see.
> Therefore when I am registering I am apt to misspell.
>
> E. M. S. I see.
> But if you ask me to correct it of course I can.   R."

With regard to "fishing" and making use of indications given by the sitter, it seems likely that with the
most transparent honesty this would be likely to happen ;
because Rector, or any other scribe, is evidently in the
position of receiving ideas by a sort of dictation, and

need not always be able clearly to discriminate their
source, whether from the ultra-material or from the
material side. For instance, the Myers$_P$ control
attempted to speak about the Odes of Horace, and
did so ; but Rector, after writing " Odes" without difficulty, appeared doubtful about the word, and wrote
"Odessus," "Odesesis," etc., and finally half accepted Mrs.
Sidgwick's suggestion " Odyssey " ;—a good instance of
how ready Rector is to accept a misleading suggestion,
even when what he has independently written is right ;
and also of discontinuity of consciousness between Rector
and the real communicator, who in this case was
obviously trying to talk about the Odes of Horace in
order to connect them with the quotations from *Abt
Vogler* just previously made.

CHAPTER XXIV

BRIEF SUMMARY OF OTHER EXPERIENCES AND COMMENT THEREUPON

SOME rather striking sittings were held by a lady named Mrs. Grove, whose deceased friends, a Mr. Marble and some others, sent many appropriate messages, which were in many respects akin to those which had been received by the same sitter through other mediums.

Her friends were perfectly obscure people, totally unknown to Mrs. Piper, and unknown in any district in which Mrs. Piper had been; hence these utterances have an importance of their own, more akin to that of the time when Phinuit showed himself able to deal with the concerns of miscellaneous strangers. They are reported in the *Proceedings* of the Society for Psychical Research (Part LVIII.), but I do not repeat them here, though I repeat an experiment made in connexion with them :—

EXPERIMENT ON THE RECOGNITION OF A PHOTOGRAPH OF ONE OF THE CONTROLS

The waking stages of the last sitting of the first Edgbaston series, in December 1906, and of the first of the second series, in May 1907,—with an interval between them of five months,—are worth recording because of an experiment I made in connexion with the likeness of a person supposed to have been communicating during the trance (in this case Mr. Marble): the point being to see whether there would be any recognition of a photograph by the automatist before her state had become entirely normal,—that is during the sort of period in which it is customarily possible dimly to remember dreams (see page 275). This stage is referred to by Dr. Hodgson on page 401 of vol. xiii.—where he calls it Mrs. Piper's subliminal stage, and says that it is a condition in which she frequently has visions of the distant or departing "communicators."

On the first occasion I waited rather a long time before trying the experiment,—something more than an hour,—and the recognition was uncertain; but faint as it was, it seemed to be a residual effect of the trance; since it was not permanent, and by next day had entirely disappeared.

On the second occasion I tried directly after the waking stage was complete; and then the recognition was immediate and certain. But in a few minutes it had become vague and dim, and before the end of the day it had again completely ceased.

Sequel to sitting No. 13, which had lasted from 11.10 to 1.10 on 3rd December 1906

After lunch I took eleven photographs of men, and asked Mrs. Piper if she had ever seen any of them. She looked over them, hesitating on the one representing Mr. Joseph Marble for some time, and then picked that out and said she had seen that man somewhere, but she could not remember where. Nothing was said by me during the process, of course.

Next day, in the evening, I tested Mrs. Piper again with another set of photographs of men, partly the same and partly different, but containing among others the critical one. This time, however, it was looked at without comment and without interest, and no remembrance of the appearance seemed to persist. She remembered the fact of having recognised one before; but when asked to do it again, she picked out, after much hesitation, a different one as a possibility, and said that she thought it had been found in America that the memory evaporated in time, and that it was strongest within an hour of the sitting. The test made the day before had been made about an hour and a half after a sitting at which "Mr. Marble" had been one of the communicators.

Sequel to Waking Stage of No. 14 *on* 19*th May* 1907

> (A number of men's photographs were placed in a row before her as soon as she had come to: she immediately pounced on one without the slightest hesitation.)

That is the man I saw. I saw him. That is the man I saw. I saw him up there: such a nice face. I could see him. I could see Mr. Hodgson pushing him up to the front.

> [The selection was correct; the photograph was one of the person she calls Joe, *i.e.* of the late Mr. Joseph Marble.]
> (*An hour or so later.* I again put the photographs in front of her. She looked at them as if for the first time, and said)

I do not know the photographs.

> (She then hesitated long over the right one, saying she had "seen him somewhere," but finished up by saying)

No, I do not know.

COMMENT

The result of this experiment, with other experiences relating to the description of the personal appearance of a person spoken of in the trance, has satisfied me that— whatever may be the cause—a visual likeness of the people supposed to be communicating in the trance is sometimes really impressed at the time upon the sub-conscious mind of Mrs. Piper. A veridical dream impression seems to be caused in these cases; but like other dream impressions it fades. The visual impression is merely an extension of the impression of character and of speech, which is also impressed upon the same stratum of her subconsciousness, and is of a similarly evanescent character.

During trance undoubtedly her subconsciousness is thus, at least occasionally, in touch with a simulacrum or hallucinatory representation of a deceased person,—whatever be the cause,—a telepathic impression received from the sitter perhaps, or, as appears more likely, from the surviving influence of the deceased person.

That much is certain ; and to deny that, is merely to refuse to be informed by facts of experience. But of what nature this evanescent but for a time vivid impression of appearance and character and personality really is, is a more difficult question, on which at present I do not feel competent to express an opinion. For what it is worth, however, my instinct leads me to judge that it is not solely due to a telepathic impulse from the sitter—in spite of the fact that the sympathy and understanding of the sitter is a great help, and indeed a determining cause why one set of impressions is produced and not a totally different set. Undoubtedly the existence of real interest and affection on the part of a person present is an awakening cause of a particular veridical impression. It is that which determines the selection, out of the infinite multitude of other impressions which otherwise might equally well be produced. But although sympathy of this kind is the selective and determining cause, I do not feel that it is the creative or constructive cause. It appears to me that there is an agency or energy lying ready, which is capable of arousing in the subconsciousness of an entranced person, or of persons endowed with automatic faculty, a vast multitude of impressions—good bad and indifferent ; and that out of this multitude of possible impressions some are selected with more or less discrimination as appropriate to a particular case,—the presence of a sitter being the detent or trigger which liberates or guides the energy in one direction and not in another.

On the whole, these experiences, with many others which are omitted, tend to render certain the existence of some outside intelligence or control, distinct from the consciousness, and as far as I can judge from the sub-consciousness also, of Mrs. Piper or other medium. And they tend to render probable the working hypo-thesis, on which I choose to proceed, that that version of the nature of the intelligences which they themselves present and favour is something like the truth. In other words, I feel that we are in secondary or tertiary touch —at least occasionally—with some stratum of the surviv-ing personality of the individuals who are represented as sending messages.

I call the touch secondary, because it is always through the medium and not direct; and I call it generally tertiary, because it represents itself as nearly always operating through an agency or medium on that side also—an agency which calls itself " Rector " or " Phinuit." That these latter impersonations are really themselves individuals, I do not venture either to assert or deny ; but it is difficult or impossible to bring them to book, and an examination of their nature may be deferred : it is the impersonation of verifiable or terrestrially known individuals to which it behoves us in the first instance to pay attention.

From this point of view the sittings in the Mrs. Grove case—at some of which I was present—must be regarded as among the most strictly *evidential* of all ; for a decided unity of character and of message is preserved, no matter through what medium the communication comes.   Similar messages had come when Mrs. Grove had sat with Mrs. Thompson and other mediums.

Deductions

A careful analysis and examination of the facts, both for and against the genuine activity of deceased Communicators, has been made by Dr. Hodgson, and will be found in his Report in *Proceedings*, vol. xiii. pages 357–412.   (Extracts are quoted above in Chapter XVIII.) He is led distinctly to countenance, and indeed to champion, a cautious and discriminating form of spiritistic theory,—not as a working hypothesis only, but as truly representing part of the facts.   His experience was so large, and his critical faculty so awake, that such a conclusion of his is entitled to the gravest consideration. If I had to pronounce a prematurely decided opinion, my own view would agree with his.

The old series of sittings with Mrs. Piper convinced me of survival, for reasons which I should find it hard to formulate in any strict fashion, but that was their distinct effect.   They also made me suspect—or more than suspect—that surviving intelligences were in some cases consciously communicating,—yes, in some few cases consciously ; though more usually the messages came in all probability from an unconscious stratum, being received by the medium in an inspirational manner analogous to psychometry.

The hypothesis of surviving intelligence and personality,—not only surviving but anxious and able with difficulty to communicate,—is the simplest and most straightforward, and the only one that fits all the facts. But the process of communication is sophisticated by many influences, so that it is very difficult, perhaps at present impossible, to disentangle and exhibit clearly the part that each plays.

One thing that conspicuously suggests itself is that we are here made aware, through these trivial but illuminating facts, of a process which by religious people has always been recognised and insisted on, viz. the direct interaction of incarnate with discarnate mind,—that is to say, an intercourse between mind and mind in more than one grade of existence, by means apart from, and independent of, the temporary mechanism of the body.

The facts indeed open the way to a perception of the influence of spirit generally, as a guiding force in human and terrestrial affairs,—active not under the exceptional circumstances of trance alone, but always and constantly and normally,—so uniformly active in fact that by ordinary people the agency is undetected and unperceived. Most people are far too busy to attend : they are too thoroughly occupied with what for the time are certainly extremely important affairs. A race of inspired people would be hopelessly unpractical,—though Society is usually grateful for the existence and utterance of a few individuals of this type.

The fact that these communications are obtained through subconscious agency is sometimes held to militate against their importance as a subject of study. But have not men of genius sometimes testified that brilliant ideas do surge up into their consciousness from some submerged stratum, at a time when they are incompletely awake to the things of this world? And ordinary people are aware that a brown study favours the conscious reception of something presumably akin to inspiration, by relegating ordinary experience to the background, and thereby enabling new and unfamiliar ideas to enter or germinate in the mind.

A trance, or any state of complete unconsciousness, renders the normal though obscure activity of an unfamiliar psychical region still more manifest. Not indeed to the patient—who is unaware of the whole phenomenon, or remembers it only after the indistinct and temporary fashion of a dream—but to an observer or experimenter, who is allowed to enlarge his experience and to receive impressions by deputy; thereby attaining, at second hand, some of the privileges of intuition or clairvoyance, or even of genius, while he himself remains in an ordinary and business-like condition. His experience in fact may be regarded as an undeserved, and therefore only moderately valuable, kind of vicarious inspiration.

CHAPTER XXV

INTRODUCTION TO THE STUDY OF CROSS-CORRESPONDENCE

THE subject of cross-correspondence is so large and complicated that any one who wishes to form an opinion on it is bound to study the detailed publications by Mr. Piddington, Mrs. Verrall, Miss Johnson, and others, in recent volumes of the *Proceedings* of the Society for Psychical Research. It would be impossible otherwise to give the critical and substantial study which the elaborate literary references demand. Whatever else they are, they are eminently communications from a man of letters, to be interpreted by scholars, and they are full of obscure classical allusions. And parenthetically I may here state, as a noteworthy fact, that nowadays even through Mrs. Piper such scholarly allusions are obtained,—not obvious and elementary ones, but such as exhibit a range of reading far beyond that of ordinary people—beyond my own for instance—and beyond that of anyone present at the time. The facts on which this statement is based have not yet (October 1909) been published.

Returning to the general subject of cross-correspondence,— the main feature of this kind of communication is that we are required to study, not the phenomena exhibited by a single medium actuated by a number of ostensible controls, as heretofore, but conversely the utterance of one ostensible control effected through the contributory agency of several different mediums;—who write automatically quite independently of each other, who are at a distance from each other, who are sometimes unknown to each other, and who at first were unaware that any kind of correspondence was going on.

In many cases, moreover, the messages as separately obtained were quite unintelligible, and only exhibited a meaning when they were subsequently put together by another person. So that the content of the message was in no living mind until the correspondences were detected by laborious criticism a year or two later; then at last the several parts were unified and the whole message and intention made out.

The object of this ingenious and complicated effort clearly is to prove that there is some definite intelligence underlying the phenomena, distinct from that of any of the automatists, by sending fragments of a message or literary reference which shall be unintelligible to each separately—so that no effective mutual telepathy is possible between them,—thus eliminating or trying to eliminate what had long been recognised by all members of the Society for Psychical Research as the most troublesome and indestructible of the semi-normal hypotheses. And the further object is evidently to prove as far as possible, by the substance and quality of the message, that it is characteristic of the one particular personality who is ostensibly communicating, and of no other.

That has clearly been the aim of the communicators themselves. Whether or not they have been successful

is a question which it may take some time and study
finally and conclusively to decide.

If a student is to form a first hand judgment of any
value on this subject, he must, as I have said, read in full
the elaborate papers of Mr. Piddington and Miss Johnson
and Mrs. Verrall in the important recent volumes of the
Proceedings of the Society ; which is no light task.

DISCOVERY OF CROSS-CORRESPONDENCES

But as giving the best introductory and purely initial
account of this large and evidently growing subject, I
will quote from the paper of our Research Officer, Miss
Johnson, her Chapter VII. called "The Theory of
Cross-correspondences," since it was through her patient
care and perspicacity that the existence of such things,
on the way to something like their present striking form,
was first demonstrated.

It opens with a quotation from the writings of
F. W. H. Myers, which illustrates his attitude to the
subject when living :—

"It is not we who are in reality the discoverers here.   The experiments which are being made are not the work of earthly skill.   All that
we can contribute to the new result is an attitude of patience, attention,
care ; an honest readiness to receive and weigh whatever may be
given into our keeping by intelligences beyond our own.   Experiments,
I say, there are ; probably experiments of a complexity and difficulty
which surpass our imagination ; but they are made from the other side
of the gulf, by the efforts of spirits who discern pathways and possibilities which for us are impenetrably dark."—(*Human Personality*,
vol. ii. p. 275.)

And then it continues :—

In *Human Personality* Mr. Myers hints more than
once at a favourite theory of his that the influence of
science on modern thought is not confined to this life

alone, but may be carried on into the next, and so tend to improve the evidence for communication from the dead.   The latter, he suggests, are coming to understand more and more clearly what constitutes really good evidence, and may gradually discover better means of producing it.   [In the above passage he formulates this conjecture most clearly, and] it would seem from our recent investigations that some such experiments as he there foreshadowed may actually be taking place.

Mr. Myers and Dr. Hodgson made attempts at different times to obtain connections between the utterances—either spoken or written—of different automatists. It is by no means easy even to obtain suitable conditions for trying such experiments, and unfortunately, as far as I am aware, no complete record of these attempts seems to exist.   Some references to them, however, occur in a number of letters written by Mr. Myers to Mrs. Thompson ; for instance on October 24th, 1898, he wrote as follows :

" Dr. Hodgson is staying on in America for the winter, sitting with Mrs. Piper.   It would be grand if we could get communication between the 'controls' on each side."

Some interesting connections between the automatisms of Mrs. Thompson and those of other sensitives were already recorded in Mr. Piddington's paper, "On the Types of Phenomena displayed in Mrs. Thompson's Trance," in *Proceedings*, S.P.R., vol. xviii. pp. 104–307.

But the most notable development of cross-correspondence, and the first appearance of a really complicated and remarkably evidential type of them, have taken place since Mr. Myers's death.

This was shown first in Mrs. Verrall's script, and a considerable section of her *Report* on it (*Proc.* vol. xx. pp. 205–275) is devoted to an account of the cross-correspondences between her script and the script or automatic speech of other automatists.

In studying these in proof in the early part of 1906 —says Miss Johnson, our Research Officer—I was struck by the fact that in some of the most remarkable instances the statements in the script of one writer were by no means a simple reproduction of statements in the script of the other, but seemed to represent different aspects of the same idea, one supplementing or completing the other. Thus, in one case (p. 223), Mrs. Forbes's script, purporting to come from her son Talbot, stated that he must now leave her, since he was looking for a sensitive who wrote automatically, in order that he might obtain corroboration of her own writing. Mrs. Verrall, on the same day, wrote of a fir-tree planted in a garden, and the script was signed with a sword and suspended bugle. The latter was part of the badge of the regiment to which Talbot Forbes had belonged, and Mrs. Forbes had in her garden some fir-trees, grown from seed sent to her by her son. These facts were unknown to Mrs. Verrall.

In another case (pp. 241–245)—too complicated to summarise here—Mrs. Forbes produced, on November 26th and 27th, 1902, references, absolutely meaningless to herself, to a passage in the *Symposium* which Mrs. Verrall had been reading on these days. These references also applied appropriately to an obscure sentence in Mrs. Verrall's own script of November 26th; and on December 18th, attempts were made in Mrs. Forbes's script to give a certain test word, "Dion" or "Dy," which, it was stated, "will be found in Myers' own. . . ." Mrs. Verrall interpreted the test word at the time, for reasons given, as "Diotima,', and a description of the same part of the *Symposium*, including the mention of Diotima, did occur in *Human Personality*, which was published about three months later, in February 1903. Further references to the *Symposium* appeared in Mrs. Forbes's script in the early part of 1903 (see Mrs. Verrall's *Report*, p. 246).

In another case (pp. 269–271), October 16th, 1904, Mrs. Verrall's script gave details, afterwards verified, of what Mrs. Forbes was doing ; and immediately afterwards Mrs. Verrall had a mental impression of Mrs. Forbes sitting in her drawing-room, with the figure of her son standing looking at her.   Mrs. Forbes's script of the same day, purporting to come from her son, stated that he was present and wished she could see him, and that a test was being given for her at Cambridge.

I became convinced through the study of these cases that there was some special purpose in the particular form they took,—all the more because in Mrs. Verrall's script statements were often associated with them, apparently to draw attention to some peculiar kind of test,—described, *e.g.* as superposing certain things on others, when all would be clear.

The characteristic of these cases—or at least of some of them—is that we do not get in the writing of one automatist anything like a mechanical verbatim reproduction of phrases in the other ; we do not even get the same idea expressed in different ways,—as might well result from direct telepathy between them.   What we get is a fragmentary utterance in one script, which seems to have no particular point or meaning, and another fragmentary utterance in the other, of an equally pointless character ; but when we put the two together, we see that they supplement one another, and that there is apparently one coherent idea underlying both, but only partially expressed in each.

It occurred to me, then, that by this method, if by any, it might be possible to obtain evidence more conclusive than any obtained hitherto of the action of a third intelligence, external to the minds of both automatists.   If we simply find the same idea expressed— even though in different forms—by both of them, it may, as I have just said, most easily be explained by telepathy between them ; but it is much more difficult to suppose that the telepathic perception of *one* fragment could lead to the production of *another* fragment which can only, after careful comparison, be seen to be related to the first.

The weakness of all well-authenticated cases of apparent telepathy from the dead is, of course, that they can generally be explained by telepathy from the living. If the knowledge displayed by the medium is possessed by any person certainly existing,—that is, any living person,—we must refer it to that source rather than to a person whose existence is uncertain,—that is, a dead person. To do otherwise would be to beg the whole question at issue, for the very thing to be proved is the existence of the dead person.

Hitherto the evidence for survival has depended on statements that seem to show the control's recollection of incidents in his past life. It would be useless for him to communicate telepathically anything about his present life, because there could be no proof of the truth of the communication. This is the fundamental difference between the types of evidence for telepathy from the living and for telepathy from the dead.

Now, telepathy relating to the present, such as we sometimes get between living persons, must be stronger evidentially than telepathy relating to the past, because it is much easier to exclude normal knowledge of events in the present than of events in the past. But it has been supposed impossible that we could ever get this kind of evidence for telepathy from the dead; since events in the present are either known to some living person,—in which case we could not exclude his telepathic agency,—or they are unknown to any living person, in which case it would be difficult or impossible to prove that they had occurred.

In these cross-correspondences, however, we find apparently telepathy relating to the present,—that is, the corresponding statements are approximately con- temporaneous,—and to events in the present which, to all intents and purposes, are unknown to any living person; since the meaning and point of her script is often uncomprehended by each automatist until the solution is found through putting the two scripts together. At the same time we have proof of what has occurred [*i.e.* some special indication that a correspondence is being attempted] in the scripts themselves. Thus it appears that this method is directed towards satisfying our evidential requirements.

Now, granted the possibility of communication, it may be supposed that within the last few years a certain group of persons have been trying to communicate with us, who are sufficiently well instructed to know all the objections that reasonable sceptics have urged against the previous evidence, and sufficiently intelligent to realise to the full all the force of these objections. It may be supposed that these persons have invented a new plan,—the plan of cross-correspondences,—to meet the sceptics' objections. There is no doubt that the cross-correspondences are a characteristic element in the scripts that we have been collecting in the last few years,—the scripts of Mrs. Verrall, Mrs. Forbes, Mrs. Holland, and, still more recently, Mrs. Piper. And the important point is that the element is a new one. We have reason to believe, as I have shown above, that the idea of making a statement in one script *complementary* of a statement in another had not occurred to Mr. Myers in his lifetime,—for there is no reference to it in any of his written utterances on the subject that I have been able to discover. Neither did those who have been investigating automatic script since his death invent this plan, if plan it be. It was not the automatists themselves that detected it, but a student of their scripts ; it has every appearance of being an element imported from outside ; it suggests an independent invention, an active intelligence constantly at work in the present, not a mere echo or remnant of individualities of the past.

Yes, it suggests an independent invention—*an active*

intelligence constantly at work in the present, not a mere echo or remnant of individualities of the past.

And so the matter has gone on developing, and a still further and more elaborate system of evidently experimental and designed cross-correspondence has now been discovered by Mr. Piddington in the scripts of the automatists mentioned, when independently compared together ; with veiled statements in those same scripts which symbolically but definitely claim that such correspondences are to be found if looked for.   Those so far discovered are reported in the Society's *Proceedings*—a series of documents upon a consideration of which I do not propose to enter, since at this stage they are not capable of effective abridgement.

Summary

Summarising once more our position as regards cross-correspondence—we have in the course of the last few years been driven to recognise that the controls are pertinaciously trying to communicate now one now another definite idea by means of two or more different automatists, whom at the same time they are trying to prevent from communicating telepathically or unconsciously with one another ; and that in order to achieve this deliberate aim the controls express the factors of the idea in so veiled a form that each writer indites her own share without understanding it.   Yet some identifying symbol or phrase is often included in each script, so as to indicate to a critical examiner that the correspondence is intended and not accidental ; and, moreover, the idea thus co-operatively expressed is so definite that, when once the clue is found, no room is left for doubt as to the proper interpretation.

That is precisely what we have quite recently again and again obtained.   We are told by the communicators that there are other correspondences not yet detected by us ; and by more careful collation of the documents this has already been found true.   The evidence needs careful and critical study ; it is not in itself sensational, but it affords strong evidence of the intervention of a mind behind and independent of the automatist.

If this be so—says the present President of the Society for Psychical Research, Mrs. Sidgwick—the question what mind this is becomes of extreme interest and importance.   Can it be a mind still in the body ? or have we got into relation with minds which have survived bodily death and are endeavouring by means of the cross-correspondences to produce evidence of their operation ?   If this last hypothesis be the true one, it would mean that intelligent co-operation between other than embodied human minds and our own, in experiments of a new kind intended to prove continued existence, has become possible ; and we should be justified in feeling that we are entering on a new and very important stage of the Society's work.

Consider for a moment the purport and full bearing of a judgment which, though still in form hypothetical, I hold for my own part to be fully justified :—
Intelligent co-operation between other than embodied human minds than our own . . . has become possible.

It is surely difficult to over-estimate the importance of so momentous an induction when it can finally be made.

Man's practical outlook upon the universe is entering upon a new phase.   Simultaneously with the beginning of a revolutionary increase in his powers of physical locomotion—which will soon be extended into a third dimension and no longer limited to a solid or liquid surface—his power of reciprocal mental intercourse also is in process of being enlarged ; for there are signs that it will some day be no longer limited to contemporary denizens of earth, but will permit a utilisation of knowledge and powers superior to his own, even to the extent of ultimately attaining trustworthy information concerning other conditions of existence.

CHAPTER XXVI

TENTATIVE CONCLUSION

I F we now try to summarise once more the position at which we have so far arrived—which I have endeavoured to express in the concluding paragraph of the preceding chapter—we shall represent it somewhat as follows :—

The evidence for the survival of man, that is for the persistence of human intelligence and individual personality beyond bodily death, has always been cumulative ; and now, through recent developments of the ancient phenomenon of automatic writing, it is beginning to be crucial.

The fame of Mrs. Piper has spread into all lands, and I should think the fame of Mrs. Verrall also. In these recent cases of automatism the Society has been singularly fortunate, for in the one we have a Medium who has been under strict supervision and competent management for the greater part of her psychical life ; and in the other we have one of the sanest and acutest of our own investigators fortunately endowed with some power herself,—some power of acting as translator or interpreter between the psychical and the physical worlds. There are also other ladies to some extent concerned in the recent unsensational but most intelligent phenomena, —especially the one known as Mrs. Holland,—who are likewise above any suspicion of duplicity. But, indeed, the whole thing has been so conducted that no duplicity, either conscious or unconscious, can rationally be suspected : everything has been deposited at the time with responsible persons outside the sphere of influence, and we are at liberty to learn what we can from the record of the phenomena, unperturbed by any moral suspicions.

And what do we find?

We find deceased friends—some of them well known to us and active members of the Society while alive— especially Gurney, Myers, and Hodgson—constantly purporting to communicate, with the express purpose of patiently proving their identity and giving us cross-correspondences between different mediums. We also find them answering specific questions in a manner characteristic of their known personalities and giving evidence of knowledge appropriate to them.

Not easily or early do we make this admission. In spite of long conversations with what purported to be the surviving intelligence of these friends and investigators, we were by no means convinced of their identity by mere general conversation,—even when of a friendly and intimate character, such as in normal cases would be considered amply and overwhelmingly sufficient for the identification of friends speaking, let us say, through a telephone or a typewriter. We required definite and crucial proof—a proof difficult even to imagine as well as difficult to supply.

The ostensible communicators realise the need of such proof just as fully as we do, and have done their best to satisfy the rational demand. Some of us think they have succeeded, others are still doubtful.

The following is Mrs. Verrall's conclusion after years of first-hand experience and careful testing :—

It cannot be denied that the "communicator" of the Piper sittings and of my own script presents a consistent personality dramatically resembling that of the person whom he claims to be.

I entirely acquiesce in this judgment. In fact, I am of those who, though they would like to see further and still stronger and more continued proofs, are of opinion that a good case has been made out, and that as the best working hypothesis at the present time it is legitimate to grant that lucid moments of intercourse with deceased persons may in the best cases supervene ; —amid a mass of supplementary material, quite natural under the circumstances, but mostly of a presumably subliminal and less evidential kind.

The boundary between the two states—the known and the unknown—is still substantial, but it is wearing thin in places ; and like excavators engaged in boring a tunnel from opposite ends, amid the roar of water and other noises, we are beginning to hear now and again the strokes of the pickaxes of our comrades on the other side.

So we presently come back out of our tunnel into the light of day, and relate our experience to a busy and incredulous, or in some cases too easily credulous, world. We expect to be received with incredulity ; though doubtless we shall be told in some quarters that it is all stale news, that there has been access to the other side of the mountain range from time immemorial, and that our laboriously constructed tunnel was quite unnecessary. Agile climbers may have been to the top and peeped over. Flying messages from the other side may have arrived ; pioneers must have surveyed the route. But we, like the navvies, are unprovided with wings, we dig and work on the common earth, our business is to pierce

22

the mountain at some moderate elevation, and construct a permanent road or railway for the service of humanity.

What we have to announce, then, is no striking novelty, no new method of communication, but only the reception, by old but developing methods, of carefully constructed evidence of identity more exact and more nearly complete than perhaps ever before. Carefully constructed evidence, I say. The constructive ingenuity exists quite as much on the other side of the partition as on our side: there has been distinct co-operation between those on the material and those on the immaterial side; and we are at liberty, not indeed to announce any definite conclusion, but to adopt as a working hypothesis the ancient doctrine of a possible intercourse of intelligence between the material and some other, perhaps ethereal, order of existence.

Some people have expected or hoped to communicate with Mars; it appears likely that recognised communication may some day occur with less removed, and indeed less hypothetical, dwellers in (or perhaps not in) the realm of space.

But let us not jump to the conclusion that the idea of "space" no longer means anything to persons removed from the planet. They are no longer in touch with *matter* truly, and therefore can no longer appeal to our organs of sense, as they did when they had bodies for that express purpose; but, for all we know, they may exist in the ether and be as aware of space and of the truths of geometry, though not of geography, as we are. Let us not be too sure that their condition and surroundings are altogether and utterly different from those of mankind. That is one of the things we may gradually find out not to be true.

Meanwhile is there anything that provisionally and tentatively we can say that is earnestly taught to those who are willing to make the hypothesis that the communications are genuine?

The first thing we learn, perhaps the only thing we clearly learn in the first instance, is *continuity*. There is no such sudden break in the conditions of existence as may have been anticipated; and no break at all in the continuous and conscious identity of genuine character and personality. Essential belongings, such as memory, culture, education, habits, character, and affection,—all these, and to a certain extent tastes and interests,—for better for worse, are retained. Terrestrial accretions, such as worldly possessions, bodily pain and disabilities, these for the most part naturally drop away.

Meanwhile it would appear that knowledge is not suddenly advanced—it would be unnatural if it were,— we are not suddenly flooded with new information, nor do we at all change our identity; but powers and faculties are enlarged, and the scope of our outlook on the universe may be widened and deepened, if effort here has rendered the acquisition of such extra insight legitimate and possible.

On the other hand, there are doubtless some whom the removal of temporary accretion and accidents of existence will leave in a feeble and impoverished condition; for the things are gone in which they trusted, and they are left poor indeed. Such doctrines have been taught, on the strength of vision and revelation— quite short of any recognised Divine revelation—for more than a century. The visions of Swedenborg, divested of their exuberant trappings, are not wholly unreal, and are by no means wholly untrue. There is

a general consistency in the doctrines that have thus
been taught through various sensitives, and all I do is
to add my testimony to the rational character of the
general survey of the universe indicated by Myers in
his great and eloquent work.

CHAPTER XXVII

IN MEMORY OF MYERS

I T behoves me who have learnt so much from the
Pioneers and Founders of the Society for Psychical
Research not to conclude this book,—which
attempts to set forth in some detail an outline of the
less orthodox facts by which among other things I
have been led to my views concerning the universe,—
without emphasising the debt I owe to those who have
immediately preceded me in this study; and I can
discharge the debt most compactly by quoting here
the Address which I gave to the Society for Psychical
Research shortly after the death of its President of
1900—on the occasion when it fell to my lot to succeed
him in the Chair.

In Memory of F. W. H. Myers

’Αρνύμενος ἥν τε ψυχὴν καὶ νόστον ἑταίρων

Who would have thought a year ago, when our
Secretary and joint Founder at length consented to be
elected President, that we should so soon be lamenting
his decease?

When Henry Sidgwick died, the Society was
orphaned; and now it is left desolate. Of the original
chief founders, Professor Barrett alone remains; for

341

Mr. Podmore, the only other member of the first Council still remaining on it, was not one of the actual founders of the Society. Neither the wisdom of Sidgwick nor the energy and power of Myers can by any means be replaced. Our loss is certain, but the blow must not be paralysing. Rather it must stimulate those that remain to fresh exertions, must band us together, determined that a group of workers called together for a pioneering work, for the founding and handing on to posterity of a new science, must not be permitted to disband and scatter till their work is done. That work will not be done in our lifetime; it must continue with what energy and wisdom we can muster, and we must be faithful to the noble leaders who summoned us together, and laid this burden to our charge.

I, unworthy, am called to this Chair. I would for every reason that it could have been postponed; but it is the wish of your Council; I am told that it was the wish of Myers, and I regard it as a duty from which I must not shrink.

The last communication which my predecessor made was in memory of Henry Sidgwick: my own first communication must be in memory of Frederic Myers.

To how many was he really known? I wonder. Known in a sense he was to all, except the unlettered and the ignorant. Known in reality he was to very few. But to the few who were privileged to know him, his is a precious memory: a memory which will not decay with the passing of the years. I was honoured with his intimate friendship. I esteem it one of the privileges of my life.

To me, though not to me alone, falls the duty of

doing some justice to his memory. I would that I might be inspired for the task.

I was not one of those who knew him as a youth, and my acquaintance with him ripened gradually. Our paths in life were wide apart, and our powers were different: our powers, but not our tastes. He could instruct me in literature and most other things, I could instruct him in science; he was the greedier learner of the two. I never knew a man more receptive, nor one with whom it was a greater pleasure to talk. His grasp of science was profound: I do not hesitate to say it, though many who did not really know him will fail to realise that this was possible; nor was he fully conscious of it himself. Even into some of the more technical details, when they were properly presented, he could and did enter, and his mind was in so prepared a state that any fact once sown in it began promptly to take root and bud. It was not a detailed knowledge of science that he possessed, of course, but it was a grasp, a philosophic grasp, of the meaning and bearing of it all,—not unlike the accurately comprehending grasp of Tennyson. And again and again in his writings do we find the facts, which his mind had thus from many sources absorbed, utilised for the purpose of telling and brilliant illustrations, and made to contribute each its quota to his Cosmic scheme.

For that is what he was really doing, all through this last quarter of a century: he was laying the foundation for a cosmic philosophy, a scheme of existence as large and comprehensive and well founded as any that have appeared.

Do I mean that he achieved such a structure? I do not. A philosophy of that kind is not to be constructed by the labour of one man, however brilliant; and Myers laboured almost solely on the psychological side.   He would be the first to deprecate any exaggeration of what he has done; but he himself would have admitted this,—that he strenuously and conscientiously sought facts, and endeavoured to construct his cosmic foundation by their aid and in their light, and not in the dark gropings of his own unaided intelligence.

To me it has seemed that most philosophers suffer from a dearth of facts.   In the past necessarily so, for the scientific exploration of the physical universe is, as it were, a thing of yesterday.   Our cosmic outlook is very different from that of the ancients, is different even from that of philosophers of the middle of last century, before the spectroscope was invented, before Darwin and Wallace wrote, before many discoveries connected with less familiar household words than these: in the matter of physical science alone the most recent philosopher must needs have some advantage.   But this is a small item in his total outfit, mental phenomena must contribute the larger part of that; and the facts of the mind have been open—it is generally assumed—from all antiquity.   This is in great degree true, and philosophers have always recognised and made use of these facts, especially those of the mind in its normal state.   Yet in modern science we realise that to understand a thing thoroughly it must be observed not only in its normal state but under all the conditions into which it can be thrown by experiment,—every variation being studied and laid under contribution to the general understanding of the whole.

And, I ask, did any philosopher ever know the facts of the mind in health and in disease more profoundly, with more detailed and intimate knowledge, drawn from personal inquiry, and from the testimony of all the savants of Europe, than did Frederic Myers? He laid under contribution every abnormal condition studied in the Salpêtrière, in hypnotic trance, in delirium, every state of the mind in placidity and in excitement. He was well acquainted with the curious facts of multiple personality, of clairvoyant vision, of hallucinations, automatisms, self-suggestion, of dreams, and of the waking visions of genius.

It will be said that Hegel, and to some extent Kant also, as well as other philosophers, recognised some ultra-normal mental manifestations, and allowed a place for clairvoyance in their scheme. All honour to those great men for doing so, in advance of the science of their time; but how could they know all that we know to-day? Fifty years ago the facts even of hypnotism were not by orthodox science accepted; such studies as were made, were made almost surreptitiously, here and there, by some truth-seeker clear-sighted enough to out-step the fashion of his time and to look at things with his own eyes. But only with difficulty could he publish his observations, and doubtless many were lost for fear of ridicule and the contempt of his professional brethren.

But now it is different: not so different as it ought to be, even yet; but facts previously considered occult are now investigated and recorded and published in every country of Europe. The men who observe them are too busy to unify them; they each contribute their portion, but they do not grasp the whole: the grasping of the whole is the function of a philosopher. I assert that Myers was that philosopher.

Do I then in my own mind place him on a pedestal

by the side of Plato and Kant? God forbid! I am
not one to juggle with great names and apportion
merit to the sages of mankind. Myers' may not
be a name which will sound down the ages as an
achiever and builder of a system of truth; but I do
claim for him that as an earnest pioneer and industrious
worker and clear-visioned student, he has laid a foundation, perhaps not even a foundation but a corner-stone,
on ground more solid than has ever been available
before; and I hold that the great quantity of knowledge
now open to any industrious truth-seeker gives a man
of modest merit and of self-distrustful powers, a lever,
a fulcrum, more substantial than those by which the
great men of antiquity and of the middle ages were
constrained to accomplish their mighty deeds.

Myers left behind two unpublished volumes on
Human Personality,—left them, alas, not finished, not
finally finished; how nearly finished I do not know.
I read fractions of them as they left his pen, and to me
they seemed likely to be an epoch-making work.

They are doubtless finished enough: more might
have been done, they might have been better ordered,
more highly polished, more neatly dove-tailed, had he
lived; but they represent for all time his real life work,
that for which he was willing to live laborious days;
they represent what he genuinely conceived to be a
message of moment to humanity: they are his legacy
to posterity; and in the light of the facts contained in
them he was willing and even eager to die.

The termination of his life, which took place at Rome
in presence of his family, was physically painful owing to
severe attacks of difficult breathing which constantly preceded sleep; but his bearing under it all was so patient
and elevated as to extort admiration from the excellent

Italian doctor who attended him. And in a private letter
by an eye-witness his departure was described as "a
spectacle for the Gods ; it was most edifying to see how
a genuine conviction of immortality can make a man
indifferent to what to ordinary people is so horrible."

In the intervals of painful breathing he quoted from
one of his own poems ("The Renewal of Youth,"—
which he preferred to earlier and better-known poems
of his, and from which alone I quote) :

> "Ah, welcome then that hour which bids thee lie
> In anguish of thy last infirmity !
> Welcome the toss for ease, the gasp for air,
> The visage drawn, and Hippocratic stare ;
> Welcome the darkening dream, the lost control,
> The sleep, the swoon, the arousal of the soul !"

Death he did not dread. That is true ; and his clear
and happy faith was the outcome entirely of his scientific
researches. The years of struggle and effort and
systematic thought had begotten in him a confidence as
absolute and supreme as is to be found in the holiest
martyr or saint. By this I mean that it was not possible
for any one to have a more absolute and childlike confidence that death was a mere physical event. To him
it was an adversity which must happen to the body, but
it was not one of those evil things which may assault and
hurt the soul.

An important and momentous event truly, even as
birth is ; a temporary lapse of consciousness, even as
trance may be ; a waking up to strange and new surroundings, like a more thorough emigration than any that can
be undertaken on a planet ; but a destruction or lessening
of power, no whit. Rather an enhancement of existence,
an awakening from this earthly dream, a casting off of
the trammels of the flesh, and putting on of a body more

adapted to the needs of an emancipated spirit, a wider
field of service,—a gradual opportunity of re-uniting with
the many who have gone before.   So he believed, on
what he thought a sure foundation of experience, and
in the strength of that belief he looked forward hopefully
to perennial effort and unending progress :

> "Say, could aught else content thee? which were best,
> After so brief a battle an endless rest,
> Or the ancient conflict rather to renew,
> By the old deeds strengthened mightier deeds to do?"

Such was his faith : by this he lived, and in this he
died.   Religious men in all ages have had some such
faith, perhaps a more restful and less strenuous faith ;
but to Myers the faith did not come by religion : he
would have described himself as one who walked by
sight and knowledge rather than by faith, and his eager
life-long struggle for knowledge was in order that he
might by no chance be mistaken.

To some, conviction of this kind would be impossible
—they are the many who know not what science is.   To
others, conviction of this kind seems unnecessary—they
are the favoured ones who feel that they have grasped all
needed truth by revelation or by intuition.   But by a few
here and there, even now, this avenue to knowledge
concerning the unseen is felt to be open.   Myers believed
that hereafter it would become open to all.   He knew
that the multitude could appreciate science no more,
perhaps less, than they can appreciate religion ; but he
knew further that when presently any truth becomes
universally accepted by scientific men, it will penetrate
downwards and be accepted by ordinary persons, as they
now accept any other established doctrine,—such as the
planetary position of the earth in the solar system, or the
evolution of species,—not because they have really made

a study of the matter, but because it is a part of the atmosphere into which they were born.

If continuity of existence and intelligence across the gulf of death really can ever be thus proved, it surely is a desirable and worthy object for science to aim at. There be some religious men of little faith who resent this attempted intrusion of scientific proof into their arena ; as if they had a limited field which could be encroached upon. Those men do not realise, as Myers did, the wealth of their inheritance. They little know the magnitude of the possibilities of the universe, the unimagined scope of the regions still, and perhaps for ever, beyond the grasp of what we now call science.

There was a little science in my youth which prided itself upon being positive knowledge, and sought to pour scorn upon the possibility, say, of prayer or of any mode of communication between this world and a purely hypothetical other. Honest and true and brilliant though narrow men held these beliefs and promulgated these doctrines for a time : they did good service in their day by clearing away some superstition, and, with their healthy breezy common-sense, freeing the mind from cant,—that is, from the conventional utterance of phrases embodying beliefs only half held. I say no word against the scientific men of that day, to whom were opposed theologians of equal narrowness and of a more bitter temper. But their warlike energy, though it made them effective crusaders, left their philosophy defective and their science unbalanced. It has not fully re-attained equilibrium yet. With Myers the word Science meant something much larger, much more comprehensive : it meant a science and a philosophy and a religion combined. It meant, as it meant to Newton, an attempt at a true cosmic scheme. His was no purblind outlook

on a material universe limited and conditioned by our
poor senses.   He had an imagination wider than that
of most men.   Myers spoke to me once of the possibility
that the parts of an atom move perhaps inside the atom
in astronomical orbits, as the planets move in the solar
system, each spaced out far away from others and not
colliding, but altogether constituting the single group or
system we call the atom,—a microcosm akin to the
visible cosmos ; which again might be only an atom of
some larger whole.   I was disposed at that time to
demur.   I should not demur now ; the progress of
science within the last few years of the nineteenth
century makes the first part of this thesis extremely
probable.   On the latter part too there is more to be
said than is generally known.   Physics and astronomy
are rapidly advancing in this direction.

Nor was it only upon material things that he looked
with the eye of prescience and of hope.   I never knew
a man so hopeful concerning his ultimate destiny.   He
once asked me whether I would barter—if it were
possible—my unknown destiny, whatever it might be,
for as many æons of unmitigated and wise terrestrial
happiness as might last till the secular fading of the sun,
and then an end.

He would not !   No limit could satisfy him.   That
which he was now he only barely knew,—for to him not
the whole of each personality is incarnate in this mortal
flesh, the subliminal self still keeps watch and ward
beyond the threshold, and is in touch always with another
life,—but that which he might come to be hereafter he
could by no means guess : οὔπω ἐφανερώθη τί ἐσόμεθα.
Gradually and perhaps through much suffering, from
which indeed he sensitively shrank, but through which
nevertheless he was ready to go, he believed that a

being would be evolved out of him,—"even," as he would say, "out of *him*,"—as much higher in the scale of creation as he now was above the meanest thing that crawls.

Nor yet an end. Infinity of infinities—he could conceive no end, of space or time or existence, nor yet of development : though an end of the solar system and therefore of mankind seemed to him comparatively imminent—

> "That hour may come when Earth no more can keep
> Tireless her year-long voyage thro' the deep ;
> Nay, when all planets, sucked and swept in one,
> Feed their rekindled solitary sun ;—
> Nay, when all suns that shine, together hurled,
> Crash in one infinite and lifeless world :—
> Yet hold thou still, what worlds soe'er may roll,
> Naught bear they with them master of the soul ;
> In all the eternal whirl, the cosmic stir,
> All the eternal is akin to her ;
> She shall endure, and quicken, and live at last,
> When all save souls has perished in the past."

Infinite progress, infinite harmony, infinite love,—these were the things which filled and dominated his existence. Limits for him were repellent and impossible. Limits conditioned by the flesh and by imperfection,—by rebellion, blindness, and error,—these are obvious, these he admitted and lamented to the full ; but ultimate limits, impassable barriers, cessation of development, a highest in the scale of being beyond which it was impossible to go,—these he would not admit, these seemed to him to contradict all that he had gleaned of the essence and meaning of existence.

Principalities and Powers on and on, up and up, without limit now and for ever,—this was the dominant note of his mind ; and if he seldom used the word God except in poetry, or employed the customary phrases, it was because everything was so supremely real to him ; and " God," the personified totality of existence, too blinding a conception to conceive.

For practical purposes something less lofty served, and he could return from cosmic speculations to the simple everyday life, which is for all of us the immediate business in hand, and which, if patiently pursued, seemed to him to lead to more than could be desired or deserved—

> " Live thou and love ! so best and only so
> Can thy one soul into the One Soul flow,—
> Can thy small life to Life's great centre flee,
> And thou be nothing, and the Lord in thee."

This is an expression of himself : it was not so much his creed as himself. He with his whole being and personality—at first slowly and painfully, with many rebuffs and after much delay and hesitation, but in the end richly and enthusiastically—rose to this height of emotion, of conviction, and of serenity ; though perhaps to few he showed it.

> " Either we cannot or we hardly dare
> Breathe forth that vision into earthly air ;
> And if ye call us dreamers, dreamers then
> Be we esteemed amid you waking men ;
> Hear us or hear not as ye choose ; but we
> Speak as we can, and are what we must be."

Not that he believed easily : let no man think that his faith came easily and cost him nothing. He has himself borne witness to the struggle, the groanings that could not be uttered. His was a keenly emotional nature. What he felt, he felt strongly ; what he believed, he believed in no half-hearted or conventional manner. When he doubted, he doubted fiercely ; but the pain of the doubt only stimulated him to effort, to struggle ; to know at least the worst, and doubt no longer. He was content with no half knowledge, no clouded faith, he must know or he must suffer, and in the end he believed that he knew.

Seeker after Truth and Helper of his comrades

is a line in his own metre, though not a quotation, which runs in my mind as descriptive of him; suggested doubtless by that line from the Odyssey which, almost in a manner at his own request, I have placed in the fore-front of this essay. For he speaks of himself in an infrequent autobiographical sentence as having "often a sense of great solitude, and of an effort beyond my strength; 'striving,'—as Homer says of Odysseus in a line which I should wish graven on some tablet in my memory,—'striving to save my own soul and my comrades' homeward way.'"

But the years of struggle and effort brought in the end ample recompense, for they gave him a magnificent power to alleviate distress. He was able to communicate something of his assurance to others, so that more than one bereaved friend learned to say with him—

"What matter if thou hold thy loved ones prest
Still with close arms upon thy yearning breast,
Or with purged eyes behold them hand in hand
Come in a vision from that lovely land,—
Or only with great heart and spirit sure
Deserve them and await them and endure;
Knowing well, no shocks that fall, no years that flee,
Can sunder God from these, or God from thee;
Nowise so far thy love from theirs can roam
As past the mansions of His endless home."

To how many a sorrowful heart his words have brought hope and comfort, letters, if ever published, will one day prove. The deep personal conviction behind his message drove it home with greater force,

23

nor did it lose influence because it was enfranchised
from orthodox traditions, and rang with no hollow professional note.

There are those who lament that with his undoubted
powers as a man of letters he to some extent deserted
the sunny fields of pure literature for the rugged tracts
of scientific inquiry; but indeed the two were closely
blended. It is, as Dr. Walter Leaf has said, impossible to appreciate Myers without insisting on this
interfusion :—

The essay on his best-beloved Virgil is perhaps that
of all his utterances which gives us most of his literary
self. And the very heart of Virgil was to him in the
famous speech of Anchises to Æneas in Elysium
(*Æn.* vi. 724–755), where the poet " who meant, as we
know, to devote to philosophy the rest of his life after
the completion of the ' Æneid ' " propounds " an answer
to the riddle of the universe in an unexpectedly definite
form."

This ultimate subordination of form to substance, of
art to thought, is the whole story of Myers's literary
work. His art gained all the more because it was not
pursued as a primary aim, and the obvious rewards
of it were little sought. Those only who followed the
working of his aspirations will adequately recognise his
mastery, and see how for him style was but the expression of his inmost soul. In his wonderful fragments
of Virgilian translation he reached his height. The
poet who was ever his truest ideal is transfused till the
Roman and the Englishman blend in one passion,
human and divine, and the triumphant song is taken up
and proclaimed again after two thousand years—

> " To God again the enfranchised soul must tend,
> He is her home, her Author is her end ;
> No death is hers ; when earthly eyes grow dim
> Starlike she soars and Godlike melts in Him."

INDEX

Printed by
MORRISON & GIBB LIMITED,
Edinburgh

A CATALOGUE OF BOOKS PUBLISHED BY METHUEN AND COMPANY: LONDON 36 ESSEX STREET W.C.

CONTENTS

SEPTEMBER 1909

A CATALOGUE OF
MESSRS. METHUEN'S
PUBLICATIONS

In this Catalogue the order is according to authors. An asterisk denotes that the book is in the press.

Colonial Editions are published of all Messrs. METHUEN'S Novels issued at a price above 2s. 6d., and similar editions are published of some works of General Literature. Colonial editions are only for circulation in the British Colonies and India.

All books marked net are not subject to discount, and cannot be bought at less than the published price. Books not marked net are subject to the discount which the bookseller allows.

Messrs. METHUEN'S books are kept in stock by all good booksellers. If there is any difficulty in seeing copies, Messrs. Methuen will be very glad to have early information, and specimen copies of any books will be sent on receipt of the published price *plus* postage for net books, and of the published price for ordinary books.

I.P.L. represents Illustrated Pocket Library.

PART I.—GENERAL LITERATURE

Abraham (George D.). THE COMPLETE MOUNTAINEER. With 75 Illustrations. *Second Edition. Demy 8vo.* 15s. *net.*

Acatos (M. J.). See Junior School Books.

Addleshaw (Percy). SIR PHILIP SIDNEY. With 12 Illustrations. *Demy 8vo.* 10s. 6d. *net.*

Adeney (W. F.), M.A. See Bennett (W. H.)

Ady (Cecilia M.). A HISTORY OF MILAN UNDER THE SFORZA. With 20 Illustrations and a Map. *Demy 8vo.* 10s. 6d. *net.*

Aeschylus. See Classical Translations.

Ainsworth (W. Harrison). See I.P.L.

Aldis (Janet). THE QUEEN OF LETTER WRITERS, MARQUISE DE SÉVIGNÉ, DAME DE BOURBILLY, 1626-96. With 18 Illustrations. *Second Edition. Demy 8vo.* 12s. 6d. *net.*

Alexander (William), D.D., Archbishop of Armagh. THOUGHTS AND COUNSELS OF MANY YEARS. *Demy 16mo.* 2s. 6d.

Aiken (Henry). See I.P.L.

Allen (Charles C.). See Textbooks of Technology.

Allen (L. Jessie). See Little Books on Art.

Allen (J. Romilly), F.S.A. See Antiquary's Books.

Almack (E.), F.S.A. See Little Books on Art.

Amherst (Lady). A SKETCH OF EGYPTIAN HISTORY FROM THE EARLIEST TIMES TO THE PRESENT DAY. With many Illustrations and Maps. *A New and Cheaper Issue. Demy 8vo.* 7s. 6d. *net.*

Anderson (F. M.). THE STORY OF THE BRITISH EMPIRE FOR CHILDREN. With 42 Illustrations. *Cr. 8vo.* 2s.

Anderson (J. G.), B.A., NOUVELLE GRAMMAIRE FRANÇAISE, À L'USAGE DES ÉCOLES ANGLAISES. *Crown 8vo.* 2s.

EXERCICES DE GRAMMAIRE FRANÇAISE. *Cr. 8vo.* 1s. 6d.

Andrewes (Bishop). PRECES PRIVATAE. Translated and edited, with Notes, by F. E. BRIGHTMAN. M.A., of Pusey House, Oxford. *Cr. 8vo.* 6s.

See also Library of Devotion.

'Anglo-Australian.' AFTER-GLOW MEMORIES. *Cr. 8vo.* 6s.

Anon. THE BUDGET, THE LAND AND THE PEOPLE. *Second Edition. Crown 8vo.* 6d. *net.*

HEALTH, WEALTH, AND WISDOM. *Crown 8vo.* 1s. *net.*

THE WESTMINSTER PROBLEMS BOOK. Prose and Verse. Compiled from *The Saturday Westminster Gazette* Competitions, 1904-1907. *Cr. 8vo.* 3s. 6d. *net.*

VENICE AND HER TREASURES. With many Illustrations. *Round corners. Fcap. 8vo.* 5s. *net.*

Aristotle. THE ETHICS OF. Edited, with an Introduction and Notes by JOHN BURNET, M.A., *Cheaper issue. Demy 8vo.* 10s. 6d. *net.*

Asman (H. N.), M.A., B.D. See Junior School Books.

Atkins (H. G.). See Oxford Biographies.

Atkinson (C. M.). JEREMY BENTHAM. *Demy 8vo.* 5s. *net.*

Atkinson (C. T.), M.A., Fellow of Exeter College, Oxford, sometime Demy of Magdalen College. A HISTORY OF GERMANY, from 1713 to 1815. With 35 Maps and Plans *Demy 8vo.* 15s. *net.*

Atkinson (T. D.). ENGLISH ARCHITECTURE. With 196 Illustrations. *Fcap. 8vo.* 3s. 6d. net.

A GLOSSARY OF TERMS USED IN ENGLISH ARCHITECTURE. With 265 Illustrations. *Second Edition. Fcap. 8vo.* 3s. 6d. net.

Atteridge (A. H.). NAPOLEON'S BROTHERS. With 24 Illustrations. *Demy 8vo.* 18s. net.

Auden (T.), M.A., F.S.A. See Ancient Cities.

Aurelius (Marcus). WORDS OF THE ANCIENT WISE. Thoughts from Epictetus and Marcus Aurelius. Edited by W. H. D. ROUSE, M.A., Litt. D. *Fcap. 8vo.* 3s. 6d. net.
See also Standard Library.

Austen (Jane). See Standard Library, Little Library and Mitton (G. E.).

Aves (Ernest). CO-OPERATIVE INDUSTRY. *Crown 8vo.* 5s. net.

Bacon (Francis). See Standard Library and Little Library.

Bagot (Richard). THE LAKES OF NORTHERN ITALY. With 37 Illustrations and a Map. *Fcap. 8vo.* 5s. net.

Bailey (J. C.), M.A. See Cowper (W.).

*****Bain (R. Nisbet).** THE LAST KING OF POLAND AND HIS CONTEMPORARIES. With 16 Illustrations. *Demy 8vo.* 10s. 6d. net.

Baker (W. G.), M.A. See Junior Examination Series.

Baker (Julian L.), F.I.C., F.C.S. See Books on Business.

Balfour (Graham). THE LIFE OF ROBERT LOUIS STEVENSON. With a Portrait. *Fourth Edition in one Volume. Cr. 8vo. Buckram, 6s.*

Ballard (A.), B.A., LL.D. See Antiquary's Books.

Bally (S. E.). See Commercial Series.

Barham (R. H.). See Little Library.

Baring (The Hon. Maurice). WITH THE RUSSIANS IN MANCHURIA. *Third Edition. Demy 8vo.* 7s. 6d. net.

A YEAR IN RUSSIA. *Second Edition. Demy 8vo.* 10s. 6d. net.

RUSSIAN ESSAYS AND STORIES. *Second Edition. Cr. 8vo.* 5s. net.
Also published in a Colonial Edition.

Baring=Gould (S.). THE LIFE OF NAPOLEON BONAPARTE. With nearly 200 Illustrations, including a Photogravure Frontispiece. *Second Edition. Wide Royal 8vo.* 10s. 6d. net.

THE TRAGEDY OF THE CÆSARS: A STUDY OF THE CHARACTERS OF THE CÆSARS OF THE JULIAN AND CLAUDIAN HOUSES. With numerous Illustrations from Busts, Gems, Cameos, etc. *Sixth Edition. Royal 8vo.* 10s. 6d. net.

A BOOK OF FAIRY TALES. With numerous Illustrations by A. J. GASKIN.

Second Edition. Cr. 8vo. Buckram. 6s., also *Medium 8vo.* 6d.

OLD ENGLISH FAIRY TALES. With numerous Illustrations by F. D. BEDFORD. *Third Edition. Cr. 8vo. Buckram.* 6s.

THE VICAR OF MORWENSTOW. Revised Edition. With a Portrait. *Third Edition. Cr. 8vo.* 3s. 6d.

OLD COUNTRY LIFE. With 69 Illustrations. *Fifth Edition. Large Crown 8vo.* 6s.

A GARLAND OF COUNTRY SONG: English Folk Songs with their Traditional Melodies. Collected and arranged by S. BARING-GOULD and H. F. SHEPPARD. *Demy 4to.* 6s.

SONGS OF THE WEST: Folk Songs of Devon and Cornwall. Collected from the Mouths of the People. By S. BARING-GOULD, M.A., and H. FLEETWOOD SHEPPARD, M.A. New and Revised Edition, under the musical editorship of CECIL J. SHARP. *Large Imperial 8vo.* 5s. net.

A BOOK OF NURSERY SONGS AND RHYMES. Edited by S. BARING-GOULD. Illustrated. *Second and Cheaper Edition. Large Cr. 8vo.* 2s. 6d. net.

STRANGE SURVIVALS: SOME CHAPTERS IN THE HISTORY OF MAN. Illustrated. *Third Edition. Cr. 8vo.* 2s. 6d. net.

YORKSHIRE ODDITIES: INCIDENTS AND STRANGE EVENTS. *Fifth Edition. Cr. 8vo.* 2s. 6d. net.

THE BARING-GOULD SELECTION READER. Arranged by G. H. ROSE. Illustrated. *Crown 8vo.* 1s. 6d.

THE BARING-GOULD CONTINUOUS READER. Arranged by G. H. ROSE. Illustrated. *Crown 8vo.* 1s. 6d.

A BOOK OF CORNWALL. With 33 Illustrations. *Second Edition. Cr. 8vo.* 6s.

A BOOK OF DARTMOOR. With 60 Illustrations. *Second Edition. Cr. 8vo.* 6s.

A BOOK OF DEVON. With 35 Illustrations. *Third Edition. Cr. 8vo.* 6s.

A BOOK OF NORTH WALES. With 49 Illustrations. *Cr. 8vo.* 6s.

A BOOK OF SOUTH WALES. With 57 Illustrations. *Cr. 8vo.* 6s.

A BOOK OF BRITTANY. With 69 Illustrations. *Second Edition Cr. 8vo.* 6s.

A BOOK OF THE RHINE: From Cleve to Mainz. With 8 Illustrations in Colour by TREVOR HADDEN, and 48 other Illustrations. *Second Edition. Cr. 8vo.* 6s.

A BOOK OF THE RIVIERA. With 40 Illustrations. *Cr. 8vo.* 6s.

A BOOK OF THE PYRENEES. With 25 Illustrations. *Cr. 8vo.* 6s.
See also Little Guides.

Barker (Aldred F.). See Textbooks of Technology.

Barker (E.), M.A. (Late) Fellow of Merton College, Oxford. THE POLITICAL THOUGHT OF PLATO AND ARISTOTLE. *Demy 8vo.* 10s. 6d. net.

Barnes (W. E.), D.D. See Churchman's Bible.

Barnett (Mrs. P. A.). See Little Library.
Baron (R. R. N.), M.A. FRENCH PROSE COMPOSITION. *Fourth Edition. Cr. 8vo. 2s. 6d. Key,* 3s. *net.*
See also Junior School Books.
Barron (H. M.), M.A., Wadham College, Oxford. TEXTS FOR SERMONS. With a Preface by Canon SCOTT HOLLAND. *Cr. 8vo.* 3s. 6d.
Bartholomew (J. G.), F.R.S.E See Robertson (C. G.).
Bastable (C. F.), LL.D. THE COMMERCE OF NATIONS. *Fourth Ed. Cr. 8vo.* 2s. 6d.
Bastian (H. Charlton), M.A., M.D., F.R.S. THE EVOLUTION OF LIFE. With Diagrams and many Photomicrographs. *Demy 8vo.* 7s. 6d. *net.*
Batson (Mrs. Stephen). A CONCISE HANDBOOK OF GARDEN FLOWERS. *Fcap. 8vo.* 3s. 6d.
THE SUMMER GARDEN OF PLEASURE. With 36 Illustrations in Colour by OSMUND PITTMAN. *Wide Demy 8vo.* 15s. *net.*
Bayley (R. Child). THE COMPLETE PHOTOGRAPHER. With over 100 Illustrations. With Note on Direct Colour Process. *Third Edition. Demy 8vo.* 10s. 6d. *net.*
Beard (W. S.). EASY EXERCISES IN ALGEBRA FOR BEGINNERS. *Cr. 8vo.* 1s. 6d. With Answers. 1s. 9d.
See also Junior Examination Series and Beginner's Books.
Beckett (Arthur). ┆THE SPIRIT OF THE DOWNS : Impressions and Reminiscences of the Sussex Downs. With 20 Illustrations in Colour by STANLEY INCHBOLD. *Demy 8vo.* 10s. 6d. *net.*
Beckford (Peter). THOUGHTS ON HUNTING. Edited by J. OTHO PAGET, and Illustrated by G. H. JALLAND. *Second Edition. Demy 8vo.* 6s.
Beckford (William). See Little Library.
Beeching (H. C.), M.A., Canon of Westminster. See Library of Devotion.
Beerbohm (Max). A BOOK OF CARICATURES. *Imperial 4to.* 21s. *net.*
Begbie (Harold). MASTER WORKERS. Illustrated. *Demy 8vo.* 7s. 6d. *net.*
Behmen (Jacob). DIALOGUES ON THE SUPERSENSUAL LIFE. Edited by BERNARD HOLLAND. *Fcap. 8vo.* 3s. 6d.
Bell (Mrs. Arthur G.). THE SKIRTS OF THE GREAT CITY. With 16 Illustrations in Colour by ARTHUR G. BELL, 17 other Illustrations, and a Map. *Second Edition. Cr. 8vo.* 6s.
Belloc (H.) PARIS. With 7 Maps and a Frontispiece in Photogravure. *Second Edition, Revised. Cr. 8vo.* 6s.
HILLS AND THE SEA. *Second Edition. Crown 8vo.* 6s.
ON NOTHING AND KINDRED SUBJECTS. *Second Edition. Fcap. 8vo.* 5s.
*ON EVERYTHING. *Fcap. 8vo.* 5s.
MARIE ANTOINETTE. With 35 Portraits

and Illustrations, and 22 Maps. *Demy 8vo.* 15s. *net.*
THE PYRENEES. With 46 Sketches by the Author, and 22 Maps. *Second Edition. Demy 8vo.* 7s. 6d. *net.*
Bellot (H. H. L.), M.A. See Jones (L. A. A.).
Bennett (Joseph). FORTY YEARS OF MUSIC, 1865-1905. With 24 Illustrations. *Demy 8vo.* 16s. *net.*
Bennett (W. H.), M.A. A PRIMER OF THE BIBLE. *Fifth Edition. Cr. 8vo.* 2s. 6d.
Bennett (W. H.) and Adeney (W. F.). A BIBLICAL INTRODUCTION. With a concise Bibliography. *Fifth Edition. Cr. 8vo.* 7s. 6d.
Benson (Archbishop) GOD'S BOARD. Communion Addresses. *Second Edition. Fcap. 8vo.* 3s. 6d. *net.*
Benson (A. C.), M.A. See Oxford Biographies.
Benson (R. M.). THE WAY OF HOLINESS. An Exposition of Psalm cxix. Analytical and Devotional.
Bernard (E. R.), M.A., Canon of Salisbury THE ENGLISH SUNDAY: ITS ORIGINS AND ITS CLAIMS. *Fcap. 8vo.* 1s. 6d.
Berry (W. Grinton), M.A. FRANCE SINCE WATERLOO. With 16 Illustrations and Maps. *Cr. 8vo.* 6s.
Beruete (A. de). See Classics of Art.
Betham-Edwards (Miss). HOME LIFE IN FRANCE. With 20 Illustrations. *Fifth Edition. Crown 8vo.* 6s.
Bethune-Baker (J. F.), M.A. See Handbooks of Theology.
Bindley (T. Herbert), B.D. THE OECUMENICAL DOCUMENTS OF THE FAITH. With Introductions and Notes. *Second Edition. Cr. 8vo.* 6s. *net.*
Binns (H. B.). THE LIFE OF WALT WHITMAN. Illustrated. *Demy 8vo.* 10s. 6d. *net.*
Binyon (Mrs. Laurence). NINETEENTH CENTURY PROSE. Selected and arranged by. *Crown 8vo.* 6s.
Binyon (Laurence). THE DEATH OF ADAM AND OTHER POEMS. *Cr. 8vo.* 3s. 6d. *net.*
See also Blake (William).
Birch (Walter de Gray), LL.D., F.S.A. See Connoisseur's Library.
Birnstingl (Ethel). See Little Books on Art.
Blackmantle (Bernard). See I.P.L.
Blair (Robert). See I.P.L.
Blake (William). THE LETTERS OF WILLIAM BLAKE, TOGETHER WITH A LIFE BY FREDERICK TATHAM. Edited from the Original Manuscripts, with an Introduction and Notes, by ARCHIBALD G. B. RUSSELL. With 12 Illustrations. *Demy 8vo.* 7s. 6d. *net.*
ILLUSTRATIONS OF THE BOOK OF JOB. With General Introduction by LAURENCE BINYON. *Quarto.* 21s. *net.*
See also I.P.L., and Little Library.

Bloom (J. Harvey), M.A. See Antiquary's Books.

Blouet (Henri). See Beginner's Books.

Boardman (T. H.), M.A. See French (W.).

Bode (Wilhelm), Ph.D. See Classics of Art.

Bodley (J. E. C.) THE CORONATION OF EDWARD VII. *Demy 8vo.* 21s. net. By Command of the King.

Body (George), D.D. THE SOUL'S PILGRIMAGE : Devotional Readings from the Published and Unpublished writings of George Body, D.D. Selected and arranged by J. H. BURN, B.D., F.R.S.E. *Demy 16mo.* 2s. 6d.

Bona (Cardinal). See Library of Devotion.

Bonnor (Mary L.). See Little Books on Art.

Boon (F. C.)., B.A. See Commercial Series.

Borrow (George). See Little Library.

Bos (J. Ritzema). AGRICULTURAL ZOOLOGY. Translated by J. R. AINSWORTH DAVIS, M.A. With 155 Illustrations. *Second Edition. Cr. 8vo.* 3s. 6d.

Botting (C. G.), B.A. EASY GREEK EXERCISES. *Cr. 8vo.* 2s. See also Junior Examination Series.

Boulting (W.) TASSO AND HIS TIMES. With 24 Illustrations. *Demy 8vo.* 10s. 6d. net.

Boulton (E. S.), M.A. GEOMETRY ON MODERN LINES. *Cr. 8vo.* 2s.

Boulton (William B.). SIR JOSHUA REYNOLDS, P.R.A. With 49 Illustrations. *Second Edition. Demy 8vo.* 7s. 6d. net.

Bovill (W. B. Forster). HUNGARY AND THE HUNGARIANS. With 16 Illustrations in Colour by WILLIAM PASCOE, 12 other Illustrations and a Map. *Demy 8vo.* 7s. 6d. net.

Bowden (E. M.). THE IMITATION OF BUDDHA : Being Quotations from Buddhist Literature for each Day in the Year. *Fifth Edition. Cr. 16mo.* 2s. 6d.

Bower (E.), B.A. See New Historical Series.

Boyle (W.). CHRISTMAS AT THE ZOO. With Verses by W. BOYLE and 24 Coloured Pictures by H. B. NEILSON. *Super Royal 16mo.* 2s.

Brabant (F. G.), M.A. RAMBLES IN SUSSEX. With 30 Illustrations. *Crown 8vo.* 6s. See also Little Guides.

Bradley (A. G.). ROUND ABOUT WILTSHIRE. With 14 Illustrations, in Colour by T. C. GOTCH, 16 other Illustrations, and a Map. *Second Edition. Cr. 8vo.* 6s. THE ROMANCE OF NORTHUMBERLAND. With 16 Illustrations in Colour by FRANK SOUTHGATE, R.B.A., and 12 from Photographs. *Second Edition. Demy 8vo.* 7s. 6d net.

Bradley (John W.). See Little Books on Art.

Braid (James), Open Champion, 1901, 1905 and 1906. ADVANCED GOLF. With 88 Photographs and Diagrams. *Fifth Edition. Demy 8vo.* 10s. 6d. net.

Braid (James) and Others. GREAT GOLFERS IN THE MAKING. Edited by HENRY LEACH. With 24 Illustrations. *Second Edition. Demy 8vo.* 7s. 6d. net.

Brailsford (H. N.). MACEDONIA: ITS RACES AND THEIR FUTURE. With 32 Illustrations and 2 Maps. *Demy 8vo.* 12s. 6d. net.

Brentano (C.). See Simplified German Texts.

Brightman (F. E.), M.A. See Andrewes (Lancelot).

Brock (A. Clutton). SHELLEY: THE MAN AND THE POET. With 12 Illustrations. *Demy 8vo.* 7s. 6d. net.

Brodrick (Mary) and Morton (A. Anderson). A CONCISE DICTIONARY OF EGYPTIAN ARCHÆOLOGY. A Hand-Book for Students and Travellers. With 80 Illustrations and many Cartouches. *Cr. 8vo.* 3s. 6d.

Brooks (E. E.), B.Sc. (Lond.), Leicester Municipal Technical School, and **James (W. H. N.), A.M.I.E.E., A.R.C.Sc.,** Municipal School of Technology, Manchester. See Textbooks of Technology.

Brown (S. E.), M.A., B.Sc., Senior Science Master at Uppingham. A PRACTICAL CHEMISTRY NOTE-BOOK FOR MATRICULATION AND ARMY CANDIDATES. Easy Experiments on the Commoner Substances. *Cr. 4to.* 1s. 6d. net.

Brown (J. Wood), M.A. THE BUILDERS OF FLORENCE. With 74 Illustrations by HERBERT RAILTON. *Demy 4to.* 18s. net.

Browne (Sir Thomas). See Standard Library.

Brownell (C. L.). THE HEART OF JAPAN. Illustrated. *Third Edition. Cr. 8vo.* 6s. Also *Medium 8vo.* 6d.

Browning (Robert). See Little Library.

Bryant (Walter W.), B.A., F.R.A.S., F.R. Met. Soc., of the Royal Observatory, Greenwich. A HISTORY OF ASTRONOMY. With 47 Illustrations. *Demy 8vo.* 7s. 6d .net.

Buckland (Francis T.). CURIOSITIES OF NATURAL HISTORY. Illustrated by H. B. NEILSON. *Cr. 8vo.* 3s. 6d.

Buckton (A. M.) THE BURDEN OF ENGELA. *Second Edition. Cr. 8vo.* 3s. 6d. net.

EAGER HEART : A Mystery Play. *Seventh Edition. Cr. 8vo.* 1s. net.

KINGS IN BABYLON : A Drama. *Cr. 8vo.* 1s. net.

SONGS OF JOY. *Cr. 8vo.* 1s. net.

Budge (E. A. Wallis). THE GODS OF THE EGYPTIANS. With over 100 Coloured Plates and many Illustrations. *Two Volumes. Royal 8vo.* £3, 3s. net.

Buist Massac (H.). THE COMPLETE AERONAUT. With many Illustrations. *Demy 8vo.* 12s. 6d. net.

Bull (Paul), Army Chaplain. GOD AND OUR SOLDIERS. *Second Edition. Cr. 8vo.* 6s.

Bulley (Miss). See Dilke (Lady).

Bunyan (John). THE PILGRIM'S PRO-GRESS. Edited, with an Introduction by C. H. FIRTH, M.A. With 39 Illustrations by R. ANNING BELL. *Crown 8vo. 6s.* See also Standard Library and Library of Devotion.

Burch (G. J.), M.A., F.R.S. A MANUAL OF ELECTRICAL SCIENCE. Illustrated. *Cr. 8vo. 3s.*

Burgess (Gelett). GOOPS AND HOW TO BE THEM. Illustrated. *Small 4to. 6s.*

Burke (Edmund). See Standard Library.

Burn (A. E.), D.D., Rector of Handsworth and Prebendary of Lichfield. See Handbooks of Theology.

Burn (J. H.), B.D., F.R.S.E. THE CHURCHMAN'S TREASURY OF SONG: Gathered from the Christian poetry of all ages. Edited by. *Fcap. 8vo. 3s. 6d. net.* See also Library of Devotion.

Burnet (John), M.A. See Aristotle.

Burns (Robert), THE POEMS. Edited by ANDREW LANG and W. A. CRAIGIE. With Portrait. *Third Edition. Wide Demy 8vo, gilt top. 6s.* See also Standard Library.

Burnside (W. F.), M.A. OLD TESTAMENT HISTORY FOR USE IN SCHOOLS. *Third Edition. Cr. 8vo. 3s. 6d.*

Burton (Alfred). See I.P.L.

Bury (J. B.), M.A., Litt. D. See Gibbon (Edward).

Bussell (F. W.), D.D. CHRISTIAN THEOLOGY AND SOCIAL PROGRESS (The Bampton Lectures of 1905). *Demy 8vo. 10s. 6d. net.*

Butler (Joseph), D.D. See Standard Library.

Butlin (F. M.). AMONG THE DANES. With 12 Illustrations in Colour by ELLEN WILKINSON, and 15 from Photographs. *Demy 8vo. 7s. 6d. net.*

Cain (Georges), Curator of the Carnavalet Museum, Paris. WALKS IN PARIS. Translated by A. R. ALLINSON, M.A. With a Frontispiece in Colour by MAXWELL ARMFIELD, and 118 other Illustrations. *Demy 8vo. 7s. 6d. net.*

Caldecott (Alfred), D.D. See Handbooks of Theology.

Calderwood (D. S.), Headmaster of the Normal School, Edinburgh. TEST CARDS IN EUCLID AND ALGEBRA. In three packets of 40, with Answers. *1s.* each. Or in three books, price *2d., 2d.,* and *3d.*

Cameron (Mary Lovett). OLD ETRURIA AND MODERN TUSCANY. With 32 Illustrations. *Crown 8vo. 7s. 6d. net.*

Cannan (Edwin), M.A. See Smith (Adam).

Canning (George). See Little Library.

Capey (E. F. H.). See Oxford Biographies.

Carden (Robert W.). THE CITY OF GENOA. With 12 Illustrations in Colour by WILLIAM PARKINSON, and 20 other Illustrations. *Demy 8vo. 10s. 6d. net.*

Careless (John). See I.P.L.

Carlyle (Thomas). THE FRENCH REVOLUTION. Edited by C. R. L. FLETCHER, Fellow of Magdalen College, Oxford. *Three Volumes. Cr. 8vo. 18s.* THE LETTERS AND SPEECHES OF OLIVER CROMWELL. With an Introduction by C. H. FIRTH, M.A., and Notes and Appendices by Mrs. S. C. LOMAS. *Three Volumes. Demy 8vo. 18s. net.*

Carlyle (R. M. and A. J.), M.A. See Leaders of Religion.

Carmichael (Philip). ALL ABOUT PHILIPPINE. With 8 Illustrations. *Cr. 8vo. 2s. 6d.*

Carpenter (Margaret Boyd). THE CHILD IN ART. With 50 Illustrations. *Second Edition. Large Cr. 8vo. 6s.*

*****Carter (George),** M.A. THE STORY OF MILTON'S 'PARADISE LOST.' *Crown 8vo. 1s. 6d.*

Cavanagh (Francis), M.D. (Edin.). See New Library of Medicine.

Celano (Brother Thomas of). THE LIVES OF FRANCIS OF ASSISI. Translated by A. G. FERRERS HOWELL. With a Frontispiece. *Cr. 8vo. 5s. net.*

Chambers (A. M.). A CONSTITUTIONAL HISTORY OF ENGLAND. *Crown 8vo. 6s.*

Chamisso (A. von). See Simplified German Texts.

Chandler (Arthur), Bishop of Bloemfontein. ARA CŒLI : AN ESSAY IN MYSTICAL THEOLOGY. *Third Edition. Crown 8vo. 3s. 6d. net.*

Channer (C. C.) and Roberts (M. E.). LACEMAKING IN THE MIDLANDS, PAST AND PRESENT. With 17 full-page Illustrations. *Cr. 8vo. 2s. 6d.*

Chapman (S. J.). See Books on Business.

Chatterton (Thomas). See Standard Library.

Chesterfield (Lord), THE LETTERS OF THE EARL OF CHESTERFIELD TO HIS SON. Edited, with an Introduction by C. STRACHEY, with Notes by A. CALTHROP. *Two Volumes. Cr. 8vo. 12s.*

Chesterton (G. K.). CHARLES DICKENS. With two Portraits in Photogravure. *Fifth Edition. Cr. 8vo. 6s.* ALL THINGS CONSIDERED. *Fourth Edition. Fcap. 8vo. 5s.* TREMENDOUS TRIFLES. *Fcap. 8vo. 5s.*

Childe (Charles P.), B.A., F.R.C.S. See New Library of Medicine.

Cicero. See Classical Translations.

Clapham (J. H.), Professor of Economics in the University of Leeds. THE WOOLLEN AND WORSTED INDUSTRIES. With 21 Illustrations and Diagrams. *Cr. 8vo. 6s.*

Clarke (F. A.), M.A. See Leaders of Religion.

Clausen (George), A.R.A., R.W.S. SIX LECTURES ON PAINTING. With 16

Illustrations. *Third Edition. Large Post 8vo. 3s. 6d. net.*

AIMS AND IDEALS IN ART. Eight Lectures delivered to the Students of the Royal Academy of Arts. With 32 Illustrations. *Second Edition. Large Post 8vo. 5s. net.*

Clay (Rotha Mary). See Antiquary's Books.

Cleather (A. L.). See Wagner (R.).

Clinch (G.), F.G.S. See Antiquary's Books and Little Guides.

Clough (W. T.) and Dunstan (A. E.). See Junior School Books and Textbooks of Science.

Clouston (T. S.), M.D., C.C.D., F.R.S.E. See New Library of Medicine.

Coast (W. G.), B.A. EXAMINATION PAPERS IN VERGIL. *Cr. 8vo. 2s.*

Cobb (W. F.), M.A. THE BOOK OF PSALMS : with an Introduction and Notes. *Demy 8vo. 10s. 6d. net.*

*Cockshott (Winifred), St. Hilda's Hall, Oxford. THE PILGRIM FATHERS, THEIR CHURCH AND COLONY. With 12 Illustrations. *Demy 8vo. 7s. 6d. net.*

Collingwood (W. G.), M.A. THE LIFE OF JOHN RUSKIN. With Portrait. *Sixth Edition. Cr. 8vo. 2s. 6d. net.*

Collins (W. E.), M.A. See Churchman's Library.

Colvill (Helen H.). ST. TERESA OF SPAIN. With 20 Illustrations. *Demy 8vo. 7s. 6d. net.*

Combe (William). See I.P.L.

Conrad (Joseph). THE MIRROR OF THE SEA: Memories and Impressions. *Third Edition. Cr. 8vo. 6s.*

Cook (A. M.), M.A., and Marchant (E. C.), M.A. PASSAGES FOR UNSEEN TRANSLATION. Selected from Latin and Greek Literature. *Fourth Ed. Cr. 8vo. 3s. 6d.*
LATIN PASSAGES FOR UNSEEN TRANSLATION. *Cr. 8vo. 1s. 6d.*

Cooke-Taylor (R. W.). THE FACTORY SYSTEM. *Cr. 8vo. 2s. 6d.*

Coolidge (W. A. B.), M.A. THE ALPS. With many Illustrations. *Demy 8vo. 7s. 6d. net.*

Cooper (C. S.), F.R.H.S. See Westell (W.P.)

Corkran (Alice). See Little Books on Art.

Cotes (Rosemary). DANTE'S GARDEN. With a Frontispiece. *Second Edition. Fcap. 8vo. 2s. 6d.; leather, 3s. 6d. net.*
BIBLE FLOWERS. With a Frontispiece and Plan. *Fcap. 8vo. 2s. 6d. net.*

Cotton (Charles). See I.P.L. and Little Library.

Coulton (G. G.). CHAUCER AND HIS ENGLAND. *Second Edition. Demy 8vo. 10s. 6d. net.*

Cowley (Abraham). See Little Library.

Cowper (William). THE POEMS. Edited with an Introduction and Notes by J. C. BAILEY, M.A. Illustrated, including two unpublished designs by WILLIAM BLAKE. *Demy 8vo. 10s. 6d. net.*

Cox (J. Charles). See Ancient Cities, Antiquary's Books, and Little Guides.

Cox (Harold), B.A., M.P. LAND NATIONALIZATION AND LAND TAXATION. *Second Edition revised. Cr. 8vo. 3s. 6d. net.*

Crabbe (George). See Little Library.

Craik (Mrs.). See Little Library.

Crane (C. P.), D.S.O. See Little Guides.

Crane (Walter), R.W.S. AN ARTIST'S REMINISCENCES. With 123 Illustrations by the Author and others from Photographs. *Second Edition. Demy 8vo. 18s. net.*
INDIA IMPRESSIONS. With 84 Illustrations from Sketches by the Author. *Second Edition. Demy 8vo. 7s. 6d. net.*

Crashaw (Richard). See Little Library.

Crispe (T. E.), K.C. REMINISCENCES OF A K.C. With Portraits. *Demy 8vo. 10s. 6d. net.*

Cross (J. A.), M.A. THE FAITH OF THE BIBLE. *Fcap. 8vo. 2s. 6d. net.*

*Crowley (Ralph H.). THE HYGIENE OF SCHOOL LIFE. *Cr. 8vo. 3s. 6d. net.*

Cruikshank (G.). THE LOVING BALLAD OF LORD BATEMAN. With 11 Plates. *Cr. 16mo. 1s. 6d. net.*

Crump (B.). See Wagner (R.).

Cruttwell (C. T.), M.A., Canon of Peterborough. See Handbooks of English Church History.

Cunynghame (H. H.), C.B. See Connoisseur's Library.

Cutts (E. L.), D.D. See Leaders of Religion.

Daniell (G. W.), M.A. See Leaders of Religion.

Dante (Alighieri). LA COMMEDIA DI DANTE. The Italian Text edited by PAGET TOYNBEE, M.A., D.Litt. *Cr. 8vo. 6s.*
THE DIVINE COMEDY. Translated by H. F. CARY. Edited with a Life of Dante and Introductory Notes by PAGET TOYNBEE, M.A., D.Litt. *Demy 8vo. 6d.*
THE PURGATORIO OF DANTE. Translated into Spenserian Prose by C. GORDON WRIGHT. With the Italian text. *Fcap. 8vo. 2s. 6d. net.*
See also Little Library, Toynbee (Paget), and Vernon (Hon. W. Warren).

Darley (George). See Little Library.

D'Arcy (R. F.), M.A. A NEW TRIGONOMETRY FOR BEGINNERS. With numerous diagrams. *Cr. 8vo. 2s. 6d.*

Daudet (Alphonse). See Simplified French Texts.

Davenport (Cyril). See Connoisseur's Library and Little Books on Art.

Davenport (James). THE WASHBOURNE FAMILY. With 15 Illustrations and a Map. *Royal 8vo. 21s. net.*

Davey (Richard.) THE PAGEANT OF LONDON. With 40 Illustrations in Colour by JOHN FULLEYLOVE, R.I. *In Two Volumes. Demy 8vo. 15s. net.*
See also Romantic History.

Davies (Gerald S.). See Classics of Art.

Davies (W. O. P.). See Junior Examination Series.

Davis (H. W. C.), M.A., Fellow and Tutor of Balliol College. ENGLAND UNDER THE NORMANS AND ANGEVINS : 1066-1272. With Maps and Illustrations. *Demy 8vo.* 10s. 6d. net.

Dawson (Nelson). See Connoisseur's Library.

Dawson (Mrs. Nelson). See Little Books on Art.

Deane (A. C.). See Little Library.

Deans (Storry R.). THE TRIALS OF FIVE QUEENS : KATHARINE OF ARAGON, ANNE BOLEYN, MARY QUEEN OF SCOTS, MARIE ANTOINETTE and CAROLINE OF BRUNSWICK. With 12 Illustrations. *Demy 8vo.* 10s. 6d. net.

Dearmer (Mabel). A CHILD'S LIFE OF CHRIST. With 8 Illustrations in Colour by E. FORTESCUE-BRICKDALE. *Large Cr. 8vo.* 6s.

*****D'Este (Margaret).** IN THE CANARIES WITH A CAMERA. Illustrated. *Cr. 8vo* 7s. 6d. net.

Delbos (Leon). THE METRIC SYSTEM. *Cr. 8vo.* 2s.

Demosthenes. AGAINST CONON AND CALLICLES. Edited by F. DARWIN SWIFT, M.A. *Second Edition. Fcap. 8vo.* 2s.

Dickens (Charles). See Little Library, I.P.L., and Chesterton (G. K.).

Dickinson (Emily). POEMS. *Cr. 8vo.* 4s. 6d. net.

Dickinson (G. L.), M.A., Fellow of King's College, Cambridge. THE GREEK VIEW OF LIFE. *Sixth Edition. Cr. 8vo.* 2s. 6d.

Dilke (Lady), Bulley (Miss), and Whitley (Miss). WOMEN'S WORK. *Cr. 8vo.* 2s. 6d.

Dillon (Edward), M.A. See Connoisseur's Library, Little Books on Art, and Classics of Art.

Ditchfield (P. H.), M.A., F.S.A. THE STORY OF OUR ENGLISH TOWNS. With an Introduction by AUGUSTUS JESSOPP, D.D. *Second Edition. Cr. 8vo.* 6s.
OLD ENGLISH CUSTOMS : Extant at the Present Time. *Cr. 8vo.* 6s.
ENGLISH VILLAGES. With 100 Illustrations. *Second Edition. Cr. 8vo.* 2s. 6d. net.
THE PARISH CLERK. With 31 Illustrations. *Third Edition. Demy 8vo.* 7s. 6d. net.
THE OLD-TIME PARSON. With 17 Illustrations. *Second Edition. Demy 8vo.* 7s. 6d. net.

Dixon (W. M.), M.A. A PRIMER OF TENNYSON. *Third Edition. Cr. 8vo.* 2s. 6d.
ENGLISH POETRY FROM BLAKE TO BROWNING. *Second Edition. Cr. 8vo.* 2s. 6d.

Dobbs (W. J.), M.A. See Textbooks of Science.

Doney (May). SONGS OF THE REAL. *Cr. 8vo.* 3s. 6d. net.

Douglas (Hugh A.). VENICE ON FOOT. With the Itinerary of the Grand Canal. With 75 Illustrations and 11 Maps. *Fcap. 8vo.* 5s. net.

Douglas (James). THE MAN IN THE PULPIT. *Cr. 8vo.* 2s. 6d. net.

Dowden (J.), D.D., Lord Bishop of Edinburgh. FURTHER STUDIES IN THE PRAYER BOOK. *Cr. 8vo.* 6s.
See also Churchman's Library.

Drage (G.). See Books on Business.

Driver (S. R.), D.D., D.C.L., Regius Professor of Hebrew in the University of Oxford. SERMONS ON SUBJECTS CONNECTED WITH THE OLD TESTAMENT. *Cr. 8vo.* 6s.
See also Westminster Commentaries.

Dry (Wakeling). See Little Guides.

Dryhurst (A. R.). See Little Books on Art.

*****Duff (Nora).** MATILDA OF TUSCANY. With many Illustrations. *Demy 8vo.* 10s. 6d. net.

Duguid (Charles). See Books on Business.

Dumas (Alexandre). THE CRIMES OF THE BORGIAS AND OTHERS. With an Introduction by R. S. GARNETT. With 9 Illustrations. *Cr. 8vo.* 6s
THE CRIMES OF URBAIN GRANDIER AND OTHERS. With 8 Illustrations. *Cr. 8vo.* 6s.
THE CRIMES OF THE MARQUISE DE BRINVILLIERS AND OTHERS. With 8 Illustrations. *Cr. 8vo.* 6s.
THE CRIMES OF ALI PACHA AND OTHERS. With 8 Illustrations. *Cr. 8vo.* 6s.
MY MEMOIRS. Translated by E. M. WALLER. With an Introduction by ANDREW LANG. With Frontispieces in Photogravure. In six Volumes. *Cr. 8vo.* 6s. *each volume.*
VOL. I. 1802-1821. VOL. IV. 1830-1831.
VOL. II. 1822-1825. VOL. V. 1831-1832.
VOL. III. 1826-1830. VOL. VI. 1832-1833.
MY PETS. Newly translated by A. R. ALLINSON, M.A. With 16 Illustrations by V. LECOMTE. *Cr. 8vo.* 6s.
See also Simplified French Texts.

Duncan (David), D.Sc., LL.D. THE LIFE AND LETTERS OF HERBERT SPENCER. With 17 Illustrations. *Demy 8vo.* 15s.

Dunn (J. T.), D.Sc., and Mundella (V. A.). GENERAL ELEMENTARY SCIENCE. With 114 Illustrations. *Second Edition. Cr. 8vo.* 3s. 6d.

Dunn=Pattison (R. P.). NAPOLEON'S MARSHALS. With 20 Illustrations. *Demy 8vo. Second Edition.* 12s. 6d. net.

Dunstan (A. E.), B.Sc. (Lond.). See Textbooks of Science, and Junior School Books.

Durham (The Earl of). A REPORT ON CANADA. With an Introductory Note. *Demy 8vo.* 4s. 6d. net.

Dutt (W. A.). THE NORFOLK BROADS. With coloured Illustrations by FRANK SOUTHGATE, R.B.A. *Second Edition. Cr. 8vo.* 6s.

WILD LIFE IN EAST ANGLIA. With 16 Illustrations in colour by FRANK SOUTHGATE, R.B.A. *Second Edition. Demy 8vo. 7s. 6d. net.*

SOME LITERARY ASSOCIATIONS OF EAST ANGLIA. With 16 Illustrations in Colour by W. DEXTER, R.B.A., and 16 other Illustrations. *Demy 8vo.* 10s. 6d. net. See also Little Guides.

Earle (John), Bishop of Salisbury. MICROCOSMOGRAPHIE, OR A PIECE OF THE WORLD DISCOVERED. *Post 16mo.* 2s. net.

Edmonds (Major J. E.), R.E.; D.A.Q.-M.G. See Wood (W. Birkbeck).

Edwardes (Tickner). THE LORE OF THE HONEY BEE. With, 24 Illustrations. *Cr. 8vo.* 6s.

Edwards (Clement), M.P. RAILWAY NATIONALIZATION. *Second Edition, Revised. Crown 8vo.* 2s. 6d. net.

Edwards (W. Douglas). See Commercial Series.

Egan (Pierce). See I.P.L.

Egerton (H. E.), M.A. A HISTORY OF BRITISH COLONIAL POLICY. *Second Ed., Revised. Demy 8vo.* 7s. 6d. net.

Ellaby (C. G.). See Little Guides.

Ellerton (F. G.). See Stone (S. J.).

Epictetus. See Aurelius (Marcus).

Erasmus. A Book called in Latin ENCHIRIDION MILITIS CHRISTIANI, and in English the Manual of the Christian Knight. *Fcap. 8vo.* 3s. 6d. net.

Erckmann-Chatrian. See Simplified French Texts.

Evagrius. See Byzantine Texts.

Ewald (Carl). TWO LEGS, AND OTHER STORIES. Translated from the Danish by ALEXANDER TEIXEIRA DE MATTOS. Illustrated by AUGUSTA GUEST. *Large Cr. 8vo.* 6s.

Ezekiel. See Westminster Commentaries.

Facon (H. T.), B.A. See Junior Examination Series.

Fairbrother (W. H.), M.A. THE PHILOSOPHY OF T. H. GREEN. *Second Edition. Cr. 8vo.* 3s. 6d.

Fea (Allan). THE FLIGHT OF THE KING. With over 70 Sketches and Photographs by the Author. *New and revised Edition. Demy 8vo.* 7s. 6d. net.

SECRET CHAMBERS AND HIDING-PLACES. With 80 Illustrations. *New and revised Edition. Demy 8vo.* 7s. 6d. net.

JAMES II. AND HIS WIVES. With 40 Illustrations. *Demy 8vo.* 10s. 6d. net.

Fell (E. F. B.). THE FOUNDATIONS OF LIBERTY. *Cr. 8vo.* 5s. net.

Ferrier (Susan). See Little Library.

Fidler (T. Claxton), M.Inst. C.E. See Books on Business.

Fielding (Henry). See Standard Library.

Finn (S. W.), M.A. See Junior Examination Series.

Firth (J. B.). See Little Guides.

Firth (C. H.), M.A., Regius Professor of Modern History at Oxford. CROM-

WELL'S ARMY: A History of the English Soldier during the Civil Wars, the Commonwealth, and the Protectorate. *Cr. 8vo.* 6s.

*Firth (Edith E.). See Beginner's Books and Junior School Books.

FitzGerald (Edward). THE RUBÁIYÁT OF OMAR KHAYYÁM. Printed from the Fifth and last Edition. With a Commentary by Mrs. STEPHEN BATSON, and a Biography of Omar by E. D. ROSS. *Cr. 8vo.* 6s. See also Miniature Library.

FitzGerald (H. P.). A CONCISE HANDBOOK OF CLIMBERS, TWINERS, AND WALL SHRUBS. Illustrated. *Fcap. 8vo.* 3s. 6d. net.

Fitzpatrick (S. A. O.). See Ancient Cities.

Flecker (W. H.), M.A., D.C.L., Headmaster of the Dean Close School, Cheltenham. THE STUDENT'S PRAYER BOOK. THE TEXT OF MORNING AND EVENING PRAYER AND LITANY. With an Introduction and Notes. *Cr. 8vo.* 2s. 6d.

Fletcher (C. R. L.), M.A. *See* Carlyle (Thomas).

Fletcher (J. S.). A BOOK OF YORKSHIRE. With 16 Illustrations in Colour by WAL PAGET and FRANK SOUTHGATE, R.B.A., 16 other Illustrations and a Map. *Demy 8vo.* 7s. 6d. net.

Flux (A. W.), M.A., William Dow Professor of Political Economy in M'Gill University, Montreal. ECONOMIC PRINCIPLES. *Demy 8vo.* 7s. 6d. net.

Foat (F. W. G.), D.Litt., M.A. A LONDON READER FOR YOUNG CITIZENS. With Plans and Illustrations. *Cr. 8vo.* 1s. 6d.

Ford (H. J.), M.A., Assistant Master at Bristol Grammar School. See Junior School Books.

Forel (A.). THE SENSES OF INSECTS. Translated by MACLEOD YEARSLEY. With 2 Illustrations. *Demy 8vo.* 10s. 6d. net.

Fortescue (Mrs. G.). See Little Books on Art.

Fouqué (La Motte). SINTRAM AND HIS COMPANIONS. Translated by A. C. FARQUHARSON. With 20 Illustrations by EDMUND J. SULLIVAN, and a Frontispiece in Photogravure from an engraving by ALBRECHT DÜRER. *Demy 8vo.* 7s. 6d. net. *Half White Vellum, 10s. 6d. net.* See also Simplified German Texts.

Fraser (J. F.). ROUND THE WORLD ON A WHEEL. With 100 Illustrations. *Fifth Edition Cr. 8vo.* 6s.

French (W.), M.A. See Textbooks of Science.

Freudenreich (Ed. von). DAIRY BACTERIOLOGY. A Short Manual for Students. Translated by J. R. AINSWORTH DAVIS, M.A. *Second Edition. Revised. Cr. 8vo.* 2s. 6d.

Fursdon (F. R. M). FRENCH AND ENGLISH PARALLELS. *Fcap. 8vo.* 3s. 6d. net.

Fyvie (John). TRAGEDY QUEENS OF THE GEORGIAN ERA. With 16 Illustrations. *Second Ed. Demy 8vo.* 12s. 6d. net.

A 2

Gallaher (D.) and Stead (W. J.). THE COMPLETE RUGBY FOOTBALLER, ON THE NEW ZEALAND SYSTEM. With 35 Illustrations. *Second Ed. Demy 8vo. 10s. 6d. net.*

Gallichan (W. M.). See Little Guides.

Galton (Sir Francis), F.R.S.; D.C.L., Oxf.; Hon. Sc.D., Camb.; Hon. Fellow Trinity College, Cambridge. MEMORIES OF MY LIFE. With 8 Illustrations. *Third Edition. Demy 8vo. 10s. 6d. net.*

Gambado (Geoffrey, Esq.). See I.P.L.

Garnett (Lucy M. J.). THE TURKISH PEOPLE: THEIR SOCIAL LIFE, RELIGIOUS BELIEFS AND INSTITUTIONS, AND DOMESTIC LIFE. With 21 Illustrations. *Demy 8vo. 10s. 6d. net.*

Gaskell (Mrs.). See Little Library, Standard Library and Sixpenny Novels.

Gasquet, the Right Rev. Abbot, O.S.B. See Antiquary's Books.

Gee (Henry), D.D., F.S.A. See Handbooks of English Church History.

George (H. B.), M.A., Fellow of New College, Oxford. BATTLES OF ENGLISH HISTORY. With numerous Plans. *Fourth Edition Revised. Cr. 8vo. 3s. 6d.*
A HISTORICAL GEOGRAPHY OF THE BRITISH EMPIRE. *Fourth Edition. Cr. 8vo. 3s. 6d.*

Gibbins (H. de B.), Litt.D., M.A. INDUSTRY IN ENGLAND: HISTORICAL OUTLINES. With 5 Maps. *Fifth Edition. Demy 8vo. 10s. 6d.*
THE INDUSTRIAL HISTORY OF ENGLAND. With Maps and Plans. *Fifteenth Edition, Revised. Cr. 8vo. 3s.*
ENGLISH SOCIAL REFORMERS. *Second Edition. Cr. 8vo. 2s. 6d.*
   See also Hadfield (R. A.)., and Commercial Series.

Gibbon (Edward). MEMOIRS OF MY LIFE AND WRITINGS. Edited by G. BIRKBECK HILL, LL.D. *Cr. 8vo. 6s.*
*THE DECLINE AND FALL OF THE ROMAN EMPIRE. Edited, with Notes, Appendices, and Maps, by J. B. BURY. M.A., Litt.D., Regius Professor of Modern History at Cambridge. Illustrated. *In Seven Volumes. Demy 8vo. Gilt top. Each 10s. 6d. net.*

Gibbs (Philip). THE ROMANCE OF GEORGE VILLIERS: FIRST DUKE OF BUCKINGHAM, AND SOME MEN AND WOMEN OF THE STUART COURT. With 20 Illustrations. *Second Edition. Demy 8vo. 15s. net.*

Gibson (E. C. S.), D.D., Lord Bishop of Gloucester. See Westminster Commentaries, Handbooks of Theology, and Oxford Biographies.

Gilbert (A. R.). See Little Books on Art.

Gloag (M. R.) and Wyatt (Kate M.). A BOOK OF ENGLISH GARDENS. With 24 Illustrations in Colour. *Demy 8vo. 10s. 6d. net.*

Glover (T. R.), M.A., Fellow and Classical Lecturer of St. John's College, Cambridge. THE CONFLICT OF RELIGIONS IN THE EARLY ROMAN EMPIRE. *Third Edition. Demy 8vo. 7s. 6d. net.*

Godfrey (Elizabeth). A BOOK OF REMEMBRANCE. Being Lyrical Selections for every day in the Year. Arranged by. *Second Edition. Fcap. 8vo. 2s. 6d. net.*
ENGLISH CHILDREN IN THE OLDEN TIME. With 32 Illustrations. *Second Edition. Demy 8vo. 7s. 6d. net.*

Godley (A. D.), M.A., Fellow of Magdalen College, Oxford. OXFORD IN THE EIGHTEENTH CENTURY. With 16 Illustrations. *Second Edition. Demy 8vo. 7s. 6d. net.*
   Also published in a Colonial Edition.
LYRA FRIVOLA. *Fourth Edition. Fcap. 8vo. 2s. 6d.*
VERSES TO ORDER. *Second Edition. Fcap. 8vo. 2s. 6d.*
SECOND STRINGS. *Fcap. 8vo. 2s. 6d.*

Goldsmith (Oliver). See I.P.L. and Standard Library.

Goll (August). CRIMINAL TYPES IN SHAKESPEARE. Authorised Translation from the Danish by Mrs. CHARLES WEEKES. *Cr. 8vo. 5s. net.*

Gomme (G. L.). See Antiquary's Books.

Gordon (Lina Duff) (Mrs. Aubrey Waterfield). HOME LIFE IN ITALY: LETTERS FROM THE APENNINES. With 13 Illustrations by AUBREY WATERFIELD and 15 Illustrations from Photographs. *Second Edition. Demy 8vo. 10s. 6d. net.*

Gorst (Rt. Hon. Sir John). See New Library of Medicine.

Gostling (Frances M.). THE BRETONS AT HOME. With 12 Illustrations in Colour by GASTON FANTY LESCURE, and 32 from Photographs. *Demy 8vo. 10s. 6d. net.*

Goudge (H. L.), M.A., Principal of Wells Theological College. See Westminster Commentaries.

Graham (Harry). A GROUP OF SCOTTISH WOMEN. With 16 Illustrations. *Second Edition. Demy 8vo. 10s. 6d. net.*

Graham (P. Anderson). THE RURAL EXODUS. The Problem of the Village and the Town. *Cr. 8vo. 2s. 6d.*

Grahame (Kenneth). THE WIND IN THE WILLOWS. With a Frontispiece by GRAHAM ROBERTSON. *Fourth Edition. Cr. 8vo. 6s.*

Granger (F. S.), M.A., Litt.D. PSYCHOLOGY. *Third Edition. Cr. 8vo. 2s. 6d.*
THE SOUL OF A CHRISTIAN. *Cr. 8vo. 6s.*

Gray (E. M'Queen). GERMAN PASSAGES FOR UNSEEN TRANSLATION. *Cr. 8vo. 2s. 6d.*

Gray (P. L.), B.Sc. THE PRINCIPLES OF MAGNETISM AND ELECTRICITY. With 181 Diagrams. *Cr. 8vo. 3s. 6d.*

Green (G. Buckland), M.A., late Fellow of St. John's College, Oxon. NOTES ON

GREEK AND LATIN SYNTAX. *Second Ed. revised. Crown 8vo.* 3s. 6d.

Green (Mary Anne Everett). ELIZABETH; ELECTRESS PALATINE AND QUEEN OF BOHEMIA. Revised by her Niece S. C. LOMAS. With a Prefatory Note by A. W. WARD, Litt.D. *Demy 8vo.* 10s. 6d. net.

Greenidge (A. H. J.), M.A., D.Litt. A HISTORY OF ROME: From the Tribunate of Tiberius Gracchus to the end of the Jugurthine War, B.C. 133-104. *Demy 8vo.* 10s. 6d. net.

Gregory (Miss E. C.). See Library of Devotion.

Grubb (H. C.). See Textbooks of Technology.

Gwynn (Stephen), M.P. A HOLIDAY IN CONNEMARA. With 16 Illustrations. *Demy 8vo.* 10s. 6d. net.

Hadfield (R. A.) and Gibbins (H. de B.). A SHORTER WORKING DAY. *Cr. 8vo.* 2s. 6d.

*****Hall (Cyril).** THE YOUNG CARPENTER. With Diagrams, and Illustrations. *Cr. 8vo.* 5s.

Hall (Hammond). THE YOUNG ENGINEER: OR MODERN ENGINES AND THEIR MODELS. With 85 Illustrations. *Second Edition. Cr. 8vo.* 5s.

Hall (Mary). A WOMAN'S TREK FROM THE CAPE TO CAIRO. With 64 Illustrations and 2 Maps. *Second Edition. Demy 8vo.* 16s. net.

Hamel (Frank). FAMOUS FRENCH SALONS. With 20 Illustrations. *Third Edition. Demy 8vo.* 12s. 6d. net.

Hannay (D.). A SHORT HISTORY OF THE ROYAL NAVY. Vol. I., 1217-1688. Vol. II., 1689-1815. *Demy 8vo. Each* 7s. 6d. net.

Hannay (James O.), M.A. THE SPIRIT AND ORIGIN OF CHRISTIAN MONASTICISM. *Cr. 8vo.* 6s. THE WISDOM OF THE DESERT. *Fcap. 8vo.* 3s. 6d. net.

Hardie (Martin). See Connoisseur's Library.

Hare (A. T.), M.A. THE CONSTRUCTION OF LARGE INDUCTION COILS. With 35 Illustrations. *Demy 8vo.* 6s.

Harker (Alfred), M.A., F.R.S., Fellow of St. John's College, and Lecturer in Petrology in the University of Cambridge. THE NATURAL HISTORY OF IGNEOUS ROCKS. With 112 Diagrams and 2 Plates. *Demy 8vo.* 12s. 6d. net.

Harper (Charles G.). THE AUTOCAR ROAD-BOOK. In three Volumes. *Crown 8vo. Each* 7s. 6d. net.
Vol. I.—SOUTH OF THE THAMES.

Harvey (Alfred), M.B. See Ancient Cities and Antiquary's Books.

Hawthorne (Nathaniel). See Little Library.

*****Headley (F. W.).** DARWINISM AND MODERN SOCIALISM. *Cr. 8vo.* 5s. net.

Heath (Frank R.). See Little Guides.

Heath (Dudley). See Connoisseur's Library.

Henderson (B. W.), Fellow of Exeter College, Oxford. THE LIFE AND PRINCIPATE OF THE EMPEROR NERO. Illustrated. *New and cheaper issue. Demy 8vo.* 7s. 6d. net.
AT INTERVALS. *Fcap 8vo.* 2s. 6d. net.

Henderson (M. Sturge). GEORGE MEREDITH: NOVELIST, POET, REFORMER. With a Portrait in Photogravure. *Second Edition. Crown 8vo.* 6s.

Henderson (T. F.). See Little Library and Oxford Biographies.

Henderson (T. F.), and Watt (Francis). SCOTLAND OF TO-DAY. With 20 Illustrations in colour and 24 other Illustrations. *Second Edition. Cr. 8vo.* 6s.

Henley (W. E.). ENGLISH LYRICS. CHAUCER TO POE, 1340-1849. *Second Edition. Cr. 8vo.* 2s. 6d. net.

Henley (W. E.) and Whibley (C.) A BOOK OF ENGLISH PROSE, CHARACTER, AND INCIDENT, 1387-1649. *Cr. 8vo.* 2s. 6d. net.

Herbert (George). See Library of Devotion.

Herbert of Cherbury (Lord). See Miniature Library.

Hett (Walter S.), B.A. A SHORT HISTORY OF GREECE TO THE DEATH OF ALEXANDER THE GREAT. With 3 Maps and 4 Plans. *Cr. 8vo.* 3s. 6d.

Hewins (W. A. S.), B.A. ENGLISH TRADE AND FINANCE IN THE SEVENTEENTH CENTURY. *Cr. 8vo.* 2s. 6d.

Hewitt (Ethel M.) A GOLDEN DIAL. A Day Book of Prose and Verse. *Fcap. 8vo.* 2s. 6d. net.

Hey (H.), Inspector, Surrey Education Committee, and **Rose (G. H.),** City and Guilds Woodwork Teacher. A WOODWORK CLASS-BOOK. Pt. I. Illustrated. *4to.* 2s.

Heywood (W.). See St. Francis of Assisi.

Hill (Clare). See Textbooks of Technology.

*****Hill (George Francis).** ONE HUNDRED MASTERPIECES OF SCULPTURE. with 101 Illustrations. *Demy 8vo.* 10s. 6d. net.

Hill (Henry), B.A., Headmaster of the Boy's High School, Worcester, Cape Colony. A SOUTH AFRICAN ARITHMETIC. *Cr. 8vo.* 3s. 6d.

Hind (C. Lewis). DAYS IN CORNWALL. With 16 Illustrations in Colour by WILLIAM PASCOE, and 20 other Illustrations and a Map. *Second Edition. Cr. 8vo.* 6s.

Hirst (F. W.) See Books on Business.

Hobhouse (L. T.), late Fellow of C.C.C., Oxford. THE THEORY OF KNOWLEDGE. *Demy 8vo.* 10s. 6d. net.

Hobson (J. A.), M.A. INTERNATIONAL TRADE: A Study of Economic Principles. *Cr. 8vo.* 2s. 6d. net.
PROBLEMS OF POVERTY. An Inquiry

into the Industrial Condition of the Poor. *Seventh Edition.* *Cr. 8vo. 2s. 6d.*
THE PROBLEM OF THE UNEMPLOYED. *Fourth Edition. Cr. 8vo. 2s. 6d.*

Hodgetts (E. A. Brayley). THE COURT OF RUSSIA IN THE NINETEENTH CENTURY. With 20 Illustrations. *Two Volumes. Demy 8vo. 24s. net.*

Hodgkin (T.), D.C.L. See Leaders of Religion.

Hodgson (Mrs. W.) HOW TO IDENTIFY OLD CHINESE PORCELAIN. With 40 Illustrations. *Second Edition. Post 8vo. 6s.*

Holden-Stone (G. de). See Books on Business.

Holdich (Sir T. H.), K.C.I.E., C.B., F.S.A. THE INDIAN BORDERLAND, 1880-1900. With 22 Illustrations and a Map. *Second Edition. Demy 8vo. 10s. 6d. net.*

Holdsworth (W. S.), D.C.L. A HISTORY OF ENGLISH LAW. *In Four Volumes. Vols. I., II., III. Demy 8vo.* Each 10s. 6d. net.

Holland (Clive). TYROL AND ITS PEOPLE. With 16 Illustrations in Colour by ADRIAN STOKES, and 31 other Illustrations. *Demy 8vo. 10s. 6d. net.*

Holland (H. Scott), Canon of St. Paul's. See Newman (J. H.).

Hollings (M. A.), M.A. See Six Ages of European History.

Hollway=Calthrop (H. C.), late of Balliol College, Oxford ; Bursar of Eton College. PETRARCH : HIS LIFE, WORK, AND TIMES. With 24 Illustrations. *Demy 8vo. 12s. 6d. net.*

Holmes (T. Scott). See Ancient Cities.

Holyoake (G. J.). THE CO-OPERATIVE MOVEMENT OF TO-DAY. *Fourth Ed. Cr. 8vo. 2s. 6d.*

Hone (Nathaniel J.). See Antiquary's Books.

Hook (A.) HUMANITY AND ITS PROBLEMS. *Cr. 8vo. 5s. net.*

Hoppner. See Little Galleries.

Horace. See Classical Translations.

Horsburgh (E. L. S.), M.A. LORENZO THE MAGNIFICENT : AND FLORENCE IN HER GOLDEN AGE. With 24 Illustrations and 2 Maps. *Second Edition. Demy 8vo. 15s. net.*
WATERLOO : With Plans. *Second Edition. Cr. 8vo. 5s.*
See also Oxford Biographies.

Horth (A. C.). See Textbooks of Technology.

Horton (R. F.), D.D. See Leaders of Religion.

Hosie (Alexander). MANCHURIA. With 30 Illustrations and a Map. *Second Edition. Demy 8vo. 7s. 6d. net.*

How (F. D.). SIX GREAT SCHOOLMASTERS. With 13 Illustrations. *Second Edition. Demy 8vo. 7s. 6d.*

Howell (A. G. Ferrers). FRANCISCAN DAYS. Being Selections for every day in the year from ancient Franciscan writings. *Cr. 8vo. 3s. 6d. net.*

Howell (G.). TRADE UNIONISM—NEW AND OLD. *Fourth Edition. Cr. 8vo. 2s. 6d.*

Huggins (Sir William), K.C.B., O.M., D.C.L., F.R.S. THE ROYAL SOCIETY ; OR, SCIENCE IN THE STATE AND IN THE SCHOOLS. With 25 Illustrations. *Wide Royal 8vo. 4s. 6d. net.*

Hughes (C. E.). THE PRAISE OF SHAKESPEARE. An English Anthology. With a Preface by SIDNEY LEE. *Demy 8vo. 3s. 6d. net.*

Hugo (Victor). See Simplified French Texts.

*Hutton (Samuel F.). THE CLERK OF OXFORD IN FICTION. With 12 Illustrations. *Demy 8vo. 15s. net.*

Hume (Martin), M.A. See Romantic History.

Hutchinson (Horace G.) THE NEW FOREST. Illustrated in colour with 50 Pictures by WALTER TYNDALE and 4 by LUCY KEMP-WELCH. *Third Edition. Cr. 8vo. 6s.*

Hutton (A. W.), M.A. See Leaders of Religion and Library of Devotion.

Hutton (Edward). THE CITIES OF UMBRIA. With 20 Illustrations in Colour by A. PISA, and 12 other Illustrations. *Third Edition. Cr. 8vo. 6s.*
THE CITIES OF SPAIN. With 24 Illustrations in Colour, by A. W. RIMINGTON, 20 other Illustrations and a Map. *Third Edition. Cr. 8vo. 6s.*
FLORENCE AND THE CITIES OF NORTHERN TUSCANY, WITH GENOA. With 16 Illustrations in Colour by WILLIAM PARKINSON, and 16 other Illustrations. *Second Edition. Cr. 8vo. 6s.*
ENGLISH LOVE POEMS. Edited with an Introduction. *Fcap. 8vo. 3s. 6d. net.*
COUNTRY WALKS ABOUT FLORENCE. With 32 Drawings by ADELAIDE MARCHI and 20 other Illustrations. *Fcap. 8vo. 5s. net.*
IN UNKNOWN TUSCANY. With an Appendix by WILLIAM HEYWOOD. With 8 Illustrations in Colour and 20 others. *Second Edition. Demy 8vo. 7s. 6d. net.*
*ROME. With 16 Illustrations in Colour by MAXWELL ARMFIELD, and 12 other Illustrations. *Cr. 8vo. 6s.*

Hutton (R. H.). See Leaders of Religion.

Hutton (W. H.), M.A. THE LIFE OF SIR THOMAS MORE. With Portraits after Drawings by HOLBEIN. *Second Edition. Cr. 8vo. 5s.*
See also Leaders of Religion.

Hyde (A. G.) GEORGE HERBERT AND HIS TIMES. With 32 Illustrations. *Demy 8vo. 10s. 6d. net.*

Hyett (F. A.). FLORENCE : HER HISTORY AND ART TO THE FALL OF THE REPUBLIC. *Demy 8vo. 7s. 6d. net.*

Ibsen (Henrik). BRAND. A Drama. Translated by WILLIAM WILSON. *Third Edition. Cr. 8vo. 3s. 6d.*

Inge (W. R.), M.A., Fellow and Tutor of Hertford College, Oxford. CHRISTIAN MYSTICISM. (The Bampton Lectures of 1899.) *Demy 8vo. 12s. 6d. net.*
See also Library of Devotion.

Innes (A. D.), M.A. A HISTORY OF THE BRITISH IN INDIA. With Maps and Plans. *Cr. 8vo.* 6s.
ENGLAND UNDER THE TUDORS. With Maps. *Second Edition. Demy 8vo.* 10s. 6d. net.
*Innes (Mary).** SCHOOLS OF PAINTING. With 76 Illustrations. *Cr. 8vo.* 5s. net.
Isaiah. See Churchman's Bible.
Jackson (C. E.), B.A. See Textbooks of Science.
Jackson (S.), M.A. See Commercial Series.
Jackson (F. Hamilton). See Little Guides.
Jacob (F.), M.A. See Junior Examination Series.
Jeans (J. Stephen). TRUSTS, POOLS, AND CORNERS AS AFFECTING COMMERCE AND INDUSTRY. *Cr. 8vo.* 2s. 6d.
See also Books on Business.
Jebb (Camilla). A STAR OF THE SALONS : JULIE DE LESPINASSE. With 20 Illustrations. *Demy 8vo.* 10s. 6d. net.
Jeffery (Reginald W.), M.A. THE HISTORY OF THE THIRTEEN COLONIES OF NORTH AMERICA 1497-1763. With 8 Illustrations and a Map. *Demy 8vo.* 7s. 6d. net.
Jeffreys (D. Gwyn). DOLLY'S THEATRICALS. *Super Royal 16mo.* 2s. 6d.
Jenks (E.), M.A., B.C.L. AN OUTLINE OF ENGLISH LOCAL GOVERNMENT. *Second Ed.* Revised by R. C. K. ENSOR, M.A. *Cr. 8vo.* 2s. 6d.
Jenner (Mrs. H.). See Little Books on Art.
Jennings (A. C.), M.A. See Handbooks of English Church History.
Jennings (Oscar), M.D. EARLY WOODCUT INITIALS. *Demy 4to.* 21s. net.
*Jerningham (Charles Edward).** THE MAXIMS OF MARMADUKE. *Crown 8vo.* 5s.
Jessopp (Augustus), D.D. See Leaders of Religion.
Jevons (F. B.), M.A., Litt.D., Principal of Hatfield Hall, Durham. RELIGION IN EVOLUTION. *Cr. 8vo.* 3s. 6d. net.
See also Churchman's Library and Handbooks of Theology.
Johnson (A. H.), M.A. See Six Ages of European History.
Johnston (Sir H. H.), K.C.B. BRITISH CENTRAL AFRICA. With nearly 200 Illustrations and Six Maps. *Third Edition. Cr. 4to.* 18s. net.
Jones (H.). See Commercial Series.
Jones (H. F.). See Textbooks of Science.
Jones (L. A. Atherley), K.C., M.P., and **Bellot (Hugh H. L.)**, M.A., D.C.L. THE MINER'S GUIDE TO THE COAL MINES REGULATION ACTS AND THE LAW OF EMPLOYERS AND WORKMEN. *Cr. 8vo.* 2s. 6d. net.
COMMERCE IN WAR. *Royal 8vo.* 21s. net.
Jones (R. Compton), M.A. POEMS OF THE INNER LIFE. Selected by. *Thirteenth Edition. Fcap. 8vo.* 2s. 6d. net.

Jonson (Ben). See Standard Library.
Julian (Lady) of Norwich. REVELATIONS OF DIVINE LOVE. Ed. by GRACE WARRACK. *Third Ed. Cr. 8vo.* 3s. 6d.
Juvenal. See Classical Translations.
'Kappa.' LET YOUTH BUT KNOW : A Plea for Reason in Education. *Cr. 8vo.* 3s. 6d. net.
Kaufmann (M.), M.A. SOCIALISM AND MODERN THOUGHT. *Second Edition Revised and Enlarged. Cr. 8vo.* 2s. 6d. net.
Keats (John). THE POEMS. Edited with Introduction and Notes by E. de SÉLINCOURT, M.A. With a Frontispiece in Photogravure. *Second Edition Revised. Demy 8vo.* 7s. 6d. net.
REALMS OF GOLD. Selections from the Works of. *Fcap. 8vo.* 3s. 6d. net.
See also Little Library and Standard Library.
Keble (John). THE CHRISTIAN YEAR. With an Introduction and Notes by W. LOCK, D.D., Warden of Keble College. Illustrated by R. ANNING BELL. *Third Edition. Fcap. 8vo.* 3s. 6d. ; *padded morocco*, 5s.
See also Library of Devotion.
Kelynack (T. N.), M.D., M.R.C.P. See New Library of Medicine.
Kempis (Thomas à). THE IMITATION OF CHRIST. With an Introduction by DEAN FARRAR. Illustrated by C. M. GERE. *Third Edition. Fcap. 8vo.* 3s. 6d.; *padded morocco.* 5s.
Also Translated by C. BIGG, D.D. *Cr. 8vo.* 3s. 6d.
See also Montmorency (J. E. G. de)., Library of Devotion, and Standard Library.
Kennedy (James Houghton), D.D., Assistant Lecturer in Divinity in the University of Dublin. See St. Paul.
Kerr (S. Parnell). GEORGE SELWYN AND THE WITS. With 16 Illustrations. *Demy 8vo.* 12s. 6d. net.
Kimmins (C. W.), M.A. THE CHEMISTRY OF LIFE AND HEALTH. Illustrated. *Cr. 8vo.* 2s. 6d.
Kinglake (A. W.). See Little Library.
Kipling (Rudyard). BARRACK-ROOM BALLADS. 91th Thousand. *Twenty-sixth Edition. Cr. 8vo.* 6s. Also *Fcap. 8vo, Leather.* 5s.
THE SEVEN SEAS. 79th Thousand. *Fifteenth Edition. Cr. 8vo.* 6s. Also *Fcap. 8vo, Leather.* 5s.
THE FIVE NATIONS. 66th Thousand. *Fifth Edition. Cr. 8vo.* 6s. Also *Fcap. 8vo, Leather.* 5s.
DEPARTMENTAL DITTIES. *Seventeenth Edition. Cr. 8vo.* 6s. Also *Fcap. 8vo, Leather.* 5s.
Knight (Albert E.). THE COMPLETE CRICKETER. With 50 Illustrations. *Demy 8vo.* 7s. 6d. net.
Knowling (R. J.), M.A., Professor of New Testament Exegesis at King's College, London. See Westminster Commentaries.

Knox (Winifred F.). THE COURT OF A SAINT. With 16 Illustrations. *Demy 8vo.* 10s. 6d. net.

Kropotkin (Prince). THE TERROR IN RUSSIA. *Seventh Edition. Cr. 8vo.* 2d. net.

Laboulaye (Edouard). See Simplified French Texts.

Lamb (Charles and Mary), THE WORKS. Edited by E. V. LUCAS. Illustrated. *In Seven Volumes. Demy 8vo.* 7s. 6d. each. See also Little Library and Lucas (E. V.)

Lambert (F. A. H.). See Little Guides.

Lambros (Professor S. P.). See Byzantine Texts.

Lane-Poole (Stanley). A HISTORY OF EGYPT IN THE MIDDLE AGES. With 101 Illustrations and a Map. *Cr. 8vo.* 6s.

Langbridge (F.), M.A. BALLADS OF THE BRAVE : Poems of Chivalry, Enterprise, Courage, and Constancy. *Third Edition. Cr. 8vo.* 2s. 6d.

Lankester (Sir E. Ray), K.C.B., F.R.S. SCIENCE FROM AN EASY CHAIR. With many Illustrations, of which 2 are in Colour. *Cr. 8vo.* 6s.

Law (William). See Library of Devotion and Standard Library.

Leach (Henry). THE SPIRIT OF THE LINKS. *Cr. 8vo.* 6s. See also Braid (James).

Le Braz (Anatole). THE LAND OF PARDONS. Translated by FRANCES M. GOSTLING. With 12 Illustrations in Colour by T. C. GOTCH, and 40 other Illustrations. *Third Edition. Crown 8vo.* 6s.

Lees (Beatrice). See Six Ages of European History.

Lees (Frederick). A SUMMER IN TOURAINE. With 12 Illustrations in Colour by MAXWELL ARMFIELD, and 87 from Photographs. Also a Map. *Second Edition. Demy 8vo.* 10s. 6d. net.

Lehmann (R. C.), M.P. THE COMPLETE OARSMAN. With 59 Illustrations. *Demy 8vo.* 10s. 6d. net.

Lewes (V. B.), M.A. AIR AND WATER. Illustrated. *Cr. 8vo.* 2s. 6d.

Lewis (B. M. Gwyn). A CONCISE HANDBOOK OF GARDEN SHRUBS. With 20 Illustrations. *Fcap. 8vo.* 3s. 6d. net.

Lindsay (Lady Mabel). ANNI DOMINI : A Gospel Study. *In Two Volumes. Super Royal 8vo.* 10s. net.

Lindsay (W. M.), Fellow of Jesus College, Oxford. See Plautus.

Lisle (Fortunéede). See Little Books on Art.

Littlehales (H.). See Antiquary's Books.

Llewellyn (Owen) and Raven-Hill (L.). THE SOUTH-BOUND CAR. With 85 Illustrations. *Crown 8vo.* 6s.

Lock (Walter), D.D., Warden of Keble College. ST. PAUL, THE MASTER-BUILDER. *Second Ed. Cr. 8vo.* 3s. 6d. THE BIBLE AND CHRISTIAN LIFE. *Cr. 8vo.* 6s. See also Keble (J.) and Leaders of Religion.

Locker (F.). See Little Library.

Lodge (Sir Oliver), F.R.S. THE SUBSTANCE OF FAITH, ALLIED WITH SCIENCE : A Catechism for Parents and Teachers. *Ninth Ed. Cr. 8vo.* 2s net. MAN AND THE UNIVERSE : A Study OF THE INFLUENCE OF THE ADVANCE IN SCIENTIFIC KNOWLEDGE UPON OUR UNDERSTANDING OF CHRISTIANITY. *Sixth Edition. Demy 8vo.* 7s. 6d. net. *THE SURVIVAL OF MAN : A Study OF UNRECOGNISED HUMAN FACULTY. *Demy 8vo.* 7s. 6d. net.

Lodge (Eleanor C.). See Six Ages of European History.

Lofthouse (W. F.), M.A. ETHICS AND ATONEMENT. With a Frontispiece. *Demy 8vo.* 5s. net.

Longfellow (H. W.). See Little Library.

Lorimer (George Horace). LETTERS FROM A SELF-MADE MERCHANT TO HIS SON. *Seventeenth Edition. Cr. 8vo.* 3s. 6d. OLD GORGON GRAHAM. *Second Edition. Cr. 8vo.* 6s.

*Lorimer (Norma).** BY THE WATERS OF EGYPT. With 12 Illustrations in Colour by BENTON FLETCHER, and other Illustrations. *Demy 8vo.* 16s. net.

Lover (Samuel). See I.P.L.

Lucas (E. V.). THE LIFE OF CHARLES LAMB. With 28 Illustrations. *Fourth and Revised Edition in One Volume. Demy 8vo.* 7s. 6d. net. A WANDERER IN HOLLAND. With 20 Illustrations in Colour by HERBERT MARSHALL, 34 Illustrations after old Dutch Masters, and a Map. *Ninth Edition. Cr. 8vo.* 6s. A WANDERER IN LONDON. With 16 Illustrations in Colour by NELSON DAWSON, 36 other Illustrations and a Map. *Seventh Edition. Cr. 8vo.* 6s. A WANDERER IN PARIS. With 16 Illustrations in Colour by WALTER DEXTER, and 32 from Photographs after Old Masters. *Second Edition. Cr. 8vo.* 6s. THE OPEN ROAD : a Little Book for Wayfarers. *Fifteenth Edition. Fcap. 8vo.* 5s. ; *India Paper,* 7s. 6d. THE FRIENDLY TOWN : a Little Book for the Urbane. *Fourth Edition. Fcap. 8vo.* 5s. : *India Paper,* 7s. 6d. FIRESIDE AND SUNSHINE. *Fourth Edition. Fcap. 8vo.* 5s. CHARACTER AND COMEDY. *Fourth Edition. Fcap. 8vo.* 5s. THE GENTLEST ART. A Choice of Letters by Entertaining Hands. *Fifth Edition. Fcap. 8vo.* 5s. A SWAN AND HER FRIENDS. With 24 Illustrations. *Demy 8vo.* 12s. 6d. net. HER INFINITE VARIETY : A Feminine Portrait Gallery. *Fourth Edition. Fcap. 8vo.* 5s. LISTENER'S LURE : An Oblique Narration. *Fifth Edition. Fcap. 8vo.* 5s.

*GOOD COMPANY: A RALLY OF MEN. *Fcap. 8vo. 5s.*
ONE DAY AND ANOTHER: A VOLUME OF ESSAYS. *Fcap. 8vo. 5s.*
OVER BEMERTON'S: AN EASY-GOING CHRONICLE. *Sixth Edition. Fcap. 8vo. 5s. net.*
See also Lamb (Charles).
Lucian. See Classical Translations.
Lyde (L. W.), M.A. See Commercial Series.
Lydon (Noel S.). A PRELIMINARY GEOMETRY. With numerous Diagrams. *Cr. 8vo. 1s.*
See also Junior School Books.
Lyttelton (Hon. Mrs. A.). WOMEN AND THEIR WORK. *Cr. 8vo. 2s. 6d.*
M. (R.). THE THOUGHTS OF LUCIA HALIDAY. With some of her Letters. Edited by R. M. *Fcap. 8vo. 2s. 6d. net.*
Macaulay (Lord). CRITICAL AND HISTORICAL ESSAYS. Edited by F. C. MONTAGUE, M.A. *Three Volumes. Cr. 8vo. 18s.*
M'Allen (J. E. B.), M.A. See Commercial Series.
McCabe (Joseph) (formerly Very Rev. F. ANTONY, O.S.F.). THE DECAY OF THE CHURCH OF ROME. *Demy 8vo. 7s. 6d. net.*
MacCunn (Florence A.). MARY STUART. With 44 Illustrations, including a Frontispiece in Photogravure. *New and Cheaper Edition. Large Cr. 8vo. 6s.*
See also Leaders of Religion.
McDermott (E. R.). See Books on Business.
McDougall (William), M.A. (Oxon., M.B. (Cantab.). AN INTRODUCTION TO SOCIAL PSYCHOLOGY. *Cr. 8vo. 5s. net.*
M'Dowall (A. S.). See Oxford Biographies.
MacFie (Ronald C.), M.A., M.B. See New Library of Medicine.
Mackay (A. M.), B.A. See Churchman's Library.
Mackenzie (W. Leslie), M.A., M.D., D.P.H., etc. THE HEALTH OF THE SCHOOL CHILD. *Cr. 8vo. 2s. 6d.*
Macklin (Herbert W.), M.A. See Antiquary's Books.
M'Neile (A. H.), B.D. See Westminster Commentaries.
'Mdlle Mori' (Author of). ST. CATHERINE OF SIENA AND HER TIMES. With 28 Illustrations. *Second Edition. Demy 8vo. 7s. 6d. net.*
Maeterlinck (Maurice). THE BLUE BIRD: A FAIRY PLAY IN FIVE ACTS. Translated by ALEXANDER TEIXERA DE MATTOS. *Second Edition. Fcap. 8vo. Deckle Edges. 3s. 6d. net.*
Magnus (Laurie), M.A. A PRIMER OF WORDSWORTH. *Cr. 8vo. 2s. 6d.*
Mahaffy (J. P.), Litt.D. A HISTORY OF THE EGYPT OF THE PTOLEMIES. With 79 Illustrations. *Cr. 8vo. 6s.*
Maitland (F. W.), M.A., LL.D. ROMAN CANON LAW IN THE CHURCH OF ENGLAND. *Royal 8vo. 7s. 6d.*
Major (H.), B.A., B.Sc. A HEALTH AND

TEMPERANCE READER. *Cr. 8vo. 1s.*
Malden (H. E.), M.A. ENGLISH RECORDS. A Companion to the History of England. *Cr. 8vo. 3s. 6d.*
THE RIGHTS AND DUTIES OF A CITIZEN. *Seventh Edition. Cr. 8vo. 1s. 6d.*
See also School Histories.
Marchant (E. C.), M.A., Fellow of Peterhouse, Cambridge. A GREEK ANTHOLOGY. *Second Edition. Cr. 8vo. 3s. 6d.*
See also Cook (A. M.).
Marett (R. R.), M.A., Fellow and Tutor of Exeter College, Oxford. THE THRESHOLD OF RELIGION. *Cr. 8vo. 3s. 6d net.*
Marks (Jeannette), M.A. ENGLISH PASTORAL DRAMA from the Restoration to the date of the publication of the 'Lyrical Ballads' (1660-1798). *Cr. 8vo. 5s. net.*
Marr (J. E.), F.R.S., Fellow of St John's College, Cambridge. THE SCIENTIFIC STUDY OF SCENERY. *Third Edition.* Revised. Illustrated. *Cr. 8vo. 6s.*
AGRICULTURAL GEOLOGY. Illustrated. *Cr. 8vo. 6s.*
Marriott (Charles). A SPANISH HOLIDAY. With 8 Illustrations by A. M. FOWERAKER, R.B.A., and 22 other Illustrations. *Demy 8vo. 7s. 6d. net.*
Marriott (J. A. R.), M.A. THE LIFE AND TIMES OF LORD FALKLAND. With 23 Illustrations. *Second Edition. Demy 8vo. 7s. 6d. net.*
See also Six Ages of European History.
Marvell (Andrew). See Little Library.
Masefield (John). SEA LIFE IN NELSON'S TIME. With 16 Illustrations. *Cr. 8vo. 3s. 6d. net.*
ON THE SPANISH MAIN: or, SOME ENGLISH FORAYS IN THE ISTHMUS OF DARIEN. With 22 Illustrations and a Map. *Demy 8vo. 10s. 6d. net.*
A SAILOR'S GARLAND. Selected and Edited by. *Second Ed. Cr. 8vo. 3s. 6d. net.*
AN ENGLISH PROSE MISCELLANY. Selected and Edited by. *Cr. 8vo. 6s.*
Maskell (A.). See Connoisseur's Library.
Mason (A. J.), D.D. See Leaders of Religion.
Masterman (C. F. G.), M.A., M.P. TENNYSON AS A RELIGIOUS TEACHER. *Cr. 8vo. 6s.*
THE CONDITION OF ENGLAND. *Second Edition. Cr. 8vo. 6s.*
Masterman (J. H. B.), M.A. See Six Ages of European History.
Matheson (E. F.). COUNSELS OF LIFE. *Fcap. 8vo. 2s. 6d. net.*
Maude (J. H.), M.A. See Handbooks of English Church History.
May (Phil). THE PHIL MAY ALBUM. *Second Edition. 4to. 1s. net.*
Mayne (Ethel Colburn). ENCHANTERS OF MEN. With 24 Illustrations. *Demy 8vo. 10s. 6d. net.*

Meakin (Annette M. B.), Fellow of the Anthropological Institute. WOMAN IN TRANSITION. *Cr. 8vo.* 6s.
GALICIA: THE SWITZERLAND OF SPAIN. With 105 Illustrations and a Map. *Demy 8vo.* 12s. 6d. net.
*****Medley (D. J.),** M.A., Professor of History in the University of Glasgow. ORIGINAL ILLUSTRATIONS OF ENGLISH CONSTITUTIONAL HISTORY, COMPRISING A SELECTED NUMBER OF THE CHIEF CHARTERS AND STATUTES. *Cr. 8vo.* 7s. 6d. net.
Mellows (Emma S.). A SHORT STORY OF ENGLISH LITERATURE. *Cr. 8vo.* 3s. 6d.
Mérimée (P.). See Simplified French Texts.
Methuen (A. M. S.), M.A. THE TRAGEDY OF SOUTH AFRICA. *Cr. 8vo.* 2s. net. Also *Cr. 8vo.* 3d. net.
ENGLAND'S RUIN : DISCUSSED IN FOURTEEN LETTERS TO A PROTECTIONIST. *Ninth Edition. Cr. 8vo.* 3d. net.
Meynell (Everard). COROT AND HIS FRIENDS. With 28 Illustrations. *Demy 8vo* 10s. 6d. net.
Miles (Eustace), M.A. LIFE AFTER LIFE: OR, THE THEORY OF REINCARNATION. *Cr. 8vo.* 2s. 6d. net.
THE POWER OF CONCENTRATION : How TO ACQUIRE IT. *Third Edition. Cr. 8vo.* 3s. 6d. net.
Millais (J. G.). THE LIFE AND LETTERS OF SIR JOHN EVERETT MILLAIS, President of the Royal Academy. With many Illustrations, of which 2 are in Photogravure. *New Edition. Demy 8vo.* 7s. 6d. net.
See also Little Galleries.
Millin (G. F.). PICTORIAL GARDENING. With 21 Illustrations. *Crown 8vo.* 3s. 6d. net.
Millis (C. T.), M.I.M.E. See Textbooks of Technology.
Milne (J. G.), M.A. A HISTORY OF EGYPT UNDER ROMAN RULE. With 143 Illustrations. *Cr. 8vo.* 6s.
Milton (John). A DAY BOOK OF MILTON. Edited by R. F. TOWNDROW. *Fcap. 8vo.* 2s. 6d. net.
See also Little Library and Standard Library.
Minchin (H. C.), M.A. See Peel (R.).
Mitchell (P. Chalmers), M.A. OUTLINES OF BIOLOGY. With 74 Illustrations. *Second Edition. Cr. 8vo.* 6s.
Mitton (G. E.). JANE AUSTEN AND HER TIMES. With 21 Illustrations. *Second and Cheaper Edition. Large Cr. 8vo.* 6s.
Moffat (Mary M.). QUEEN LOUISA OF PRUSSIA. With 20 Illustrations. *Fourth Edition. Crown 8vo.* 6s.
Moil (A.). See Books on Business.
Moir (D. M.). See Little Library.
Molinos (Dr. Michael de). See Library of Devotion.
Money (L. G. Chiozza), M.P. RICHES

AND POVERTY. *Eighth Edition Demy 8vo.* 5s. net. Also *Cr. 8vo.* 1s. net.
Montagu (Henry), Earl of Manchester. See Library of Devotion.
Montaigne. A DAY BOOK OF. Edited by C. F. POND. *Fcap. 8vo.* 2s. 6d. net.
Montgomery (H. B.) THE EMPIRE OF THE EAST. With a Frontispiece in Colour and 18 other Illustrations. *Second Edition. Demy 8vo.* 7s. 6d. net.
Montmorency (J. E. G. de), B.A., LL.B. THOMAS À KEMPIS, HIS AGE AND BOOK. With 22 Illustrations. *Second Edition. Demy 8vo.* 7s. 6d. net.
Moore (H. E.). BACK TO THE LAND. *Cr. 8vo.* 2s. 6d.
*****Moore (T. Sturge).** ART AND LIFE. Illustrated *Cr. 8vo.* 5s. net.
Moorhouse (E. Hallam). NELSON'S LADY HAMILTON. With 51 Portraits. *Second Edition. Demy 8vo.* 7s. 6d. net.
Moran (Clarence G.). See Books on Business.
More (Sir Thomas). See Standard Library.
Morfill (W. R.), Oriel College, Oxford. A HISTORY OF RUSSIA FROM PETER THE GREAT TO ALEXANDER II. With 12 Maps and Plans. *Cr. 8vo.* 3s. 6d.
Morich (R. J.). See School Examination Series.
Morley (Margaret W.), Founded on. THE BEE PEOPLE. With 74 Illustrations. *Sq. Crown 8vo.* 2s. 6d.
LITTLE MITCHELL: THE STORY OF A MOUNTAIN SQUIRREL TOLD BY HIMSELF. With 26 Illustrations. *Sq. Cr. 8vo.* 2s. 6d.
Morris (J.). THE MAKERS OF JAPAN. With 24 Illustrations. *Demy 8vo.* 12s. 6d. net.
Morris (Joseph E.). See Little Guides.
Morton (A. Anderson). See Brodrick (M.).
Moule (H. C. G.), D.D., Lord Bishop of Durham. See Leaders of Religion.
Muir (M. M. Pattison), M.A. THE CHEMISTRY OF FIRE. Illustrated. *Cr. 8vo.* 2s. 6d.
Mundella (V. A.), M.A. See Dunn (J. T.).
Munro (R.), M.A., LL.D. See Antiquary's Books.
Musset (Alfred de). See Simplified French Text.
Myers (A. Wallis), THE COMPLETE LAWN TENNIS PLAYER. With 90 Illustrations. *Second Edition. Demy 8vo.* 10s. 6d. net.
Naval Officer (A). See I. P. L.
Newman (Ernest). See New Library of Music.
Newman (George), M.D., D.P.H., F.R.S.E. See New Library of Medicine.
Newman (J. H.) and others. See Library of Devotion.
Newsholme (Arthur), M.D., F.R.C.P. See New Library of Medicine.
Nichols (Bowyer). See Little Library.
Nicklin (T.), M.A. EXAMINATION PAPERS IN THUCYDIDES. *Cr. 8vo.* 2s.
Nimrod. See I. P. L.
Norgate (G. Le Grys). THE LIFE OF

SIR WALTER SCOTT. With 53 Illustra-
tions by JENNY WYLIE. *Demy 8vo. 7s. 6d. net.*
Norway (A. H.). NAPLES. PAST AND
PRESENT. With 25 Coloured Illustrations
by MAURICE GREIFFENHAGEN. *Third
Edition. Cr. 8vo. 6s.*
Novalis. THE DISCIPLES AT SAÏS and
OTHER FRAGMENTS. Edited by Miss UNA
BIRCH. *Fcap. 8vo. 3s. 6d. net.*
Officer (An). See I. P. L.
Oldfield (W. J.), M.A., Prebendary of
Lincoln. A PRIMER OF RELIGION.
BASED ON THE CATECHISM OF THE CHURCH
OF ENGLAND. *Crown 8vo. 2s. 6d.*
Oldham (F. M.), B.A. See Textbooks of
Science.
Oliphant (Mrs.). See Leaders of Religion.
Oliver, Thomas, M.D. See New Library of
Medicine.
Oman (C. W. C.), M.A., Fellow of All Souls',
Oxford. A HISTORY OF THE ART
OF WAR IN THE MIDDLE AGES.
Illustrated. *Demy 8vo. 10s. 6d. net.*
ENGLAND BEFORE THE CONQUEST.
With Maps. *Demy 8vo. 10s. 6d. net.*
Oppé (A. P.). See Classics of Art.
Ottley (R. L.), D.D. See Handbooks of
Theology and Leaders of Religion.
Overton (J. H.). See Leaders of Religion.
Owen (Douglas). See Books on Business.
Oxford (M. N.), of Guy's Hospital. A HAND-
BOOK OF NURSING. *Fifth Edition.
Cr. 8vo. 3s. 6d.*
Pakes (W. C. C.). THE SCIENCE OF
HYGIENE. Illustrated. *Demy 8vo. 15s.*
Parker (Eric). THE BOOK OF THE
ZOO; BY DAY AND NIGHT. With 24
Illustrations from Photographs by HENRY
IRVING. *Cr. 8vo. 6s.*
Parker (Gilbert), M.P. A LOVER'S
DIARY. *Fcap. 8vo. 5s.*
Parkes (A. K.). SMALL LESSONS ON
GREAT TRUTHS. *Fcap. 8vo. 1s. 6d.*
Parkinson (John). PARADISI IN SOLE
PARADISUS TERRESTRIS, OR A
GARDEN OF ALL SORTS OF PLEA-
SANT FLOWERS. *Folio. £3, 3s. net.*
Parsons (Mrs. C.). GARRICK AND HIS
CIRCLE. With 36 Illustrations. *Second
Edition. Demy 8vo. 12s. 6d. net.*
THE INCOMPARABLE SIDDONS. With
20 Illustrations. *Demy 8vo. 12s. 6d. net.*
Pascal. See Library of Devotion.
Paston (George). SOCIAL CARICA-
TURE IN THE EIGHTEENTH
CENTURY. With 214 Illustrations. *Im-
perial Quarto. £2, 12s. 6d. net.*
LADY MARY WORTLEY MONTAGU
AND HER TIMES. With 24 Illustra-
tions. *Second Edition. Demy 8vo. 15s. net.*
See also Little Books on Art and I.P.L.
Patmore (K. A.). THE COURT OF
LOUIS XIII. With 16 Illustrations. *Demy
8vo. 10s. 6d. net.*
Patterson (A. H.). NOTES OF AN EAST
COAST NATURALIST. Illustrated in
Colour by F. SOUTHGATE, R.B.A. *Second
Edition. Cr. 8vo. 6s.*

NATURE IN EASTERN NORFOLK.
With 12 Illustrations in Colour by FRANK
SOUTHGATE, R.B.A. *Second Edition. Cr.
8vo. 6s.*
WILD LIFE ON A NORFOLK ESTU-
ARY. With 40 Illustrations by the Author,
and a Prefatory Note by Her Grace the
DUCHESS OF BEDFORD. *Demy 8vo.
10s. 6d. net.*
*MAN AND NATURE ON TIDAL
WATERS. With Illustrations by the
Author. *Cr. 8vo. 6s.*
Peacock (Netta). See Little Books on Art.
Peake (C. M. A.), F.R.H.S. A CON-
CISE HANDBOOK OF GARDEN
ANNUAL AND BIENNIAL PLANTS.
With 24 Illustrations. *Fcap. 8vo. 3s. 6d. net.*
Peel (Robert), and **Minchin (H. C.),** M.A.
OXFORD. With 100 Illustrations in
Colour. *Cr. 8vo. 6s.*
Peel (Sidney), late Fellow of Trinity College,
Oxford, and Secretary to the Royal Com-
mission on the Licensing Laws. PRACTI-
CAL LICENSING REFORM. *Second
Edition. Cr. 8vo. 1s. 6d.*
Pentin (Herbert), M.A. See Library of
Devotion.
Petrie (W. M. Flinders), D.C.L., LL.D., Pro-
fessor of Egyptology at University College.
A HISTORY OF EGYPT. Fully Illus-
trated. *In six volumes. Cr. 8vo. 6s. each.*
VOL. I. FROM THE EARLIEST KINGS TO
XVITH DYNASTY. *Sixth Edition.*
VOL. II. THE XVIITH AND XVIIITH
DYNASTIES. *Fourth Edition.*
VOL. III. XIXTH TO XXXTH DYNASTIES.
VOL. IV. EGYPT UNDER THE PTOLEMAIC
DYNASTY. J. P. MAHAFFY, Litt.D.
VOL. V. EGYPT UNDER ROMAN RULE. J. G.
MILNE, M.A.
VOL. VI. EGYPT IN THE MIDDLE AGES.
STANLEY LANE-POOLE, M.A.
RELIGION AND CONSCIENCE IN
ANCIENT EGYPT. Lectures delivered
at University College, London. Illustrated.
Cr. 8vo. 2s. 6d.
SYRIA AND EGYPT, FROM THE TELL
EL AMARNA LETTERS. *Cr. 8vo. 2s. 6d.*
EGYPTIAN TALES. Translated from the
Papyri. First Series, IVth to XIIth Dynasty.
Edited by W. M. FLINDERS PETRIE. Illus-
trated by TRISTRAM ELLIS. *Second Edi-
tion. Cr. 8vo. 3s. 6d.*
EGYPTIAN TALES. Translated from the
Papyri. Second Series. XVIIIth to XIXth
Dynasty. Illustrated by TRISTRAM ELLIS.
Crown 8vo. 3s. 6d.
EGYPTIAN DECORATIVE ART. A
Course of Lectures delivered at the Royal
Institution. Illustrated. *Cr. 8vo. 3s. 6d.*
Phillips (W. A.). See Oxford Biographies.
Phillpotts (Eden). MY DEVON YEAR.
With 38 Illustrations by J. LEY PETHY-
BRIDGE. *Second and Cheaper Edition.
Large Cr. 8vo. 6s.*
UP - ALONG AND DOWN - ALONG.
Illustrated by CLAUDE SHEPPERSON.
Cr. 4to. 5s. net.

A 3

Phythian (J. Ernest). TREES IN NATURE, MYTH, AND ART. With 24 Illustrations. *Crown 8vo.* 6s.

Plarr (Victor G.). M.A. See School Histories.

Plato. See Standard Library.

Plautus. THE CAPTIVI. Edited, with an Introduction, Textual Notes, and a Commentary, by W. M. LINDSAY, Fellow of Jesus College, Oxford. *Demy 8vo.* 10s. 6d. net.

Plowden-Wardlaw (J. T.), B.A. See School Examination Series.

Podmore (Frank). MODERN SPIRITUALISM. *Two Volumes. Demy 8vo.* 21s. net.
MESMERISM AND CHRISTIAN SCIENCE : A Short History of Mental Healing. *Demy 8vo.* 10s. 6d. net.

Pollard (Alice). See Little Books on Art.

Pollard (Alfred W.). THE SHAKESPEARE'S FOLIOS AND QUARTOS. With numerous Facsimiles. *Folio. One Guinea net.*

Pollard (Eliza F.). See Little Books on Art.

Pollock (David), M.I.N.A. See Books on Business.

Potter (M. C.), M.A., F.L.S. AN ELEMENTARY TEXT-BOOK OF AGRICULTURAL BOTANY. Illustrated. *Third Edition. Cr. 8vo.* 4s. 6d.

Power (J. O'Connor). THE MAKING OF AN ORATOR. *Cr. 8vo.* 6s.

Price (Eleanor C.). A PRINCESS OF THE OLD WORLD. With 21 Illustrations. *Demy 8vo.* 12s. 6d. net.

Price (L. L.), M.A., Fellow of Oriel College, Oxon. A HISTORY OF ENGLISH POLITICAL ECONOMY FROM ADAM SMITH TO ARNOLD TOYNBEE. *Fifth Edition. Cr. 8vo.* 2s. 6d.

Protheroe (Ernest). THE DOMINION OF MAN. GEOGRAPHY IN ITS HUMAN ASPECT. With 32 full-page Illustrations. *Second Edition. Cr. 8vo.* 2s.

Psellus. See Byzantine Texts.

Pullen-Burry (B.). IN A GERMAN COLONY; or, FOUR WEEKS IN NEW BRITAIN. With 8 Illustrations and 2 Maps. *Cr. 8vo.* 5s. net.

Pycraft (W. P.). BIRD LIFE. With 2 Illustrations in Colour by G. E. LODGE, and others from Drawings and Photographs. *Demy 8vo.* 10s. 6d. net.

'Q' (A. T. Quiller Couch). THE GOLDEN POMP. A PROCESSION OF ENGLISH LYRICS FROM SURREY TO SHIRLEY. *Second and Cheaper Edition. Cr. 8vo.* 2s. 6d. net.

G. R. and E. S. MR. WOODHOUSE'S CORRESPONDENCE. *Cr. 8vo.* 6s.
Also published in a Colonial Edition.

Rackham (R. B.), M.A. See Westminster Commentaries.

Ragg (Laura M.). THE WOMEN ARTISTS OF BOLOGNA. With 20 Illustrations. *Demy 8vo.* 7s. 6d. net.

Ragg (Lonsdale). B.D., Oxon. DANTE

AND HIS ITALY. With 32 Illustrations. *Demy 8vo.* 12s. 6d. net.

Rahtz (F. J.), M.A., B.Sc. HIGHER ENGLISH. *Fourth Edition. Cr. 8vo.* 3s. 6d.
JUNIOR ENGLISH. *Second Edition. Cr. 8vo.* 1s. 6d.

Randolph (B. W.), D.D. See Library of Devotion.

Rannie (D. W.), M.A. A STUDENT'S HISTORY OF SCOTLAND. *Cr. 8vo.* 3s. 6d.
WORDSWORTH AND HIS CIRCLE. With 20 Illustrations. *Demy 8vo.* 12s. 6d. net.

Rashdall (Hastings), M.A., Fellow and Tutor of New College, Oxford. DOCTRINE AND DEVELOPMENT. *Cr. 8vo.* 6s.

Raven (J. J.), D.D., F.S.A. See Antiquary's Books.

Raven-Hill (L.). See Llewellyn (Owen).

Rawlings (Gertrude Burford). COINS AND HOW TO KNOW THEM. With 206 Illustrations. *Second Edition. Cr. 8vo.* 6s.

Rawstorne (Lawrence, Esq.). See I.P.L.

Raymond (Walter). See School Histories.

Rea (Lilian). THE LIFE AND TIMES OF MARIE MADELEINE COUNTESS OF LA FAYETTE. With 20 Illustrations. *Demy 8vo.* 10s. 6d. net.

Read (C. Stanford), M.B. (Lond.), M.R.C.S., L.R.C.P. FADS AND FEEDING. *Cr. 8vo.* 2s. 6d.

Real Paddy (A). See I.P.L.

Reason (W.), M.A. UNIVERSITY AND SOCIAL SETTLEMENTS. Edited by *Cr. 8vo.* 2s. 6d.

Redpath (H. A.), M.A., D.Litt. See Westminster Commentaries.

Rees (J. D.), C.I.E., M.P. THE REAL INDIA. *Second Edition. Demy 8vo.* 10s. 6d. net.

Reich (Emil), Doctor Juris. WOMAN THROUGH THE AGES. With 36 Illustrations. *Two Volumes. Demy 8vo.* 21s. net.

Reynolds (Sir Joshua). See Little Galleries.

Rhodes (W. E.). See School Histories.

Ricketts (Charles). See Classics of Art.

Richardson (Charles). THE COMPLETE FOXHUNTER. With 46 Illustrations, of which 4 are in Colour. *Second Edition. Demy 8vo.* 12s. 6d. net.

Richmond (Wilfrid), Chaplain of Lincoln's Inn. THE CREED IN THE EPISTLES. *Cr. 8vo.* 2s. 6d. net.

Riehl (W. H.). See Simplified German Texts.

Roberts (M. E.). See Channer (C. C.).

Robertson (A.), D.D., Lord Bishop of Exeter. REGNUM DEI. (The Bampton Lectures of 1901.) *A New and Cheaper Edition. Demy 8vo.* 7s. 6d. net.

Robertson (C. Grant), M.A., Fellow of All Souls' College, Oxford. SELECT STATUTES, CASES, AND CONSTITUTIONAL DOCUMENTS, 1660-1832. *Demy 8vo.* 10s. 6d. net.

Robertson (C. Grant) and Bartholomew (J. G.), F.R.S.E., F.R.G.S. A HISTORICAL AND MODERN ATLAS OF THE BRITISH EMPIRE. *Demy Quarto.* 4s. 6d. net.

Robertson (Sir G. S.), K.C.S.I. CHITRAL: THE STORY OF A MINOR SIEGE. With 8 Illustrations. *Third Edition. Demy 8vo.* 10s. 6d. net.

Robinson (Cecilia). THE MINISTRY OF DEACONESSES. With an Introduction by the late Archbishop of Canterbury. *Cr. 8vo.* 3s. 6d.

Robinson (F. S.). See Connoisseur's Library.

Rochefoucauld (La). See Little Library.

Rodwell (G.), B.A. NEW TESTAMENT GREEK. A Course for Beginners. With a Preface by WALTER LOCK, D.D., Warden of Keble College. *Fcap. 8vo.* 3s. 6d.

Roe (Fred). OLD OAK FURNITURE. With many Illustrations by the Author, including a frontispiece in colour. *Second Edition. Demy 8vo.* 10s. 6d. net.

Rogers (A. G. L.), M.A. See Books on Business.

Roland. See Simplified French Texts.

Romney (George). See Little Galleries.

Roscoe (E. S.). See Little Guides.

Rose (Edward). THE ROSE READER. Illustrated. *Cr. 8vo.* 2s. 6d. Also in 4 Parts. *Parts I. and II.* 6d. each ; *Part III.* 8d. ; *Part IV.* 10d.

Rose (G. H.). See Hey (H.) and Baring-Gould (S).

Rowntree (Joshua). THE IMPERIAL DRUG TRADE. A RE-STATEMENT OF THE OPIUM QUESTION. *Third Edition Revised. Cr. 8vo.* 2s. net.

Royde-Smith (N. G.). THE PILLOW BOOK : A GARNER OF MANY MOODS. Collected by. *Second Edition. Cr. 8vo.* 4s. 6d. net.

POETS OF OUR DAY. Selected, with an Introduction, by. *Fcap. 8vo.* 5s.

Rubie (A. E.), D.D. See Junior School Books.

Rumbold (The Right Hon. Sir Horace). Bart., G. C. B., G. C. M. G. THE AUSTRIAN COURT IN THE NINETEENTH CENTURY. With 16 Illustrations. *Demy 8vo.* 18s. net.

Russell (Archibald G. B.). See Blake (William.)

Russell (W. Clark). THE LIFE OF ADMIRAL LORD COLLINGWOOD. With 12 Illustrations by F. BRANGWYN. *Fourth Edition. Cr. 8vo.* 6s.

Ryley (M. Beresford). QUEENS OF THE RENAISSANCE. With 24 Illustrations. *Demy 8vo.* 10s. 6d. net.

Sainsbury (Harrington), M.D., F.R.C.P. PRINCIPIA THERAPEUTICA. *Demy 8vo.* 7s. 6d. net.
See also New Library of Medicine.

St. Anselm. See Library of Devotion.

St. Augustine. See Library of Devotion.

St. Bernard. See Library of Devotion.

St. Cyres (Viscount) See Oxford Biographies.

St. Francis of Assisi. THE LITTLE FLOWERS OF THE GLORIOUS MESSER, AND OF HIS FRIARS. Done into English, with Notes by WILLIAM HEYWOOD. With 40 Illustrations from Italian Painters. *Demy 8vo.* 5s. net.
See also Library of Devotion and Standard Library.

St. Francis de Sales. See Library of Devotion.

St. James. See Churchman's Bible and Westminster Commentaries.

St. Luke. See Junior School Books.

St. Mark. See Junior School Books and Churchman's Bible.

St. Matthew. See Junior School Books.

St. Paul. SECOND AND THIRD EPISTLES OF PAUL THE APOSTLE TO THE CORINTHIANS. Edited by JAMES HOUGHTON KENNEDY, D.D., Assistant Lecturer in Divinity in the University of Dublin. With Introduction, Dissertations, and Notes by J. SCHMITT. *Cr. 8vo.* 6s. See also Churchman's Bible and Westminster Commentaries.

'Saki' (H. Munro). REGINALD. *Second Edition. Fcap. 8vo.* 2s. 6d. net.

Salmon (A. L.). See Little Guides.

Sanders (Lloyd). THE HOLLAND HOUSE CIRCLE. With 24 Illustrations. *Second Edition. Demy 8vo.* 12s. 6d. net.

Sathas (C.). See Byzantine Texts.

Schmitt (John). See Byzantine Texts.

Schofield (A. T.), M.D., Hon. Phys. Freidenham Hospital. See New Library of Medicine.

Scudamore (Cyril). See Little Guides.

Scupoli (Dom. L.). See Library of Devotion.

Ségur (Madame de). See Simplified French Texts.

Sélincourt (E. de.) See Keats (John).

Sélincourt (Hugh de). GREAT RALEGH. With 16 Illustrations. *Demy 8vo.* 10s. 6d. net.

Sells (V. P.), M.A. THE MECHANICS OF DAILY LIFE. Illustrated. *Cr. 8vo.* 2s. 6d.

Selous (Edmund). TOMMY SMITH'S ANIMALS. Illustrated by G. W. ORD. *Eleventh Edition. Fcap. 8vo.* 2s. 6d.
School Edition, 1s. 6d.

TOMMY SMITH'S OTHER ANIMALS. Illustrated by AUGUSTA GUEST. *Fifth Edition. Fcap. 8vo.* 2s. 6d.
School Edition, 1s. 6d.

Senter (George), B.Sc. (Lond.), Ph.D. See Textbooks of Science.

Shakespeare (William).
THE FOUR FOLIOS, 1623 ; 1632 ; 1664 ; 1685. Each £4, 4s. net, or a complete set, £12, 12s. net.
Folios 2, 3 and 4 are ready.
THE POEMS OF WILLIAM SHAKESPEARE. With an Introduction and Notes

by GEORGE WYNDHAM. *Demy* 8vo. *Buckram, gilt top*, 10s. 6d.
See also Arden Shakespeare, Standard Library and Little Quarto Shakespeare.

Sharp (A.). VICTORIAN POETS. *Cr. 8vo.* 2s. 6d.

Sharp (Cecil). See Baring-Gould (S.).

Sharp (Elizabeth). See Little Books on Art.

Shedlock (J. S.) THE PIANOFORTE SONATA. *Cr. 8vo.* 5s.

Shelley (Percy B.). See Standard Library.

Sheppard (H. F.), M.A. See Baring-Gould (S.).

Sherwell (Arthur), M.A. LIFE IN WEST LONDON. *Third Edition. Cr. 8vo.* 2s. 6d.

Shipley (Mary E.). AN ENGLISH CHURCH HISTORY FOR CHILDREN. With a Preface by the Bishop of Gibraltar. With Maps and Illustrations. *Cr. 8vo. Each part* 2s. 6d. net.
PART I.—To the Norman Conquest.
PART II.—To the Reformation.

Sichel (Walter). See Oxford Biographies.

Sidgwick (Mrs. Alfred). HOME LIFE IN GERMANY. With 16 Illustrations. *Second Edition. Demy* 8vo. 10s. 6d. net.

Sime (John). See Little Books on Art.

Simonson (G. A.). FRANCESCO GUARDI. With 41 Plates. *Imperial 4to.* £2, 2s. net.

Sketchley (R. E. D.). See Little Books on Art.

Skipton (H. P. K.). See Little Books on Art.

Sladen (Douglas). SICILY: The New Winter Resort. With over 200 Illustrations. *Second Edition. Cr. 8vo.* 5s. net.

Smallwood (M. G.). See Little Books on Art.

Smedley (F. E.). See I.P.L.

Smith (Adam). THE WEALTH OF NATIONS. Edited with an Introduction and numerous Notes by EDWIN CANNAN, M.A. *Two volumes. Demy* 8vo. 21s. net.

Smith (H. Bompas), M.A. A NEW JUNIOR ARITHMETIC. *Crown 8vo.* Without Answers, 2s. With Answers, 2s. 6d.

Smith (H. Clifford). See Connoisseur's Library.

Smith (Horace and James). See Little Library.

Smith (R. Mudie). THOUGHTS FOR THE DAY. Edited by. *Fcap. 8vo.* 3s. 6d. net.

Smith (Nowell C.). See Wordsworth (W).

Smith (John Thomas). A BOOK FOR A RAINY DAY: Or, Recollections of the Events of the Years 1766-1833. Edited by WILFRED WHITTEN. Illustrated. *Wide Demy* 8vo. 12s. 6d. net.

Snell (F. J.). A BOOK OF EXMOOR. Illustrated. *Cr. 8vo.* 6s.

Snowden (C. E.). A HANDY DIGEST OF BRITISH HISTORY. *Demy* 8vo. 4s. 6d.

Sophocles. See Classical Translations.

Sornet (L. A.), and **Acatos (M. J.)** See Junior School Books.

Southey (R.). ENGLISH SEAMEN. Edited by DAVID HANNAY.
Vol. I. (Howard, Clifford, Hawkins, Drake, Cavendish). *Second Edition. Cr. 8vo.* 6s.
Vol. II. (Richard Hawkins, Grenville, Essex, and Raleigh). *Cr. 8vo.* 6s.
See also Standard Library.

Souvestre (E.). See Simplified French Texts.

Spence (C. H.), M.A. See School Examination Series.

Spicer (A. Dykes), M.A. THE PAPER TRADE. A Descriptive and Historical Survey. With Diagrams and Plans. *Demy* 8vo. 12s. 6d. net.

Spooner (W. A.), M.A. See Leaders of Religion.

Spragge (W. Horton), M.A. See Junior School Books.

Staley (Edgcumbe). THE GUILDS OF FLORENCE. Illustrated. *Second Edition. Royal* 8vo. 16s. net.

Stanbridge (J. W.), B.D. See Library of Devotion.

'Stancliffe.' GOLF DO'S AND DONT'S. *Second Edition. Fcap. 8vo.* 1s.

Stead (D. W.). See Gallaher (D.).

Stedman (A. M. M.), M.A.
INITIA LATINA: Easy Lessons on Elementary Accidence. *Eleventh Edition. Fcap. 8vo.* 1s.
FIRST LATIN LESSONS. *Eleventh Edition. Cr. 8vo.* 2s.
FIRST LATIN READER. With Notes adapted to the Shorter Latin Primer and Vocabulary. *Seventh Edition.* 18mo. 1s. 6d.
EASY SELECTIONS FROM CÆSAR. The Helvetian War. *Fourth Edition.* 18mo. 1s.
EASY SELECTIONS FROM LIVY. The Kings of Rome. *Second Edition.* 18mo. 1s. 6d.
EASY LATIN PASSAGES FOR UNSEEN TRANSLATION. *Twelfth Ed. Fcap. 8vo.* 1s. 6d.
EXEMPLA LATINA. First Exercises in Latin Accidence. With Vocabulary. *Fourth Edition. Cr. 8vo.* 1s.
EASY LATIN EXERCISES ON THE SYNTAX OF THE SHORTER AND REVISED LATIN PRIMER. With Vocabulary. *Twelfth Edition. Cr. 8vo.* 1s. 6d. KEY, 3s. net.
THE LATIN COMPOUND SENTENCE: Rules and Exercises. *Second Edition. Cr. 8vo.* 1s. 6d. With Vocabulary. 2s.
NOTANDA QUAEDAM: Miscellaneous Latin Exercises on Common Rules and Idioms. *Fifth Edition. Fcap. 8vo.* 1s. 6d. With Vocabulary. 2s. KEY, 2s. net.
LATIN VOCABULARIES FOR REPETITION: Arranged according to Subjects. *Sixteenth Edition. Fcap. 8vo.* 1s. 6d.
A VOCABULARY OF LATIN IDIOMS. 18mo. *Fourth Edition.* 1s.

STEPS TO GREEK. *Fourth Edition.*
18*mo.* 1*s.*
A SHORTER GREEK PRIMER. *Third Edition. Cr. 8vo.* 1*s. 6d.*
EASY GREEK PASSAGES FOR UNSEEN TRANSLATION. *Fourth Edition, revised. Fcap. 8vo.* 1*s. 6d.*
GREEK VOCABULARIES FOR RE-PETITION. Arranged according to Subjects. *Fourth Edition. Fcap. 8vo.* 1*s 6d.*
GREEK TESTAMENT SELECTIONS. For the use of Schools. With Introduction, Notes, and Vocabulary. *Fourth Edition. Fcap. 8vo.* 2*s. 6d.*
STEPS TO FRENCH. *Ninth Edition.* 18*mo.* 8*d.*
FIRST FRENCH LESSONS. *Ninth Edition. Cr. 8vo.* 1*s.*
EASY FRENCH PASSAGES FOR UNSEEN TRANSLATION. *Sixth Edition. Fcap. 8vo.* 1*s. 6d.*
EASY FRENCH EXERCISES ON ELEMENTARY SYNTAX. With Vocabulary. *Fourth Edition. Cr. 8vo.* 2*s. 6d.* KEY. 3*s. net.*
FRENCH VOCABULARIES FOR RE-PETITION : Arranged according to Subjects. *Fourteenth Edition. Fcap. 8vo.* 1*s.*
See also School Examination Series.
Steel (R. Elliott), M.A., F.C.S. THE WORLD OF SCIENCE. With 147 Illustrations. *Second Edition. Cr. 8vo.* 2*s. 6d.*
See also School Examination Series.
Stephenson (C.), of the Technical College, Bradford, and **Suddards (F.)** of the Yorkshire College, Leeds. A TEXTBOOK DEALING WITH ORNAMENTAL DESIGN FOR WOVEN FABRICS. With 66 full-page Plates and numerous Diagrams in the Text. *Third Edition. Demy 8vo.* 7*s. 6d.*
Sterne (Laurence). See Little Library.
Steuart (Katherine). BY ALLAN WATER. *Second Edition. Cr. 8vo.* 6*s.*
RICHARD KENNOWAY AND HIS FRIENDS. A Sequel to 'By Allan Water.' *Demy 8vo.* 7*s. 6d. net.*
Stevenson (R. L.) THE LETTERS OF ROBERT LOUIS STEVENSON TO HIS FAMILY AND FRIENDS. Selected and Edited by SIDNEY COLVIN. *Eighth Edition.* 2 *vols. Cr. 8vo.* 12*s.*
VAILIMA LETTERS. With an Etched Portrait by WILLIAM STRANG. *Seventh Edition. Cr. 8vo. Buckram.* 6*s.*
THE LIFE OF R. L. STEVENSON See Balfour (G.).
Stevenson (M. I.). FROM SARANAC TO THE MARQUESAS. Being Letters written by Mrs. M. I. STEVENSON during 1887-88. *Cr. 8vo.* 6*s. net.*
LETTERS FROM SAMOA, 1891-95. Edited and arranged by M. C. BALFOUR With many Illustrations. *Second Edition Cr. 8vo.* 6*s. net.*
Stoddart (Anna M.). See Oxford Biographies.

Stokes (F. G.), B.A. HOURS WITH RABELAIS. From the translation of SIR T. URQUHART and P. A. MOTTEUX. With a Portrait in Photogravure. *Cr. 8vo.* 3*s. 6d. net.*
Stone (S. J.). POEMS AND HYMNS. With a Memoir by F. G. ELLERTON, M.A. With Portrait. *Cr. 8vo.* 6*s.*
Storr (Vernon F.), M.A., Canon of Winchester. DEVELOPMENT AND DIVINE PURPOSE *Cr. 8vo.* 5*s. net.*
Story (Alfred T.). AMERICAN SHRINES IN ENGLAND. With 4 Illustrations in Colour, and 19 other Illustrations. *Crown 8vo.* 6*s.*
See also Little Guides.
Straker (F.). See Books on Business.
Streane (A. W.), D.D. See Churchman's Bible.
Streatfeild (R. A.). MODERN MUSIC AND MUSICIANS. With 24 Illustrations. *Second Ed. Demy 8vo.* 7*s. 6d. net.*
See also New Library of Music.
Stroud (Henry), D.Sc., M.A. ELEMENTARY PRACTICAL PHYSICS. With 115 Diagrams. *Second Edit., revised. Cr. 8vo.* 4*s. 6d.*
Sturch (F.), Staff Instructor to the Surrey County Council. MANUAL TRAINING DRAWING (WOODWORK). With Solutions to Examination Questions, Orthographic, Isometric and Oblique Projection. With 50 Plates and 140 Figures. *Foolscap.* 5*s. net.*
Suddards (F.). See Stephenson (C.).
Surtees (R. S.). See I.P.L.
Sutherland (William). OLD AGE PENSIONS IN THEORY AND PRACTICE, WITH SOME FOREIGN EXAMPLES. *Cr. 8vo.* 3*s. 6d. net.*
*****Swanton (E. W.),** Member of the British Mycological Society. FUNGI AND HOW TO KNOW THEM. With 16 Coloured Plates by M. K. SPITTAL, and 32 Black and White Plates. *Cr. 8vo.* 5*s. net.*
Symes (J. E.), M.A. THE FRENCH REVOLUTION. *Second Edition. Cr. 8vo.* 2*s. 6d.*
Sympson (E. Mansel), M.A., M.D. See Ancient Cities.
Tabor (Margaret E.). THE SAINTS IN ART. With 20 Illustrations. *Fcap. 8vo.* 3*s. 6d. net.*
Tacitus. AGRICOLA. Edited by R. F. DAVIS, M.A. *Cr. 8vo.* 2*s.*
GERMANIA. By the same Editor. *Cr. 8vo.* 2*s.*
See also Classical Translations.
Tallack (W.). HOWARD LETTERS AND MEMORIES. *Demy 8vo.* 10*s. 6d. net.*
Tatham (Frederick). See Blake (William).
Tauler (J.). See Library of Devotion.
Taylor (A. E.). THE ELEMENTS OF METAPHYSICS. *Second Edition. Demy 8vo.* 10*s. 6d. net.*
Taylor (F. G.), M.A. See Commercial Series.
Taylor (I. A.). See Oxford Biographies.

Taylor (John W.). THE COMING OF THE SAINTS. With 26 Illustrations. *Demy 8vo. 7s. 6d. net.*

Taylor (T. M.), M.A., Fellow of Gonville and Caius College, Cambridge. A CONSTITUTIONAL AND POLITICAL HISTORY OF ROME. To the Reign of Domitian. *Cr. 8vo. 7s. 6d.*

Teasdale-Buckell (G. T.). THE COMPLETE SHOT. With 53 Illustrations. *Third Edition. Demy 8vo. 12s. 6d. net.*

Tennyson (Alfred, Lord). EARLY POEMS. Edited, with Notes and an Introduction, by J. CHURTON COLLINS, M.A. *Cr. 8vo. 6s.*

IN MEMORIAM, MAUD, AND THE PRINCESS. Edited by J. CHURTON COLLINS, M.A. *Cr. 8vo. 6s.*

See also Little Library.

Terry (C. S.). See Oxford Biographies.

Terry (F. J.), B.A. ELEMENTARY LATIN. *Cr. 8vo. 2s.*

TEACHER'S HANDBOOK TO ELEMENTARY LATIN. Containing the necessary supplementary matter to Pupil's edition. *Cr. 8vo. 3s. 6d. net.*

Thackeray (W. M.). See Little Library.

Theobald (F. V.), M.A. INSECT LIFE. Illustrated. *Second Edition Revised. Cr. 8vo. 2s. 6d.*

Thibaudeau (A. C.). BONAPARTE AND THE CONSULATE. Translated and Edited by G. K. FORTESQUE, LL.D. With 12 Illustrations. *Demy 8vo. 10s. 6d. net.*

Thompson (A. H.). See Little Guides.

Thompson (Francis). SELECTED POEMS OF FRANCIS THOMPSON. With a Biographical Note by WILFRID MEYNELL. With a Portrait in Photogravure. *Second Edition. Fcap. 8vo. 5s. net.*

Thompson (A. P.). See Textbooks of Technology.

*****Thomson (J. M.),** Fellow and Dean of Divinity of Magdalen College, Oxford. JESUS ACCORDING TO ST. MARK. *Cr. 8vo. 5s.*

Tileston (Mary W.). DAILY STRENGTH FOR DAILY NEEDS. *Sixteenth Edition. Medium 16mo. 2s. 6d. net.* Also an edition in superior binding, 6s.

Tompkins (H. W.), F.R.H.S. See Little Books on Art and Little Guides.

Toynbee (Paget), M.A., D.Litt. IN THE FOOTPRINTS OF DANTE. A Treasury of Verse and Prose from the works of Dante. *Small Cr. 8vo. 4s. 6d. net.*

DANTE IN ENGLISH LITERATURE: FROM CHAUCER TO CARY. *Two vols. Demy 8vo. 21s. net.*

See also Oxford Biographies and Dante.

Tozer (Basil). THE HORSE IN HISTORY. With 25 Illustrations. *Cr. 8vo. 6s.*

Tremayne (Eleanor E.). See Romantic History.

Trench (Herbert). DEIRDRE WEDDED, AND OTHER POEMS. *Second and Revised Edition. Large Post 8vo. 6s.*

NEW POEMS. *Second Edition. Large Post 8vo. 6s.*

APOLLO AND THE SEAMAN. *Large Post 8vo. Paper, 1s. 6d. net; cloth, 2s 6d. net.*

Trevelyan (G. M.), Fellow of Trinity College, Cambridge. ENGLAND UNDER THE STUARTS. With Maps and Plans. *Third Edition. Demy 8vo. 10s. 6d. net.*

ENGLISH LIFE THREE HUNDRED YEARS AGO : Being the first two chapters of *England under the Stuarts.* Edited by J. TURRAL, B.A. *Cr. 8vo. 1s.*

Triggs (Inigo H.), A.R.I.B.A. TOWN PLANNING: PAST, PRESEMT, AND POSSIBLE. With 173 Illustrations. *Wide Royal 8vo. 15s. net.*

Troutbeck (G. E.). See Little Guides.

Tyler (E. A.), B.A., F.C.S. See Junior School Books.

Tyrrell-Gill (Frances). See Little Books on Art.

Unwin (George). See Antiquary's Books.

Vardon (Harry). THE COMPLETE GOLFER. With 63 Illustrations. *Tenth Edition. Demy 8vo. 10s. 6d. net.*

Vaughan (Henry). See Little Library.

Vaughan (Herbert M.), B.A. (Oxon.). THE LAST OF THE ROYAL STUARTS, HENRY STUART, CARDINAL, DUKE OF YORK. With 20 Illustrations. *Second Edition. Demy 8vo. 10s. 6d. net.*

THE MEDICI POPES (LEO X. AND CLEMENT VII. With 20 Illustrations. *Demy 8vo. 15s. net.*

THE NAPLES RIVIERA. With 25 Illustrations in Colour by MAURICE GREIFFENHAGEN. *Second Edition. Cr. 8vo. 6s.*

Vernon (Hon. W. Warren), M.A. READINGS ON THE INFERNO OF DANTE. With an Introduction by the Rev. Dr. MOORE. *In Two Volumes. Second Edition. Cr. 8vo. 15s. net.*

READINGS ON THE PURGATORIO OF DANTE. With an Introduction by the late DEAN CHURCH. *In Two Volumes. Third Edition. Cr. 8vo. 15s. net.*

READINGS ON THE PARADISO OF DANTE. With an Introduction by the BISHOP OF RIPON. *In Two Volumes. Second Edition. Cr. 8vo. 15s. net.*

Vincent (J. E.). THROUGH EAST ANGLIA IN A MOTOR CAR. With 16 Illustrations in Colour by FRANK SOUTHGATE, R.B.A., and a Map. *Cr. 8vo. 6s.*

Voegelin (A.), M.A. See Junior Examination Series.

Waddell (Col. L. A.), LL.D., C.B. LHASA AND ITS MYSTERIES. With a Record of the Expedition of 1903-1904. With 155 Illustrations and Maps. *Third and Cheaper Edition. Medium 8vo. 7s. 6d. net.*

Wade (G. W.), D.D. OLD TESTAMENT HISTORY. With Maps. *Sixth Edition. Cr. 8vo. 6s.*

Wade (G. W.), D.D., and **Wade (J. H.),** M.A. See Little Guides.

Wagner (Richard). RICHARD WAG-

NER'S MUSIC DRAMAS: Interpretations, embodying Wagner's own explanations. By ALICE LEIGHTON CLEATHER and BASIL CRUMP. *In Three Volumes. Fcap 8vo. 2s. 6d. each.*
VOL. I.—THE RING OF THE NIBELUNG. *Third Edition.*
VOL. II.—PARSIFAL, LOHENGRIN, and THE HOLY GRAIL.
VOL. III.—TRISTAN AND ISOLDE.

Waineman (Paul). A SUMMER TOUR IN FINLAND. With 16 Illustrations in Colour by ALEXANDER FEDERLEY, 16 other Illustrations and a Map. *Demy 8vo. 10s. 6d. net.*

Walkley (A. B.). DRAMA AND LIFE. *Cr. 8vo. 6s.*

Wall (J. C.). See Antiquary's Books.

Wallace-Hadrill (F.), Second Master at Herne Bay College. REVISION NOTES ON ENGLISH HISTORY. *Cr. 8vo. 1s.*

Walters (H. B.). See Little Books on Art and Classics of Art.

Walton (F. W.), M.A. See School Histories.

Walton (Izaak) and **Cotton (Charles).** See I.P.L. and Little Library.

Waterhouse (Elizabeth). WITH THE SIMPLE-HEARTED: Little Homilies to Women in Country Places. *Second Edition. Small Pott 8vo. 2s. net.*
COMPANIONS OF THE WAY. Being Selections for Morning and Evening Reading. Chosen and arranged by ELIZABETH WATERHOUSE. *Large Cr. 8vo. 5s. net.*
THOUGHTS OF A TERTIARY. *Small Pott 8vo. 1s. net.*
See also Little Library.

Watt (Francis). See Henderson (T. F.).

Weatherhead (T. C.), M.A. EXAMINATION PAPERS IN HORACE. *Cr. 8vo. 2s.*
See also Junior Examination Series.

***Webb (George W.),** B.A. A SYSTEMATIC GEOGRAPHY OF THE BRITISH ISLES. With Maps and Diagrams. *Cr. 8vo. 1s.*

Webber (F. C.). See Textbooks of Technology.

***Weigall (Arthur E. P.).** A GUIDE TO THE ANTIQUITIES OF UPPER EGYPT: From Abydos to the Sudan Frontier. With 67 Maps, and Plans. *Cr. 8vo. 7s. 6d. net.*

Weir (Archibald), M.A. AN INTRODUCTION TO THE HISTORY OF MODERN EUROPE. *Cr. 8vo. 6s.*

Welch (Catharine). THE LITTLE DAUPHIN. With 16 Illustrations. *Cr. 8vo. 6s.*

Wells (Sidney H.) See Textbooks of Science.

Wells (J.), M.A., Fellow and Tutor of Wadham College. OXFORD AND OXFORD LIFE. *Third Edition. Cr. 8vo. 3s. 6d.*
A SHORT HISTORY OF ROME. *Ninth Edition.* With 3 Maps. *Cr. 8vo. 3s. 6d.*
See also Little Guides.

Wesley (John). See Library of Devotion.

Westell (W. Percival). THE YOUNG NATURALIST. With 8 Coloured Plates

by C. F. NEWALL, and many other Illustrations. *Cr. 8vo. 6s.*

Westell (W. Percival), F.L.S., M.B.O.U., and **Cooper (C. S.),** F.R.H.S. THE YOUNG BOTANIST. With 8 Coloured and 63 Black and White Plates drawn from Nature, by C. F. NEWALL. *Cr. 8vo. 3s. 6d. net.*

Whibley (C.). See Henley (W. E.).

Whibley (L.), M.A., Fellow of Pembroke College, Cambridge. GREEK OLIGARCHIES: THEIR ORGANISATION AND CHARACTER. *Cr. 8vo. 6s.*

White (Eustace E.). THE COMPLETE HOCKEY PLAYER. With 32 Illustrations. *Second Edition. Demy 8vo. 5s. net.*

White (George F.), Lieut.-Col. A CENTURY OF SPAIN AND PORTUGAL. *Demy 8vo. 12s. 6d. net.*

White (Gilbert). See Standard Library.

Whitfield (E. E.), M.A. See Commercial Series.

Whitehead (A. W.). GASPARD DE COLIGNY, ADMIRAL OF FRANCE. With 26 Illustrations and 10 Maps and Plans. *Demy 8vo. 12s. 6d. net.*

Whiteley (R. Lloyd), F.I.C., Principal of the Municipal Science School, West Bromwich. AN ELEMENTARY TEXTBOOK OF INORGANIC CHEMISTRY. *Cr. 8vo. 2s. 6d.*

Whitley (Miss). See Dilke (Lady).

Whitling (Miss L.), late Staff Teacher of the National Training School of Cookery. THE COMPLETE COOK. With 42 Illustrations. *Demy 8vo. 7s. 6d. net.*

Whitten (W.). See Smith (John Thomas).

Whyte (A. G.), B.Sc. See Books on Business.

Wilberforce (Wilfrid). See Little Books on Art.

Wilde (Oscar). DE PROFUNDIS. *Twelfth Edition. Cr. 8vo. 5s. net.*
THE WORKS OF OSCAR WILDE. *In 12 Volumes. Fcap. 8vo. 5s. net each volume.*
I. THE DUCHESS OF PADUA. II. LADY WINDERMERE'S FAN. III. A WOMAN OF NO IMPORTANCE. IV. THE IMPORTANCE OF BEING EARNEST. V. AN IDEAL HUSBAND. VI. DE PROFUNDIS and PRISON LETTERS. VII. INTENTIONS. VIII. ESSAYS. IX. A HOUSE OF POMEGRANATES. X. LORD ARTHUR SAVILE'S CRIME and the PORTRAIT OF MR. W. H. XI. POEMS. XII. SALOMÉ, A FLORENTINE TRAGEDY, and LA SAINTE COURTISANE.

Wilkins (W. H.), B.A. THE ALIEN INVASION. *Cr. 8vo. 2s. 6d.*

Williams (H. Noel). THE WOMEN BONAPARTES. The Mother and three Sisters of Napoleon. With 36 Illustrations. *In Two Volumes. Demy 8vo. 24s net.*
A ROSE OF SAVOY: MARIE ADELÉIDE OF SAVOY, DUCHESSE DE BOURGOGNE, MOTHER OF LOUIS XV. With a Frontispiece in Photogravure and 16 other Illustrations. *Demy 8vo. 15s. net.*

Williams (A.). PETROL PETER: or Pretty Stories and Funny Pictures. Illustrated in Colour by A. W. MILLS. *Demy 4to.* 3s. 6d. net.

Williamson (M. G.), M.A. See Ancient Cities.

Williamson (W.), B.A. See Junior Examination Series, Junior School Books, and Beginner's Books.

Wilmot-Buxton (E. M.), F.R. Hist. S. MAKERS OF EUROPE. Outlines of European History for the Middle Forms of Schools. With 12 Maps. *Tenth Edition. Cr. 8vo.* 3s. 6d.

THE ANCIENT WORLD. With Maps and Illustrations. *Cr. 8vo.* 3s. 6d.

A BOOK OF NOBLE WOMEN. With 16 Illustrations. *Cr. 8vo.* 3s. 6d.

A HISTORY OF GREAT BRITAIN: FROM THE COMING OF THE ANGLES TO THE YEAR 1870. With 20 Maps. *Cr. 8vo.* 3s. 6d. See also Beginner's Books and New Historical Series.

Wilson(Bishop.). See Library of Devotion.

Wilson (A. J.). See Books on Business.

Wilson (H. A.). See Books on Business.

Wilton (Richard), M.A. LYRA PASTORALIS : Songs of Nature, Church, and Home. *Pott 8vo.* 2s. 6d.

Winbolt (S. E.), M.A. EXERCISES IN LATIN ACCIDENCE. *Cr. 8vo.* 1s. 6d.

LATIN HEXAMETER VERSE: An Aid to Composition. *Cr. 8vo.* 3s. 6d. KEY, 5s. net.

Windle (B. C. A.), D.Sc.,F.R.S., F.S.A. See Antiquary's Books, Little Guides, Ancient Cities, and School Histories.

Wood (Sir Evelyn), F. M., V.C., G.C.B., G.C.M.G. FROM MIDSHIPMAN TO FIELD-MARSHAL. With Illustrations, and 29 Maps. *Fifth and Cheaper Edition. Demy 8vo.* 7s. 6d. net.

THE REVOLT IN HINDUSTAN. 1857-59. With 8 Illustrations and 5 Maps. *Second Edition. Cr. 8vo.* 6s.

Wood (J. A. E.). See Textbooks of Technology.

Wood (J. Hickory). DAN LENO. Illustrated. *Third Edition. Cr. 8vo.* 6s.

Wood (W. Birkbeck), M.A., late Scholar of Worcester College, Oxford, and **Edmonds (Major J. E.), R.E., D.A.Q.-M.G.** A HISTORY OF THE CIVIL WAR IN

THE UNITED STATES. With an Introduction by H. SPENSER WILKINSON. With 24 Maps and Plans. *Second Edition. Demy 8vo.* 12s. 6d. net.

Wordsworth (Christopher), M.A. See Antiquary's Books.

Wordsworth (W.). THE POEMS OF. With an Introduction and Notes by NOWELL C. SMITH, late Fellow of New College, Oxford. *In Three Volumes. Demy 8vo.* 15s. net.

POEMS BY WILLIAM WORDSWORTH. Selected with an Introduction by STOPFORD A. BROOKE. With 40 Illustrations by E. H. NEW, including a Frontispiece in Photogravure. *Cr. 8vo.* 7s. 6d. net. See also Little Library.

Wordsworth (W.) and Coleridge (S. T.). See Little Library.

Wright (Arthur), D.D., Fellow of Queen's College, Cambridge. See Churchman's Library.

Wright (C. Gordon). See Dante.

Wright (J. C.). TO-DAY. Thoughts on Life for every day. *Demy 16mo.* 1s. 6d. net.

Wright (Sophie). GERMAN VOCABULARIES FOR REPETITION. *Fcap. 8vo.* 1s. 6d.

Wyatt (Kate M.). See Gloag (M. R.).

Wylde (A. B.). MODERN ABYSSINIA. With a Map and a Portrait. *Demy 8vo.* 15s. net.

Wyllie (M. A.). NORWAY AND ITS FJORDS. With 16 Illustrations, in Colour by W. L. WYLLIE, R.A., and 17 other Illustrations. *Crown 8vo.* 6s.

Wyndham (George). See Shakespeare (William).

Yeats (W. B.). A BOOK OF IRISH VERSE. *Revised and Enlarged Edition. Cr. 8vo.* 3s. 6d.

Young (Filson). THE COMPLETE MOTORIST. With 138 Illustrations. *New Edition (Seventh), with many additions. Demy 8vo.* 12s. 6d. net.

THE JOY OF THE ROAD: An Appreciation of the Motor Car. With a Frontispiece in Photogravure. *Small Demy 8vo.* 5s. net.

Zachariah of Mitylene. See Byzantine Texts.

Zimmern (Antonia). WHAT DO WE KNOW CONCERNING ELECTRICITY? *Fcap. 8vo.* 1s. 6d. net.

Ancient Cities

General Editor, B. C. A. WINDLE, D.Sc., F.R.S.

Cr. 8vo. 4s. 6d. net.

BRISTOL. By Alfred Harvey, M.B. Illustrated by E. H. New.

CANTERBURY. By J. C. Cox, LL.D., F.S.A. Illustrated by B. C. Boulter.

CHESTER. By B. C. A. Windle, D.Sc. F.R.S. Illustrated by E. H. New.

DUBLIN. By S. A. O. Fitzpatrick. Illustrated by W. C. Green.

EDINBURGH. By M. G. Williamson, M.A. Illustrated by Herbert Railton.

LINCOLN. By E. Mansel Sympson, M.A., M.D. Illustrated by E. H. New.

SHREWSBURY. By T. Auden, M.A., F.S.A. Illustrated by Katharine M. Roberts.

WELLS and GLASTONBURY. By T. S. Holmes. Illustrated by E. H. New.

The Antiquary's Books

General Editor, J. CHARLES COX, LL.D., F.S.A

Demy 8vo. 7s. 6d. net.

ARCHÆOLOGY AND FALSE ANTIQUITIES. By R. Munro, LL.D. With 81 Illustrations.

BELLS OF ENGLAND, THE. By Canon J. J. Raven, D.D., F.S.A. With 60 Illustrations. *Second Edition.*

BRASSES OF ENGLAND, THE. By Herbert W. Macklin, M.A. With 85 Illustrations. *Second Edition.*

CELTIC ART IN PAGAN AND CHRISTIAN TIMES. By J. Romilly Allen, F.S.A. With 44 Plates and numerous Illustrations.

DOMESDAY INQUEST, THE. By Adolphus Ballard, B.A., LL.B. With 27 Illustrations.

ENGLISH CHURCH FURNITURE. By J. C. Cox, LL.D., F.S.A., and A. Harvey, M.B. With 121 Illustrations. *Second Edition.*

ENGLISH COSTUME. From Prehistoric Times to the End of the Eighteenth Century. By George Clinch, F.G.S. With 131 Illustrations.

ENGLISH MONASTIC LIFE. By the Right Rev. Abbot Gasquet, O.S.B. With 50 Illustrations, Maps and Plans. *Third Edition.*

ENGLISH SEALS. By J. Harvey Bloom. With 93 Illustrations.

FOLK-LORE AS AN HISTORICAL SCIENCE. By G. L. Gomme. With 28 Illustrations.

GILDS AND COMPANIES OF LONDON, THE. By George Unwin. With 37 Illustrations.

MANOR AND MANORIAL RECORDS, THE. By Nathaniel J. Hone. With 54 Illustrations.

MEDIÆVAL HOSPITALS OF ENGLAND, THE. By Rotha Mary Clay. With many Illustrations.

OLD SERVICE BOOKS OF THE ENGLISH CHURCH. By Christopher Wordsworth, M.A., and Henry Littlehales. With 38 Coloured and other Illustrations.

PARISH LIFE IN MEDIÆVAL ENGLAND. By the Right Rev. Abbott Gasquet, O.S.B. With 39 Illustrations. *Second Edition.*

REMAINS OF THE PREHISTORIC AGE IN ENGLAND. By B. C. A. Windle, D.Sc., F.R.S. With 94 Illustrations. *Second Edition.*

ROYAL FORESTS OF ENGLAND, THE. By J. C. Cox, LL.D., F.S.A. With 25 Plates and 23 other Illustrations.

SHRINES OF BRITISH SAINTS. By J. C. Wall. With 28 Plates and 50 other Illustrations.

The Arden Shakespeare

Demy 8vo. 2s. 6d. *net each volume.*

An edition of Shakespeare in single Plays. Edited with a full Introduction, Textual Notes, and a Commentary at the foot of the page.

ALL'S WELL THAT ENDS WELL. Edited by W. O. Brigstocke.

ANTONY AND CLEOPATRA. Edited by R. H. Case.

CYMBELINE. Edited by E. Dowden.

COMEDY OF ERRORS, THE. Edited by Henry Cuningham.

HAMLET. Edited by E. Dowden. *Second Edition.*

JULIUS CAESAR. Edited by M. Macmillan.

KING HENRY V. Edited by H. A. Evans.

KING HENRY VI. PT. I. Edited by H. C. Hart.

KING HENRY VI. PT. II. Edited by H. C. Hart and C. K. Pooler.

KING LEAR. Edited by W. J. Craig.

KING RICHARD III. Edited by A. H. Thompson.

LIFE AND DEATH OF KING JOHN, THE. Edited by Ivor B. John.

LOVE'S LABOUR'S LOST. Edited by H. C. Hart.

*MACBETH. Edited by H. Cuningham.

MEASURE FOR MEASURE. Edited by H. C. Hart.

MERCHANT OF VENICE, THE. Edited by C. K. Pooler.

MERRY WIVES OF WINDSOR, THE. Edited by H. C. Hart.

A MIDSUMMER NIGHT'S DREAM. Edited by H. Cuningham.

OTHELLO. Edited by H. C. Hart.

PERICLES. Edited by K. Deighton.

ROMEO AND JULIET. Edited by Edward Dowden.

TAMING OF THE SHREW, THE. Edited by R. Warwick Bond.

TEMPEST, THE. Edited by M. Luce.

TIMON OF ATHENS. Edited by K. Deighton.

TITUS ANDRONICUS. Edited by H. B. Baildon.

TROILUS AND CRESSIDA. Edited by K. Deighton.

TWO GENTLEMEN OF VERONA, THE. Edited by R. W. Bond.

TWELFTH NIGHT. Edited by M. Luce.

The Beginner's Books

Edited by W. WILLIAMSON, B.A.

EASY DICTATION AND SPELLING. By W. Williamson, B.A. *Seventh Ed. Fcap. 8vo.* 1s.

EASY EXERCISES IN ARITHMETIC. Arranged by W. S. Beard. *Third Edition. Fcap. 8vo.* Without Answers, 1s. With Answers. 1s. 3d.

EASY FRENCH RHYMES. By Henri Blouet. *Second Edition.* Illustrated. *Fcap. 8vo.* 1s.

AN EASY POETRY BOOK. Selected and arranged by W. Williamson, B.A. *Second Edition. Cr. 8vo.* 1s.

EASY STORIES FROM ENGLISH HISTORY. By E. M. Wilmot-Buxton, F.R.Hist.S. *Fifth Edition. Cr. 8vo.* 1s.

A FIRST HISTORY OF GREECE. By E. E. Firth. With 7 Maps. *Cr. 8vo.* 1s. 6d.

STORIES FROM ROMAN HISTORY. By E. M. Wilmot-Buxton. *Second Edition. Cr. 8vo.* 1s. 6d.

STORIES FROM THE OLD TESTAMENT. By E. Wilmot-Buxton. *Cr. 8vo.* 1s. 6d.

Books on Business

Cr. 8vo.   2s. 6d. net.

AUTOMOBILE INDUSTRY, THE. G. Holden-Stone.

BREWING INDUSTRY, THE. J. L. Baker, F.I.C., F.C.S. With 28 Illustrations.

BUSINESS OF ADVERTISING, THE. C. G. Moran, With 11 Illustrations.

BUSINESS SIDE OF AGRICULTURE, THE. A. G. L. Rogers.

BUSINESS OF INSURANCE, THE. A. J. Wilson.

CIVIL ENGINEERING. C. T. Fidler. With 15 Illustrations.

COTTON INDUSTRY AND TRADE, THE. S. J. Chapman. With 8 Illustrations.

THE ELECTRICAL INDUSTRY : LIGHTING, TRACTION, AND POWER. A. G. Whyte,

IRON TRADE OF GREAT BRITAIN, THE. J. S. Jeans. With 12 Illustrations.

LAW IN BUSINESS. H. A. Wilson.

MINING AND MINING INVESTMENTS. A. Moil.

MONEY MARKET, THE. F. Straker.

MONOPOLIES, TRUSTS, AND KARTELLS. F. W. Hirst.

PORTS AND DOCKS. Douglas Owen.

RAILWAYS. E. R. McDermott.

SHIPBUILDING INDUSTRY THE : Its History, Practice, Science, and Finance. David Pollock, M.I.N.A.

STOCK EXCHANGE, THE. C. Duguid. *Second Edition.*

TRADE UNIONS. G. Drage.

Byzantine Texts

Edited by J. B. BURY, M.A., Litt.D.

THE SYRIAC CHRONICLE KNOWN AS THAT OF ZACHARIAH OF MITYLENE. Translated by F. J. Hamilton, D.D., and E. W. Brooks. *Demy 8vo.* 12s. 6d. net.

EVAGRIUS. Edited by L. Bidez and Léon Parmentier. *Demy 8vo.* 10s. 6d. net.

THE HISTORY OF PSELLUS. Edited by C. Sathas. *Demy 8vo.* 15s. net.

ECTHESIS CHRONICA AND CHRONICON ATHENARUM. Edited by Professor S. P. Lambros. *Demy 8vo.* 7s. 6d. net.

THE CHRONICLE OF MOREA. Edited by John Schmitt. *Demy 8vo.* 15s. net.

The Churchman's Bible

General Editor, J. H. BURN, B.D., F.R.S.E.

Fcap. 8vo.   1s. 6d. net each.

THE EPISTLE OF ST. PAUL THE APOSTLE TO THE GALATIANS. Explained by A. W. Robinson, M.A. *Second Edition.*

ECCLESIASTES. Explained by A. W. Streane, D.D.

THE EPISTLE OF ST. PAUL THE APOSTLE TO THE PHILIPPIANS. Explained by C. R. D. Biggs, D.D. *Second Edition.*

THE EPISTLE OF ST. JAMES. Explained by H. W. Fulford M.A.

ISAIAH. Explained by W. E. Barnes, D.D. *Two Volumes.* With Map. 2s. net each.

THE EPISTLE OF ST. PAUL THE APOSTLE TO THE EPHESIANS. Explained by G. H. Whitaker, M.A.

THE GOSPEL ACCORDING TO ST. MARK. Explained by J. C. Du Buisson, M.A. 2s. 6d. net.

THE EPISTLE OF PAUL THE APOSTLE TO THE COLOSSIANS AND PHILEMON. Explained by H. J. C. Knight. 2s. net.

The Churchman's Library

General Editor, J. H. BURN, B.D., F.R.S.E.

Crown 8vo. 3s. 6d. each.

THE BEGINNINGS OF ENGLISH CHRISTIANITY. By W. E. Collins, M.A. With Map.

THE CHURCHMAN'S INTRODUCTION TO THE OLD TESTAMENT. By A. M. Mackay, B.A. *Second Edition.*

EVOLUTION. By F. B. Jevons, M.A., Litt.D.

SOME NEW TESTAMENT PROBLEMS. By Arthur Wright, D.D. 6s.

THE WORKMANSHIP OF THE PRAYER BOOK: Its Literary and Liturgical Aspects. By J. Dowden, D.D. *Second Edition, Revised and Enlarged.*

Classical Translations

Crown 8vo.

AESCHYLUS—The Oresteian Trilogy (Agamemnon, Choëphoroe, Eumenides). Translated by Lewis Campbell, LL.D. 5s.

CICERO—De Oratore I. Translated by E. N. P. Moor, M.A. *Second Edition.* 3s. 6d.

CICERO—The Speeches against Cataline and Antony and for Murena and Milo. Translated by H. E. D. Blakiston, M.A. 5s.

CICERO—De Natura Deorum. Translated by F. Brooks, M.A. 3s. 6d.

CICERO—De Officiis. Translated by G. B. Gardiner, M.A. 2s. 6d.

HORACE—The Odes and Epodes. Translated by A. D. Godley, M.A. 2s.

LUCIAN—Six Dialogues Translated by S. T. Irwin, M.A. 3s. 6d.

SOPHOCLES—Ajax and Electra. Translated by E. D. Morshead, M.A. 2s. 6d.

TACITUS—Agricola and Germania. Translated by R. B. Townshend. 2s. 6d.

JUVENAL—Thirteen Satires. Translated by S. G. Owen, M.A. 2s. 6d.

Classics of Art

Edited by DR. J. H. W. LAING

Wide Royal 8vo. Gilt top.

THE ART OF THE GREEKS. By H. B. Walters. With 112 Plates and 18 Illustrations in the Text. 12s. 6d. net.

FLORENTINE SCULPTORS OF THE RENNAISANCE. Wilhelm Bode, Ph.D. Translated by Jessie Haynes. With 94 Plates. 12s. 6d. net.

GHIRLANDAIO. Gerald S. Davies, Master of the Charterhouse. With 50 Plates. *Second Edition.* 10s. 6d.

*MICHELANGELO. Gerald S. Davies, Master of the Charterhouse. With 126 Plates. 12s. 6d. net.

RUBENS. Edward Dillon, M.A. With a Frontispiece in Photogravure and 483 Plates. 25s. net.

RAPHAEL. A. P. Oppé. With a Frontispiece in Photogravure and 200 Illustrations. 12s. 6d. net.

TITIAN. Charles Ricketts. With about 220 Illustrations. 12s. 6d. net.

VELAZQUEZ. By A. de Beruete. With 94 Plates. 10s. 6d. net.

Commercial Series

Crown 8vo.

BRITISH COMMERCE AND COLONIES FROM ELIZABETH TO VICTORIA. By H. de B. Gibbins, Litt.D., M.A. *Fourth Edition.* 2s.

COMMERCIAL EXAMINATION PAPERS. By H. de B. Gibbins, Litt.D., M.A. 1s. 6d.

THE ECONOMICS OF COMMERCE, By H. de B. Gibbins, Litt.D., M.A. *Second Edition.* 1s. 6d.

A GERMAN COMMERCIAL READER. By S. E. Bally. With Vocabulary. 2s.

A COMMERCIAL GEOGRAPHY OF THE BRITISH EMPIRE. By L. W. Lyde, M.A. *Seventh Edition.* 2s.

A COMMERCIAL GEOGRAPHY OF FOREIGN NATIONS. By F. C. Boon, B.A. 2s.

A PRIMER OF BUSINESS. By S. Jackson, M.A. *Fourth Edition.* 1s. 6d.

A SHORT COMMERCIAL ARITHMETIC. By F. G. Taylor, M.A. *Fourth Edition.* 1s. 6d.

FRENCH COMMERCIAL CORRESPONDENCE. By S. E. Bally. With Vocabulary. *Fourth Edition.* 2s.

GERMAN COMMERCIAL CORRESPONDENCE. By S. E. Bally. With Vocabulary. *Second Edition.* 2s. 6d.

A FRENCH COMMERCIAL READER. By S. E. Bally. With Vocabulary. *Second Edition.* 2s.

PRECIS WRITING AND OFFICE CORRESPONDENCE. By E. E. Whitfield, M.A. *Second Edition.* 2s.

AN ENTRANCE GUIDE TO PROFESSIONS AND BUSINESS. By H. Jones. 1s. 6d.

THE PRINCIPLES OF BOOK-KEEPING BY DOUBLE ENTRY. By J. E. B. M'Allen, M.A. 2s.

COMMERCIAL LAW. By W. Douglas Edwards. *Second Edition.* 2s.

The Connoisseur's Library

Wide Royal 8vo.   25*s. net.*

MEZZOTINTS. By Cyril Davenport. With 40 Plates in Photogravure.

PORCELAIN. By Edward Dillon. With 19 Plates in Colour, 20 in Collotype, and 5 in Photogravure.

MINIATURES. By Dudley Heath. With 9 Plates in Colour, 15 in Collotype, and 15 in Photogravure.

IVORIES. By A. Maskell. With 80 Plates in Collotype and Photogravure.

ENGLISH FURNITURE. By F. S. Robinson. With 160 Plates in Collotype and one in Photogravure. *Second Edition.*

ENGLISH COLOURED BOOKS. By Martin Hardie. With 28 Illustrations in Colour and Collotype.

EUROPEAN ENAMELS. By Henry H. Cunynghame, C.B. With 54 Plates in Collotype and Half-tone and 4 Plates in Colour.

GOLDSMITHS' AND SILVERSMITHS' WORK. By Nelson Dawson. With 51 Plates in Collotype and a Frontispiece in Photogravure. *Second Edition.*

GLASS. By Edward Dillon. With 37 Illustrations in Collotype and 12 in Colour.

SEALS. By Walter de Gray Birch. With 52 Illustrations in Collotype and a Frontispiece in Photogravure.

JEWELLERY. By H. Clifford Smith. With 50 Illustrations in Collotype, and 4 in Colour. *Second Edition.*

Handbooks of English Church History

Edited by J. H. BURN, B.D.   *Crown 8vo.*   2*s.* 6*d. net.*

THE FOUNDATIONS OF THE ENGLISH CHURCH. J. H. Maude.

THE SAXON CHURCH AND THE NORMAN CONQUEST. C. T. CRUTTWELL.

THE MEDIÆVAL CHURCH AND THE PAPACY A. C. Jennings.

*THE REFORMATION PERIOD. By Henry Gee.

The Illustrated Pocket Library of Plain and Coloured Books

Fcap 8vo.   3*s.* 6*d. net each volume.*

COLOURED BOOKS

OLD COLOURED BOOKS. By George Paston. With 16 Coloured Plates. *Fcap. 8vo.* 2*s. net.*

THE LIFE AND DEATH OF JOHN MYTTON, ESQ. By Nimrod. With 18 Coloured Plates by Henry Alken and T. J. Rawlins. *Fourth Edition.*

THE LIFE OF A SPORTSMAN. By Nimrod. With 35 Coloured Plates by Henry Alken.

HANDLEY CROSS. By R. S. Surtees. With 17 Coloured Plates and 100 Woodcuts in the Text by John Leech. *Second Edition.*

MR. SPONGE'S SPORTING TOUR. By R. S. Surtees. With 13 Coloured Plates and 90 Woodcuts in the Text by John Leech.

JORROCKS' JAUNTS AND JOLLITIES. By R. S. Surtees. With 15 Coloured Plates by H. Alken. *Second Edition.*

ASK MAMMA. By R. S. Surtees. With 13 Coloured Plates and 70 Woodcuts in the Text by John Leech.

THE ANALYSIS OF THE HUNTING FIELD. By R. S. Surtees. With 7 Coloured Plates by Henry Alken, and 43 Illustrations on Wood.

THE TOUR OF DR. SYNTAX IN SEARCH OF THE PICTURESQUE. By William Combe. With 30 Coloured Plates by T. Rowlandson.

THE TOUR OF DOCTOR SYNTAX IN SEARCH OF CONSOLATION. By William Combe. With 24 Coloured Plates by T. Rowlandson.

THE THIRD TOUR OF DOCTOR SYNTAX IN SEARCH OF A WIFE. By William Combe. With 24 Coloured Plates by T. Rowlandson.

THE HISTORY OF JOHNNY QUAE GENUS: the Little Foundling of the late Dr. Syntax. By the Author of 'The Three Tours.' With 24 Coloured Plates by Rowlandson.

THE ENGLISH DANCE OF DEATH, from the Designs of T. Rowlandson, with Metrical Illustrations by the Author of 'Doctor Syntax.' *Two Volumes.*

This book contains 76 Coloured Plates.

THE DANCE OF LIFE: A Poem. By the Author of 'Doctor Syntax.' Illustrated with 26 Coloured Engravings by T. Rowlandson.

LIFE IN LONDON: or, the Day and Night Scenes of Jerry Hawthorn, Esq., and his Elegant Friend, Corinthian Tom. By Pierce Egan. With 36 Coloured Plates by I. R. and G. Cruikshank. With numerous Designs on Wood.

REAL LIFE IN LONDON: or, the Rambles and Adventures of Bob Tallyho, Esq., and his Cousin, The Hon. Tom Dashall. By an Amateur (Pierce Egan). With 31 Coloured Plates by Alken and Rowlandson, etc. *Two Volumes.*

THE LIFE OF AN ACTOR. By Pierce Egan. With 27 Coloured Plates by Theodore Lane, and several Designs on Wood.

THE VICAR OF WAKEFIELD. By Oliver Goldsmith. With 24 Coloured Plates by T. Rowlandson.

THE MILITARY ADVENTURES OF JOHNNY NEWCOME. By an Officer. With 15 Coloured Plates by T. Rowlandson.

ILLUSTRATED POCKET LIBRARY OF PLAIN AND COLOURED BOOKS—*continued.*

THE NATIONAL SPORTS OF GREAT BRITAIN. With Descriptions and 50 Coloured Plates by Henry Alken.

THE ADVENTURES OF A POST CAPTAIN. By A Naval Officer. With 24 Coloured Plates by Mr. Williams.

GAMONIA : or, the Art of Preserving Game ; and an Improved Method of making Plantations and Covers, explained and illustrated by Lawrence Rawstorne, Esq. With 15 Coloured Plates by T. Rawlins.

AN ACADEMY FOR GROWN HORSEMEN : Containing the completest Instructions for Walking, Trotting, Cantering, Galloping, Stumbling, and Tumbling. Illustrated with 27 Coloured Plates, and adorned with a Portrait of the Author. By Geoffrey Gambado, Esq.

REAL LIFE IN IRELAND, or, the Day and Night Scenes of Brian Boru, Esq., and his Elegant Friend, Sir Shawn O'Dogherty. By a Real Paddy. With 19 Coloured Plates by Heath, Marks, etc.

THE ADVENTURES OF JOHNNY NEWCOME IN THE NAVY. By Alfred Burton. With 16 Coloured Plates by T. Rowlandson.

THE OLD ENGLISH SQUIRE : A Poem. By John Careless, Esq. With 20 Coloured Plates after the style of T. Rowlandson.

THE ENGLISH SPY. By Bernard Blackmantle. An original Work, Characteristic, Satirical, Humorous, comprising scenes and sketches in every Rank of Society, being Portraits of the Illustrious, Eminent, Eccentric, and Notorious. With 72 Coloured Plates by R. CRUIKSHANK, and many Illustrations on wood. *Two Volumes.* 7s. *net.*

PLAIN BOOKS

THE GRAVE : A Poem. By Robert Blair. Illustrated by 12 Etchings executed by Louis Schiavonetti from the original Inventions of William Blake. With an Engraved Title Page and a Portrait of Blake by T. Phillips, R.A. The illustrations are reproduced in photogravure.

ILLUSTRATIONS OF THE BOOK OF JOB. Invented and engraved by William Blake. These famous Illustrations—21 in number—are reproduced in photogravure.

WINDSOR CASTLE By W. Harrison Ainsworth. With 22 Plates and 87 Woodcuts in the Text by George Cruikshank.

THE TOWER OF LONDON. By W. Harrison Ainsworth. With 40 Plates and 58 Woodcuts in the Text by George Cruikshank.

FRANK FAIRLEGH. By F. E. Smedley. With 30 Plates by George Cruikshank.

HANDY ANDY. By Samuel Lover. With 24 Illustrations by the Author.

THE COMPLEAT ANGLER. By Izaak Walton and Charles Cotton. With 14 Plates and 77 Woodcuts in the Text.

THE PICKWICK PAPERS. By Charles Dickens. With the 43 Illustrations by Seymour and Phiz, the two Buss Plates, and the 32 Contemporary Onwhyn Plates.

Junior Examination Series

Edited by A. M. M. STEDMAN, M.A. *Fcap. 8vo.* 1s.

JUNIOR ALGEBRA EXAMINATION PAPERS. By S. W. Finn, M.A.

JUNIOR ARITHMETIC EXAMINATION PAPERS. By W. S. Beard. *Fifth Edition.*

JUNIOR ENGLISH EXAMINATION PAPERS. By W. Williamson, B.A. *Second Edition.*

JUNIOR FRENCH EXAMINATION PAPERS. By F. Jacob, M.A. *Second Edition.*

JUNIOR GENERAL INFORMATION EXAMINATION PAPERS. By W. S. Beard. KEY, 3s. 6d. *net.*

JUNIOR GEOGRAPHY EXAMINATION PAPERS. By W. G. Baker, M.A.

JUNIOR GERMAN EXAMINATION PAPERS. By A. Voegelin, M.A.

JUNIOR GREEK EXAMINATION PAPERS. By T. C. Weatherhead, M.A. KEY, 3s. 6d. *net.*

JUNIOR LATIN EXAMINATION PAPERS. By C. G. Botting, B.A. *Sixth Edition.* KEY, 3s. 6d. *net.*

*JUNIOR HISTORY EXAMINATION PAPERS. By W. O. P. Davis.

Methuen's Junior School-Books

Edited by O. D. INSKIP, LL.D., and W. WILLIAMSON, B.A.

A CLASS-BOOK OF DICTATION PASSAGES. By W. Williamson, B.A. *Fourteenth Edition.* Cr. 8vo. 1s. 6d.

THE GOSPEL ACCORDING TO ST. MATTHEW. Edited by E. Wilton South, M.A. With Three Maps. Cr. 8vo. 1s. 6d.

THE GOSPEL ACCORDING TO ST. MARK. Edited by A. E. Rubie, D.D. With Three Maps. Cr. 8vo. 1s. 6d.

A JUNIOR ENGLISH GRAMMAR. By W. Williamson, B.A. With numerous passages for parsing and analysis, and a chapter on Essay Writing. *Fourth Edition.* Cr. 8vo. 2s.

A JUNIOR CHEMISTRY. By E. A. Tyler, B.A., F.C.S. With 78 Illustrations. *Fourth Edition.* Cr. 8vo. 2s. 6d.

THE ACTS OF THE APOSTLES. Edited by A. E. Rubie, D.D. Cr. 8vo. 2s.

METHUEN'S JUNIOR SCHOOL BOOKS—*continued.*

A JUNIOR FRENCH GRAMMAR. By L. A. Sornet and M. J. Acatos. *Third Edition.* *Cr. 8vo.* 2s.

ELEMENTARY EXPERIMENTAL SCIENCE. PHYSICS by W. T. Clough, A.R.C.Sc. (Lond.), F.C.S. CHEMISTRY by A. E. Dunstan, B.Sc. (Lond.), F.C.S. With 2 Plates and 154 Diagrams. *Seventh Edition. Cr. 8vo.* 2s. 6d.

A JUNIOR GEOMETRY. By Noel S. Lydon. With 276 Diagrams. *Seventh Edition. Cr. 8vo.* 2s.

ELEMENTARY EXPERIMENTAL CHEMISTRY. By A. E. Dunstan, B.Sc. (Lond.), F.C.S. With 4 Plates and 109 Diagrams. *Third Edition. Cr. 8vo.* 2s.

A JUNIOR FRENCH PROSE. By R. R. N. Baron, M.A. *Third Edition. Cr. 8vo.* 2s.

THE GOSPEL ACCORDING TO ST. LUKE. With an Introduction and Notes by William Williamson, B.A. With Three Maps. *Cr. 8vo.* 2s.

THE FIRST BOOK OF KINGS. Edited by A. E. RUBIE, D.D. With 4 Maps. *Cr. 8vo.* 2s.

A JUNIOR GREEK HISTORY. By W. H. Spragge, M.A. With 4 Illustrations and 5 Maps. *Cr. 8vo.* 2s. 6d.

A SCHOOL LATIN GRAMMAR. By H. G. Ford, M.A. *Cr. 8vo.* 2s. 6d.

A JUNIOR LATIN PROSE. By H. N. Asman, M.A., B.D. *Cr. 8vo.* 2s. 6d.

*ELEMENTARY EXPERIMENTAL ELECTRICITY AND MAGNETISM. By W. T. Clough, A.R.C.Sc. (Lond.), F.C.S. With 200 Illustrations and Diagrams. *Cr. 8vo.* 2s. 6d.

ENGLISE LITERATURE FOR SCHOOLS. By Edith E. Firth. *Cr. 8vo.* 2s. 6d.

Leaders of Religion

Edited by H. C. BEECHING, M.A., Canon of Westminster. *With Portraits.*

Cr. 8vo. 2s. *net.*

CARDINAL NEWMAN. By R. H. Hutton.
JOHN WESLEY. By J. H. Overton, M.A.
BISHOP WILBERFORCE. By G. W. Daniell, M.A.
CARDINAL MANNING. By A. W. Hutton, M.A.
CHARLES SIMEON. By H. C. G. Moule, D.D.
JOHN KNOX. By F. MacCunn. *Second Edition.*
JOHN HOWE. By R. F. Horton, D.D.
THOMAS KEN. By F. A. Clarke, M.A.
GEORGE FOX, THE QUAKER. By T. Hodgkin, D.C.L. *Third Edition.*
JOHN KEBLE. By Walter Lock, D.D.

THOMAS CHALMERS. By Mrs. Oliphant.
LANCELOT ANDREWES. By R. L. Ottley, D.D. *Second Edition.*
AUGUSTINE OF CANTERBURY. By E. L. Cutts, D.D.
WILLIAM LAUD. By W. H. Hutton, M.A. *Third Edition.*
JOHN DONNE. By Augustus Jessopp, D.D.
THOMAS CRANMER. By A. J. Mason, D.D.
BISHOP LATIMER. By R. M. Carlyle and A. J. Carlyle, M.A.
BISHOP BUTLER. By W. A. Spooner, M.A.

The Library of Devotion

With Introductions and (where necessary) Notes.

Small Pott 8vo, cloth, 2s. ; *leather,* 2s. 6d. *net.*

THE CONFESSIONS OF ST. AUGUSTINE. Edited by C. Bigg, D.D. *Sixth Edition.*
THE IMITATION OF CHRIST : called also the Ecclesiastical Music. Edited by C. Bigg, D.D. *Fifth Edition.*
THE CHRISTIAN YEAR. Edited by Walter Lock, D.D. *Fourth Edition.*
LYRA INNOCENTIUM. Edited by Walter Lock, D.D. *Second Edition.*
THE TEMPLE. Edited by E. C. S. Gibson, D.D. *Second Edition.*
A BOOK OF DEVOTIONS. Edited by J. W. Stanbridge. B.D. *Second Edition.*
A SERIOUS CALL TO A DEVOUT AND HOLY LIFE. Edited by C. Bigg, D.D. *Fourth Ed.*
A GUIDE TO ETERNITY. Edited by J. W. Stanbridge, B.D.
THE INNER WAY. By J. Tauler. Edited by A. W. Hutton, M.A.

ON THE LOVE OF GOD. By St. Francis de Sales. Edited by W. J. Knox-Little, M.A.
THE PSALMS OF DAVID. Edited by B. W. Randolph, D.D.
LYRA APOSTOLICA. By Cardinal Newman and others. Edited by Canon Scott Holland, M.A., and Canon H. C. Beeching, M.A.
THE SONG OF SONGS. Edited by B. Blaxland, M.A.
THE THOUGHTS OF PASCAL. Edited by C. S. Jerram, M.A.
A MANUAL OF CONSOLATION FROM THE SAINTS AND FATHERS. Edited by J. H. Burn, B.D.
*DEVOTIONS FROM THE APOCRYPHA. Edited, with an Introduction, by Herbert Pentin, M.A.

THE LIBRARY OF DEVOTION—*continued*.

*THE SPIRITUAL COMBAT. By Dom Lorenzo Scupoli. Newly translated, with an Introduction and Notes, by Thomas Barns, M.A.

THE DEVOTIONS OF ST. ANSELM. Edited by C. C. J. Webb, M.A.

GRACE ABOUNDING TO THE CHIEF OF SINNERS. By John Bunyan. Edited by S. C. Freer, M.A.

BISHOP WILSON'S SACRA PRIVATA. Edited by A. E. Burn, B.D.

LYRA SACRA : A Book of Sacred Verse. Edited by Canon H. C. Beeching, M.A. *Second Edition, revised.*

A DAY BOOK FROM THE SAINTS AND FATHERS. Edited by J. H. Burn, B.D.

A LITTLE BOOK OF HEAVENLY WISDOM. A Selection from the English Mystics. Edited by E. C. Gregory.

LIGHT, LIFE, and LOVE. A Selection from the German Mystics. Edited by W. R. Inge, M.A.

AN INTRODUCTION TO THE DEVOUT LIFE. By St. Francis de Sales. Translated and Edited by T. Barns, M.A.

THE LITTLE FLOWERS OF THE GLORIOUS MESSER ST. FRANCIS AND OF HIS FRIARS. Done into English by W. Heywood. With an Introduction by A. G. Ferrers Howell.

MANCHESTER AL MONDO : a Contemplation of Death and Immortality. By Henry Montagu, Earl of Manchester. With an Introduction by Elizabeth Waterhouse, Editor of 'A Little Book of Life and Death.'

THE SPIRITUAL GUIDE, which Disentangles the Soul and brings it by the Inward Way to the Fruition of Perfect Contemplation, and the Rich Treasure of Internal Peace. Written by Dr. Michael de Molinos, Priest. Translated from the Italian copy, printed at Venice, 1685. Edited with an Introduction by Kathleen Lyttelton. And a Note by Canon Scott Holland.

DEVOTIONS FOR EVERY DAY OF THE WEEK AND THE GREAT FESTIVALS. By John Wesley. Edited, with an Introduction by Canon C. Bodington.

PRECES PRIVATAE. By Lancelot Andrewes, Bishop of Winchester. Selections from the Translation by Canon F. E. Brightman. Edited, with an Introduction, by A. E. Burn, D.D.

HORAE MYSTICAE : A Day Book from the Writings of Mystics of Many Nations. Edited by E. C. Gregory.

Little Books on Art

With many Illustrations. Demy 16mo. 2s. 6d. net.

Each volume consists of about 200 pages, and contains from 30 to 40 Illustrations, including a Frontispiece in Photogravure.

ALBRECHT DÜRER. J. Allen.
ARTS OF JAPAN, THE. E. Dillon.
BOOKPLATES. E. Almack.
BOTTICELLI. Mary L. Bonnor.
BURNE-JONES. F. de Lisle.
CHRIST IN ART. Mrs. H. Jenner.
CLAUDE. E. Dillon.
CONSTABLE. H. W. Tompkins.
COROT. A. Pollard and E. Birnstingl.
ENAMELS. Mrs. N. Dawson.
FREDERIC LEIGHTON. A. Corkran.
GEORGE ROMNEY. G. Paston.
GREEK ART. H. B. Walters.
GREUZE AND BOUCHER. E. F. Pollard
HOLBEIN. Mrs. G. Fortescue.

ILLUMINATED MANUSCRIPTS. J. W. Bradley.
JEWELLERY. C. Davenport.
JOHN HOPPNER. H. P. K. Skipton.
SIR JOSHUA REYNOLDS. J. Sime.
MILLET. N. Peacock.
MINIATURES. C. Davenport.
OUR LADY IN ART. Mrs. H. Jenner.
RAPHAEL. A. R. Dryhurst. *Second Edition.*
REMBRANDT. Mrs. E. A. Sharp.
TURNER. F. Tyrrell-Gill.
VANDYCK. M. G. Smallwood.
VELASQUEZ. W. Wilberforce and A. R. Gilbert.
WATTS. R. E. D. Sketchley.

The Little Galleries

Demy 16mo. 2s. 6d. net.

Each volume contains 20 plates in Photogravure, together with a short outline of the life and work of the master to whom the book is devoted.

A LITTLE GALLERY OF REYNOLDS.
A LITTLE GALLERY OF ROMNEY.
A LITTLE GALLERY OF HOPPNER.

A LITTLE GALLERY OF MILLAIS.
A LITTLE GALLERY OF ENGLISH POETS.

The Little Guides

With many Illustrations by E. H. NEW and other artists, and from photographs.

Small Pott 8vo, cloth, 2s. 6d. net.; leather, 3s. 6d. net.

The main features of these Guides are (1) a handy and charming form ; (2) illustrations from photographs and by well-known artists; (3) good plans and maps ; (4) an adequate but compact presentation of everything that is interesting in the natural features, history, archæology, and architecture of the town or district treated.

CAMBRIDGE AND ITS COLLEGES. A. H. Thompson. *Second Edition.*
ENGLISH LAKES, THE. F. G. Brabant.
ISLE OF WIGHT. THE. G. Clinch.
MALVERN COUNTRY, THE B. C. A. Windle.
NORTH WALES. A. T. Story.
OXFORD AND ITS COLLEGES. J. Wells. *Eighth Edition.*
SHAKESPEARE'S COUNTRY. B. C. A. Windle. *Third Edition.*
ST. PAUL'S CATHEDRAL. G. Clinch.
WESTMINSTER ABBEY. G. E. Troutbeck. *Second Edition.*

BUCKINGHAMSHIRE. E. S. Roscoe.
CHESHIRE. W. M. Gallichan.
CORNWALL. A. L. Salmon.
DERBYSHIRE. J. C. Cox.
DEVON. S. Baring-Gould.
DORSET. F. R. Heath. *Second Edition.*
ESSEX. J. C. Cox.
HAMPSHIRE. J. C. Cox.

HERTFORDSHIRE. H. W. Tompkins.
KENT. G. Clinch.
KERRY. C. P. Crane.
MIDDLESEX. J. B. Firth.
MONMOUTHSHIRE. G. W. Wade and J. H. Wade.
NORFOLK. W. A. Dutt.
NORTHAMPTONSHIRE. W. Dry.
OXFORDSHIRE. F. G. Brabant.
SOMERSET. G. W. and J. H. Wade.
SUFFOLK. W. A. Dutt.
SURREY. F. A. H. Lambert.
SUSSEX. F. G. Brabant. *Second Edition.*
YORKSHIRE, THE EAST RIDING. J. E. Morris.
YORKSHIRE, THE NORTH RIDING. J. E. Morris.

BRITTANY. S. Baring-Gould.
NORMANDY. C. Scudamore.
ROME. C. G. Ellaby.
SICILY. F. H. Jackson.

The Little Library

With Introductions, Notes, and Photogravure Frontispieces.

Small Pott 8vo. Each Volume, cloth, 1s. 6d. net ; leather, 2s. 6d. net.

Anon. A LITTLE BOOK OF ENGLISH LYRICS. *Second Edition.*
Austen (Jane). PRIDE AND PREJUDICE. Edited by E. V. LUCAS. *Two Vols.*
NORTHANGER ABBEY. Edited by E. V. LUCAS.
Bacon (Francis). THE ESSAYS OF LORD BACON. Edited by EDWARD WRIGHT.
Barham (R. H.). THE INGOLDSBY LEGENDS. Edited by J. B. ATLAY. *Two Volumes.*
Barnett (Mrs. P. A.). A LITTLE BOOK OF ENGLISH PROSE. *Second Edition.*
Beckford (William). THE HISTORY OF THE CALIPH VATHEK. Edited by E. DENISON ROSS.
Blake (William). SELECTIONS FROM WILLIAM BLAKE. Edited by M. PERUGINI.
Borrow (George). LAVENGRO. Edited by F. HINDES GROOME. *Two Volumes.*
THE ROMANY RYE. Edited by JOHN SAMPSON.
Browning (Robert). SELECTIONS FROM THE EARLY POEMS OF ROBERT BROWNING. Edited by W. HALL GRIFFIN, M.A.

Canning (George). SELECTIONS FROM THE ANTI-JACOBIN : with GEORGE CANNING'S additional Poems. Edited by LLOYD SANDERS.
Cowley (Abraham). THE ESSAYS OF ABRAHAM COWLEY. Edited by H. C. MINCHIN.
Crabbe (George). SELECTIONS FROM GEORGE CRABBE. Edited by A. C. DEANE.
Craik (Mrs.). JOHN HALIFAX, GENTLEMAN. Edited by ANNIE MATHESON. *Two Volumes.*
Crashaw (Richard). THE ENGLISH POEMS OF RICHARD CRASHAW. Edited by EDWARD HUTTON.
Dante (Alighieri). THE INFERNO OF DANTE. Translated by H. F. CARY. Edited by PAGET TOYNBEE, M.A., D.Litt.
THE PURGATORIO OF DANTE. Translated by H. F. CARY. Edited by PAGET TOYNBEE, M.A., D.Litt.
THE PARADISO OF DANTE. Translated by H. F. CARY. Edited by PAGET TOYNBEE, M.A., D.Litt.
Darley (George). SELECTIONS FROM THE POEMS OF GEORGE DARLEY. Edited by R. A. STREATFEILD.

THE LITTLE LIBRARY—*continued*.

Deane (A. C.). A LITTLE BOOK OF LIGHT VERSE.

Dickens (Charles). CHRISTMAS BOOKS. *Two Volumes.*

Ferrier (Susan). MARRIAGE. Edited by A. GOODRICH - FREER and LORD IDDESLEIGH. *Two Volumes.*
THE INHERITANCE. *Two Volumes.*

Gaskell (Mrs.). CRANFORD. Edited by E. V. LUCAS. *Second Edition.*

Hawthorne (Nathaniel). THE SCARLET LETTER. Edited by PERCY DEARMER.

Henderson (T. F.). A LITTLE BOOK OF SCOTTISH VERSE.

Keats (John). POEMS. With an Introduction by L. BINYON, and Notes by J. MASEFIELD.

Kinglake (A. W.). EOTHEN. With an Introduction and Notes. *Second Edition.*

Lamb (Charles). ELIA, AND THE LAST ESSAYS OF ELIA. Edited by E. V. LUCAS.

Locker (F.). LONDON LYRICS. Edited by A. D. GODLEY, M.A. A reprint of the First Edition.

Longfellow (H. W.). SELECTIONS FROM LONGFELLOW. Edited by L. M. FAITHFULL.

Marvell (Andrew). THE POEMS OF ANDREW MARVELL. Edited by E. WRIGHT.

Milton (John). THE MINOR POEMS OF JOHN MILTON. Edited by H. C. BEECHING, M.A.

Moir (D. M.). MANSIE WAUCH. Edited by T. F. HENDERSON.

Nichols (J. B. B.). A LITTLE BOOK OF ENGLISH SONNETS.

Rochefoucauld (La). THE MAXIMS OF LA ROCHEFOUCAULD. Translated by Dean STANHOPE. Edited by G. H. POWELL.

Smith (Horace and James). REJECTED ADDRESSES. Edited by A. D. GODLEY, M.A.

Sterne (Laurence). A SENTIMENTAL JOURNEY. Edited by H. W. PAUL.

Tennyson (Alfred, Lord). THE EARLY POEMS OF ALFRED, LORD TENNYSON. Edited by J. CHURTON COLLINS, M.A.
IN MEMORIAM. Edited by H. C. BEECHING, M.A.
THE PRINCESS. Edited by ELIZABETH WORDSWORTH.
MAUD. Edited by ELIZABETH WORDSWORTH.

Thackeray (W. M.). VANITY FAIR. Edited by S. GWYNN. *Three Volumes.*
PENDENNIS. Edited by S. GWYNN. *Three Volumes.*
ESMOND. Edited by S. GWYNN.
CHRISTMAS BOOKS. Edited by S. GWYNN.

Vaughan (Henry). THE POEMS OF HENRY VAUGHAN. Edited by EDWARD HUTTON.

Walton (Izaak). THE COMPLEAT ANGLER. Edited by J. BUCHAN.

Waterhouse (Elizabeth). A LITTLE BOOK OF LIFE AND DEATH. Edited by. *Twelfth Edition.*

Wordsworth (W.). SELECTIONS FROM WORDSWORTH. Edited by NOWELL C. SMITH.

Wordsworth (W.) and Coleridge (S. T.). LYRICAL BALLADS. Edited by GEORGE SAMPSON.

The Little Quarto Shakespeare

Edited by W. J. CRAIG. With Introductions and Notes.

Pott 16*mo. In* 40 *Volumes. Leather, price* 1*s. net each volume.*

Mahogany Revolving Book Case. 10*s. net.*

Miniature Library

Reprints in miniature of a few interesting books which have qualities of humanity, devotion, or literary genius.

EUPHRANOR: A Dialogue on Youth. By Edward FitzGerald. From the edition published by W. Pickering in 1851. *Demy* 32*mo. Leather,* 2*s. net.*

THE LIFE OF EDWARD, LORD HERBERT OF CHERBURY. Written by himself. From the edition printed at Strawberry Hill in the year 1764. *Demy* 32*mo. Leather,* 2*s. net.*

POLONIUS: or Wise Saws and Modern Instances. By Edward FitzGerald. From the edition published by W. Pickering in 1852. *Demy* 32*mo. Leather,* 2*s. net.*

THE RUBÁIYÁT OF OMAR KHAYYÁM. By Edward FitzGerald. From the 1st edition of 1859, *Fourth Edition. Leather,* 1*s. net.*

A New Historical Series

Edited by the Rev. H. N. ASMAN, M.A., B.D.

*STORIES FROM ANCIENT HISTORY. By E. Bower, B.A. *Cr. 8vo. 1s. 6d.*

*STORIES FROM MODERN HISTORY. By E. M. Wilmot-Buxton, F.R.Hist.S. *Cr. 8vo. 1s.6d.*

The New Library of Medicine

Edited by C. W. SALEEBY, M.D., F.R.S.Edin. *Demy 8vo.*

CARE OF THE BODY, THE. F. Cavanagh. *Second Edition. 7s. 6d. net.*
CHILDREN OF THE NATION, THE. Right Hon. Sir John Gorst. *7s. 6d. net.*
CONTROL OF A SCOURGE, THE : or, How Cancer is Curable. Chas. P. Childe. *7s. 6d. net.*
DISEASES OF OCCUPATION. Sir Thomas Oliver. *10s. 6d. net.*
DRINK PROBLEM, THE, in its Medico-Sociological Aspects. Edited by T. N. Kelynack. *7s. 6d. net.*

DRUGS AND THE DRUG HABIT. H. Sainsbury.
FUNCTIONAL NERVE DISEASES. A. T. Schofield. *7s. 6d. net.*
HYGIENE OF MIND, THE. T. S. Clouston. *Fifth Edition. 7s. 6d. net.*
INFANT MORTALITY. George Newman. *7s. 6d. net.*
PREVENTION OF TUBERCULOSIS (CONSUMPTION), THE. Arthur Newsholme. *10s. 6d. net.*
*AIR AND HEALTH. Ronald C. Macfie, M.A., M.B. *7s. 6d. net.*

The New Library of Music

Edited by ERNEST NEWMAN. *Demy 8vo. 7s. 6d. net.*

HUGO WOLF. By Ernest Newman. With 13 Illustrations.

HANDEL. By R. A. Streatfeild. With 12 Illustrations.

Oxford Biographies

Fcap. 8vo. Each volume, cloth, 2s. 6d. net ; leather, 3s. 6d. net.

DANTE ALIGHIERI. By Paget Toynbee, M.A., D.Litt. With 12 Illustrations. *Third Edition.*
GIROLAMO SAVONAROLA. By E. L. S. Horsburgh, M.A. With 12 Illustrations. *Second Edition.*
JOHN HOWARD. By E. C. S. Gibson, D.D., Bishop of Gloucester. With 12 Illustrations.
ALFRED TENNYSON. By A. C. Benson, M.A. With 9 Illustrations. *Second Edition.*
SIR WALTER RALEIGH. By I. A. Taylor. With 12 Illustrations.
ERASMUS. By E. F. H. Capey. With 12 Illustrations.
THE YOUNG PRETENDER. By C. S. Terry. With 12 Illustrations.

ROBERT BURNS. By T. F. Henderson. With 12 Illustrations.
CHATHAM. By A. S. M'Dowall. With 12 Illustrations.
FRANCIS OF ASSISI. By Anna M. Stoddart. With 16 Illustrations.
CANNING. By W. Alison Phillips. With 12 Illustrations.
BEACONSFIELD. By Walter Sichel. With 12 Illustrations.
JOHANN WOLFGANG GOETHE. By H. G. Atkins. With 16 Illustrations.
FRANÇOIS FENELON. By Viscount St Cyres. With 12 Illustrations.

Romantic History

Edited by MARTIN HUME, M.A. *With Illustrations. Demy 8vo.*

A series of attractive volumes in which the periods and personalities selected are such as afford romantic human interest, in addition to their historical importance.

THE FIRST GOVERNESS OF THE NETHERLANDS, MARGARET OF AUSTRIA. Eleanor E. Tremayne. *10s. 6d. net.*
TWO ENGLISH QUEENS AND PHILIP. Martin

Hume, M.A. *15s. net.*
THE NINE DAYS' QUEEN. Richard Davey. With a Preface by Martin Hume, M.A. With 12 Illustrations. *10s. 6d. net.*

School Examination Series

Edited by A. M. M. STEDMAN, M.A. *Crown 8vo.* 2s. 6d.

EXAMINATION PAPERS IN ENGLISH HISTORY. By J. Tait Plowden-Wardlaw, B.A.
FRENCH EXAMINATION PAPERS. By A. M. M. Stedman, M.A. *Fifteenth Edition.* KEY. *Sixth Edition.* 6s. net.
GENERAL KNOWLEDGE EXAMINATION PAPERS. By A. M. M. Stedman, M.A. *Sixth Edition.* KEY. *Fourth Edition.* 7s. net.
GERMAN EXAMINATION PAPERS. By R. J. Morich. *Seventh Edition.* KEY. *Third Edition.* 6s. net.

GREEK EXAMINATION PAPERS. By A. M. M. Stedman, M.A. *Ninth Edition.* KEY, *Fourth Edition.* 6s. net.
HISTORY AND GEOGRAPHY EXAMINATION PAPERS. By C. H. Spence, M.A. *Third Edition.*
LATIN EXAMINATION PAPERS. By A. M. M. Stedman, M.A. *Fourteenth Edition.* KEY. *Seventh Edition.* 6s. net.
PHYSICS EXAMINATION PAPERS. By R. E. Steel, M.A., F.C.S.

School Histories

Illustrated. Crown 8vo. 1s. 6d.

A SCHOOL HISTORY OF WARWICKSHIRE. By B. C. A. Windle, D.Sc., F.R.S.
A SCHOOL HISTORY OF SOMERSET. By Walter Raymond. *Second Edition.*
A SCHOOL HISTORY OF LANCASHIRE. By W. E. Rhodes, M.A.

A SCHOOL HISTORY OF SURREY. By H. E Malden, M.A.
A SCHOOL HISTORY OF MIDDLESEX. By V. G. Plarr, M.A., and F. W. Walton, M.A.

Simplified French Texts

Edited by T. R. N. CROFTS, M.A.

Fcap 8vo. 1s.

ABDALLAH. By Edouard Laboulaye. Adapted by J. A. Wilson.
*DEUX CONTES. By P. Mérimée. Adapted by J. F. Rhoades.
*EDMOND DANTÈS. By A. Dumas. Adapted by M. Ceppi.
JEAN VALJEAN. By Victor Hugo. Adapted by F. W. M. Draper, M.A.
LA BATAILLE DE WATERLOO. By Erckmann-Chatrian. Adapted by G. H. Evans.
LA BOUILLIE AU MIEL. By A. Dumas. Adapted by P. B. Ingham, M.A.
LA CHANSON DE ROLAND. Adapted by H. Rieu, M.A. *Second Edition.*
LE CONSCRIT DE 1813. By Erckmann-Chatrian. Adapted by H. Rieu.

LE DOCTEUR MATHÉUS. By Erckmann-Chatrian. Adapted by W. P. Fuller, M.A.
*LE DUC DE BEAUFORT. By A. Dumas. Adapted by P. B. Ingham, M.A.
L'EQUIPAGE DE LA BELLE-NIVERNAISE. By Alphonse Daudet. Adapted by T. R. N. Crofts, M.A.
L'HISTOIRE D'UNE TULIPE. By A. Dumas. Adapted by T. R. N. Crofts, M.A. *Second Edition.*
L'HISTOIRE DE PIERRE ET CAMILLE. By A. de Musset. Adapted by J. B. Patterson, M.A.
MÉMOIRES DE CADICHON. By Madam de Ségur. Adapted by J. F. Rhoades.
*D'AJACCIO À SAINT HÉLÈNE. By A. Dumas. Adapted by F. W. M. DRAPER, M.A.
REMY LE CHEVRIER. By E. Souvestre. Adapted by E. E. Chottin, B-es-L.

Simplified German Texts

Edited by T. R. G. CROFTS, M.A. *Fcap. 8vo.* 1s.

DER MULLER AM RHEIN. By C. Brentano. Adapted by Florence A. Ryan.
DIE GESCHICHTE VON PETER SCHLEMIHL. By A. v. Chamisso. Adapted by R. C. Perry.

DIE NOTHELFER. By W. H. Riehl. Adapted by P. B. Ingham, M.A.
UNDINE UND HULDBRAND. By La Motte Fouqué. Adapted by T. R. N. Crofts, M.A.

Six Ages of European History

Edited by A. H. JOHNSON, M.A. With Maps. *Crown 8vo. 2s. 6d.*

AGE OF THE ENLIGHTENED DESPOT, THE, 1660-1789. A. H. Johnson.
CENTRAL PERIOD OF THE MIDDLE AGE, THE, 918-1273. Beatrice A. Lees.
DAWN OF MEDIÆVAL EUROPE, THE, 476-918. J. H. B. Masterman.

END OF THE MIDDLE AGE, THE, 1273-1453. E. C. Lodge.
EUROPE IN RENAISSANCE AND REFORMA-TION, 1453-1659. M. A. Hollings.
REMAKING OF MODERN EUROPE, THE, 1789-1878. J. A. R. Marriott.

Methuen's Standard Library

Cloth, 1s. net; double volumes, 1s. 6d. net.   *Paper, 6d. net; double volume, 1s. net.*

THE MEDITATIONS OF MARCUS AURELIUS. Translated by R. Graves.
SENSE AND SENSIBILITY. Jane Austen.
ESSAYS AND COUNSELS and THE NEW ATLANTIS. Francis Bacon, Lord Verulam.
RELIGIO MEDICI and URN BURIAL. Sir Thomas Browne. The text collated by A. R. Waller.
THE PILGRIM'S PROGRESS. John Bunyan.
REFLECTIONS ON THE FRENCH REVOLUTION. Edmund Burke.
THE POEMS AND SONGS OF ROBERT BURNS. Double Volume.
THE ANALOGY OF RELIGION, NATURAL AND REVEALED. Joseph Butler.
MISCELLANEOUS POEMS. T. CHATTERTON.
THE ROWLEY POEMS. T. Chatterton.
TOM JONES. Henry Fielding. Treble Vol.
CRANFORD. Mrs. Gaskell.
THE POEMS AND PLAYS OF OLIVER GOLDSMITH.
THE CASE IS ALTERED. EVERY MAN IN HIS HUMOUR. EVERY MAN OUT OF HIS HUMOUR. Ben Jonson.
CYNTHIA'S REVELS. POETASTER. Ben Jonson.

THE POEMS OF JOHN KEATS. Double volume. The Text has been collated by E. de Sélincourt.
ON THE IMITATION OF CHRIST. By Thomas à Kempis. Translation by C. Bigg.
A SERIOUS CALL TO A DEVOUT AND HOLY LIFE. W. Law.
PARADISE LOST. John Milton.
EIKONOKLASTES AND THE TENURE OF KINGS AND MAGISTRATES. John Milton.
UTOPIA AND POEMS. Sir Thomas More.
THE REPUBLIC OF PLATO. Translated by Sydenham and Taylor. Double Volume. Translation revised by W. H. D. Rouse.
THE LITTLE FLOWERS OF ST. FRANCIS. Translated by W. Heywood.
THE WORKS OF WILLIAM SHAKESPEARE. In 10 volumes.
THE POEMS OF PERCY BYSSHE SHELLEY. In 4 volumes. With Introductions by C. D. Locock.
THE LIFE OF NELSON. Robert Southey.
THE NATURAL HISTORY AND ANTIQUITIES OF SELBORNE. Gilbert White.

Textbooks of Science

Edited by G. F. GOODCHILD, M.A., B.Sc., and G. R. MILLS, M.A.

Fully Illustrated.

COMPLETE SCHOOL CHEMISTRY, THE. By F. M. Oldham, B.A. With 126 Illustrations. *Third Edition. Cr. 8vo. 4s. 6d.*
ELEMENTARY SCIENCE FOR PUPIL TEACHERS. PHYSICS SECTION. By W. T. Clough, A.R.C.Sc. (Lond.), F.C.S. CHEMISTRY SECTION. By A. E. Dunstan, B.Sc. (Lond.), F.C.S. With 2 Plates and 10 Diagrams. *Cr. 8vo. 2s.*
EXAMPLES IN ELEMENTARY MECHANICS, Practical, Graphical, and Theoretical. By W. J. Dobbs, M.A. With 52 Diagrams. *Cr. 8vo. 5s.*
EXAMPLES IN PHYSICS. By C. E. Jackson, M.A. *Cr. 8vo. 2s. 6d.*
FIRST YEAR PHYSICS. By C. E. Jackson, M.A. With 51 Diagrams. *Cr. 8vo. 1s. 6d.*
OUTLINES OF PHYSICAL CHEMISTRY. By George Senter, B.Sc. (Lond.), Ph.D. With many Diagrams. *Cr. 8vo. 3s. 6d.*

ORGANIC CHEMISTRY, AN, FOR SCHOOLS AND TECHNICAL INSTITUTES. By A. E. Dunstan, B.Sc. (Lond.), F.C.S. With many Illustrations. *Cr. 8vo. 2s. 6d.*
PLANT LIFE, Studies in Garden and School. By Horace F. Jones, F.C.S. With 320 Illustrations. *Cr. 8vo. 3s. 6d.*
PRACTICAL CHEMISTRY. Part I. W. French, M.A. *Fifth Edition. Cr. 8vo. 1s. 6d.*
PRACTICAL CHEMISTRY. Part II. W. French, M.A., and T. H. Boardman, M.A. *Cr. 8vo. 1s. 6d.*
*PRACTICAL CHEMISTRY FOR SCHOOLS AND TECHNICAL INSTITUTES, A. By A. E. Dunstan, B.Sc. (Lond.), F.C.S. *Cr. 8vo. 3s. 6d.*
PRACTICAL MECHANICS. S. H. Wells. *Fourth Edition. Cr. 8vo. 3s. 6d.*
TECHNICAL ARITHMETIC AND GEOMETRY. By C. T. Millis, M.I.M.E. *Cr. 8vo. 3s. 6d.*

Textbooks of Technology
Fully Illustrated.

BUILDERS' QUANTITIES. By H. C. Grubb. *Cr. 8vo. 4s. 6d.*

CARPENTRY AND JOINERY. By F. C. Webber. *Fifth Edition. Cr. 8vo. 3s. 6d.*

ELECTRIC LIGHT AND POWER: An Introduction to the Study of Electrical Engineering. By E. E. Brooks, B.Sc. (Lond.). and W. H. N. James, A.M.I.E.E., A.R.C.Sc. *Cr. 8vo. 4s. 6d.*

ENGINEERING WORKSHOP PRACTICE. By C. C. Allen. *Cr. 8vo. 3s. 6d.*

HOW TO MAKE A DRESS. By J. A. E. Wood. *Fourth Edition. Cr. 8vo. 1s. 6d.*

INSTRUCTION IN COOKERY. A. P. THOMSON. *Cr. 8vo. 2s. 6d.*

INTRODUCTION TO THE STUDY OF TEXTILE DESIGN, AN. By Aldred F. Barker. *Demy 8vo. 7s. 6d.*

MILLINERY, THEORETICAL AND PRACTICAL. By Clare Hill. *Fourth Edition. Cr. 8vo. 2s.*

RÉPOUSSÉ METAL WORK. By A. C. Horth. *Cr. 8vo. 2s. 6d.*

Handbooks of Theology

THE DOCTRINE OF THE INCARNATION. By R. L. Ottley, D.D. *Fourth Edition revised. Demy 8vo. 12s. 6d.*

A HISTORY OF EARLY CHRISTIAN DOCTRINE. By J. F. Bethune-Baker, M.A. *Demy 8vo. 10s. 6d.*

AN INTRODUCTION TO THE HISTORY OF RELIGION. By F. B. Jevons. M.A., Litt.D. *Fourth Edition. Demy 8vo. 10s. 6d.*

AN INTRODUCTION TO THE HISTORY OF THE CREEDS. By A. E. Burn, D.D. *Demy 8vo. 10s. 6d.*

THE PHILOSOPHY OF RELIGION IN ENGLAND AND AMERICA. By Alfred Caldecott, D.D. *Demy 8vo. 10s. 6d.*

THE XXXIX. ARTICLES OF THE CHURCH OF ENGLAND. Edited by E. C. S. Gibson, D.D. *Sixth Edition. Demy 8vo. 12s. 6d.*

The Westminster Commentaries
General Editor, WALTER LOCK, D.D., Warden of Keble College,
Dean Ireland's Professor of Exegesis in the University of Oxford.

THE ACTS OF THE APOSTLES. Edited by R. B. Rackham, M.A. *Demy 8vo. Fourth Edition. 10s. 6d.*

THE FIRST EPISTLE OF PAUL THE APOSTLE TO THE CORINTHIANS. Edited by H. L. Goudge, M.A. *Second Ed. Demy 8vo. 6s.*

A COMMENTARY ON EXODUS. By A. H. M'Neile, B.D. With a Map and 3 Plans. *Demy 8vo. 10s. 6d.*

THE BOOK OF EZEKIEL. Edited H. A. Redpath, M.A., D.Litt. *Demy 8vo. 10s. 6d.*

THE BOOK OF GENESIS. Edited with Introduction and Notes by S. R. Driver, D.D. *Seventh Edition Demy 8vo. 10s. 6d.*

THE BOOK OF JOB. Edited by E. C. S. Gibson, D.D. *Second Edition. Demy 8vo. 6s.*

THE EPISTLE OF ST. JAMES. Edited with Introduction and Notes by R. J. Knowling, D.D. *Demy 8vo. 6s.*

PART II.—FICTION

Albanesi (E. Maria). SUSANNAH AND ONE OTHER. *Fourth Edition. Cr. 8vo. 6s.*

THE BLUNDER OF AN INNOCENT. *Second Edition. Cr. 8vo. 6s.*

CAPRICIOUS CAROLINE. *Second Edition. Cr. 8vo. 6s.*

LOVE AND LOUISA. *Second Edition. Cr. 8vo. 6s. Also Medium 8vo. 6d.*

PETER, A PARASITE. *Cr. 8vo. 6s.*

THE BROWN EYES OF MARY. *Third Edition. Cr. 8vo. 6s.*

I KNOW A MAIDEN. *Third Edition. Cr. 8vo. 6s. Also Medium 8vo. 6d.*

THE INVINCIBLE AMELIA: OR, THE POLITE ADVENTURESS. *Third Edition. Cr. 8vo. 3s. 6d.*

Annesley (Maude). THIS DAY'S MADNESS. *Cr. 8vo. 6s.*

Anstey (F.). A BAYARD FROM BENGAL. *Medium 8vo. 6d.*

Austen (Jane). PRIDE AND PREJUDICE. *Medium 8vo. 6d.*

Aveling (Francis). ARNOUL THE ENGLISHMAN. *Cr. 8vo. 6s.*

Bagot (Richard). A ROMAN MYSTERY. *Third Edition. Cr. 8vo. 6s. Also Medium 8vo. 6d.*

THE PASSPORT. *Fourth Edition. Cr. 8vo. 6s.*

TEMPTATION. *Fifth Edition. Cr. 8vo. 6s.*

ANTHONY CUTHBERT. *Fourth Edition Cr. 8vo. 6s.*

LOVE'S PROXY. *A New Edition. Cr. 8vo. 6s.*

DONNA DIANA. *Second Edition. Cr. 8vo. 6s.* Also *Medium 8vo. 6d.*

CASTING OF NETS. *Twelfth Edition. Cr. 8vo. 6s.* Also *Medium 8vo. 6d.*

Balfour (Andrew). BY STROKE OF SWORD. *Medium 8vo. 6d.*

Ball (Oona H.) (Barbara Burke). THEIR OXFORD YEAR. With 16 Illustrations *Cr. 8vo. 6s.*

BARBARA GOES TO OXFORD. With 16 Illustrations. *Third Edition. Cr. 8vo. 6s.*

Baring-Gould (S.). ARMINELL. *Fifth Edition. Cr. 8vo. 6s.* Also *Medium 8vo. 6d.*

URITH. *Fifth Edition. Cr. 8vo. 6s.* Also *Medium 8vo. 6d.*

IN THE ROAR OF THE SEA. *Seventh Edition. Cr. 8vo. 6s.* Also *Medium 8vo. 6d.*

CHEAP JACK ZITA. *Medium 8vo. 6d.*

MARGERY OF QUETHER. *Third Edition. Cr. 8vo. 6s.*

THE QUEEN OF LOVE. *Fifth Edition. Cr. 8vo. 6s.* Also *Medium 8vo. 6d.*

JACQUETTA. *Third Edition. Cr. 8vo. 6s.*

KITTY ALONE. *Fifth Edition. Cr. 8vo. 6s.* Also *Medium 8vo. 6d.*

NOÉMI. Illustrated. *Fourth Edition. Cr. 8vo. 6s.* Also *Medium 8vo. 6d.*

THE BROOM-SQUIRE. Illustrated. *Fifth Edition. Cr. 8vo. 6s.* Also *Medium 8vo. 6d.*

DARTMOOR IDYLLS. *Cr. 8vo. 6s.*

GUAVAS THE TINNER. Illustrated. *Second Edition. Cr. 8vo. 6s.*

BLADYS OF THE STEWPONEY. Illustrated. *Second Edition. Cr. 8vo. 6s.*

PABO THE PRIEST. *Cr. 8vo. 6s.*

WINEFRED. Illustrated. *Second Edition. Cr. 8vo. 6s.* Also *Medium 8vo. 6d.*

ROYAL GEORGIE. Illustrated. *Cr. 8vo. 6s.*

CHRIS OF ALL SORTS. *Cr. 8vo. 6s.*

IN DEWISLAND. *Second Ed. Cr. 8vo. 6s.*

THE FROBISHERS. *Crown 8vo. 6s.* Also *Medium 8vo. 6d.*

DOMITIA. Illus. *Second Ed. Cr. 8vo. 6s.*

MRS. CURGENVEN OF CURGENVEN. *Crown 8vo. 6s.*

LITTLE TU'PENNY. *Medium 8vo. 6d.*

FURZE BLOOM. *Medium 8vo. 6d.*

Barnett (Edith A.). A WILDERNESS WINNER. *Second Edition. Cr. 8vo. 6s.*

Barr (James). LAUGHING THROUGH A WILDERNESS. *Cr. 8vo. 6s.*

Barr (Robert). IN THE MIDST OF ALARMS. *Third Edition. Cr. 8vo. 6s.* Also *Medium 8vo. 6d.*

THE COUNTESS TEKLA. *Fourth Edition. Cr. 8vo. 6s.* Also *Medium 8vo. 6d.*

THE MUTABLE MANY. *Third Edition. Cr. 8vo. 6s.* Also *Medium 8vo. 6d.*

THE TEMPESTUOUS PETTICOAT. Illustrated. *Third Edition. Cr. 8vo. 6s.*

JENNIE BAXTER JOURNALIST. *Medium 8vo. 6d.*

Begbie (Harold). THE CURIOUS AND DIVERTING ADVENTURES OF SIR JOHN SPARROW; or, THE PROGRESS OF AN OPEN MIND. With a Frontispiece. *Second Edition. Cr. 8vo. 6s.*

Belloc (H.), EMMANUEL BURDEN, MERCHANT. With 36 Illustrations by G. K. CHESTERTON. *Second Ed. Cr. 8vo. 6s.*

A CHANGE IN THE CABINET. *Second Edition. Cr. 8vo. 6s.*

Benson (E. F.) DODO : A DETAIL OF THE DAY. *Fifteenth Edition. Cr. 8vo. 6s.* Also *Medium 8vo. 6d.*

THE VINTAGE. *Medium 8vo. 6d.*

Benson (Margaret). SUBJECT TO VANITY. *Cr. 8vo. 3s. 6d.*

Birmingham (George A.). THE BAD TIMES. *Second Edition. Cr. 8vo. 6s.*

SPANISH GOLD. *Fourth Edition. Cr. 8vo. 6s.*

THE SEARCH PARTY. *Cr. 8vo. 6s.*

Bowles (G. Stewart). A GUN-ROOM DITTY BOX. *Second Ed. Cr. 8vo. 1s. 6d.*

Bretherton (Ralph Harold). THE MILL. *Cr. 8vo. 6s.*

AN HONEST MAN. *Second Edition. Cr. 8vo. 6s.*

Brontë (Charlotte). SHIRLEY. *Medium 8vo. 6d.*

Burton (J. Bloundelle). ACROSS THE SALT SEAS. *Medium 8vo. 6d.*

Caffyn (Mrs.) ('Iota'). ANNE MAULE-VERER. *Medium 8vo. 6d.*

Campbell (Mrs. Vere). FERRIBY. *Second Edition. Cr. 8vo. 6s.*

Capes (Bernard). THE EXTRAORDINARY CONFESSIONS OF DIANA PLEASE. *Third Edition. Cr. 8vo. 6s.*

A JAY OF ITALY. *Fourth Ed. Cr. 8vo. 6s.*

LOAVES AND FISHES. *Second Edition. Cr. 8vo. 6s.*

A ROGUE'S TRAGEDY. *Second Edition. Cr. 8vo. 6s.*

THE GREAT SKENE MYSTERY. *Second Edition. Cr. 8vo. 6s.*

THE LOVE STORY OF ST. BEL. *Second Edition. Cr. 8vo. 6s.*

THE LAKE OF WINE. *Medium 8vo. 6d.*

Carey (Wymond). LOVE THE JUDGE. *Second Edition. Cr. 8vo. 6s.*

Castle (Agnes and Egerton). FLOWER O' THE ORANGE, and Other Tales. With a Frontispiece in Colour by A. H. Buckland. *Third Edition. Cr. 8vo. 6s.*

Charlton (Randal). MAVE. *Second Edition. Cr. 8vo. 6s.*

THE VIRGIN WIDOW. *Cr. 8vo. 6s.*

Chesney (Weatherby). THE MYSTERY OF A BUNGALOW. *Second Edition. Cr. 8vo. 6s.*

Clifford (Mrs. W. K.). THE GETTING WELL OF DOROTHY. Illustrated by GORDON BROWNE. *Second Edition. Cr. 8vo. 3s. 6d.*

A FLASH OF SUMMER. *Medium 8vo. 6d.*

MRS. KEITH'S CRIME. *Medium 8vo. 6d.*

Conrad (Joseph). THE SECRET AGENT: A Simple Tale. *Fourth Ed. Cr. 8vo. 6s.*

A SET OF SIX. *Fourth Edition. Cr. 8vo. 6s.*

Corbett (Julian). A BUSINESS IN GREAT WATERS. *Third Edition. Cr. 8vo. 6s.* Also *Medium 8vo. 6d.*

Corelli (Marie). A ROMANCE OF TWO WORLDS. *Twenty-Ninth Ed. Cr. 8vo. 6s.*

VENDETTA. *Twenty-Seventh Edition. Cr. 8vo. 6s.*

THELMA. *Thirty-Ninth Ed. Cr. 8vo. 6s.*

ARDATH: THE STORY OF A DEAD SELF. *Nineteenth Edition. Cr. 8vo. 6s.*

THE SOUL OF LILITH. *Sixteenth Edition. Cr. 8vo. 6s.*

WORMWOOD. *Sixteenth Ed. Cr. 8vo. 6s.*

BARABBAS: A DREAM OF THE WORLD'S TRAGEDY. *Forty-Fourth Edition. Cr. 8vo. 6s.*

THE SORROWS OF SATAN. *Fifty-Fifth Edition. Cr. 8vo. 6s.*

THE MASTER CHRISTIAN. *Twelfth Edition. 177th Thousand. Cr. 8vo. 6s.*

TEMPORAL POWER: A STUDY IN SUPREMACY. *Second Edition. 150th Thousand. Cr. 8vo. 6s.*

GOD'S GOOD MAN: A SIMPLE LOVE STORY. *Thirteenth Edition.* 150th Thousand. *Cr. 8vo. 6s.*

HOLY ORDERS: THE TRAGEDY OF A QUIET LIFE. *Second Edition.* 120th *Thousand. Crown 8vo. 6s.*

THE MIGHTY ATOM. *Twenty-seventh Edition. Cr. 8vo. 6s.*

BOY: a Sketch. *Eleventh Edition. Cr. 8vo. 6s.*

CAMEOS. *Thirteenth Edition. Cr. 8vo. 6s.*

Cotes (Mrs. Everard). See Duncan (Sara Jeannette).

Cotterell (Constance). THE VIRGIN AND THE SCALES. Illustrated. *Second Edition. Cr. 8vo. 6s.*

Crockett (S. R.), LOCHINVAR. Illustrated. *Third Edition. Cr. 8vo. 6s.* Also *Medium 8vo. 6d.*

THE STANDARD BEARER. *Cr. 8vo. 6s.*

Croker (Mrs. B. M.). THE OLD CANTONMENT. *Cr. 8vo. 6s.*

JOHANNA. *Second Edition. Cr. 8vo. 6s.* Also *Medium 8vo. 6d.*

THE HAPPY VALLEY. *Fourth Edition. Cr. 8vo. 6s.*

A NINE DAYS' WONDER. *Third Edition. Cr. 8vo. 6s.*

PEGGY OF THE BARTONS. *Seventh Ed. Cr. 8vo. 6s.* Also *Medium 8vo. 6d.*

ANGEL. *Fifth Edition. Cr. 8vo. 6s.* Also *Medium 8vo. 6d.*

A STATE SECRET. *Third Edition. Cr. 8vo. 3s. 6d.* Also *Medium 8vo. 6d.*

KATHERINE THE ARROGANT. *Fifth Edition. Cr. 8vo. 6s.*

Crosbie (Mary). DISCIPLES. *Second Ed. Cr. 8vo. 6s.*

Cuthell (Edith E.). ONLY A GUARD-ROOM DOG. Illustrated by W. PARKINSON. *Crown 8vo. 3s. 6d.*

Dawson (Warrington). THE SCAR. *Second Edition. Cr. 8vo. 6s.*

THE SCOURGE. *Cr. 8vo. 6s.*

Deakin (Dorothea). THE YOUNG COLUMBINE. With a Frontispiece by LEWIS BAUMER. *Cr. 8vo. 6s.*

Deane (Mary). THE OTHER PAWN. *Cr. 8vo. 6s.*

Doyle (A. Conan). ROUND THE RED LAMP. *Eleventh Edition. Cr. 8vo. 6s.* Also *Medium 8vo. 6d.*

Dumas (Alexandre). See page 46.

Duncan (Sara Jeannette) (Mrs. Everard Cotes). THOSE DELIGHTFUL AMERICANS. *Medium 8vo. 6d.*

A VOYAGE OF CONSOLATION. Illustrated. *Third Edition. Cr. 8vo. 6s.* Also *Medium 8vo. 6d.*

COUSIN CINDERELLA. *Second Edition. Cr. 8vo. 6s.*

THE BURNT OFFERING. *Cr. 8vo. 6s.*

Eldridge (George D.). IN THE POTTER'S HOUSE. *Cr. 8vo. 6s.*

Eliot (George). THE MILL ON THE FLOSS. *Medium 8vo. 6d.*

Erskine (Mrs. Steuart). THE MAGIC PLUMES. *Cr. 8vo. 6s.*

Fenn (G. Manville). SYD BELTON; or, The Boy who would not go to Sea. Illustrated by GORDON BROWNE. *Second Ed. Cr. 8vo. 3s. 6d.*

Findlater (J. H.). THE GREEN GRAVES OF BALGOWRIE. *Fifth Edition. Cr. 8vo. 6s.* Also *Medium 8vo. 6d.*

THE LADDER TO THE STARS. *Second Edition. Cr. 8vo. 6s.*

Findlater (Mary). A NARROW WAY. *Third Edition. Cr. 8vo. 6s.*
OVER THE HILLS. *Second Edition. Cr. 8vo. 6s.*
THE ROSE OF JOY. *Third Edition. Cr. 8vo. 6s.*
A BLIND BIRD'S NEST. With 8 Illustrations. *Second Edition. Cr. 8vo. 6s.*
Fitzpatrick (K.) THE WEANS AT ROWALLAN. Illustrated. *Second Edition. Cr. 8vo. 6s.*
Francis (M. E.). (Mrs. Francis Blundell). STEPPING WESTWARD. *Second Edition. Cr. 8vo. 6s.*
MARGERY O' THE MILL. *Third Edition. Cr. 8vo. 6s.*
HARDY-ON-THE-HILL. *Third Edition. Cr. 8vo. 6s.*
GALATEA OF THE WHEATFIELD. *Second Edition. Cr. 8vo. 6s.*
Fraser (Mrs. Hugh). THE SLAKING OF THE SWORD. *Second Edition. Cr. 8vo. 6s.*
GIANNELLA. *Cr. 8vo. 6s.*
IN THE SHADOW OF THE LORD. *Third Edition. Crown 8vo. 6s.*
Fry (B. and C. B.). A MOTHER'S SON. *Fifth Edition. Cr. 8vo. 6s.*
Fuller-Maitland (Ella). BLANCHE ESMEAD. *Second Edition. Cr. 8vo. 6s.*
Gallon (Tom). RICKERBY'S FOLLY. *Medium 8vo. 6d.*
Gaskell (Mrs.). CRANFORD. *Medium 8vo. 6d.*
MARY BARTON. *Medium 8vo. 6d.*
NORTH AND SOUTH. *Medium 8vo. 6d.*
Gates (Eleanor). THE PLOW-WOMAN. *Cr. 8vo. 6s.*
Gerard (Dorothea). HOLY MATRIMONY. *Medium 8vo. 6d.*
MADE OF MONEY. *Medium 8vo. 6d.*
THE IMPROBABLE IDYL. *Third Edition. Cr. 8vo. 6s.*
THE BRIDGE OF LIFE. *Cr. 8vo. 6s.*
THE CONQUEST OF LONDON. *Medium 8vo. 6d.*
Gibbs (Philip). THE SPIRIT OF REVOLT. *Second Edition. Cr. 8vo. 6s.*
Gissing (George). THE TOWN TRAVELLER. *Medium 8vo. 6d.*
THE CROWN OF LIFE. *Cr. 8vo. 6s.* Also *Medium 8vo. 6d.*
Glanville (Ernest). THE INCA'S TREASURE. Illustrated. *Cr. 8vo. 3s. 6d.* Also *Medium 8vo. 6d.*
THE KLOOF BRIDE. *Medium 8vo. 6d.*
Gleig (Charles). BUNTER'S CRUISE. Illustrated. *Cr. 8vo. 3s. 6d.* Also *Medium 8vo. 6d.*
Grimm (The Brothers). GRIMM'S FAIRY TALES. Illustrated. *Medium 8vo. 6d.*

Haig (J. C.). IN THE GRIP OF THE TRUSTS: A STORY OF 1914. *Cr. 8vo. 1s. net.*
Hamliton (M.). THE FIRST CLAIM. *Second Edition. Cr. 8vo. 6s.*
Harraden (Beatrice). IN VARYING MOODS. *Fourteenth Edition. Cr. 8vo. 6s.*
THE SCHOLAR'S DAUGHTER. *Fourth Edition. Cr. 8vo. 6s.*
HILDA STRAFFORD and THE REMITTANCE MAN. *Twelfth Ed. Cr. 8vo. 6s.*
INTERPLAY. *Fifth Edition. Cr. 8vo. 6s.*
Harrod (F.) (Frances Forbes Robertson). THE TAMING OF THE BRUTE. *Cr. 8vo. 6s.*
Hart (Mabel). SISTER K. *Cr. 8vo. 6s.*
Hichens (Robert). THE PROPHET OF BERKELEY SQUARE. *Second Edition. Cr. 8vo. 6s.*
TONGUES OF CONSCIENCE. *Third Edition. Cr. 8vo. 6s.*
FELIX. *Sixth Edition. Cr. 8vo. 6s.*
THE WOMAN WITH THE FAN. *Seventh Edition. Cr. 8vo. 6s.*
BYEWAYS. *Cr. 8vo. 6s.*
THE GARDEN OF ALLAH. *Eighteenth Edition. Cr. 8vo. 6s.*
THE BLACK SPANIEL. *Cr. 8vo. 6s.*
THE CALL OF THE BLOOD. *Seventh Edition. Cr. 8vo. 6s.*
BARBARY SHEEP. *Second Edition. Cr. 8vo. 3s. 6d.*
Hope (Anthony). THE GOD IN THE CAR. *Eleventh Edition. Cr. 8vo. 6s.*
A CHANGE OF AIR. *Sixth Ed. Cr. 8vo. 6s.* Also *Medium 8vo. 6d.*
A MAN OF MARK. *Sixth Ed. Cr. 8vo. 6s.* Also *Medium 8vo. 6d.*
THE CHRONICLES OF COUNT ANTONIO. *Sixth Edition. Cr. 8vo. 6s.* Also *Medium 8vo. 6d.*
PHROSO. Illustrated by H. R. MILLAR. *Eighth Edition. Cr. 8vo. 6s.* Also *Medium 8vo. 6d.*
SIMON DALE. Illustrated. *Eighth Edition. Cr. 8vo. 6s.*
THE KING'S MIRROR. *Fourth Edition. Cr. 8vo. 6s.*
QUISANTE. *Fourth Edition. Cr. 8vo. 6s.*
THE DOLLY DIALOGUES. *Cr. 8vo. 6s.* Also *Medium 8vo. 6d.*
A SERVANT OF THE PUBLIC. Illustrated. *Fourth Edition. Cr. 8vo. 6s.*
TALES OF TWO PEOPLE. With a Frontispiece by A. H. BUCKLAND. *Third Ed. Cr. 8vo. 6s.*
THE GREAT MISS DRIVER. With a Frontispiece by A. H. BUCKLAND. *Fourth Edition. Cr. 8vo. 6s.*

FICTION

Hornung (E. W.). DEAD MEN TELL NO TALES. *Medium 8vo. 6d.*

Housman (Clemence). THE LIFE OF SIR AGLOVALE DE GALIS. *Cr. 8vo. 6s.*

Hueffer (Ford Madox). AN ENGLISH GIRL: A ROMANCE. *Second Edition. Cr. 8vo. 6s.*

MR. APOLLO: A JUST POSSIBLE STORY. *Second Edition. Cr. 8vo. 6s.*

Hutten (Baroness von). THE HALO. *Fifth Edition. Cr. 8vo. 6s.*

Hyne (C. J. Cutcliffe). MR. HORROCKS, PURSER. *Fourth Edition. Cr. 8vo. 6s.*

PRINCE RUPERT, THE BUCCANEER. Illustrated. *Third Edition. Cr. 8vo. 6s.*

Ingraham (J. H.). THE THRONE OF DAVID. *Medium 8vo. 6d.*

Jacobs (W. W.). MANY CARGOES. *Thirty-first Edition. Cr. 8vo. 3s. 6d.*

SEA URCHINS. *Fifteenth Edition.. Cr. 8vo. 3s. 6d.*

A MASTER OF CRAFT. Illustrated by WILL OWEN. *Eighth Edition. Cr. 8vo. 3s. 6d.*

LIGHT FREIGHTS. Illustrated by WILL OWEN and Others. *Seventh Edition. Cr. 8vo. 3s. 6d.*

THE SKIPPER'S WOOING. *Ninth Edition. Cr. 8vo. 3s. 6d.*

AT SUNWICH PORT. Illustrated by WILL OWEN. *Ninth Edition. Cr. 8vo. 3s.6d.*

DIALSTONE LANE. Illustrated by WILL OWEN. *Seventh Edition. Cr. 8vo. 3s. 6d.*

ODD CRAFT. Illustrated by WILL OWEN. *Third Edition. Cr. 8vo. 3s. 6d.*

THE LADY OF THE BARGE. Illustrated. *Eighth Edition. Cr. 8vo. 3s. 6d.*

SALTHAVEN. Illustrated by WILL OWEN. *Second Edition. Cr. 8vo. 3s. 6d.*

SAILORS' KNOTS. *Cr. 8vo. 3s. 6d.*

James (Henry). THE SOFT SIDE. *Second Edition. Cr. 8vo. 6s.*

THE BETTER SORT. *Cr. 8vo. 6s.*

THE GOLDEN BOWL. *Third Edition. Cr. 8vo. 6s.*

Keays (H. A. Mitchell). HE THAT EATETH BREAD WITH ME. *Cr. 8vo. 6s.*

Kester (Vaughan). THE FORTUNES OF THE LANDRAYS. *Cr. 8vo. 6s.*

Lawless (Hon. Emily). WITH ESSEX IN IRELAND. *Cr. 8vo. 6s.*

Le Queux (William). THE HUNCHBACK OF WESTMINSTER. *Third Ed. Cr. 8vo. 6s.* Also *Medium 8vo. 6d.*

THE CLOSED BOOK. *Third Edition. Cr. 8vo. 6s.*

THE VALLEY OF THE SHADOW. Illustrated. *Third Edition. Cr. 8vo. 6s.*

BEHIND THE THRONE. *Third Edition. Cr. 8vo. 6s.*

THE CROOKED WAY. *Second Edition. Cr. 8vo. 6s.*

Levett-Yeats (S. K.). ORRAIN. *Second Edition. Cr. 8vo. 6s.* Also *Medium 8vo. 6d.*

THE TRAITOR'S WAY. *Medium 8vo. 6d.*

Linton (E. Lynn). THE TRUE HISTORY OF JOSHUA DAVIDSON. *Medium 8vo. 6d.*

London (Jack). WHITE FANG. With a Frontispiece by CHARLES RIVINGSTON BULL. *Sixth Edition. Cr. 8vo. 6s.*

Lubbock (Basil). DEEP SEA WARRIORS. Illustrated. *Second Edition. Cr. 8vo. 6s.*

*Lucas (St. John). THE FIRST ROUND. *Cr. 8vo. 6s.*

Lyall (Edna). DERRICK VAUGHAN, NOVELIST. *43rd Thousand. Cr. 8vo. 3s. 6d.* Also *Medium 8vo. 6d.*

Maartens (Maarten). THE NEW RELIGION: A MODERN NOVEL. *Third Edition. Cr. 8vo. 6s.*

BROTHERS ALL; MORE STORIES OF DUTCH PEASANT LIFE. *Third Edition. Cr. 8vo. 6s.*

THE PRICE OF LIS DORIS. *Cr. 8vo. 6s.*

M'Carthy (Justin H.). THE LADY OF LOYALTY HOUSE. Illustrated. *Third Edition. Cr. 8vo. 6s.*

THE DRYAD. *Second Edition. Cr. 8vo. 6s.*

THE DUKE'S MOTTO. *Third Edition. Cr. 8vo. 6s.*

Macdonald (Ronald). A HUMAN TRINITY. *Second Edition. Cr. 8vo. 6s.*

Macnaughtan (S.). THE FORTUNE OF CHRISTINA M'NAB. *Fourth Edition. Cr. 8vo. 6s.*

Malet (Lucas). COLONEL ENDERBY'S WIFE. *Fourth Edition. Cr. 8vo. 6s.*

A COUNSEL OF PERFECTION. *Second Edition. Cr. 8vo. 6s.* Also *Medium 8vo. 6d.*

THE WAGES OF SIN. *Sixteenth Edition. Cr. 8vo. 6s.*

THE CARISSIMA. *Fifth Ed. Cr. 8vo. 6s.* Also *Medium 8vo. 6d.*

THE GATELESS BARRIER. *Fifth Edition. Cr. 8vo. 6s.*

THE HISTORY OF SIR RICHARD CALMADY. *Seventh Edition. Cr. 8vo. 6s.*

Mann (Mrs. M. E.). OLIVIA'S SUMMER. *Second Edition. Cr. 8vo. 6s.*

A LOST ESTATE. *A New Ed. Cr. 8vo. 6s.* Also *Medium 8vo. 6d.*

THE PARISH OF HILBY. *A New Edition. Cr. 8vo. 6s.*

THE PARISH NURSE. *Fourth Edition. Cr. 8vo. 6s.*

GRAN'MA'S JANE. *Cr. 8vo. 6s.*

MRS. PETER HOWARD. *Second Edition.* *Cr. 8vo.* 6s. Also *Medium 8vo.* 6d.
A WINTER'S TALE. *A New Edition.* *Cr. 8vo.* 6s. Also *Medium 8vo.* 6d.
ONE ANOTHER'S BURDENS. *A New Edition. Cr. 8vo.* 6s. Also *Medium 8vo.* 6d.
ROSE AT HONEYPOT. *Third Ed. Cr. 8vo.* 6s.
THERE WAS ONCE A PRINCE. Illustrated by M. B. MANN. *Cr. 8vo.* 3s. 6d.
WHEN ARNOLD COMES HOME. Illustrated by M. B. MANN. *Cr. 8vo.* 3s. 6d.
THE EGLAMORE PORTRAITS. *Third Edition. Cr. 8vo.* 6s.
THE MEMORIES OF RONALD LOVE. *Cr. 8vo.* 6s.
THE SHEEP AND THE GOATS. *Third Edition. Cr. 8vo.* 6s.
A SHEAF OF CORN. *Second Edition. Cr. 8vo.* 6s.
THE HEART-SMITER. *Second Edition. Cr. 8vo.* 6s.
AVENGING CHILDREN. *Cr. 8vo.* 6s.
THE PATTEN EXPERIMENT. *Medium 8vo.* 6d.
THE CEDAR STAR. *Medium 8vo.* 6d.
Marchmont (A. W.). MISER HOADLEY'S SECRET. *Medium 8vo.* 6d.
A MOMENT'S ERROR. *Medium 8vo.* 6d.
Marriott (Charles). GENEVRA. *Second Edition. Cr. 8vo.* 6s.
Marryat (Captain). PETER SIMPLE *Medium 8vo.* 6d.
JACOB FAITHFUL. *Medium 8vo.* 6d.
Marsh (Richard). THE TWICKENHAM PEERAGE. *Second Edition. Cr. 8vo.* 6s. Also *Medium 8vo.* 6d.
THE MARQUIS OF PUTNEY. *Second Edition. Cr. 8vo.* 6s.
IN THE SERVICE OF LOVE. *Third. Edition. Cr. 8vo.* 6s.
THE GIRL AND THE MIRACLE. *Third Edition. Cr. 8vo.* 6s.
THE COWARD BEHIND THE CURTAIN. *Cr. 8vo.* 6s.
THE SURPRISING HUSBAND. *Second Edition. Cr. 8vo.* 6s.
A ROYAL INDISCRETION. *Cr. 8vo.* 6s.
A METAMORPHOSIS. *Medium 8vo.* 6d.
THE GODDESS. *Medium 8vo.* 6d.
THE JOSS. *Medium 8vo.* 6d.
Marshall (Archibald). MANY JUNES. *Second Edition. Cr. 8vo.* 6s.
THE SQUIRE'S DAUGHTER. *Cr. 8vo.* 6s.
Mason (A. E. W.). CLEMENTINA. Illustrated. *Third Edition. Cr. 8vo.* 6s. Also *Medium 8vo.* 6d.
Mathers (Helen). HONEY. *Fourth Ed. Cr. 8vo.* 6s. Also *Medium 8vo.* 6d.

GRIFF OF GRIFFITHSCOURT. *Second Edition. Cr. 8vo.* 6s. Also *Medium 8vo.* 6d.
THE FERRYMAN *Second Edition. Cr. 8vo.* 6s.
TALLY-HO! *Fourth Edition. Cr. 8vo.* 6s.
SAM'S SWEETHEART. *Medium 8vo.* 6d.
Maud (Constance). A DAUGHTER OF FRANCE. With a Frontispiece. *Second Edition. Cr. 8vo.* 6s.
Maxwell (W. B.). VIVIEN. *Ninth Edition. Cr. 8vo.* 6s.
THE RAGGED MESSENGER. *Third Edition. Cr. 8vo.* 6s.
FABULOUS FANCIES. *Cr. 8vo.* 6s.
THE GUARDED FLAME. *Seventh Edition. Cr. 8vo.* 6s.
ODD LENGTHS. *Second Ed. Cr. 8vo.* 6s.
HILL RISE. *Fourth Edition. Cr. 8vo.* 6s.
THE COUNTESS OF MAYBURY: BETWEEN YOU AND I. *Fourth Edition. Cr. 8vo.* 6s.
Meade (L. T.). DRIFT. *Second Edition. Cr. 8vo.* 6s. Also *Medium 8vo.* 6d.
RESURGAM. *Second Edition. Cr. 8vo.* 6s.
VICTORY. *Cr. 8vo.* 6s.
A GIRL OF THE PEOPLE. Illustrated. *Fourth Edition. Cr. 8vo.* 3s. 6d.
HEPSY GIPSY. Illustrated. *Cr. 8vo.* 2s. 6d.
THE HONOURABLE MISS: A STORY OF AN OLD-FASHIONED TOWN. Illustrated. *Second Edition. Cr. 8vo.* 3s. 6d.
Melton (R.). CÆSAR'S WIFE. *Second Edition. Cr. 8vo.* 6s.
Meredith (Ellis). HEART OF MY HEART. *Cr. 8vo.* 6s.
Miller (Esther). LIVING LIES. *Third Edition. Cr. 8vo.* 6s. Also *Medium 8vo.* 6d.
Mitford (Bertram). THE SIGN OF THE SPIDER. Illustrated. *Sixth Edition. Cr. 8vo.* 3s. 6d. Also *Medium 8vo.* 6d.
IN THE WHIRL OF THE RISING. *Third Edition. Cr. 8vo.* 6s.
THE RED DERELICT. *Second Edition. Cr. 8vo.* 6s.
Molesworth (Mrs.). THE RED GRANGE. Illustrated. *Second Edition. Cr. 8vo.* 3s. 6d.
Montgomery (K. L.). COLONEL KATE. *Second Edition. Cr. 8vo.* 6s.
Montresor (F. F.). THE ALIEN. *Third Edition. Cr. 8vo.* 6s. Also *Medium 8vo.* 6d.
Morrison (Arthur). TALES OF MEAN STREETS. *Seventh Edition. Cr. 8vo.* 6s.
A CHILD OF THE JAGO. *Fifth Edition. Cr. 8vo.* 6s.
THE HOLE IN THE WALL. *Fourth Edition. Cr. 8vo.* 6s. Also *Medium 8vo.* 6d.

L G Parsons
The More
Exmouth

Nov 22/09